Theory in
Economic Anthropology

SOCIETY FOR ECONOMIC ANTHROPOLOGY (SEA) MONOGRAPHS

Deborah Winslow, University of New Hampshire
General Editor, Society for Economic Anthropology

Monographs for the Society for Economic Anthropology contain original essays that explore the connections between economics and social life. Each year's volume focuses on a different theme in economic anthropology. Earlier volumes were published with the University Press of America, Inc. (#1–15, 17), and Rowman & Littlefield, Inc. (#16). The monographs are now published jointly by AltaMira Press and the Society for Economic Anthropology (http://nautarch.tamu.edu/anth/sea/).

No. 1.   Sutti Ortiz, ed., *Economic Anthropology: Topics and Theories.*

No. 2.   Sidney M. Greenfield and Arnold Strickon, eds., *Entrepreneurship and Social Change.*

No. 3.   Morgan D. Maclachlan, ed., *Household Economies and their Transformation.*

No. 4.   Stuart Plattner, ed., *Markets and Marketing.*

No. 5.   John W. Bennett and John R. Brown, eds., *Production and Autonomy: Anthropological Studies and Critiques of Development.*

No. 6.   Henry J. Rutz and Benjamin S. Orlove, eds., *The Social Economy of Consumption.*

No. 7.   Christina Gladwin and Kathleen Truman, eds., *Food and Farm: Current Debates and Policies.*

No. 8.   M. Estellie Smith, ed., *Perspectives on the Informal Economy.*

No. 9.   Hill Gates and Alice Littlefield, eds., *Marxist Trends in Economic Anthropology.*

No. 10. Sutti Ortiz and Susan Lees, eds., *Understanding Economic Process.*

No. 11. Elizabeth M. Brumfiel, ed., *The Economic Anthropology of the State.*

No. 12. James M. Acheson, ed., *Anthropology and Institutional Economics.*

No. 13. Richard E. Blanton, Peter N. Peregrine, Deborah Winslow, and Thomas D. Hall, eds., *Economic Analysis Beyond the Local System.*

No. 14. Robert C. Hunt and Antonio Gilman, eds., *Property in Economic Context.*

No. 15. David B. Small and Nicola Tannenbaum, eds., *At the Interface: The Household and Beyond.*

No. 16. Angelique Haugerud, M. Priscilla Stone, and Peter D. Little, eds., *Commodities and Globalization: Anthropological Perspectives.*

No. 17. Martha W. Rees & Josephine Smart, eds., *Plural Globalities in Multiple Localities: New World Border.*

Theory in Economic Anthropology

Edited By
Jean Ensminger

Published in cooperation with the
Society for Economic Anthropology

ALTAMIRA
PRESS

A Division of Rowman and Littlefield Publishers, Inc.
Walnut Creek • Lanham • New York • Oxford

AltaMira Press
A Division of Rowman & Littlefield Publishers, Inc.
1630 North Main Street, #367
Walnut Creek, CA 94596
www.altamirapress.com

Rowman & Littlefield Publishers, Inc.
4720 Boston Way
Lanham, MD 20706

12 Hid's Copse Road
Cumnor Hill, Oxford OX2 9JJ, England

Published in cooperation with the Society for Economic Anthropology

British Library Cataloguing in Publication Information Available

Library of Congress Cataloging-in-Publication Data

Theory in economic anthropology / edited by Jean Ensminger.
    p. cm.
Includes bibliographical references and index.
ISBN 0-7591-0205-8 (cloth : alk. paper) — ISBN 0-7591-0206-6 (pbk. : alk. paper)
    1. Economic anthropology.

GN448 .T54 2002
306.3—dc21

                                                                                    2001046113

Printed in the United States of America

Contents

Acknowledgments

The editor wishes to express deep appreciation to a number of parties who made this volume possible. Jane Guyer and Timothy Earle organized a lovely conference at Northwestern University (upon which this volume draws) in combination with the fortieth anniversary of the Program for African Studies. Deborah Winslow took over as the series editor for the Society of Economic Anthropology during the course of this production. This event is one of the most beneficial things to happen to the organization. She is a superb organizer and the most perfectly gracious, but persistent, prodder one could find—perfect qualities in an editor. As the volume editor I also could not have been more fortunate in the cooperativeness of the individuals who made contributions to this book and in the insightfulness and thoroughly detailed comments of two anonymous outside reviewers. Last, this volume represents the first in the series since it was taken over by AltaMira Press, and it has been a delight to deal with them on this inaugural venture.

Introduction

Theory in Economic Anthropology at the Turn of the Century

Jean Ensminger

The last decade of the twentieth century was not kind to economic anthropology. In the heyday of postmodern sentiments, the type of research that has always been the forte of economic anthropology was at best underappreciated, at worst, scorned, slandered, and ignored. As the social sciences move on from the excesses of those times, it is likely that many of the solid ethnographic, empirical studies that have been the foundation of economic anthropology will once again come into vogue. Meanwhile, those who have continued in the rigorous methodological tradition that has been associated with this subdiscipline have preserved the technical and analytical skills necessary to survive into the next generation and guarantee the continuity of the discipline as a serious social science. Further, there is evidence that many exciting new theoretical ideas are entering anthropology through the engagement of economic anthropologists with others across disciplinary boundaries.

This volume is largely drawn from papers presented at the annual conference of the Society for Economic Anthropology in 1998. This conference was hosted by Northwestern University and served also to celebrate the fortieth anniversary of the founding of the Program of African Studies there by Melville J. Herskovits, the noted economic anthropologist and Africanist. The theme of the conference was designed to take the pulse of theory in economic anthropology seventeen years after the first meeting of the society and publication of the first volume in this series, which focused upon theory in economic anthropology (Ortiz 1983). It should be noted that two areas of considerable interest to economic anthropologists are somewhat underrepresented in this volume because they are the central themes of the next two volumes: gender and development. These issues are so pervasive in the field, however, that they clearly are intertwined in a number of the chapters represented here. Most especially, both gender and development are the primary themes in Gwako's chapter 1. Development issues also figure prominently in the chapters by Acheson, Ensminger, Winslow, Cohen, Obukhova and Guyer, and Hansen (chapters 2, 3, 8, 9, 10, and 11).

As the economic gap between rich and poor countries grows ever more apparent (Landes 1998), the work of economic anthropologists who can shed light on the underlying causes of this disparity in economic performance has never been more needed. Indeed, the World Bank (1997) has in recent years demonstrated increasing appreciation of the role of institutions and social capital in understanding the underperformance of developing economies. As is evident in this volume, economic anthropologists write extensively on institutions and social capital (see especially Gwako, Acheson, Ensminger, Earle, and Bell). There has perhaps never been a time when economic anthropologists are likely to be as well received by their colleagues in economics, political economy, and development. Economic anthropologists still have the expertise so much in demand by other disciplines that are stronger in theory, but lack the bottom-up understanding of what makes small economies on the ground function—sometimes well, sometimes poorly. In order to take best advantage of the synergies across disciplines, however, it is increasingly imperative that anthropologists speak the language of general theory in the social sciences. These chapters demonstrate how this dialogue is being incorporated into the research agendas of economic anthropologists. Gwako, Acheson, and Earle write in a framework influenced by new institutional economics; Gwako, Ensminger, and Henrich engage the rational choice debate raging in political science, economics, and economic sociology; Winslow and Cohen place their studies in the theoretical tradition of geographers and others dealing with spatial and transnational studies; and Hansen and Wilk work in the area of consumption and draw from theory in marketing and consumer research.

We see evidence in these chapters of the many strengths that economic anthropologists bring to the understanding of less developed economies. Many of the chapters take a historical perspective on their subject (see especially Winslow, and Obukhova and Guyer) while Earle takes an even longer evolutionary perspective. These studies highlight the advantage of an anthropological approach that is able to benefit from either longitudinal data collected in the same area over time (see especially Winslow), or a perspective that self-consciously attempts to place data in an evolutionary time frame. Here economic anthropology is especially well served by our archaeological colleagues (see Earle) who think in (and have data on) far longer time periods than is the norm for cultural anthropologists. In all of these cases, one appreciates the power of an analysis that affords the study of change over time and adds a dynamic element to more static analyses that depend more on cross-sectional data.

A number of the chapters connect with the past by tracing the theoretical roots of current thinking in the context of rich theoretical traditions in anthropology, whether these be Marxism (see especially Bell and Cohen), Chayanovian household economics (see Durrenberger and Tannenbaum), exchange theory (see Hunt), or the institutionalism of Karl Polanyi (see Bell). These chapters update the theory of classical scholars and discuss them in the context of contemporary data and current debates in the literature.

There is also considerable disagreement among economic anthropologists over the very usefulness of grand theory itself (see especially Henrich and Wilk). One of the most potent debates that divides economic anthropologists relates to the proper role for agency, rational choice, and methodological individualism in the analysis of behavior in small-scale societies. These debates were central to the transactional approaches of Bailey (1969), Barth (1981), and others in the 1960s and 1970s, and also had a major place in the great formalist/substantivist debates of the same era. Scholars today are especially divided over the place of strategic action versus behaviors driven by social norms and embeddedness in the institutional structures of society. This division highlights the extent to which the Polanyi debate (see Bell) is still with us. Gwako's chapter is very much in the tradition of recent rational choice approaches in new institutional economics and political science. Ensminger's chapter also deals with economic preferences, but provides evidence from experimental economics on the ways in which assumptions of narrow economic self-interest appear to be violated. Henrich discusses at length the rationality concept in conjunction with the history of economic anthropology. Coming from the new institutional economic tradition, Acheson's chapter nicely bridges many of these debates by addressing the way in which strategic actors attempt to change institutions to suit their own desires.

The chapters in this volume fall into five categories that represent current theoretical concerns in the discipline: the new institutionalism; debates about wealth, exchange, and the evolution of social institutions; the relationship between small producers and the wider world; the role of commodity change and the formal/informal sector; and the role of grand theory.

Part I. The New Institutionalism

The section of the book dealing with new institutional approaches highlights the current interest in this area across a wide swath of the social sciences (see especially the recent issue of the *Journal of Institutional and Theoretical Economics* devoted to this topic, particularly Miller 1998, Knight 1998, and Ensminger 1998; and see an earlier volume in this series devoted to the topic, Acheson 1994). Influenced by the new institutional economics, Laban Gwako addresses an issue of enormous import in African development—property rights. The World Bank and the Land Tenure Center at the University of Wisconsin, Madison, recently carried out a number of studies cross-culturally in which they failed to find a significant relationship between land tenure security and agricultural productivity. Yet there is considerable theoretical literature in the new institutional economics that points to the relevance of secure property rights in motivating greater incentives for agricultural production. Gwako argues in this chapter that the error in those studies stems from a failure to analyze property rights at the subhousehold level. When measured at the level of the household, it is essentially men's property rights that are being measured, but it is women who do much of the agricultural work in Africa. Gwako tested this hypothesis among the Maragoli of Kenya and found that when one examines women's property rights by plot at the subhousehold level, it is a good predictor in regression analyses of the level of agricultural output on that plot. Gwako demonstrates that the main mechanism by which this occurs is the selective application of agricultural inputs by women to the plots over which they control the outputs. Further, he provides quantitative and qualitative data from participant observation and interviews with women farmers that document their knowledge of this phenomenon and the manner in which they divert inputs to raise the productivity of their own plots.

In a very different discussion also drawing upon the new institutional economics and rational choice theory, James Acheson presents an overview of industrial organization. New institutional economists have made significant amendments to the neoclassical tradition. Among them is the assumption that market failures are common, and when this is the case people will develop alternative institutions, including firms, to solve their problems. Transaction costs are a central explanatory variable in new institutional analyses. It is now recognized that one reason why people don't transact in the market is because the costs of doing so may outweigh the gains. It is costly to acquire information about the quality of labor and products, it is costly to monitor labor and suppliers, and it is costly to negotiate and enforce contracts. For these reasons, some exchange occurs in markets, but other exchange is internalized within the firm or in hybrid organizations. The state plays a key role in reducing transaction costs, as for example

by establishing the rule of law that allows contracts to be enforced. Acheson is one of the first to apply these theoretical insights to industrial production in the developing world rather than to the more typical focus on issues tied into the agrarian economy (see Ensminger 1992). These theoretical insights will be of increasing relevance to anthropologists as the developing economies they tend to study move more and more toward industrial production and grapple with the proper role of the state in ensuring efficient economic organization. In the last part of chapter 2, Acheson deals with the interesting question of what kind of state and how much state is optimal for economic performance. While it is widely assumed that neoclassical economists view the state more as an impediment to economic development rather than a benefit, one of the insights of new institutional economics is that states provide extremely necessary institutions for the efficient functioning of markets and firms. Individuals and organizations, however, have strong vested interests in what kinds of institutions the state forms, and consequently they attempt to institute those that most serve their ends, whether these are of benefit to the common good or not.

In chapter 3, Ensminger discusses experimental methods that offer some promise for measuring economic preferences and norms cross-culturally. The chapter provides some evidence from experimental economics which challenges some fundamental economic assumptions about narrowly self-interested behavior. Ensminger presents some of the early findings from a project that is being carried out in conjunction with a number of other anthropologists (including Henrich, this volume) running economic experiments around the world to examine the levels of cooperation, self-interest, and altruism in less developed economies. The data presented here are from the Orma cattle herders of northeastern Kenya. Experimental economists have accumulated considerable data from the United States and other developed market economies that consistently demonstrate high levels of cooperation and fair-mindedness. The evidence presented in this chapter shows that, among the Orma and across the other societies where anthropologists have run experiments to date, market integration is positively correlated with fair-mindedness. Aside from the theoretical contribution, this paper also goes into considerable detail on the methods themselves. Anticipating that anthropologists may wish to add these methods to their existing tools, Ensminger provides insights from early pilot studies on how to actually adapt the methods of experimental economics to the unique and challenging situations typically faced by anthropologists a long way from the nearest laboratory.

Part II. Rethinking Wealth, Exchange, and the Evolution of Social Institutions

Earle's chapter beautifully bridges the interests of the preceding authors who are dealing largely with institutions, and those of this section who are dealing with a broader range of issues, including both institutions and exchange, which are very much the focus of this chapter as well. Earle challenges the widespread economic notion that sociocultural complexity correlates with commodity flows. Based on archaeological data from complex societies in Hawaii and Denmark, he argues that it is the system of finance that supports new institutions and that institutional finance, not sociocultural complexity per se, determines the amount of exchange. Exchange may be largely in staple commodities or it may be in wealth goods. Thus, if the exchange is in staples, as opposed to wealth goods, higher levels of exchange do not necessarily correlate with higher levels of institutional complexity. Wealth goods are important, Earle argues, because early institutions were built by ceremonially symbolic exchange and this occurred through gift exchange of wealth goods.

Hunt's chapter on economic exchanges and transfers should be of value especially to students trying to come to grips with an extensive vocabulary used by economic anthropologists. He pays considerable attention to the historical roots of central concepts in the general domains of exchange and distribution. His discussion of generalized, balanced, and negative exchange is especially helpful for questioning the very notion that these usages have anything to do with exchange. Here he suggests the term "transfers" as more appropriate. In Sahlins' classic use of the terms, after all, there is little actually exchanged in the extreme cases of negative reciprocity (theft) or generalized reciprocity (pure gift). The value of differentiating true transfers from exchanges is highlighted by the clarity that is afforded by not implying that these transfers are ever likely to be reciprocated, even over the course of decades. Hunt concludes chapter 5 by suggesting that we have less information about these behaviors in part because we have lumped transfers with exchanges. If we are to understand real transfers, including charitable contributions, it is essential that we more carefully use terminology that will not obscure the differences among these quite distinct types of allocations.

Duran Bell's chapter also revisits some classic issues and the work of leading theoreticians who have had enormous impact on economic anthropology. Bell argues that Polanyi's definition of capitalism as an unregulated market system is quite at odds with Marx's focus on capital, which he views as the central defining concept in Marx's use of the term. Further, he faults Polanyi for being unable to incorporate the well-being of workers into his analysis, which, according to Bell, places him squarely in the neoliberal camp, much at odds with a Marxist perspective. Bell argues that Polanyi's analysis of the destitution of workers in England stems from the destruction of the traditional culture and groups rather than from the meagerness of wages. Bell asks what it is about capitalism that erodes traditional communities. In Bell's discussion of Marx, the emphasis is shifted to control of new forms of capital and the role of the state in defense of new systems of capitalism at the expense of community and workers. Here Bell gets to a central point of chapter 6, which is that Polanyi tends to see the state benefiting the workers, which Marx and Bell clearly do not.

Part III. Small Producers Interacting with the Wider World

Appropriate for this volume, Durrenberger and Tannenbaum begin chapter 7 with a discussion of the meaning of theory in anthropology. Like Wilk, whose chapter closes out the volume, they argue in favor of more midlevel theory in anthropology, and their chapter is a nice illustration of exactly what they are talking about. The authors' theoretical stance begins with a set of assumptions about the categories appropriate for understanding household economics. Following Chayanov, they start with the assumption that peasants are rational, but in order to understand the logic of peasant decision making it is necessary to understand the constraints under which individual households are operating, and here one must look to the larger political economy for an explanation. The authors draw upon their case study material from Shan and Lisu villages in Thailand. They find that peasant behavior is consistent with Chayanov's logic about the effect of worker-to-consumer ratios on the tolerance level for work and drudgery. But a final accounting of peasant decision making requires the incorporation of political economy variables, as these set the actual preferences for the trade-off between drudgery and leisure in the utility function. For the hierarchical Shan, there is more individual return to drudgery in the form of wealth exchange for prestige, while for the egalitarian Lisu, there is not. This chapter nicely illustrates the way in which many economic anthropologists work through the logic of their case study material to unearth theoretical perspectives that are compatible with what they see on the ground.

The next two chapters in this section of the volume share a strong interdisciplinary orientation, but diverge in their discussion of the spatial landscape. Deborah Winslow provides, in chapter 8, an easily accessible overview of the literature on landscape studies and effectively introduces this subject to economic anthropology with an application to her long-term field site in Sri Lanka. Winslow has found spatial analysis particularly useful as the population she studies self-consciously begins to move about the regional landscape—both physically and socially. The potters studied by Winslow have in recent years benefited from a tremendous increase in economic well-being. They are using this newfound wealth to distance themselves from the low status of their potting past as they branch across the landscape into new occupations and new social statuses that deny their past. Winslow nicely documents these patterns with marriage data showing the decline in local endogamy over time and the increasing tendency to marry farther away. In this part of the analysis Winslow also incorporates agency, as she notes the strategies being used by individuals to "renegotiate the traditional 'ethnoscape' of caste and class." This is a particularly interesting case, as, in the process of moving strategically away from their lower status, individuals are actually giving up the potentially higher economic returns of life as potters.

Jeffrey Cohen provides an overview of a different spatial/global literature. Cohen's focus in chapter 9 is upon the transnational literature. Cohen examines three phases of research on social change in Mesoamerica to understand the historical roots of current thinking that makes up transnational studies: functionalist arguments, dependency and world systems theory, and market-centered research. While transnational analyses share a focus upon the greater interconnectedness of societies due to shared economic, cultural, social, and communication networks, an examination of the roots of some of these perspectives clearly points to underlying differences among the practitioners. The functionalists view transnationalism as destabilizing and disruptive of local systems. Cohen challenges these theorists for essentializing and romanticing indigenous systems; here transnationalism is viewed as a moral threat to community and identity. Dependency theorists are praised by Cohen for adding history and critical thinking about the political economy changes associated with transnationalism, but Cohen faults the dependency advocates for stripping local populations of their agency and rendering them pawns at the mercy of what goes on in the core nations. Finally, Cohen discusses the market-centered framework from which some transnational scholars work. He finds promise in the ability of this approach to take account of individual and household decision making in a purposeful and strategic manner. This approach also offers the most promise in affording the possibility of incorporating local class and status variability.

Part IV. Commodity Chains and the Formal/Informal Sector Distinction

The next two chapters follow closely the theme of the previous section as they both trace commodity changes across great regions. In addition,

Obukhova and Guyer go a long way toward updating the anthropology of the informal economy that was the subject of a previous volume in this series (Smith 1990). They make the point in chapter 10 that in this era of failed and ineffective states (Congo, Russia, and Somalia, to name a few), the line between the formal and informal economy is less clear than ever before. To examine this process, the authors choose to study commodities that are produced locally and largely for a domestic market. Their focus is upon commodity chains, wherever that may lead. For example, while the production of newspapers in Nigeria is part of the formal economy, the distribution is carried out largely by the informal economy. The economic history of the Soviet Union shows how the vodka commodity trade has shifted back and forth under conditions of high volatility. They argue persuasively by example for a more ethnographic approach to the study of commodity trade. One of the most intriguing findings they unearth by following the Nigerian commodity chain down the line is that preexisting social connections are not necessarily privileged over competence; personal capacities such as business acumen are rewarded further up the commodity chain as individuals prove themselves in the lower rungs.

Karen Tranberg Hansen introduces economic anthropologists to a little-known but huge trade in second-hand clothing that links the developed economies of the West with those of Africa, in particular. Hansen notes correctly that economic anthropology has tended to place more emphasis upon production, distribution, and exchange than it has upon consumption. Chapter 11 draws upon extensive fieldwork in Zambia that allows her to provide considerable detail on the cultural nature of consumption, on the issues driving demand, and on the agency of the actors involved. All the while, Hansen does not lose sight of the fact that she is dealing with a commodity that has considerable import to the well-being of the population and the meaning that this implies.

Part V. The Role for "Big Theory" in Economic Anthropology

The last section of the volume deals directly with the place of theory in economic anthropology. Richard Wilk questions how important high-level theory should be in economic anthropology. He approaches this important question by contrasting current work in the economic anthropology of consumption with an examination of consumer research and marketing. Wilk discusses three "high" theoretical traditions in the economic anthropology of consumption: the rational (market production as a mean to desired ends in the form of material consumption), the social (consumption as domination or resistance), and the cultural (the meaning of consumer goods).

Among other insights from chapter 12 is the observation that empirical work among consumer researchers is actually more likely to connect with and have an impact upon the low-level theory that is current in that discipline. This is less the case in anthropological research on consumption, Wilk argues, because we spend too much time engaging in grand theorizing and not enough doing rigorous empirical tests of our models. Wilk makes the case that, given the environmental reasons for needing to change consumption patterns, we can no longer afford the luxury of theories that do not connect with empirical research.

Closing the volume is a paper by Henrich that deals very explicitly with "big theory" questions in economic anthropology but, anticipating Wilk, formulates the argument heavily based upon the empirical record. Henrich takes on the tradition of assuming, implicitly and explicitly, that humans make many decisions through cost-benefit analysis. He provides evidence of this practice from the economic anthropology literature, which he argues has the tendency to assume a rational choice perspective. Henrich cites recent empirical evidence from experimental economics (see Ensminger, this volume), and cognitive psychology, which challenge both the ability of humans to make such calculations and the behavioral assumption that they actually do so in the real world. Instead, Henrich suggests that we consider the process by which people acquire information. Here he looks to the literature on cultural transmission, which argues that people selectively copy certain individuals and ideas. This process can in turn lead to adaptive behavioral patterns that we observe ethnographically.

Summary

So where does economic anthropology go from here? It is awfully hard to say, especially in these troubled post-postmodern times. Our entire discipline is in crisis, and the fate of economic anthropology may lie in the balance, but I would prefer to believe that it can offer a path to the future—both through participation in theoretical debates across the social sciences and in the rigor of method that has not been lost through this era in which such efforts were so underappreciated. If economic anthropologists, among others, are to lead the discipline out of the black hole of recent decades, I am convinced that it will require even more engagement with theory in the rest of the social sciences than we have experienced in the past. Anthropology has a tremendous wealth of knowledge that the other social sciences desperately need, but in order for this dialogue to have maximum impact we need to speak common theoretical languages. Whether one embraces or wishes to challenge the emerging new institutional and rational choice paradigms, to name two that are sweeping the rest of the social sciences, it is time for more anthropologists to follow the lead of many of the scholars represented in this volume and join these discussions across disciplinary boundaries.

References

Acheson, James
   1994 *Anthropology and Institutional Economics.* Monographs in Economic Anthropology, No. 12. New York: University Press of America.

Bailey, F. G.
   1969 *Stratagems and Spoils: A Social Anthropology of Politics.* Oxford: Basil Blackwell.

Barth, Fredrik
   1981 *Process and Form in Social Life: Selected Essays of Fredrik Barth, Vol. I.* London: Routledge & Kegan Paul.

Ensminger, Jean
   1992 *Making a Market: The Transformation of an African Society.* New York: Cambridge University Press.
   1998 "Anthropology and the New Institutionalism." *Journal of Institutional and Theoretical Economics* 154(4): 774–89.

Landes, David
   1998 *Wealth and Poverty of Nations: Why Some Are So Rich and Some So Poor.* New York: W. W. Norton.

Knight, Jack
   1998 "The Bases of Cooperation: Social Norms and the Rule of Law." *Journal of Institutional and Theoretical Economics* 154(4): 754–63.

Miller, Gary
   1998 "Coalitional Instability and Institutional Transformation." *Journal of Institutional and Theoretical Economics* 154(4): 764–73.

Ortiz, Sutti, ed.
   1983 *Economic Anthropology: Topics and Theories.* Monographs in Economic Anthropology, No. 12. New York: University Press of America.

Smith, Estellie, ed.
   1990 *Perspectives on the Informal Economy.* Monographs in Economic Anthropology, No. 8. New York: University Press of America.

World Bank
   1997 *The State in a Changing World: World Development Report 1997.* London: Oxford University Press.

Part I

The New Institutionalism

Chapter 1

Property Rights and Incentives for Agricultural Growth: Women Farmers' Crop Control and Their Use of Agricultural Inputs

Edwins Laban M. Gwako

Introduction

The analysis of data collected from an eighteen-month fieldwork among the Maragoli of western Kenya revealed that women's plot-level crop control significantly boosts agricultural output (Gwako 1997c). The mechanisms by which this higher agricultural output is achieved are the topics of discussion in this chapter. Policymakers in sub-Saharan African countries have paid significant attention to the pursuit of ways of accelerating the slow growth of agricultural production (Bindlish and Evenson 1997; Suda 1990). Several studies have also documented the critical role played by the use of various complementary agricultural inputs including extension service, fertilizer, hybrid seeds, and agricultural labor in enhancing agricultural output. For example, Suda (1990) notes that agricultural development policies and institutional support systems significantly affect agricultural production. However, less attention has been paid to the empirical analysis of how women farmers' plot-level crop control influences their use of these inputs.

In contemporary Kenya, the Training and Visit (T&V) system of agricultural extension service is the most commonly used approach. This system of agricultural extension service was first introduced by the World Bank in the late 1960s (Benor, Harrison, and Baxter 1984) and it involves the introduction of better production methods and new technologies to farmers at the field level (Bindlish and Evenson 1997). Training and Visit aims at closing the gap between the yields attainable using best practice technologies and the yields farmers actually achieve (Bindlish and Evenson

1997). This gap is wide in situations such as those in many sub-Saharan African countries, where farmers have little education, research and extension are unavailable, and markets and infrastructure are relatively undeveloped. Reducing such a gap under these conditions may result in a considerable and probably permanent increase in agricultural growth. The need to realize this goal in Kenya has led to increased emphasis on the organizational effectiveness of agricultural scientific information dissemination and management systems (Gathegi 1994; Suda 1990). Specific studies from western Kenya that have shown significant effects of farmers' agricultural innovation adoption on yields include Chitere (1993), Chitere and Omolo (1993), and Ongaro (1988).

Farmers' receptiveness to the dissemination of recommended innovations has significant implications for the enhancement of agricultural output. This explains why extension is a high priority in the World Bank's strategy for accelerating agricultural growth in Kenya and other sub-Saharan countries (Cleaver 1993). This strategy is aimed, not only at promoting improved practices, but also at helping farmers to become better managers and more adept at organizing their operations. As farmers' skills improve and demand for yield-increasing research and other services increases, extension services provide the blend of information input essential to stimulate agricultural output. Mbatia (1994) also found that frequency of extension visitation to the farmers enhances widespread fertilizer adoption and other new, appropriate technologies by small-scale farmers.

The Training and Visit system of agricultural extension service provides comprehensive services (e.g., for crops, livestock, and poultry) within a single line of command. In Kenya the strategy that has been developed has four key elements: regular visits by extension workers to designated contact farmers and contact groups (carefully selected to achieve a spread effect to farmers who are not in direct contact with extension); a cadre of subject matter specialists (who are trained by research scientists and who, in turn, train field-level extension workers); and the regular supervision of extension staff at all levels. Extension workers gradually disseminate technological packages to farmers, focusing on a few simple messages on each visit. The initial emphasis is on improving crop husbandry—i.e., land preparation, timing of different operations, planting densities, and fertilizer application. The strategic role assigned to extension and the resources being invested in it make it important to examine how much women farmers' crop control contributes to their receptiveness to extension services. This is particularly relevant, especially in view of the theoretical predictions made by new institutional economists.

Theoretical Context

The theoretical conceptualization guiding this chapter is derived from property rights literature, which highlights the importance of property rights in setting the incentive structure in economic production (Alston et al. 1996; Drobak and Nye 1997; Eggertsson 1990; Ensminger 1992; Libecap 1989; North and Thomas 1973; North 1981). Examining the role of incentives is relevant to the understanding of women's levels of participation in agriculture in many parts of sub-Saharan Africa. It is consistent with property rights theory to predict that low levels of yields and use of agricultural inputs are more likely to obtain on the plots in which African women have limited control over the products of their investment in the land. This is likely to be the case because the correct specification of property rights over the products of the land matters; property rights set the incentive system to which women farmers as economic actors respond.

North (1990) argues that much more attention must be directed to the institutional structure of a society in general, and to its property rights arrangements in particular, for explaining variation in economic performance. North (1987) also indicates that a major source of contrasting economic performance lies within property rights and legal structures of the society that define the incentives for saving, investment, and production. The institutional structure of a society and, in particular, the incentives defined by it underlie all economic activities and shape the direction of economic change toward growth, stagnation, or decline. In the case of women farmers, actual or anticipated benefits may provide the impetus for achieving higher yields and/or greater use of agricultural inputs. This argument is relevant to the situation in Africa, where the assignment of secure property rights over the products of the land to individual cultivators would have profound and enduring effects on economic performance in the agricultural sector. Appropriate incentives for individual actors and, in particular, guaranteeing control over the returns from land use considerably affect economic performance (Alston et al. 1997; North and Weingast 1996).

Bates (1989: 28) also defines property rights as "the power to limit the ability of other persons to enjoy the benefits to be secured from the use and enjoyment of a material good," the absence of which leads to minimal investment in land-augmenting improvements. Feder and Feeny (1993: 242) also view property rights as defining "the uses that are legitimately viewed as exclusive and who has these exclusive rights." Feder and Fenny also note that there is a relationship between property rights in land and resource allocation in agriculture. They contend that secure property rights in land have positive effects on yields. Their prediction is that with increased property rights security, agricultural output would rise through increase in use of inputs such as fertilizer, nonfamily labor, credit, and intensity of cultivation.

Property rights serve to assign the gains and losses from actions to agents, and therefore have a profound effect on resource allocation decisions and economic performance (Feder and Fenny 1993). Thus, insecure property rights over the products of the land cause lower farm productivity, while secure property rights over the products of investments in land induce higher levels of labor and management effort and higher levels of investment (Feder 1993; Feder and Feeny 1991, 1993). This is consistent with new institutional economists who hold that security of property rights in the products of land stimulates greater productivity (Eggertsson 1990; Ensminger 1992; North 1981, 1989, 1990, 1993a, 1993b).

Freedom from expropriation has also been emphasized by Alchian and Demsetz (1973) and Demsetz (1967) in their argument for a positive link between property rights and investment decisions. Individual farmers will not invest their labor and other productive resources in agricultural activities if the fruits of their investments are likely to be seized by others. A good example in the context of this study would be a husband who allocates a plot of land to a wife with the understanding that she will be able to control the output from that plot. Wives whose husbands consistently renege on the deal may work less hard on those plots and therefore achieve lower yields because they factor in the probability of losing the fruits of their labor. Secure property rights that are stable within a framework of well-defined laws and customs governing rights over the products of the land may guard against such occurrences.

Property rights theory also teaches us that efficiency requires that rights should be assigned and that they should be easy to identify and verify (Alston et al. 1996). Cornia (1994) notes that under secure property rights systems, all costs and benefits of individual action are fully internalized and thereby create motivation to greater productivity. This leads to an increase in investment as well as demand for various yield-boosting complementary agricultural inputs.

Barzel (1989), Libecap (1989), North (1990), and North and Thomas (1973) argue that security of property rights is crucial because it affects decision making regarding resource use, economic behavior, and agricultural performance. By assigning ownership to valuable assets and designating who bears the rewards and costs of resource-use decisions, property rights systems structure incentives for the economic behavior of farmers. While the theoretical importance of security in property rights has been given considerable attention in new institutional economics, empirical application of this theoretical perspective has been less explored.

Recent studies of security of property rights in land and its products in developing countries have also revealed that alterations to property rights in land are a central feature of development policy. While examining the link between property rights and investment incentives, Besley (1995) notes that land occupiers who lack secure property rights in their holdings will not expend effort in investments, the fruits of which can be seized by another person. An insecure farmer may not take any interest in increasing the output of a farm if he/she fears that another person will appropriate the yields.

It is therefore plausible that women farmers with insecure property rights over the products of their investment in the plots they cultivate may have the lowest levels of investment in their agricultural resource base (i.e., use of purchased inputs and extension service). This implies that clear and secure property rights over the products of investment in the land are essential to the acceleration of agricultural development through the enhancement of appropriate use of agricultural inputs for the purpose of increasing agricultural output. The existence of secure property rights over the products of the land can also improve the farmers' incentives to: (1) use credit, (2) intensify land use, and (3) invest in the conservation and improvement of their cultivated plots. An empirical analysis of how use of agricultural inputs is affected by women's control over the products of their investment in land will provide new insights and contribute to a better understanding of the motivations, challenges, and complexities of the daily activities of women farmers.

The results of my analyses of data from the Maragoli clearly demonstrate that women farmers' plot-level control over the products of their agricultural investment significantly predicted their agricultural output (Gwako 1997c). This outcome indicates that Maragoli women farmers were responsive to economic incentives and their behavior was consistent with new institutional economics and, in particular, property rights theory which predicts that increased property rights security should lead to improved incentives in farming. In the subsequent sections of this chapter, case study findings are presented to demonstrate how Maragoli women farmers achieved high plot-level yields through selective use of more agricultural inputs on the plots where they anticipated the greatest individual gains.

The Case Study

Fieldwork upon which this chapter is based was conducted among the Maragoli (also known as the Logoli or Avalogoli) of Mambai sublocation, in Vihiga District of the Western Province of Kenya. The Maragoli are the most numerous group in Vihiga District, which is also home to the Tiriki, Banyore, and other minority subtribes which make up the wider Abaluhya ethnic group. Abaluhya is a supraethnic term for people identifying themselves with smaller groupings in western Kenya (Curtis 1995).

The relatively autonomous Abaluhya subethnic groups form a linguistic and cultural subarea where closely related dialects are spoken, common bonds of kinship are recognized, and a large core of common customs and values prevails (Wagner 1949). Considerable dialect variation is found among the various Abaluhya subethnic groups. Members of the Abaluhya subethnic groups share and speak mutually understandable dialects of the western Bantu Luluhya language. Most contemporary Luluhya speakers have at least upper primary-level education and are also fluent speakers of both English and Kiswahili.[1] Various ethnographic studies have also pointed out that the Abaluhya subtribes are comprised of a relatively loose collection of patrilineal clans (Bradley 1995a; Kilbride and Kilbride 1990; Osogo 1966; Wagner 1949; Were 1967). The primary domestic unit among the Maragoli is the patrilineally extended family homestead.

Although the Maragoli practice both horticulture and animal husbandry, their extremely high population density has led to a loss of grazing land and, consequently, to a decline in herds.[2] Agricultural production in the Western Province of Kenya remains heavily subsistence-oriented (Curtis 1995). Agricultural land for personal subsistence is expensive and scarce. Cash cropping is small-scale, catering mostly to local markets. Most people farm on one-quarter to one-half acre of land. Wage labor positions are scarce and there is no suggestion of improvement. It is mainly women who farm, as men work or look for work in the wage labor sector, usually outside the area (Abwunza 1995; J. Moock 1975; P. Moock 1976).

Although Maragoli women have access to and use land as a productive resource, they continue to face some constraints in obtaining exclusive and absolute rights to a plot of land through purchase, inheritance, and the state titling system. Thus, while most women may not necessarily have titles to the land holdings, some of them often enjoy the right to manage plots and to use the products of their investments in those plots.

While much of the theoretical literature predicts a relationship between property rights over the products of the land and agricultural performance, and much development practice accepts this assumption, there is in fact little empirical data to support it. In fact, some of the best studies we have (Besley 1995; Bruce and Migot-Adholla 1994; Hoff et al. 1993; Migot-Adholla et al. 1991) fail to confirm this relationship. These analyses made the mistake of measuring property rights in land and its products at the household parcel level, rather than the individual plot level, which may not be the same thing at all to women in the household.

Both men and women in African households are sensitive to incentives and care more about output on their own plots (Abbas 1997; Davison 1988). A similar argument has been made by Udry (1996: 1028) based on his finding that "somewhat more household female labor per hectare is devoted to plots controlled by women than plots controlled by men." Thus control over the products of investments in land has been argued to be important in the understanding of agricultural production (Robertson and Berger 1986). Therefore, individual Maragoli women's control over the benefits that derive from their cultivated plots of land is an important consideration in the understanding of their agricultural output. Some of the Maragoli women work household land over which they, as women, have no ownership rights. In almost all cases, Maragoli women farmers only have indirect access to plots of land through their relationship with a man. Although Maragoli male household heads are the holders of titles to the land holdings, women are the key farmers on the various plots within the land parcels. However, some of the women farmers have low control over the products of their investment in the land because some of the men tend to claim women's labor and capital investments in the plots of land without paying and/or compensating them.

The hypothesis tested in this study is that women's crop control is a key determinant of their use of agricultural input at the plot level. The degree to which women control the fruits of the previous harvest of a given plot of land is hypothesized to be a key determinant of their efforts to ensure high yields through greater use of agricultural inputs on the same plot of land in the current season.

Operationalization of the Variables

The definitions of the variables used in this study are presented in the following section.[3] A woman farmer's crop control (control over the products of a plot of land) was measured as the percent of plot yield from the 1995 long rains season used by her. For example, if the total Kenya shillings (Kshs) value of plot yields for the 1995 long rains season was Kshs 16,000 and the woman farmer who had primary farming responsibility on that plot used Kshs 11,000, then her plot-level crop control equals 11,000 divided by 16,000, and then multiplied by 100, thus resulting in a plot-level crop control of nearly 69 percent. I used women's plot-level crop control for the 1995 long rains agricultural season as a predictor of their plot-level agricultural output per acre for the 1996 long rains agricultural season. Household wealth was measured in terms of the sum of the Kenya shillings replacement value of the household's owned on-farm and off-farm buildings, farm equipment, and livestock. Dependency ratio was calculated as the total number of dependents in the household (less than sixteen and greater than fifty-nine years old) divided by the number of adults (greater than fifteen and less than sixty years old). Each woman's total income was derived from the sum of all cash income and remittances in both kind and cash (in Kenya shillings) from all sources for a period of twelve months. A household was defined to include everyone with a stake in the household wealth and land holding, with some of its members living and working together on the holding for at least part of the year and recognizing the headship of one individual who may exercise authority in some but not necessarily all decisions relating to the members' farm and off-farm enterprises. I considered members of the household to include all resident and nonresident individuals and workers either living, farming, and/or eating together in a place of residence located within the research site for at least part of the year. Women's formal education was measured by establishing their completed number of years of formal schooling. Husbands' residence status was measured as either continuously absent (deceased), nonresident (lived outside the research site), or resident (lived within the research site).

The dependent variable—agricultural output per acre for each plot cultivated during the 1996 long rains agricultural season—was measured as the monetary value of the harvest in Kenya shillings based on the local market prices within the research site where most of the farmers sold their agricultural produce, divided by the plot size. Plot sizes were established by measuring their total area in acres.

Of the sample of 120 women farmers, the average plot-level crop control was nearly 59 percent, that is, the women controlled about 59 percent of the yields of all plots. Average household wealth was Kshs 79,018 ($1,437),[4] average dependency ratio was 0.9, average income of the women farmers was Kshs 17,937.5 ($326), average household size was 6.4 members, mean education was 4.4 years, average agricultural output was Kshs 12,135 ($221), and average plot size was 0.11 acres.

Crop Control and the Use of Extension Service

I found that extension workers are fully aware of the fact that women are major contributors in farming. I specifically observed that extension officers directly and closely worked with women farmers with the view of transferring extension knowledge to them. Transferring extension knowledge to women farmers who do the bulk of the farm work not only helps them as individual farmers, but also contributes to the realization of higher levels of national agricultural output and improved economic well-being of their families and communities.

The discussion that follows focuses on the effect of women farmers' crop control on their use of extension service. The results of this study suggest that crop control is an important factor influencing women farmers' efforts to seek and use extension service. According to table 1.1, a high percentage of Maragoli women farmers who sought and utilized extension service in their cultivated plots of land had very high crop control. Specifically, the percent of women farmers who sought and utilized extension service increased with increase in crop control, from 7.5 percent in the plots where women had low crop control to 45.5 percent in the plots where women had moderate crop control, 91.2 percent in the plots where women had high crop control, and 98.5 percent in the plots where women farmers had very high crop control. Overall, women sought extension for 67.6 percent of the plots they cultivated.

Table 1.1.   Cross-tabulation of plot-level crop control by whether women farmers sought and utilized extension service

Plot-level crop control	Sought and used extension service		
	No	Yes	Total
Low crop control	49	4	53
Moderate crop control	54	45	99
High crop control	5	52	57
Very high crop control	2	129	131
Total	110	230	340

More women farmers who sought and/or utilized extension service in their cultivated plots of land were members of established women's groups. Table 1.2 suggests that women who are members of women's groups sought extension help on 73.4 percent of their cultivated plots, while those who are not members sought help on only 57.9 percent of their cultivated plots. This suggests that women's groups and other associations might be important contact points for the dissemination of agricultural innovations. Abwunza (1995) also noted that women's groups among the Maragoli serve as avenues for discussing and disseminating agricultural assistance and innovations. Bindlish and Evenson (1997) have also noted that a high proportion of Kenyan farmers who reported receiving extension advice after the introduction of T&V were members of such groups. My fieldwork indicates that among the Maragoli, individual women who are not contact farmers access information about extension service through participation in women's group activities. Table 1.3 also shows that women farmers with the highest plot-level crop control are the most likely to be members of women's groups.

Table 1.2.   Cross-tabulation of membership in women's groups by whether women farmers sought and utilized extension service

		Sought and utilized extension service		
		No	Yes	Total
Membership in	No	53	3	126
women's groups	Yes	57	157	214
	Total	110	230	340

Table 1.3.   Cross-tabulation of women farmers' group membership status by their plot-level crop control

		Plot-level crop control				
		Low	Moderate	High	Very high	Total
Membership in	No	20	47	24	35	126
women's groups	Yes	33	52	33	96	214
Total		53	99	57	131	340

The hypothesis tested in the subsequent discussions is that "the higher the degree of women's plot-level crop control (controlling for income), the higher their use of complementary agricultural inputs." The specific inputs used to test this hypothesis are use of extension service, fertilizer, and hybrid seeds. No use of credit and hired labor was reported among Maragoli farmers of my research site and hence there is no need to include these two variables in the analyses. Pesticides and herbicides were reported, but in less than ten plots out of 340, which were not sufficient for statistical analysis. The stated hypothesis attempts to link theoretical predictions regarding crop control and women farmers' willingness to make efforts in investments in agricultural output.

The results of the linear regression of crop control and women farmers' utilization of extension service revealed that about 53 percent of the women farmers' use of extension service is predicted by their crop control with the following reported statistics: $r^2=.530$, $p=.001$, and $n=339$. These results suggest that crop control had a significant effect on whether women farmers sought and utilized extension service. Extension service is supposed to equip farmers with basic husbandry practices such as spacing, planting dates, improved cultivars, and fertilizer applications. The tapping of extension service also improves the farmers' knowledge of top dressing of fertilizer, plant protection chemicals, and stalk borer control.

I also performed a multiple linear regression analysis in order to establish the amount of variability in women cultivators' use of extension service that is explained by crop control, household wealth, dependency ratio, women's income, household size, years of schooling, women farmers' age, husbands' residence status, and membership in women's groups. This model yielded statistically significant results with $r^2=.542$, $p=.001$, and $n=339$. This suggests that approximately 54 percent of the use of extension service is predicted by this multiple linear regression model. However, the coefficients of the model indicate that only crop control ($p=.001$) is a statistically significant contributor in this analysis.

Crop Control and Use of Fertilizer

Studies have shown that in situations where farmers don't have sufficient composite manure for use on their farms, they tend to opt for nitrogen-fixing fertilizer (Mbatia 1994; Probert, Okalebo, and Jones 1995). Farmers consider the use of fertilizer as necessary and appropriate for improving the nutrient contents of their farms in order to enhance yields. In this section, I present results regarding Maragoli women farmers' use of fertilizer for purposes of increasing their agricultural production.

The scatter plot with a linear regression line of the relationship between women farmers' crop control and the money they spent to purchase fertilizer is presented in figure 1.1, which also shows that there is significant heterogeneity of variance. Consequently, I transformed the dependent variable (use of fertilizer). I had to add one to the original data in order to keep my sample size intact because there were many cases with 0 values that a natural log transformation would otherwise convert to missing values. Although this scatter plot nicely captures the linear relationship between crop control and fertilizer use, the cases of no fertilizer use lined upon the Y-axis are clearly outliers. These outliers are largely explained by the fact that fertilizer is inappropriate for some crops such as bananas, cassava, sweet potatoes, sugarcane, and nappier grass. Approximately

three quarters of the plots where no fertilizer was used fall into this category. I would argue, therefore, that the linear pattern exhibited in figure
1.1 is the true relationship.

Figure 1.1. A scatter plot with a linear regression line showing the relationship
between crop control and fertilizer use

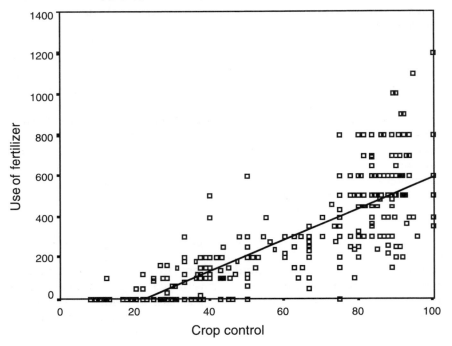

Despite the heterogeneity of variance, the linear regression analysis
above revealed a significant effect of crop control on women farmers' use
of fertilizer with the following results: r^2=.660, p=.001, and n=339. These
results suggest that nearly 60 percent of women farmers' use of fertilizer
is attributable to their crop control. These results reveal that an increase in
women farmers' plot-level crop control from zero to 100 percent is likely
to enhance their use of fertilizer by about 500 percent. The linear regression of crop control and the natural log of fertilizer use were also highly
significant with: r^2=.630, p=.001, and n=339.

Overall, these findings are consistent with the results of a study by
Mbatia (1994) which indicates that fertilizer adoption is more sensitive to
sociological and institutional factors (e.g., secure property rights over the
crop) than to economic factors such as labor and credit availabilities. It is

therefore apparent that the use of fertilizer, along with improved cropping practices learned through extension services, contributed toward the high yields attained by those women farmers who had high crop control. Most of the women farmers who enjoyed high crop control took the initiative to purchase inputs and actually sought and used advice from the ministry of agriculture's field extension workers. Thus high crop control stimulated women farmers' willingness to incur extra costs (both in time and money) for the purpose of increasing their yields.

Crop control also made significant contributions to the predicted use of fertilizer among women farmers in a multiple linear regression model. The variables entered in this multiple linear regression model are crop control, household wealth, dependency ratio, women's income, household size, years of schooling, women farmers' age, husbands' residence status, and membership in women's groups. Together these variables predicted nearly 67 percent of women farmers' use of fertilizers with r^2=.668, p=.001, and n=329. The significance of coefficients reveals that crop control is the only statistically significant predictor of women farmers' use of fertilizer.

Crop Control and Use of Hybrid Seeds

Maragoli women farmers of my research site work toward increasing production on the plots of land already in use in order to boost their yields so that they can feed their families and secure a surplus to increase cash earnings. Farmers have to make a decision to use hybrid seeds or seeds selected from the previous agricultural season's harvest. The decision to use improved seed varieties or some other alternative is influenced by several factors. The following discussions focus on the effect of crop control and all the other independent variables already explored in the previous sections of this chapter on women farmers' use of hybrid seeds.

Encouraging the use of improved seed varieties is one of the components of Kenya's agricultural extension program. However, farmers' receptiveness to the Kenya government's extension program is not homogenous and is significantly influenced by a number of considerations; the data indicates that crop control is the primary determinant of such adoption.

Figure 1.2 shows a scatter plot with a linear regression line of the relationship between crop control and use of hybrid seeds. Even though heterogeneity of variance is evident in this scatter plot, a linear relationship between crop control and the use of improved seed varieties is clearly evident. This was further ascertained through the analysis of the relationship between crop control and the natural log of use of hybrid seeds (I had to add one to the original data in order to keep my sample size intact because there were many cases with 0 values that a natural log transformation would otherwise convert to missing values). Plots where women grow crops for which there are no high-yielding varieties—such as bananas, cassava, sweet potatoes, sugarcane, and nappier grass—are clear outliers in figure 1.2.

Figure 1.2. A scatter plot with a linear regression line showing the relationship between crop control and use of hybrid seeds

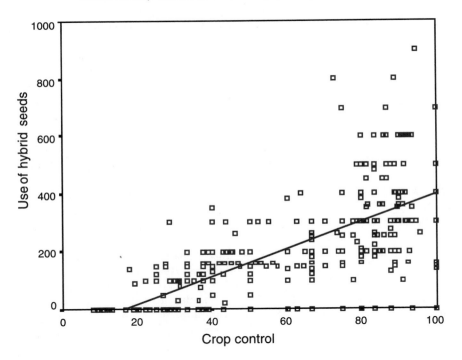

The results of linear regression analysis are consistent with the hypothesis that women with greater crop control are more likely to use yield-boosting inputs such as hybrid seeds. A summary of the coefficients of the linear regression mode are as follows: $r^2=.499$, $p=.001$, and $n=339$. These results suggest that crop control predicts nearly 50 percent of the women farmers' use of hybrid seeds. The linear regression results of crop control and the natural log of use of hybrid seeds predicted about 44 percent of women's use of hybrid seeds with $r^2=.440$, significant at $p=.001$.

Additional results from the multiple linear regression explained nearly 51 percent of women farmers' use of high-yielding seed varieties with $r^2=.507$, $p=.001$, and $n=339$. However, the only multiple regression coefficients that were found to be statistically significant from among the nine variables included in the model are crop control with $p=.001$ and dependency ratio ($p=.025$), which was found to have a negative effect on women farmers' use of hybrid seeds. Thus crop control varies positively with women farmers' use of hybrid seeds while dependency ratio has a depressive effect on their use of high-yielding seed varieties.

Crop Control and Agricultural Labor Input

In this section, I present data on the effect of crop control on the percentage of time women spend on their cultivated plots. A linear regression analysis revealed a significant effect of crop control on women farmers' agricultural labor input with the following results: $r^2=.255$, $p=.001$, and $n=339$. These results suggest that about 25 percent of the surveyed women farmers' agricultural labor input is attributable to their crop control. It would appear, therefore, that high plot-level crop control stimulated women farmers to invest extra labor in plots over which they controlled output in order to increase the agricultural output of those plots.

Women farmers' crop control also made a statistically significant contribution to the predicted value of agricultural labor input in a multiple linear regression model. In this model, I entered crop control, household wealth, dependency ratio, women's income, household size, years of schooling, women farmers' age, husbands' residence status, and membership in women's groups, which significantly predicted nearly 29 percent of farmers' agricultural labor input with $r^2=.285$, $p=.001$, and $n=339$. Multiple regression coefficients suggest that crop control and women's age were statistically significant predictors of agricultural labor input; as one might expect, women's age varies negatively with agricultural labor input.

Qualitative Discussion of Factors Affecting Use of Farm Inputs

My key informants and focus group discussants confirmed the quantitative relationships presented in this chapter. Women expressed a desire for high agricultural output but also indicated that low crop control discouraged them from realizing this objective in the plots where their husbands or some other household member(s) expropriated the products of their efforts. This appears also to be well understood by husbands, who have devised ingenious schemes for manipulating incentives to control their wives' labor.

Informants indicated that in some multicropped plots the husband may have significant control over the yields of some crop(s) while the wife has crop control over the yields of the other crop(s). For example, sometimes wives are invited to plant potatoes, onions, tomatoes, groundnuts, or beans between the rows of their husbands' tea seedlings, especially when the tea seedlings are between the ages of one and three years. Husbands control the cash earnings from the harvest of tea leaves but allow their wives to plant such crops between the tea lines in part as an incentive for them to weed the tea plants, which they cannot avoid doing in the process of weeding their own crops. Thus, while women take advantage of the economic benefits of intercropping various crops, especially cash crops and food crops (see also Njoroge and Kimemia 1995), men help solve their agency problem by indirectly motivating women to work on men's crops.

Women farmers were also aware that greater crop control caused them to respond to extension service innovations and recommendations. They believe that crop control increases their openness to new ideas and sensitivity to high-yielding seed varieties because they stand to gain from the benefits accruing from higher yields. Women farmers also know that a mix of crops allows for better crop rotation—e.g., rotating crops during the long and short rainy seasons of the year. They also believe that early maturing maize provides good results and leaves them with sufficient time for both preparing the soil and planting some other crops in the same plot(s) during the short rainy season.

Higher crop control also motivates women to do more intercropping and better crop rotation. For example, they combine recommended hybrid maize seed varieties with some other legumes during the long rains season and, thereafter, devote the same plots of land to the cultivation of legumes (e.g., groundnuts) during the short rains season in order to maximize returns. Women believe that maize planted during the long rains in plots previously used for legumes during the short rains (which fix nutrients in the soil) tend to do better than in plots used continuously for maize; this also reduces the need for nitrogen fertilizer.

Use of Credit

Not all the farmers in my sample applied for or received any loans for agricultural activities. The farmers in my research site were very reluctant to apply for loans because they feared that their land might be repossessed if they were unable to repay the loans within the stipulated period. However, a more fundamental consideration is the fact that the land holdings in the research site were too small to meet the Agricultural Finance Corporation's minimum acreage of 2 acres before a farmer's application for credit can get through the preliminary consideration stage. This requirement cuts off most of the farmers in my research site.

The focus group discussants indicated that interest-free borrowing from relatives, friends, neighbors, and women's groups is a major source of credit for Maragoli women farmers. An increasing number of Maragoli women have taken the initiative to mobilize and organize themselves into self-help groups. As active economic providers for their families, the success of their women's group movements is documented by their accumulation of cash, food, blankets, lanterns, utensils, and, even more important, their ability to borrow, lend, and provide support to each other in times of need, whether occasioned by unexpected guests or by death. Although Abwunza (1995) noted that Maragoli women groups are a major source of agricultural soft loans to their members, my findings from focus group discussants suggest that money borrowed from women's associations is mainly used for nonagricultural emergency needs such as food, sickness or death in the family, to entertain visitors, and in rare cases to pay for school fees. This expenditure pattern was also noted by Aritho (1995) who studied the effects of household income and seasonal food price changes on household expenditure patterns in Vihiga District, western Kenya.

Women farmers who cultivate French beans are provided inputs on credit by the company that buys harvested French beans. Tea farmers also receive fertilizer on credit from the Kenya Tea Development Authority for use in the tea crop. The fertilizer credit facility is extended to tea growers on condition that the Kenya Tea Development Authority recovers the cost from the farmers' monthly payments within a twelve-month period. However, some of the women farmers I interviewed indicated that their husbands usually dispose of the tea fertilizer and use the money for other non-farm-related purposes.

Conclusions

The results presented in this chapter suggest that crop control is a major predictor of women farmers' use of extension service, fertilizer, high-yielding seed varieties, and agricultural labor input. The findings presented herein also indicate that women are receptive to agricultural innovations and recommendations and that crop control plays a significant role in their responsiveness to improved farming technology. These results are therefore consistent with the hypothesis that greater crop control is more likely to encourage use of complementary farm inputs. Overall, the behavior of Maragoli women farmers is consistent with a model based on individual maximization in the context of property rights theory, which predicts that secure rights stimulate greater investments which eventually result in greater productivity.

It is significant that Maragoli women farmers' own perceptions of their behavior validated the quantitative findings presented here. The women farmers interviewed in this study believed that true increase in agricultural output comes through increased investment in land which is stimulated by secure control over the agricultural produce and cash earnings from the plots they cultivate. It was apparent to me that these women farmers were extremely responsive to secure plot-level crop control, market incentives, and other economic opportunities such as non-farm enterprises.

Secure plot-level crop control provides the motivation for higher yields, accomplished through selective application of additional agricultural inputs to the plots where control of the output was guaranteed. This study also revealed that both male and female government agricultural extension workers are consulted by women farmers; the extension workers pay visits to the plots cultivated by women farmers to deliver new information about agricultural innovations. I was informed by some of the agricultural extension workers that this approach of working with both male and, in particular, female farmers is a result of their increasing realization and awareness that women farmers contribute more of the agricultural labor than men in rural Kenya. The government is also increasingly hiring more female extension workers to facilitate and accelerate the delivery of information about agricultural innovations and recommendations to female farmers who feel more comfortable and free to discuss their needs with women extension workers.

The interviews conducted with women farmers suggested that they knew the kinds of information agricultural extension workers should provide and what they (the farmers) wanted in order to improve their yields. The agricultural extension workers also indicated that women farmers are very sensitive and paid attention to extension advice and followed instructions. However, the extension officers also indicated that women farmers will benefit more by touring the plots of the more progressive farmers in order to learn new ideas and new technology, and also by using more high-quality farm inputs such as high-yielding seed varieties, fertilizer, new crop varieties, and farm implements. Even with the availability of more and better inputs, the realization of increased productivity will largely depend on women farmers' incentives, which were found to be significantly influenced by their secure property rights over the products of their investments in agriculture. This study revealed that the productivity performance of a plot of land is mainly a function of the individual cultivators' secure property rights over the agricultural produce and cash earnings. This case study demonstrates the practical relevance of secure property rights to land not for the household, but for the cultivator; more often than not the cultivator in Africa is a woman.

Notes

1. This was one of the regions in western Kenya settled earlier by missionaries (Kaimosi Friends African Mission), which accounted for the high incidences of education and fluency in English.

2. Recent estimates indicated that the Abaluhya had a total population of about 3.5 million and was the second largest ethnic group in Kenya (Bradley 1995a; Burton and Winsor 1993). Earlier estimates of Sabatia (and Vihiga District) indicated that it had the highest rural population growth rate and rural population density in Kenya at about 1,212 persons per square kilometer (Jaetzold and Schmidt 1982; Ominde 1988; Republic of Kenya 1989a 1989b). Although some recent evidence suggests a decline in fertility among the Maragoli (Bradley 1995b; Gwako 1997a 1997b), total fertility rates, until the late 1980s, exceeded nine births per woman of childbearing age (Bradley 1995a).

3. The correlation matrix of the independent variables revealed that the only correlation above 0.40 was between age and women's education ($r=-.545$), indicating that multicollinearity was not a problem in the multiple linear regression analyses. The independent variables were therefore appropriate for use in regression analyses predicting agricultural output per acre. After evaluating the distribution of data and variance patterns, I decided to use the square root of agricultural output per acre throughout the analyses (with the exception of women whose husbands were nonresidents) because this was found to enhance conformity to the assumptions of the linear regression model. Subsequent comments regarding agricultural output should be understood as referring to the square root of agricultural output per acre (with the exception of women whose husbands were nonresidents).

4. All the 1996 U.S. dollar exchange rates reported by the Nairobi Stock Exchange averaged fifty-five Kenya shillings (Kshs) to one U.S. dollar.

References

Abbas, D. J.
  1997 "Gender Asymmetries in Intrahousehold Resource Allocation in Sub-Saharan Africa: Some Policy Implications for Land and Labour Productivity." Pp. 249–62 in *Intrahousehold Resource Allocation in Developing Countries: Models, Methods, and Policy*, L. Haddad, J. Hoddinott, and H. Alderman, eds. Baltimore: Johns Hopkins University Press.

Abwunza, J. M.
    1995   "'Silika'—To Make Our Lives Shine: Women's Groups in Maragoli, Kenya." *Anthropologica* 37(1): 27–48.
Alchian, A. A., and H. Demsetz
    1973   "The Property Rights Paradigm." *Journal of Economic History* 33(1): 16–27.
Alston, L. J., T. Eggertsson, and D. C. North, eds.
    1996   *Empirical Studies in Institutional Change*. Cambridge: Cambridge University Press.
Alston, L. J., G. D. Libecap, and B. Mueller
    1997   "Violence and the Development of Property Rights to Land in Brazilian Amazon." Pp.145–63 in *The Frontiers of New Institutional Economics*, J. N. Drobak and J. V. C. Nye, eds. San Diego: Academic Press.
Aritho, L. M.
    1995   *The Effect of Household Income and Seasonal Food Price Changes on Household Expenditure Patterns: A Case Study of Vihiga District*. Leiden, Netherlands: African Studies Center.
Barzel, Y.
    1989   *Economic Analysis of Property Rights*. Cambridge: Cambridge University Press.
Bates, R. H.
    1989   *Beyond the Miracle of the Market: The Political Economy of Agrarian Development in Kenya*. Cambridge: Cambridge University Press.
Benor, D., J. Q. Harrison, and M. Baxter
    1984   *Agricultural Extension: The Training and Visit System*. Washington D.C.: World Bank.
Besley, T.
    1995   "Property Rights and Investment Incentives: Theory and Evidence from Ghana." *Journal of Political Economy* 103(5): 903–37.
Bindlish, V., and R. E. Evenson
    1997   "The Impact of T&V Extension in Africa: The Experience of Kenya and Burkina Faso." *The World Bank Observer* 12: 183–201.
Bradley, C.
    1995a   "Luhia." Pp. 202–6 in *Encyclopedia of World Cultures* 9, J. Middleton and A. Rassam, eds. Boston: G. K. Hall.
    1995b   "Women's Empowerment and Fertility Decline in Western Kenya." Pp. 157–78 in *Situating Fertility: Anthropology and Demographic Inquiry*, S. Greenhalgh, ed. Cambridge: Cambridge University Press.
Bruce, J. W., and S. E. Migot-Adholla, eds.
    1994   *Searching for Land Tenure Security in Africa*. Dubuque: Kendall/Hunt.
Burton, V., and R. Winsor
    1993   "Society, Culture, and the Kenyan Family." Pp. 5–33 in *Kenya: The Land, the People, and the Nation*, M. Azevedo, ed. Durban: Carolina Academic Press.
Chitere, P. O.
    1993   "Sampling of Smallholder Farmers for Involvement in Farm Adoption Studies in Western Kenya." *Journal of Eastern African Research and Development* 23: 151–59.

Chitere, P. O., and B. A. Omolo
   1993   "Farmer's Indigenous Knowledge of Crop Pests and their Damage in Western Kenya." *International Journal of Pest Management* 39: 126–32.
Cleaver, K. M.
   1993   *A Strategy to Develop Agriculture in Sub-Saharan Africa: A Focus for the World Bank.* Washington D.C.: World Bank.
Cornia, G. A.
   1994   "Neglected Issues in the Decline of Africa's Agriculture: Land Tenure, Land Distribution and R&D Constraints." Pp. 217–47 in *From Adjustment to Development in Africa: Conflicts, Controversy, Convergence, Consensus?* G. A. Cornia and G. K. Helleiner, eds. New York: St. Martins.
Curtis, J. W.
   1995   *Opportunity and Obligation in Nairobi: Social Networks and Differentiation in the Political Economy of Kenya.* Hamburg: Lit.
Davison, J.
   1988   "Land and Women's Agricultural Production: The Context." Pp. 1–32 in *Agriculture, Women, and Land: The African Experience*, J. Davison, ed. Boulder, Colo.: Westview Press.
Demsetz, H.
   1967   "Towards a Theory of Property Rights." *American Economic Review Papers and Proceedings.* 57(2): 347–59.
Drobak, J. N., and J. V. C. Nye, eds.
   1997   *The Frontiers of New Institutional Economics.* San Diego: Academic Press.
Eggertsson, T.
   1990   *Economic Behavior and Institutions.* Cambridge: Cambridge University Press.
Ensminger, J.
   1992   *Making a Market: The Institutional Transformation of an African Society.* Cambridge: Cambridge University Press.
Feder, G.
   1993   "The Economics of Land and Titling in Thailand." Pp. 259–68 in *The Economics of Rural Organization: Theory, Policy, and Practice*, K. Hoff, A. Braverman, and J. E. Stiglitz, eds. New York: Oxford University Press.
Feder, G., and D. Feeny
   1991   "Land Tenure and Property Rights: Theory and Implications for Development Policy." *The World Bank Economic Review* 5(1): 135–53.
   1993   "The Theory of Land Tenure and Property Rights." Pp. 240–58 in *The Economics of Rural Organization: Theory, Policy, and Practice.* K. Hoff, A. Braverman, and J. E. Stiglitz, eds. New York: Oxford University Press.
Gathegi, J. N.
   1994   "Organizational Effectiveness of the Agricultural Scientific Information Dissemination and Management Systems in Kenya." *Journal of Agricultural and Food Information* 2: 85–101.
Gwako, E. L. M.
   1997a   "Conjugal Power in Rural Kenya Families: Its Influence on Women's Decisions about Family Size and Family Planning Practices." *Sex Roles: A Journal of Research* 36(3/4): 127–47.

1997b   "Married Women's Ideal Family Size Preferences and Family Planning Practices: Evidence From Rural Kenya." *The Social Science Journal* 34(3): 369–82.

1997c   *The Effects of Women's Land Tenure Security on Agricultural Output among the Maragoli of Western Kenya.* Ann Arbor: University Microfilm International.

Hoff, K., A. Braverman, and J. E. Stiglitz, eds.

1993   *The Economics of Rural Organization: Theory, Practice, and Policy.* Oxford: Oxford University Press.

Jaetzold, R., and H. Schmidt

1982   *Farm Management Handbook of Kenya: Volume 11/A, West Kenya.* Nairobi: Ministry of Agriculture.

Kilbride, K. P., and J. C. Kilbride

1990   *Changing Family Life in East Africa: Women and Children at Risk.* University Park: Pennsylvania State University Press.

Libecap, G. D.

1989   *Contracting for Property Rights.* Cambridge: Cambridge University Press.

Mbatia, J. N.

1994   "Fertilizer Adoption by Small-Scale Farmers in Nakuru District, Kenya." *Fertilizer Research* 38: 141–50.

Migot-Adholla, S. E., P. Hazell, B. Blarel, and F. Place

1991   "Indigenous Land Rights Systems in Sub-Saharan Africa: A Constraint on Productivity?" *The World Bank Economic Review* 5(1): 155–75.

Moock, J. L.

1975   "The Migration Process and Differential Economic Behavior in South Maragoli, Western Kenya." Ph.D. thesis, Columbia University.

Moock, P.

1976   "The Efficiency of Women as Farm Managers: Kenya." *American Journal of Agricultural Economics* 58(5): 831–35.

Njoroge, J. M., and J. K. Kimemia

1995   "Economic Benefits of Intercropping Young Arabica and Robusta Coffee with Food Crops in Kenya." *Outlook on Agriculture* 24: 27–34.

North, D. C.

1981   *Structure and Change in Economic History.* New York: Norton.

1987   "Institutions, Transaction Costs and Economic Growth." *Economic Inquiry* 25(3): 419–28.

1989   "Institutions and Economic Growth: An Historical Introduction." *World Development* 17(9): 1319–32.

1990   *Institutions, Institutional Change and Economic Performance.* Cambridge: Cambridge University Press.

1993a   "The Ultimate Sources of Economic Growth." Pp. 65–76 in *Explaining Economic Growth: Essays in Honour of Angus Maddisson*, A. Szirmai, B. V. Ark, and D. Pilat, eds. Amsterdam: North-Holland.

1993b   "Towards a Theory of Institutional Change." Pp. 61–69 in *Political Economy: Institutions, Competition and Representation: Proceedings of the Seventh International Symposium in Economic Theory and Econometrics*, W. A. Barnett, M. J. Hinich, and N. J. Schofield, eds. Cambridge: Cambridge University Press.

North, D. C., and R. P. Thomas
1973   *The Rise of the Western World: A New Economic History.* Cambridge: Cambridge University Press.
North, D. C., and B. R. Weingast
1996   "Constitutions and Commitment: The Evolution of Institutions Governing Public Choice in Seventeenth-Century England." Pp.134–65 in *Empirical Studies in Institutional Change*, L. J. Alston, T. Eggertsson, and D. C. North, eds. Cambridge: Cambridge University Press.
Ominde, S. H., ed.
1988   *Kenya's Population Growth and Development to the Year 2000 A.D.* Nairobi: Heinemann Kenya.
Ongaro, W. A.
1988   "Adoption of New Farming Technology: A Case Study of Maize Production in Western Kenya." Ph.D. dissertation, Göteborg University, Sweden.
Osogo, J.
1966   *A History of the Baluyia.* Nairobi: Oxford University Press.
Probert, M. E., J. R. Okalebo, and R. K. Jones
1995   "The Use of Manure on Smallholder Farms in Semi-Arid Eastern Kenya." *Experimental Agriculture* 31: 371–81.
Republic of Kenya
1989a   *National Development Plan 1989–1993.* Nairobi: Government Printer.
1989b   *Kakamega District Development Plan 1989–1993.* Nairobi: Government Printer.
Robertson, C. I., and I. Berger
1986   "Introduction: Analyzing Class and Gender—African Perspectives." Pp. 3–26 in *Women and Class in Africa*, C. I. Robertson and I. Berger, eds. New York: Africana Publishing.
Suda, C.
1990   "Agricultural Development Policies and Institutional Support Systems in Post-Colonial Kenya and Tanzania." *Journal of Eastern African Research and Development* 20: 104–26.
Udry, C.
1996   "Gender, Agricultural Production, and the Theory of the Household." *Journal of Political Economy* 104(5): 1010–46.
Wagner, G.
1949   *The Bantu of North Kavirondo, Vol. I.* London: Oxford University Press.
Were, G. S.
1967   *A History of the Abaluhya of Western Kenya c. 1500–1930.* Nairobi: East African Publishing.

Chapter 2

Transaction Cost Economics:
Accomplishments, Problems, and Possibilities

James M. Acheson

Introduction

The "new institutional economics" (NIE) refers to the work of a variety of social scientists concerned with the way in which institutions are generated from the decisions of individuals, and the way those institutions affect the level of productivity and exchange. It is dedicated to the idea that institutions or rule systems count. Institutions allow people to gain the benefits of coordinated activity, which has important effects on the level of productivity, efficiency, and wealth (North 1990a: vii).

Institutional economics is moving so quickly in so many different directions that it is difficult to generalize about the field, much less talk about schools of thought. A number of different subfields have emerged. One is focused on property rights and their effect on decision making (Acheson 1989: 354–57; Bromley 1989: 85–105; Demsetz 1967). The Austrian School has developed a theory of institutions and entrepreneurship (Hayak 1973; 1988). Still others are interested in rules and interaction (Axelrod 1984; Schotter 1981, 1986: 120–21). The rational choice theorists concentrate on the conditions under which people will form groups and generate rules for their mutual benefit (Buchanan 1965; Coleman 1990: 254, 272; Elster 1989a: 28 ff.; 1989b; Knight 1992: 48–64, 174–78; Olsen 1965; Taylor 1982: 50–51). Another school, closely associated with Douglass North, is concerned with the generation of basic institutions through long-term evolutionary processes (Nelson and Winter 1982; North 1983, 1984, 1990a, 1990b; North and Thomas 1973).

Most important for our purposes is "transaction cost economics," developed by Ronald Coase and Oliver Williamson, which is primarily interested in understanding how various kinds of organizations are generated in response to transaction costs (Williamson 1975, 1985, 1996). In this chapter, I will review the literature on transaction cost economics and then discuss applications to anthropology. Anthropologists are less familiar with the work of Coase and Williamson, and the potentialities for applications in anthropology are large.

Basic Concepts

The new institutional economics was considered marginal and radical not much more than a decade ago. Its marginal status was due, in part, to the fact that the practitioners of this field were concerned with rules, norms, and organizations, topics that hitherto had been the focus of anthropology, sociology, and political science. More important, institutional economics challenged the assumptions on which neoclassical economics is based, namely the idea that decision makers are rational people with perfect knowledge, engaged in exchanging homogenous goods in competitive markets. The neoclassical school sees decision makers obtaining all the information they need from market prices alone. The neoclassical school largely ignored the institutional frames within which decision makers operated. By way of contrast, the new institutional economics assumes "bounded rationality," and that information is expensive to obtain so that opportunism (self-interest with guile) is an ever-present possibility in any exchange. The atmosphere surrounding exchange is made even more uncertain by the fact that goods are not homogenous, quality is always a problem, information is rarely complete, and people do not always have secure rights to the property and services being exchanged. Market imperfections are ever present, and market failure is far from rare (Williamson 1975: 21–33). Last, but not least, the institutionalists assume that more is involved in coordinating economic activity than prices in competitive markets (Hodgson 1988: 178; Langlois 1986: 6). Institutions open opportunities and constrain decisions in a myriad of ways. If these assumptions seem blasphemous to the neoclassical economists, they seem more realistic to anthropologists and other social scientists.

Although institutional economists have worked on a wide variety of problems, six intellectual commitments are apparent in their work. First, the NIE attempts to explain the generation of institutions from the actions of individuals. For better or worse, it applies the same logic to nonmarket institutions that neoclassical economists have applied to markets.

Second, institutional economists see property rights as a key institution. Property rights are bundles of rights over goods or real estate that are enforced. No owner has all of the rights to property; some are always retained by the greater community (North 1990a: 33). Property rights are never completely enforced, and enforcement can cost a great deal. The type and security of property rights influence decisions concerning investment, conservation, and efficiency. In Eggertsson's terms (1993: 2): "It is obvious that the nature of control matters for economic actors: short-term control shortens the time horizon; uncertain control discourages potentially profitable projects; lack of control incites costly races for possession; restricted control allocates assets to inferior uses." There is, for example, a large body of literature on the common property problem which links the decision to overexploit natural resources to the absence of property rights, creating what Hardin called the "tragedy of the commons" (Acheson 1989; Hardin 1968; Scott 1955).

Third, the concept of transaction costs is central to the analyses of the institutional economists. Transaction costs refer to the time, effort, and expense of obtaining the information necessary to make an exchange, negotiate the exchange, and enforce the exchange agreement once made (Dahlman 1979: 149; Hodgson 1988: 201; Williamson 1985: 2). Institutional economists recognize that a very large number of social and cultural factors affect transaction costs. The time and effort it takes to gather information depend on such factors as literacy, communications, libraries, and transportation, while the ability to negotiate and enforce exchanges depends on a myriad of other factors, including the legal system, access to courts, standards of honesty, and standardized weights and measures. In practice, those investigating transaction costs focus on a narrow spectrum of phenomena—the costs of obtaining information on prices, markets, and business associates. In the literature, three factors are seen as the primary determinants of transaction costs. First is *frequency of exchange*, since it is easier to learn about prices, quality, etc., if there are a lot of people in the market engaged in large numbers of transactions. Second is *opportunism*, or self-interest with guile, which can include everything from outright cheating to asymmetrical information. Third and most important is *asset specificity*, which occurs when an exchange is limited to a specific location, person, or physical asset. Asset specificity lowers one's ability to bargain and increases the possibilities for opportunism (Milgrom and Roberts 1992: 28–32; Williamson 1985: 90–95; 1996: 45, 59–60).

Transaction costs can be lowered by rules or institutions that make the actions of others more predictable. The transaction costs faced by the owner of a factory are lowered by a union contract which helps to ensure a supply of labor, while a law against stealing substantially lowers the amount of time and effort needed to maintain inventories and equipment.

Fourth, one of the most important insights of the new institutional economics is that institutions stem from problems in markets. Basically this approach assumes that people obtain the goods and services they want through transactions with others. They will use the institution of the market when it is working well, but when the price system is not working well, they are able to make arrangements with each other (i.e., nonmarket institutions) to obtain the things they need. In Arrow's terms (1971: 5), "there is a wide variety of social institutions, in particular generally accepted social norms of behavior, which serve in some means as compensation for failure or limitation of the market." The new institutional economists have used this insight to account for the generation of a large number of different kinds of social arrangements, ranging from firms, markets, and property rights to clubs, families, and associations (Acheson 1994a: 6–7). Some of these arguments about the generation of nonmarket institutions are of special interest to anthropologists. Robert Bates (1994: 45–52) provides a particularly good account of the causes of market failure and the types of nonmarket institutions that result from each. Landa (1997: 1–6) argues that markets and contract law regulate exchange in modern economies, but ethnic trading networks are of critical importance in developing countries, and gift exchange systems (e.g., the Kula and potlatch) are the dominant economic institution in tribal societies.

Fifth, an important distinction needs to be made between institutions and organizations. Institutional economists define institutions as essentially sets of enforceable rules that constrain and guide human interaction. Nobel winner Douglass North defines institutions as "rules of the game" (North 1990a: 3). (Anthropologists, sociologists, and other social scientists use the term differently. Many, following Parsons, tend to define "institutions" as a cluster of statuses around a particular activity. A rule is a kind of norm.)

From the perspective of institutional economics, institutions help to lower uncertainty by ensuring the behavior of other people. As John R. Commons phrased it (1934: 705), institutions "secure expectations." A rule that we will all drive on the right-hand side of the road makes it far more certain that we will reach our destination than would be the case if there were no such rule. Institutions both constrain choices and open opportunities. A contract with a supplier to provide a raw material each day for a certain amount of money constrains both supplier and purchaser, but it also opens opportunities for a business that might not exist if the availability of the raw material at a predictable price were highly problematic.

The institutional economists see institutions as a substitute for information. If enough information were available about the intentions of others and future events, we would need no institutions.

Organizations, according to North (1990a: 4–5), are groups that come into being, given the institutions, to "win the game" or "achieve objectives." The relations between people in these organizations and between organizations are defined or constrained by the institutions (i.e., rules). Firms, trade unions, political bodies, clubs, associations, and schools are all types of organizations. In short, institutions are the rules defining interaction and competition; organizations are the units formed in accordance with these rules. The way the institutional economists view institutions and organizations is very similar to the distinction made by Bailey (1969: 4–6, 35ff) between rules and teams.

Institutions work their magic by permitting the development of more productive economic organizations. That is, opportunities for entrepreneurs as well as the aggregate level of growth for the society depend on the development of institutions and not simply technological development. Efficient institutions lower the costs of transactions and allow production and trade to flourish. North documents that the rapid development of the industrialized West is due in no small part to the development of secure property rights, money and centralized banks, commercial law, and transportation facilities (North 1990a: 9, 34, 107ff, 124; 1990b). Such institutions do not exist in Third World countries, with the result that per capita income is very low.

North and Williamson

The distinction between institutions and organizations is at the root of a central division within institutional economics itself. North focuses on institutions; Williamson is concerned with organization. North and his followers are interested in long-term, evolutionary, "invisible hand" processes determining how norms, rules, and institutions come into being in the first place (North 1990a, 1990b; Alchian 1950). These basic structural elements (i.e., property rights, contract law, central banking, governments) govern relationships between people and have long run implications for levels of growth and economic performance (Williamson 1996: 93). Williamson and others in the transaction cost economics school have focused on the ways in which firm owners have built various types of organizations using the options defined by the basic institutions or rule sets (Williamson 1975, 1979, 1985, 1996). Williamson is interested in "visible hand" processes in which people negotiate binding agreements out of existing legal structures to economize on transaction costs. The resulting agreements (called "governance structures") are the primary building blocks of firms and markets of incredible variety. These organizations are the result of private orderings, not actions of the state. The transaction cost economists do not ask how institutions come about. They simply assume that institutions exist, and then ask how business people use them as building blocks to create organizations.

North's concepts have been put to work by a number of anthropologists, most notably Jean Ensminger, who has used them to describe the development of markets and private property rights among the Orma of East Africa and the way such institutions increased development. (Ensminger 1990, 1992, 1994, 1997a, 1997b; Ensminger and Knight 1997), and David Guillet (1992a; 1992b), who has used them to understand the development of property rights and institutions to allocate water resources in Spain and Latin America. Some anthropologists are less than impressed. Wilk (1996) says that economists are "reinventing anthropology on their own without benefit of careful fieldwork."

Market Failure, Transaction Costs: The Contributions of Ronald Coase

The idea that problems in markets result in the development of nonmarket institutions was first formulated by Ronald Coase. In his 1937 paper "The Nature of the Firm," Coase argues that markets and firms are substitutable. When markets work well, people obtain what they need by using the price system; when market imperfections exist, they obtain the goods and services they need by forming firms. Coase pointed out that there would be no need for firms at all if markets were frictionless and transaction costs were low. People could obtain all they wanted by entering into a variety of market transactions. Unfortunately, markets often do not work well and people using them must overcome huge transaction costs. They form firms as a means to get around "the costs of using the price mechanism" in markets (Coase 1937: 21). From this perspective, markets and firms are quite similar. Both involve sets of contracts concerning exchanges; and they are alternative ways of obtaining goods and services. They are substitutable for each other.

But if markets and firms perform the same functions, they are still different types of organizations, involve different kinds of "rules," and have distinctive features. Markets are devoted to the exchange of goods and services through mutually agreed on exchanges in which prices give the parties to the exchange all the information they need. According to Coase, the most distinguishing feature of the firm is the "suppression of the price mechanism" so that the allocation of resources within the firm is made by "administrative fiat" (Coase 1937: 20–27; Hart 1990: 154–59; Hodgson 1988: 179–86). In addition, firms can be engaged in production. These features make firms very different from markets.

Transaction Cost Economics:
The Selection of Governance Organizations

Oliver Williamson and others interested in transaction cost economics have expanded on Coase's insight that institutions stem from market problems to delve deeply into the nature of economic organization. They have devoted themselves to understanding how different types of organizations (called "governance structures" by Williamson) are selected largely in response to transaction costs stemming from market inefficiency. Essentially, they argue that inefficient markets affect transaction costs in various ways. Entrepreneurs respond to those costs by entering into a variety of agreements with other economic actors (other firm owners, employees, banks), resulting in various kinds of economic organizations.

Most of the attention of the transaction cost economics school has been devoted to understanding the selection of various kinds of firms and markets, which stand in complex relations with each other. Recently they have extended their analysis to understand the generation of a number of other types of governance organizations such as "hybrids" and agencies.

Transaction cost economics assumes the existence of a given set of basic institutions (property rights, court system, laws, etc.) and then asks, of the myriad types of economic organizations possible (i.e., markets, firms, hybrids, and agencies), which are selected and why. These "governance structures" are seen as the result of individuals working with their own best interest in mind who enter into voluntary agreements with others in an effort to reduce transaction costs. While Williamson and his followers know that agreements between entrepreneurs are usually reinforced by legal contracts, their attention has been focused on private orderings (deals between businessmen) rather than the jural aspects of such transactions. In this sense transaction cost economics is remarkably apolitical.

Like Coase, Williamson sees markets and firms as substitutable for each other. That is, entrepreneurs can obtain the goods and services they need by going into the market and buying them from other firms or vendors, or they can make them themselves by expanding their own productive organization. Most firms do both. This means that they are involved in contracts with other firms through the market, which results in external transaction costs stemming from such problems as getting information on prices, quality of goods, and second supplier problems. They are also involved in exchanges with people in their own firm. These are associated with internal transaction costs resulting from, for example, dealing with unions, inventory control problems, or communications between divisions.

Whether the firm decides to buy or produce goods and services it needs depends on the balance of internal and external transaction costs.

external transaction costs are higher than internal transaction costs, then the owner of the firm will expand the size of their own firm and produce those goods themselves. This situation might occur if external transaction costs are elevated because of opportunism, asset specificity, if there are only a few buyers and sellers in the market, or because of problems in enforcing contracts once made. If internal transaction costs are higher than external transaction costs, then one will buy needed goods and services from other firms (Williamson 1975: 102–5; 1985: chaps. 4–6; 1986: 85–99). This might occur if union rules made it difficult to produce a good within the firm, while efficient markets made it easy to get them outside. In summary, firms respond to transaction costs by altering their size and their dependence on other firms. Thus, the size and degree of specialization of the firms that evolve stems from the relative degree of efficiency of exchanges inside and outside the firm.

During the 1970s, transaction cost economists attacked the problem of vertical integration, which they saw as closely connected to the decision to make or buy goods and services (Dugger 1993: 202; Williamson 1971, 1975). They have also devoted a great deal of attention to the appropriate amount of decentralization that should occur in firms. They have distinguished several different types of firm organizations whose units are related to each other in a variety of ways. The "U-form" firm (unitary) has one central organization that commands departments, each of which performs a distinct task (e.g., production, sales, finance, etc.); while the "M-form" firm (multidivisional) contains several separate divisions, each under a separate subadministration, which is completely responsible for producing a product or service. For example, divisions of large railroads are responsible for all railroad operations in a geographic area, while the divisions of General Motors produce and sell automobiles (e.g., Oldsmobile) (Williamson 1996: 109). J-form firms (Japanese-type) and family firms have still other traits. Similarly, they distinguished between several different kinds of markets.

The transaction cost economists have devoted a good deal of effort to understanding the behavior of people in firms and their motives. One of the questions they have asked is "how are the people in firms coordinated?" Coase's answer would seem to be that firms are controlled by "administrative fiat" from the top of the hierarchy, and those at the bottom obey out of fear. But top levels of management often do not have the information they need to effectively control the organization. As information goes from the bottom units of hierarchies to the top levels, detail is lost and information is distorted, sometimes with the strategic goals of those in lower units in mind (Williamson 1967; Miller 1992: 138ff). As the size of the organization grows, the problem of information loss becomes worse, and greatly increases internal transaction costs. Why don't employees shirk when they can get away with it? What keeps managers from making inefficient decisions when they have incentive to do so? Miller's answer is that leadership can promote cooperation and overcome selfish interests among employees (1992: 2, 179–81). Kreps (1990) argues that the goals of a firm are communicated to employees through the corporate culture and that the reputation of the employees and firms overcomes incentives for opportunism.

Entrepreneurs use a large number of different kinds of contractual arrangements to lower the transaction costs stemming from the various kinds of information problems they face. Williamson (1975, 1985, 1996) has described in detail the wide variety of such contracts occurring within and between firms in the modern world. It is very common for entrepreneurs to attempt to lower the risks and uncertainty of dealing with other firms (i.e., external transaction costs) by entering into a variety of contracts involving "hostages" (i.e., assurances specifying payments if contracts are not fulfilled) (Williamson 1996: 120ff). Firms at the same level of the market can enter into horizontal exchanges, which Williamson calls "peer exchanges," to obtain information on prices and sources of supply that they cannot obtain from the firms with which they do business (Williamson 1975: 41ff). (For example, see Acheson [1985: 118] for a description of horizontal ties between firms in the Maine lobster market.)

Internal transaction costs are lowered by other kinds of agreements. When it is difficult to monitor effort or monitor relationships (i.e., hidden action) there is a tendency to substitute contracts for spot market exchanges. Various kinds of rental, lease, and subcontracting agreements result. Many attempt to deal with "hidden type" problems within firms through contracts offering "merit pay" or incentive pay for superior performance. Owners of firms respond to some information problems by hiring "experts." Barzel (1989) points out that problems of hidden action in rural societies result in landowners and laborers entering into agreements to share the rewards and risks (e.g., varieties of share cropping agreements).

Williamson and his followers tend to see markets and firms as lying at two ends of a continuum. At one end are large, vertically integrated firms, composed of several related units and people involved in a permanent set of relationships with each other, where allocation is done by administrative fiat rather than the price system. At the other end are spot markets in which information is conveyed by price alone and people have no relationships with each other once an exchange is made (Williamson 1975). In between are a variety of organizational forms, in which the parties to the exchange maintain quasi- or fully contractual agreements with each other over the period of time. In recent years, Williamson (1996: 101) has devoted considerable attention to such organizations and has built a very elaborate model of what he calls "hybrid organizations." Most of the organizations involved are firms, but Williamson notes that governmental agencies may be involved as well.

There are many different types of hybrids. One is franchising, in which a parent firm allows others to supply goods or sell its products with stringent controls on advertising, brand name, service, location, and other terms designed to maintain product quality and the reputation of the parent firm. Another hybrid is regulated industries such as electric power companies, airlines, and railroads in which oligopolistic or monopolistic rights over a market are granted under the condition that a governmental agency be empowered to mediate between the firm and its customers regarding service, pricing, and investment. The most common hybrids are those involving long-term bilateral agreements between suppliers and purchasers. Such arrangements have been described by Macneil (1978) as "relational contracting."

Usually hybrid organizations are involved in agreements that are spelled out in a legal contract. Franchising agreements and the obligations of utilities are specified in great detail. In all cases involving hybrids, contracts are somewhat elastic since no contact or agreement can spell out all of the kinds of contingencies that may arise (Williamson 1985: 103–4). Hybrid organizations also involve some kind of asset specificity. That is, these firms have specialized skills, capital equipment, locations, dedicated assets, or brand names that make it difficult for them to redeploy these assets to other uses quickly (Williamson 1996: 59). Such firms, in short, are dependent on another firm at least in the short run. Since they are not completely free to negotiate with other firms, opportunism is an ever-present possibility. To guard against this possibility, contracts between firms involved in hybrid organizations commonly employ "hostages," which specify penalties to be paid if the terms of agreements are not met (Williamson 1996: 120ff).

Williamson (1996: 107) argues that markets, hybrids, and hierarchies are "supported by a different form of contract law" so that each is associated with different kinds of incentives, degrees of adaptability, and bureaucratic costs. Classical contract law is ideally applicable to situations in which the identity of the parties is irrelevant, and if efforts to negotiate an exchange fail, both parties are able to go their own way with minimal losses. Consequently, it applies best to spot market arrangements (Williamson 1996: 95). Hierarchies, on the other hand, are governed by the "rule of forbearance." That is, courts will not hear cases involving disputes between units of the same organization. Hybrid organizations are governed by an "elastic contracting mechanism" in which neoclassical law applies, but the terms are incomplete and allow some flexibility in recognition that all long-term contingencies cannot be predicted and specified completely (Williamson 1996: 93–99).

The three types of governance organizations differ in incentive structure. Markets have very high-powered incentives, meaning that a change in behavior or effort can have an immediate effect on compensation. Hierarchies, by way of contrast, are marked by low-powered incentives since internal organization reduces such incentives. Markets have no administrative controls, while the administration of hierarchies is very strong. Hybrids have intermediate incentive structures and administrative controls.

Whether markets, hybrids, or hierarchies are developed as the appropriate governance organization for a particular set of transactions depends on both the amount of asset specificity and transaction costs (Williamson 1996: 103–11, 115–17). If transaction costs are low (low number of disturbances) and asset specificity is low, then firms will depend on markets to obtain the goods they need. As asset specificity grows, it is more and more difficult to redeploy assets, firms become more dependent on other specific firms, and it becomes rational to form hybrids in which the partner firms are linked by long-term contracts. At very high levels of asset specificity, it becomes rational to bring all of the mutually dependent units under the same administration in a single hierarchy.

The effect of transaction costs as measured in terms of disturbances falls most heavily on hybrids. This is "because hybrid adaptations cannot be made unilaterally (as with market governance) or by fiat (as with hierarchy), but require mutual consent. Consent, however, takes time. If a hybrid mode is negotiating an adjustment to one disturbance only to be hit by another, failures of adaptation predictably obtain" (Williamson 1996: 116). If enough disturbances occur, hybrid organization will prove to be impossible, and all transactions will be organized through either markets or hierarchies (Williamson 1996: 117). If disturbances are very severe (e.g., war, revolution), then no form of governance organization will survive.

To date, most of the efforts of the transaction cost economists have gone into understanding markets and hierarchies. The possibilities may be much broader. Williamson states, "the study of economic organization in all its forms—industrial organization, labor, international trade, economic development, family organization, comparative system, and even finance—becomes grist for the transaction costs economics mill" (1996: 59). To date, he has done some work on choice of corporate financial instruments, but a great deal needs to be done if this ambitious goal is to be achieved.

In summary, Williamson has developed a generative model of the way in which organizations (i.e., markets, hybrids, and hierarchies) are produced by entrepreneurs seeking to constrain those with whom they do business. These entrepreneurs are operating within the structural constraints of their societies (norms, contract law, property rights, etc.). They also face transaction costs of various types stemming from opportunism, small numbers situations, and asset specificity. The types of organizations that emerge are the result of governance structures (authority structures) deliberately crafted through negotiations to lower transaction costs.

Transaction Cost Economics: Problems and Possibilities

Markets, Hybrids and Hierarchies: Studies by Anthropologists

Transaction cost economists have been primarily concerned with the ways in which markets, hybrids, and hierarchies have been generated from combinations of transaction costs. While anthropologists are familiar with these kinds of organizations, they have devoted relatively little attention to the issues of importance to the transaction cost economists (e.g., negotiations, and contractual arrangements between parties to trade). From this perspective, there is little on spot markets, but there are some notable exceptions. Price (1980) has described the rules governing periodic trade between hostile tribal groups who do not share a common language. Geertz (1978) describes the way information is obtained in bazaars and the role of bargaining and "clientalization" in that process. Other anthropologists working in markets with high transaction costs focus on the way in which prices are established by custom rather than market forces (Alexander and Alexander 1991; Cashdan 1990).

A few anthropologists have devoted time to studying the "institutions" or rule systems governing markets. There is some information on market rules in the literature on early empires (Berdan 1985; Polanyi 1957); and a few anthropologists have written on the rules governing exchange in auctions (Bestor 1992), while Hertz (1998) describes the rules surrounding the stock market in Shanghai.[1]

Anthropologists have also tended to ignore hierarchies (i.e., vertically integrated firms), but there are a couple of good studies. Lomnitz and Perez-Lizaur (1987) have provided a very interesting study of a large family-owned conglomerate in Mexico, Janelli (1993) gives a very good description of a Korean conglomerate, and Gates (1996) has described the firms engaged in the capitalist system of China. Very large firms are mentioned in the anthropological literature when they are engaged in export from or imports into more remote rural areas (Smith 1976). But in this literature, there is little mention of the kinds of contracts or agreements that link people in a firm together or govern exchange relationships between firms, and virtually no mention of the new institutional economics.

None of these studies focus on the selection of organizational forms as a means to lower transaction costs or uncertainty.

Interestingly enough, transaction cost economics has proven most useful to anthropologists when they have set about describing various kinds of hybrids. "Relational contracting" (Macneil 1978) of various kinds has been found in a variety of cultures ranging from Third World countries to the United States (Belshaw 1965). One of the first and most famous is the pratik relationships described by Mintz (1964) in which Haitian market women use long-term bilateral ties with each other to lower risk and uncertainty. Women who have a pratik relationship have an obligation to do business with each other if at all possible. This ensures that farm women have a market for their crops and animals at reasonable prices, while market women have a much steadier supply of produce to sell.

Relational contracting involving various kinds of long-term arrangements between buyers and sellers have also been found in the Philippines (Spoehr 1980; Szanton 1972), Nigeria (Cohen 1969); Indonesia (Dewey 1962); Bangladesh (McGregor 1994); and the United States (Acheson 1985; Ackerloff 1970; Plattner 1985, 1989, 1996; Wilson 1980). In all cases, personal ties are a substitute for information. In this regard, Plattner comments that the U.S. art market is like a "peasant marketplace." That is, risk is increased by "asymmetrical information . . . the solution is normally found in social relations" (Plattner 1996: 199).

Another type of hybrid organization is trading groups, firms linked together to transport and market goods over long distances. All of these groups involve long-term ties between traders, which are reinforced by ethnic ties and other personal links. Landa points out that such groups exist all the way from the Middle East and Far East to the Jewish diamond merchants in modern New York (Landa 1997: xii). Particularly good characterizations of such trading groups have been provided by Curtain (1984) who describes such groups historically, Abner Cohen (1969) who analyzes Hausa trade networks in Nigeria, and Alice Dewey (1962) who describes Chinese trade networks in Indonesia. Typically such groups are composed of people of a single ethnic group with certain shared traditions and religious beliefs that enhance trust and lower uncertainty. Landa and Carr specifically link the formation of such groups, which they call "ethnically homogenous middlemen groups" ("EHMGs"), to the literature on the new institutional economics. They argue convincingly that such groups lower the transaction costs of enforcing exchange agreements in a world where contract law is nonexistent (Landa 1997: 101ff). The bizarre traditions, fictive kinship ties, dietary rules, and religious cults that typify the people in such trading groups are a low-cost way of identifying group members, ensuring adherence to "club rules," and keeping outsiders out (Carr and Landa 1997: 126–36).

However, it should be noted that the kinds of hybrid organizations on which Williamson concentrates do not occur in the anthropological literature. There are, to the best of my knowledge, no studies of public utilities. With the exception of Dannhaeuser's (1985) work, there is almost no mention of franchising.

Applied Case Studies

One of the most basic theories of the transaction cost economists is that various kinds of markets, hybrids, and hierarchies are selected by entrepreneurs in response to transaction costs. Over the course of the past two decades, a number of anthropologists have used concepts from transaction cost economics to understand the genesis of institutions in a variety of settings. How well have these concepts worked? To what extent have they proven applicable to situations in other societies? The results are by no means clear. In some cases, the data reinforce aspects of the theory. In other instances, they do not.

In Third World countries, transaction costs are typically very high. Most of the conditions that facilitate obtaining information about goods and prices and negotiating enforceable contracts are absent. Communications are poor, literacy levels are low, contract law is undeveloped, property rights are insecure, enforcement of laws is spotty at best, and corruption is rampant.

According to Williamson and the other transaction cost economists, high external transaction costs should lead to vertical integration. There is at least one case study supporting this idea. Sacks points out that in Yugoslavia, markets have been replaced by a central planning system, which is not working. There is no "effective, comprehensive mechanism for influencing the allocation of resources" (1983: 23). As a result, Yugoslav firms have expanded vertically to produce much of what they need. Much of the total production of the country is done by 170 large firms. They have been able to achieve self-management by dividing these firms into divisions. Sacks argues that having large size insulates these firms from the kind of opportunism that characterizes market exchanges, but that divisionalization allows the workers to maintain their tradition of self-management in small units and gives decision makers flexibility (Sacks 1983: 58–74). In short, the organization of these large firms gives all the advantages of size foreseen by Williamson and still maintains efficiency. Sacks goes on to suggest that other large productive organizations such as "Japanese zaibatsu, the Spanish cooperatives at Mondragon or General Motors and its suppliers" might also be organizations with the same kinds of advantages.

At least one other study concludes that transaction cost economics does not work well in explaining industrial organization. Hamilton and Biggart's (1988) studies of Japan, Korea, and Taiwan indicate that transaction costs will not account for the differences observed in the size, degree of specialization, and relations between firms in these three countries. Williamson's analysis concerning the factors that should result in large firms, they say, appears to apply best to Japan, and least well to Taiwan (Hamilton and Biggert 1988: S63–S69). Firm organization, they argue, can only be explained by taking into account actions of the governments of these countries. At least two other anthropologists have found the concepts of transaction cost economics inadequate to explain certain aspects of firm organization in Third World countries. Susan Russell (1994) points out that there is rampant opportunism and cheating in one Philippine fishery. Crews steal fish since they are not in position to enforce the terms of the shares contract. Captains cannot fire crew, and thus pay crew according to the amount of fish they estimate the crewman has stolen. The system operates de facto to cheat fish consignors. Russell argues that this cheating continues because the transaction costs of letting the cheating continue are less than the transaction costs of negotiating fair and enforceable share contracts. Williamson's work would lead us to believe that cheating of this magnitude would quickly lead to effective and enforceable contracts or vertical integration. The fact that this has not occurred raises questions about Williamson's hypothesis that high external transaction costs due to opportunism lead to vertical integration or other nonmarket institutions.

Moreover, data from my own work on the furniture industry in Cuanajo, Michoacan, Mexico also do not support Williamson's hypothesis about the way organizations are generated. In Cuanajo, both internal and external transaction costs are high (Acheson 1994b: 154–56). However, firm owners are not expanding vertically to avoid high external transaction costs or entering into contracts with other firms to avoid high internal transaction costs. Rather, they use unusual strategies to lower both kinds of costs (Acheson 1994b: 154–56). They attempt to reduce the high internal transaction costs by hiring kinsmen whenever possible. They attempt to reduce the high external transaction costs by using relational markets and relying on intermediary organizations (Acheson 1994b: 157–60).

The work of other social scientists also points out that the response to high transaction costs in Third World economies is to rely on types of intermediary organizations rather than develop small firms operating in open, efficient markets. Bates demonstrates that African governments have played a pivotal role in promoting industrialization and agricultural development (1976, 1981, 1983, 1989). Here the response to high transaction costs is not efficient markets but bureaucracies (i.e., nonmarket institutions) of varying types such as centrally organized cooperatives, development authorities, marketing boards, and gigantic, vertically integrated firms that are financed and sponsored by the government. Brautigam stresses the pivotal role of intermediary organizations in the economy of Third World countries, including nongovernmental organizations (NGOs), business associations, unions, youth and women's groups (1991: 17). The intermediate organizations perform the role of markets in that they control prices, sell entire harvests, and funnel capital to rural areas (Bates 1981: 11–44; 1989: 73). They also undertake a variety of activities usually undertaken by firms in other settings (e.g., irrigation and agricultural innovation).

Other anthropologists point out that the response to high transaction costs caused by corruption or rampant bureaucracy is to depend on parallel kinds of markets, or exchange systems. One such response is to develop "informal economies" (Smith 1990); another is the "economy of favors" described by Ledeneva (1998) in Russia. Clearly the response to problems in markets outside the industrialized West is not to form large firms, but to depend on a wide variety of bureaucracies, intermediary organizations, and parallel exchange systems.

A very serious obstacle for the transaction cost economists has been posed by social scientists concerned with the role of efficiencies in generating organizations. Basically, Williamson and the other transaction cost economists argue that economic organizations are generated by people entering into contracts to economize on transaction costs. The resulting governance structure is selected with efficiency in mind. But Williamson (1996: 198ff) would admit that inefficient organizations exist, and North (1990a: 52, 92) asserts that not all rules or institutions make for economic efficiency. Several authors point to different sources of inefficiency in governments. North (1990a: 9, 73) points out that rules are "devised by those with bargaining power to create new rules." Sometimes inefficiency serves their interests better. Agents of the State sometimes make decisions with their own interests in mind rather than the best interest of the public or ruler (Moberg 1994; North 1990a: 9, 73). This often results in tariffs, subsidies, side payments, feather bedding rules, price fixing schemes, etc., that undermine economic efficiency. Nye (1997: 128) and Dugger (1993: 191) point out that state power cuts two ways where business firms are concerned. Businesses depend on many services and the infrastructure provided by states, but states are highly "predatory" toward business. Terry Moe (1990) makes a very strong case that the process of designing bureaucracies in democratic countries almost always results in sacrificing efficiency for other goals. Bureaucracies, he argues, are cobbled together by dominant groups of legislators who are forced to take into account the conflicting interests of legislators in the opposition party, presidents or chief executives, their constituents, and the bureaucrats themselves. All too often, the resulting bureaucracies are designed to work poorly, if at all.

Moreover, such bureaucracies act in ways that hamper economic growth. An especially good example is provided by Robert Higgs (1996), who shows how salmon conservation rules were the result of lobbying by fishermen who were interested in distributional issues and legislators interested in conservation of the resources. The result was regulations that outlawed the use of efficient gear but still failed to conserve the stocks.

Generative Models

What sets Williamson's work apart from the other new institutional economists is his focus on organizations, and a generative model of how various kinds of organizations are formed. Firms of varying sizes, degrees of complexity, and dependence on markets are organized to take advantage of transaction costs of varying types. It follows that, if we know the kinds of transaction costs involved, we should be able to predict a good deal about the kind of organization that will result. Williamson has come up with his own taxonomy of firms (Williamson 1975, 1985, 1986: 101–67; 1996, 120ff), and other transaction cost economists have elaborated on the types of firms and markets (e.g., Dugger 1993: 202; Joskow 1993: 117–37).

The insights of the transaction cost economists have a lot of potential for all those wishing to understand how organizations of various types are generated. Two anthropologists have developed models based on this work to explain the generation of organizations of various types.

The first is Mary Douglas, who has developed a scheme to explain the organization of opportunism in large organizations. She argues convincingly that opportunism itself is culturally embedded, and that the type of cheating and stealing observed varies with the amount of autonomy permitted in the job and the amount of cooperation needed for specific scams. The data she uses is supplied by Mars' (1984) account of occupational crime.

Basically, Douglas uses two different axes to define four different social environments (see figure 2.1). One, the horizontal axis, indicates the amount of insulation or boundary strength around a group. People are highly dependent on groups with a strong boundary, and such groups regulate the amount of interaction of their members. The vertical axis represents the degree to which the individual is insulated from the greater unit or society and is free to operate without supervision. The higher up the grid dimension, "the narrower the scope for negotiating individual options" (Douglas 1990: 110). Figure 2.1a uses these two axes to define

Figure 2.1. Mary Douglas' model of autonomy, opportunism, and industrial crime

(a)

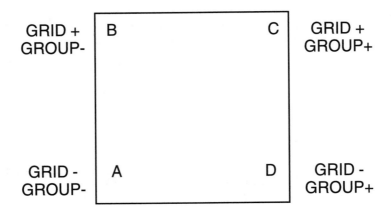

(b)

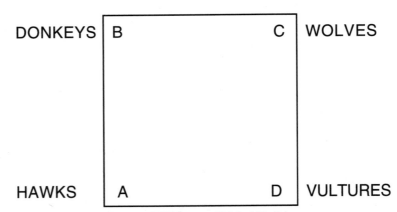

Source: Williamson 1990: 110–11.

four cells combining group boundary ("group +" indicates highly dependent on the group, or a strong boundary) and individual insulation ("grid +" indicates a role having little ability to negotiate individual options).

These two axes describe four different occupational environments, each of which presents opportunities for four different kinds of occupational criminals (Douglas 1990: 110–11), as seen in figure 2.1b. (A) "hawks" are "lone operators" who are permitted to negotiate options individually and need no collaboration for their illegal acts (e.g., a taxi driver whose earnings cannot be verified by the firm owner); (B) "donkeys" who have no individual insulation, and who do not belong to a group with a strong boundary; these people have no autonomy and thus no opportunity to cheat (e.g., assembly line workers); (C) "vultures" belong to a group that cannot be completely controlled by the employer, but whose individual autonomy is subject to bureaucratic control (e.g., a group of salesmen who negotiate with the company collectively); (D) "wolves" who have little individual autonomy, but are members of a group with a strong boundary; wolves "hunt in packs . . . and get their biggest spoils when they work in a stratified team" (Douglas 1990: 109). In wolf packs, each individual's skill is needed to pillage; there is no room for individual operators (e.g., longshoremen, airline crews looting supply lines of various kinds).

I have used the ideas of Coase and Williamson to produce a model of the types of firms generated by three different kinds of variables with a range of transaction costs (Acheson 1984). One is the relative efficiency of intermediate product markets, which governs the time and effort it takes for firms to buy and sell component parts to each other. In industries with efficient intermediate product markets, small specialized firms will be the rule. Inefficient intermediate product markets will result in larger, more complicated firms which perform more tasks for themselves. The second factor is the efficiency of final product markets (i.e., sales of completed products to consumers). If final product markets are efficient, then producing firms receive steady and predictable orders. Under these conditions, they have long production runs, can use specialized machinery, and can enter into long-term labor contracts. The result is a large firm. The third factor is organizational skill. This encompasses the kinds of skills that one learns in an MBA program, such as accounting, financial management, business law, etc., which make managers able to make better decisions concerning labor contracts, obtaining capital, utilizing technology, and responding to market inefficiencies. These skills lower the internal and external transaction costs of managing large firms with a multiplicity of divisions and complex contracts with employees, suppliers, and other firms.

The efficiency of intermediate and final product markets and the organizational skill of entrepreneurs combine in various ways to produce different types of firms. These different types of firms can be expressed in a three-dimensional, eight-cell chart below (Acheson 1984: 50). (See figure 2.2.)

Figure 2.2. Acheson's model of transaction costs and firm types

HIGH ORGANIZATION COSTS
Intermediate Product Market

	efficient	inefficient
Final Product Market — efficient	**1** small specialized firms	**2** vertical integration in production, small distribution
Final Product Market — inefficient	**3** small firm, large wholesale	**4** small firm, small wholesale

LOW ORGANIZATION COSTS
Intermediate Product Market

	efficient	inefficient
Final Product Market — efficient	**1** small specialized firms in production and distribution	**2** vertical integration in production, tend to integrate in distribution
Final Product Market — inefficient	**3** large wholesale, tendency to integrate backward into production	**4** large firms, integrated in production and distribution

Source: Acheson 1984: 51.

Institutions and Social Change

So far we have concentrated on organizations, assuming, along with the transaction cost economists, that the rules (social structure) used to construct organizations are relatively fixed, and inviolate. These rules, in combination with transaction costs, result in the selection of hierarchies and markets.

More recent work in institutional economics sees another important connection between organizations and institutions. Essentially these analysts argue that social change occurs due to the interaction of institutions and organizations. That is, organizations are constructed within the constraints and possibilities offered by institutions and culture, and, "as organizations evolve, they alter the institutions" (North 1990a: 7). Sometimes, organizations can operate to get what they want within existing rules, but in other instances, they must alter those rules to obtain their goals (Davis and North 1971: 6–7). How this occurs is very complicated and the subject of a good deal of current debate and research.

In the literature in institutional economics, there are two kinds of interactions that are generally considered to be productive of institutions. The first is strategic interactions between firms producing new, adaptive contract forms that are copied by others (North 1990a; Nelson and Winter 1982). Other changes in rules can come about as a result of bargaining between firms over distributional issues, as described by Knight (1992: 130ff). The second, and more important, source of rules is the complex set of interactions between business firms and government. Some new rules and institutions come about as a result of efforts by the state to control business firms and obtain revenue from them. Others are the by-product of lobbying efforts by business firms and associations to obtain goods, services, infrastructure, and rules desired by industry. One of the things most desired by industry is rules to give firms a competitive edge in distributive fights—e.g., subsidies, tariffs, side payments, infrastructure, tax breaks, government-sponsored research and development programs, etc. (Dugger 1993: 192–97). Sometimes, but not always, the activities of business firms result in new agencies or changes in the government itself.

However, saying that social changes come about via an interactive process involving institutions and organizations only begins to shed light on the process of change. There is no consensus on how norms or new rules are produced, or even why norms exist (Elster 1989; Taylor 1990: 224). There is a consensus that changes in rules or institutions may be the result of uncentralized (i.e., informal) processes, or centralized processes involving the power of the State to one extent or another (Knight 1992: Taylor 1990: 225ff). Changes in rules may also be the result of conscious "visible hand" solutions, or the unplanned consequence of a series to seemingly unrelated decisions ("invisible hand" solutions). Social scientists such as Veblen, Hayak, and Langlois see invisible hand solutions as the most important problem for the social sciences (Rutherford 1994: 83–92). Complicating the issue further is the fact that because rules or institutions will produce benefits for a larger group is no guarantee they will be provided. Only under certain circumstances is it possible to get people to impose rules in the common good (Acheson 1998; Ostrom 1990: 182–91; North 1990a: 12; Wade 1994: 214–17).

Summary and Assessment

The most important contribution of transaction cost economists has been to develop a model describing the way economic institutions are generated. Much of their work has gone into describing markets, hybrids, and hierarchies, which are substitutable for each other. These organizations, or "governance structures," are the result of private orderings of entrepreneurs, using the possibilities and constraints of a given institutional system to economize on transaction costs of various kinds. These transaction costs are the result of opportunism, small numbers exchange, asset specificity, and other factors producing inefficient markets.

Williamson's model is comparable to the models of John H. Holland (1998). Both argue that complex systems are the result of interactions or moves within the confines of a finite number of rules. One of Holland's examples is checkers, in which an infinitely large number of games can result from a few rules; Williamson is talking about firms and markets resulting from the negotiations of entrepreneurs maneuvering to avoid transaction costs within the confines of norms and legal principles.

Williamson's work has resulted in a good deal of discussion and controversy which will undoubtedly result in his model of governance organizations being modified and extended (Williamson and Winter 1993; Winter 1993). A more refined and elaborated model of the firm and markets will likely emerge in the near future (see Pitelis 1993). If the model is to be improved, and extended more widely, at least five different kinds of considerations need to be taken into account. Each poses interesting questions for anthropologists.

First, no way has been developed to measure transaction costs. This means that no testable hypotheses can be formulated linking the selection of organizational type with transaction costs.

Second, the transaction cost economists have focused on studying firms and markets in industrialized societies. It is by no means clear to what extent their insights can be applied to understand the firms and markets of non-Western societies. In some societies, economic organizations develop as Williamson and the other transaction cost economists would predict (e.g., the Yugoslavian firms studied by Sacks [1983]). In other places, firms do not respond in ways predicted by Williamson. This is true of the Mexican society studied by Acheson (1982, 1994b) and the Philippines community studied by Russell (1994). In other places, bureaucracies, intermediary organizations, informal economies, trading groups, or parallel exchange systems are produced, where Williamson's work would lead us to expect markets or large firms (Acheson 1994b; Bates 1976, 1981, 1983, 1989; Brautigam 1991; Ensminger 1992; Landa 1997; Ledeneva 1998; Posner 1980; Smith 1990). These findings suggest that the work of the transaction cost economists will need to be extensively modified and extended if it is to be able to account for the generation of "governance structures" in other cultures. To be sure, Coase is likely correct in saying that problems in markets will lead to the development of nonmarket organizations. But there are a lot more choices of organizations than markets, hybrids, and hierarchies. Anthropologists are especially well equipped to assess the alternative nonmarket organization. The key question remaining is, Under what conditions are various kinds of organizations selected?

Third, Williamson also makes the claim that his approach can be applied very widely to understanding a great variety of organizations such as labor arrangements, trade, development, family organization, finance, etc. (1996: 59). This may well be the case, particularly since scholars like Landa (1997) and Posner (1980) have had success applying aspects of institutional economics to kinship, ethnic trading networks, and gift exchange in far-flung societies around the globe. Moreover, Acheson (1982) and Douglas (1990) have developed models linking the generation of organizations to transaction costs of various kinds. Certainly similar models can be developed to explain the generation of other types of organizations.

But transaction cost economics likely cannot explain the development of all organizations. The work of Terry Moe (1990) points out that we cannot explain the generation of bureaucracies in terms of economizing on transaction costs. Moreover, it is very doubtful if it will be of much use in explaining traditional organizations such as the potlatch and the kula, which are likely to be the result of evolutionary, invisible hand processes rather than of visible hand negotiations. What kinds of organizations can be explained by transaction cost economics?

Fourth, the driving force producing organizations, according to Williamson, is a concern among entrepreneurs for efficiency (i.e., minimizing transaction costs). But Williamson (1996: 198ff) would admit that inefficient organizations exist, and North (1990a: 52, 92) asserts that not all rules or institutions make for economic efficiency. The work of Moe (1990), North (1990a), and Moberg (1994) suggests that government action is clearly at the root of some inefficient organizations. Is government action the sole source of inefficiency? What other factors are involved? Clearly a concern for efficiency is not the only factor driving the generation of organizations.

Fifth, institutions (social structural rules) are produced by a vastly more complicated set of processes. The basic engine of institutional change, according to North and others, is an interactive relationship between institutions and organizations, with one influencing the development of the other over the course of time. It may be true, as North indicates, that many institutions in Western societies are the result of a complex set of interactions between business firms and the State, while others are the by-product of interactions between firms themselves. It remains to be seen to what extent we can explain the generations of organizations and institutions in non-Western societies in this fashion. There is no consensus about the ways in which norms and rules are generated (Elster 1989a, 1989b: 17–49; Taylor 1990). It is becoming apparent that this question is more complicated than has been assumed.

How organizations and rules (i.e., social structure) are produced is a very basic question for social scientists. These issues deserve far more attention from anthropologists than they have received in recent decades. The work of the new institutional economists provides a useful starting point to approach them.

Note

1. There is a sizable body of anthropological literature on marketing, but most of it does not concern issues of primary interest to the transaction cost economists or to the institutional economics as a whole. Much attention has been devoted by Skinner and his students to studying markets in terms of central place theory (C. Smith 1976; Plattner 1985). A number of others have studied markets in the context of world systems theory; others have studied markets as part of the informal economy (E. Smith 1990).

References

Acheson, James M.
  1982   "Limitations on Firm Size in a Tarascan *Pueblo*." *Human Organization* 41(4):
         323–29.
  1985   "Social Organization of the Maine Lobster Market." Pp. 105–30 in *Markets and Marketing*, Stuart Plattner, ed. Monographs in Economic Anthropology, No. 4. Lanham, Md.: University Press of America.
  1984   "Constraints on Entrepreneurship: Transaction Costs and Market Efficiency." Pp. 45–53 in *Entrepreneurship and Social Change*, Sidney Greenfield

and Arnold Strickon, eds. Monographs in Economic Anthropology, No. 2. Lanham, Md.: University Press of America.

1989 "The Management of Common Property Resources." Pp. 351–78 in *Economic Anthropology*, Stuart Plattner, ed. Stanford: Stanford University Press.

1994a "Welcome to Nobel Country: An Overview of Institutional Economics." Pp. 3–41 in *Anthropology and Institutional Economics*, James M. Acheson, ed. Monographs in Economic Anthropology, No. 12. Lanham, Md.: University Press of America.

1994b "Transaction Costs and Business Strategies in a Mexican Indian Pueblo." Pp.143–65 in *Anthropology and Institutional Economics*, James M. Acheson, ed. Monographs in Economic Anthropology, No. 12. Lanham, Md.: University Press of America.

1998 "Lobster Trap Limits: A Solution to a Communal Action Problem." *Human Organization* 57(1): 43–52.

Ackerloff, George
1970 "The Market for Lemons: Quality, Uncertainty and the Market Mechanism." *Quarterly Journal of Economics* 84: 488–500.

Alchian, Armen A.
1950 "Uncertainty, Evolution and Economic Theory." *Journal of Political Economy* 58: 211–21.

Alexander, Jennifer, and Paul Alexander
1991 "What's a Fair Price? Price Setting and Trading Partnerships in Javanese Markets." *Man* 26: 493–512.

Arrow, Kenneth
1971 "Political and Economic Evaluations, Social Effects and Externalities." Pp. 3–25 in *Frontiers of Qualitative Economics*, Michael D. Intriligator, ed. Amsterdam: North-Holland Press.

Axelrod, Robert
1984 *The Evolution of Cooperation.* New York: Basic Books.

Bailey, Frederick
1969 *Strategems and Spoils.* New York: Schocken.

Bates, Robert
1976 *Rural Response to Industrialization: A Study of Village Zambia.* New Haven: Yale University Press.

1981 *Markets and States in Modern Africa: The Political Basis for Agriculture Policies.* Berkeley: University of California Press.

1983 *Essays on the Political Economy of Rural Africa.* Cambridge: Cambridge University Press.

1989 *Beyond the Miracle of the Market: The Political Economy of Agrarian Development in Rural Kenya.* Cambridge: Cambridge University Press.

1994 "Social Dilemmas and Rational Individuals." Pp. 43–66 in *Anthropology and Institutional Economics*, James M. Acheson, ed. Monographs in Economic Anthropology, No. 12. Lanham, Md.: University Press of America.

Barzel, Yoram
1989 *Economic Analysis of Property Rights.* Cambridge: Cambridge University Press.

Belshaw, Cyril
  1965   *Traditional Exchange and Modern Markets.* Englewood Cliffs, N.J: Prentice-Hall.
Berdan, Francis F.
  1985   "Markets in the Economy of Aztec Mexico." Pp. 339–67 in *Markets and Marketing,* Stuart Plattner, ed. Monographs in Economic Anthropology, No. 4. Lanham, Md.: University Press of America.
Bestor, Theodore
  1992   "Visible Hands: Auctions and Institutional Integration in the Tsukiji Wholesale Fish, Tokyo." Working paper no. 63. Columbia Graduate School of Business. New York: Columbia University Press.
Brautigam, Deborah
  1991   *Governance and Economy: A Review.* Policy and Review Department. WPS 815. Washington, D.C.: World Bank.
Bromley, Daniel
  1989   *Economic Interests and Institutions.* New York: Basil Blackwell.
Buchanan, James
  1965   "An Economic Theory of Clubs." *Economica* 32: 1–13.
Carr, Jack L., and Janet T. Landa
  1997   "The Economics of Symbols, Clan Names, and Religion." Pp.115–38 in *Trust, Ethnicity and Identity,* Janet Landa, ed. Ann Arbor: University of Michigan Press.
Cashdan, Elizabeth
  1990   "Information Costs and Customary Prices." Pp. 259–78 in *Risk and Uncertainty in Tribal and Peasant Economies,* Elizabeth Cashdan, ed. Boulder, Colo.: Westview Press.
Coase, Ronald
  1937   "The Nature of the Firm." *Economica* 4(3): 386–404. Reprinted in *The Nature of the Firm: Origins, Evolution, and Development,* Oliver E. Williamson and Sidney G. Winter, eds., pp. 18–33. 1977. New York: Oxford.
  1960   "The Problem of Social Costs." *Journal of Law and Economics* 3: 1–44.
Cohen, Abner
  1969   *Custom and Conflict in Urban Africa.* Berkeley: University of California Press.
Coleman, James S.
  1990   "Norm Generating Structures." Pp. 250–73 in *The Limits of Rationality,* Karen S. Cook and Margaret Levi, eds. Chicago: The University of Chicago Press.
Commons, John R.
  1934   *Institutional Economics: Its Place in Political Economy.* New York: MacMillan.
Curtain, Philip D.
  1984   *Cross-Cultural Trade in World History.* Cambridge: Cambridge University Press.
Dahlman, Carl
  1979   "The Problem of Externality." *Journal of Law and Economics* 22: 141–62.

Dannhaeuser, Norbert
   1985 "Urban Market Channels Under Conditions of Development: The Case
      of India and the Philippines." Pp. 179–203 in *Markets and Marketing*, Stuart
      Plattner, ed. Monographs in Economic Anthropology, No. 4. Lanham, Md.:
      University Press of America.
Davis, Lance E., and Douglass C. North
   1971 *Institutional Change and American Economic Growth*. Cambridge: Cambridge
      University Press.
Demsetz, Harold
   1967 "Toward a Theory of Property Rights." *American Economic Review* 57:
      347–59.
Dewey, Alice
   1962 *Peasant Marketing in Java*. Glencoe, Ill.: Free Press.
Douglas, Mary
   1990 "Converging on Autonomy: Anthropology and Institutional Economics."
      Pp. 98–115 in *Organization Theory*, Oliver Williamson, ed. New York: Oxford
      University Press.
Dugger, William M.
   1993 "Transaction Costs and the State." Pp. 188–216 in *Transaction Costs,
      Markets and Hierarchies*, Christos Pitelis, ed. Oxford: Basil Blackwell.
Eggertsson, Thrainn
   1993 "Economic Perspectives on Property Rights and the Economics of Insti-
      tutions." Paper given at the Beijer International Institute of Ecological
      Economics. The Royal Swedish Academy of Sciences.
Elster, Jon
   1989a "Social Norms and Economic Theory." *Journal of Economic Perspectives*
      3(4): 99–117.
   1989b *The Cement of Society*. Cambridge: Cambridge University Press.
Ensminger, Jean
   1990 "Co-opting the Elders: The Political Economy of State Incorporation in
      Africa." *American Anthropologist* 93(3): 662–75.
   1992 *Making a Market: The Institutional Transformation of an African Society*. Cam-
      bridge: Cambridge University Press.
   1994 "Transaction Costs through Time: The Case of Orma Pastoralists in East
      Africa." Pp. 69–85 in *Anthropology and Institutional Economics*, James M.
      Acheson, ed. Monographs in Economic Anthropology, No. 12. Lanham, Md.:
      University Press of America.
   1997a "Changing Property Rights: Reconciling Formal and Informal Rights to
      Land in Africa." Pp. 165–96 in *The Frontiers of the New Institutional Economics*,
      John N. Drobak and John V. C. Nye, eds. San Diego: Academic Press.
   1997b "Transaction Costs and Islam: Explaining Conversion in Africa."
      Journal of Institutional and Theoretical Economics 153(1): 1–35.
Ensminger, Jean, and Jack Knight
   1997 "Changing Social Norms: Common Property, Bride Wealth, and Clan Ex-
      ogamy." *Current Anthropology* 38(1): 1–24.

Gates, Hill
  1996 *China's Motor: A Thousand Years of Petty Capitalism*. Ithaca, N.Y.: Cornell University Press.
Geertz, Clifford
  1978 "The Bazaar Economy: Information and Search in Peasant Marketing." *American Economic Review* 68: 28–32.
Guillet, David
  1992a "Comparative Irrigation Studies: The Orbigo Valley of Spain and the Colca Valley of Peru." *Poligonos* 2: 141–50.
  1992b *Covering Ground: Communal Water Management and the State in Highland Peru*. Ann Arbor: University of Michigan Press.
Hamilton, Gary G., and Nicole W. Biggart
  1988 "Market, Culture and Authority: A Comparative Analysis of Management and Organization in the Far East." In *Organizations and Institutions: Sociological and Economic Approaches to the Analysis of Social Structure*, Christopher Winship and Sherwin Rosen, eds. Theme Issue. *American Journal of Sociology* 94: S52–S93.
Hardin, Garrett
  1968 "The Tragedy of the Commons." *Science* 162: 1243–48.
Hart, Oliver
  1990 "An Economist's Perspective on the Theory of the Firm." Pp. 154–71 in *Organization Theory: From Chester Barnard to the Present and Beyond*, Oliver Williamson, ed. Oxford: Oxford University Press.
Hayak, Friedrich
  1973 *Law, Legislation and Liberty*. Chicago: University of Chicago Press.
  1988 *The Fatal Conceit: The Errors of Socialism*. Chicago: University of Chicago Press.
Hertz, Ellen
  1998 *The Trading Crowd: An Ethnography of the Shanghai Stock Market*. Cambridge: Cambridge University Press.
Higgs, Robert
  1996 "Legally Induced Technical Regress in the Washington Salmon Fishery." Pp. 247–79 in *Empirical Studies in Instructional Change*, Lee J. Alston, Thrainn Eggertsson, and Douglass North, eds. Cambridge: Cambridge University Press.
Hodgson, Geoffrey
  1988 *Economics and Institutions: A Manifesto for a Modern Institutional Economics*. Philadelphia: University of Pennsylvania Press.
Holland, John H.
  1998 *Emergence: From Chaos to Order*. Reading, Mass.: Perseus Books.
Janelli, Roger L.
  1993 *Making Capitalism: The Social and Cultural Construction of a South Korean Conglomerate*. Stanford: Stanford University Press.
Joskow, Paul L.
  1993 "Asset Specificity and the Structure of Vertical Relationships: Empirical Evidence." Pp. 117–37 in *The Nature of the Firm: Origins, Evolution and Development*, Oliver Williamson and Sidney G. Winter, eds. New York: Oxford University Press.

Knight, Jack
1992 *Institutions and Social Conflict.* Cambridge: Cambridge University Press.
Kreps, David M.
1990 "Corporate Culture and Economic Theory." Pp. 90–143 in *Perspectives on Positive Political Economy*, James Alt and Kenneth Shepsle, eds. New York: Cambridge University Press.
Landa, Janet T.
1997 *Trust, Ethnicity and Identity.* Ann Arbor: University of Michigan Press.
Langlois, Richard N., ed.
1986 *Economics as a Process: Essays in the New Institutional Economics.* Cambridge: Cambridge University Press.
Ledeneva, Alena V.
1998 *Russia's Economy of Favors.* Cambridge: Cambridge University Press.
Lomnitz, Larissa, and Marisol Perez-Lizaur
1987 *A Mexican Elite Family: 1820–1980: Kinship, Class and Culture.* Princeton, N.J.: Princeton University Press.
Macneil, Ian
1978 "Contracts: Adjustments of Long-term Economic Relations under Classical, Neoclassical and Relational Contracts." *Northwestern University Law Review* 72: 854–97.
Mars, Gerald
1984 *Cheats at Work: An Anthropology of Occupational Crime.* London: Allen and Unwin.
McGregor, J. Alister
1994 "Village Credit and the Reproduction of Poverty in Contemporary Rural Bangladesh." Pp. 261–81 in *Anthropology and Institutional Economics*, James M. Acheson, ed. Monographs in Economic Anthropology, No. 12. Lanham, Md.: University Press of America.
Milgrom, Paul, and John Roberts
1992 *Economics, Organization and Management.* Englewood Cliffs, N.J.: Prentice-Hall.
Miller, Gary
1992 *Managerial Dilemmas: The Political Economy of Hierarchy.* New York: Cambridge University Press.
Mintz, Sidney
1964 "The Employment of Capital by Market Women in Haiti." Pp. 256–86 in *Capital, Savings and Credit in Peasant Societies*, Raymond Firth and B. S. Yamey, eds. Chicago: Aldine.
Moberg, Mark
1994 "An Agency Model of the State." Pp. 213–31 in *Anthropology and Institutional Economics*, James M. Acheson, ed. Monographs in Economic Anthropology, No. 12. Lanham, Md.: University Press of America.
Moe, Terry
1990 "The Politics of Structural Choice: Toward a Theory of Public Bureaucracy." Pp. 116–53 in *Organization Theory*, Oliver Williamson, ed. New York: Oxford University Press.

Nelson, Richard, and Sidney Winter
  1982 *An Evolutionary Theory of Economic Change.* Cambridge: Cambridge University Press.
North, Douglass
  1983 "A Theory of Economic Change." *Science* 219: 163–64.
  1984 "Government and the Cost of Exchange." *Journal of Economic History* 44: 225–64.
  1990a *Institutions, Institutional Change, and Economic Performance.* Cambridge: Cambridge University Press.
  1990b "Institutions and Their Consequences for Economic Performance." Pp. 383–401 in *The Limits of Rationality*, Karen Cook and Margaret Levi, eds. Chicago: University of Chicago Press.
North, Douglass, and Robert P. Thomas
  1973 *The Rise of the Western World: A New Economic History.* Cambridge: Cambridge University Press.
Nye, John V. C.
  1997 "Thinking about the State: Property Rights, Trade and Changing Contractual Arrangements in a World with Coercion." Pp. 121–42 in *The Frontiers of the New Institutional Economics*, John N. Drobak and John V. C. Nye, eds. San Diego: Academic Press.
Olsen, Mancur
  1965 *The Logic of Collective Action.* Cambridge: Cambridge University Press.
Ostrom, Elinor
  1990 *Governing the Commons: The Evolution of Institutions for Collective Action.* Cambridge: Cambridge University Press.
Pitelis, Christos
  1993 *Transaction Costs, Markets and Hierarchies.* Oxford: Blackwell.
Plattner, Stuart
  1985 *Markets and Marketing.* Lanham, Md.: University Press of America.
  1989 "Economic Behavior in Markets." Pp. 209–21 in *Economic Anthropology*, Stuart Plattner, ed. Stanford: Stanford University Press.
  1996 *High Art Down Home: An Economic Ethnography of a Local Art Market.* Chicago: University of Chicago Press.
Polyani, Karl
  1957 *The Great Transformation: The Political and Economic Origins of Our Time.* Boston: Beacon Press.
Posner, Richard A.
  1980 "A Theory of Primitive Society, with Special Reference to Law." *Journal of Law and Economics* 23: 1–53.
Price, John
  1980 "On Silent Trade." *Research in Economic Anthropology* 3: 75–96.
Russell, Susan
  1994 "Institutionalizing Opportunism: Cheating on Baby Purse Seiners in Batangas Bay, Philippines." Pp. 87–108 in *Anthropology and Institutional Economics*, James M. Acheson, ed. Monographs in Economic Anthropology, No. 12. Lanham, Md.: University Press of America.

Rutherford, Malcolm
  1994   *Institutions in Economics: The Old and the New Institutionalism.* Cambridge: Cambridge University Press.
Sacks, Stephen R.
  1983   *Self-Management and Efficiency: Large Corporations in Yugoslavia.* London: Allen and Unwin.
Schotter, Andrew
  1981   *Economic Theory of Institutions.* Cambridge: Cambridge University Press.
  1986   "The Evolution of Rules." Pp. 117–33 in *Economics as a Process: Essays in the New Institutional Economics,* Richard Langlois, ed. Cambridge: Cambridge University Press.
Scott, Anthony
  1955   "The Fishery: the Objectives of Sole Ownership." *Journal of Political Economy* 63: 116–34.
Smith, Carol
  1976   *Regional Analysis, Vols. 1 and 2.* New York: Academic Press.
Smith, Estellie, ed.
  1990   *Perspectives on the Informal Economy.* SEA Monographs in Economic Anthropology, No. 8. Lanham, Md.: University Press of America.
Spoehr, Alexander
  1980   *Protein from the Sea.* Ethnological Monograph No. 32. Department of Anthropology: University of Pittsburgh.
Szanton, Maria C. B.
  1972   *A Right to Survive: Subsistence Marketing in a Lowland Philippine Town.* University Park: Pennsylvania State University Press.
Taylor, Michael
  1982   *Community, Anarchy and Liberty.* Cambridge: Cambridge University Press.
  1990   "Cooperation and Rationality: Notes on the Collective Action Problem and Its Solution." Pp. 222–40 in *The Limits of Rationality,* Karen Cook and Margaret Levi, eds. Chicago: University of Chicago Press.
Wade, Robert
  1994   *Village Republics: Economic Conditions for Collective Action in South India.* San Francisco: ICS Press.
Wilk, Richard
  1996   *Economies and Cultures: Foundations of Economic Anthropology.* Boulder, Colo.: Westview Press.
Williamson, Oliver
  1971   "The Vertical Integration of Production: Market Failure Considerations." *American Economic Review* 61: 112–23.
  1975   *Markets and Hierarchies: Analysis and Anti-trust Implications.* New York: Free Press.
  1979   "Transaction-Cost Economics: The Governance of Contractual Relations." *The Journal of Law and Economics* 22(October): 233–61.
  1985   *The Economic Institutions of Capitalism.* New York: Free Press.
  1986   *Economic Organization: Firms, Markets and Policy Control.* New York: New York University Press.
  1996   *The Mechanisms of Governance.* Oxford: Oxford University Press.

Williamson, Oliver
   1967   "Hierarchical Control and Optimum Firm Size." *Journal of Political Economy* 75(2): 123–38.
Williamson, Oliver, and Sidney G. Winter, eds.
   1993   *The Nature of the Firm: Origins, Evolution, and Development.* New York: Oxford University Press.
Wilson, James
   1980   "Adaptation to Uncertainty and Small Numbers Exchange: The New England Fish Market." *Bell Journal of Economics* 11: 491–504.
Winter, Sidney G.
   1993   "On Coase, Competence and the Corporation." Pp. 179–95 in *The Nature of the Firm: Origins, Evolution, and Development,* Oliver Williamson and Sidney G. Winter, eds. New York: Oxford University Press.

Chapter 3

Experimental Economics: A Powerful New Method for Theory Testing In Anthropology

Jean Ensminger

Experimental economics offers much promise as a method for anthropologists to test important theoretical assumptions regarding economic preferences, social norms, and social capital. While there is much theoretical speculation about the role of self-interest in human behavior and the counter-veiling force of social norms in maintaining cooperation, there is actually little empirical data to defend many theoretical speculations (see Green and Shapiro 1994; Friedman 1995; and Ostrom 1998). Anthropologists have the opportunity to enter this burgeoning field with powerful cross-cultural data that could move these important theoretical debates in interesting directions.

Experimental economists have taught us a great deal in recent years about the ways in which people in developed societies routinely violate simple assumptions about narrowly self-interested behavior (Fehr and Schmidt 1999; Davis and Holt 1993; Hagel and Roth 1995). We have learned that fair-mindedness, trust, and contributions to the common good are frequently observed in one-shot anonymous games played for real money. Until recently, very few economic experiments had been run in non-Western societies. The few non-Western society studies that we do have (some examples are: Cameron 1999; Kachelmeier and Shehata 1997; Roth et al. 1991; Yamagishi and Yamagishi 1994) show some cross-cultural variation relative to the United States, but it is not great. Until recently, there were virtually no studies from less developed societies. That all changed when Joseph Henrich, then a doctoral student at UCLA, decided to run the ultimatum game among Machiguenga Indians in Peru (Henrich 2000). His results were startling. It turned out that the Machiguenga play such games more like "economic men" than do typical members of highly developed Western societies. This result prompted members of the MacArthur Foundation's Preference Network to fund about a dozen anthropologists to replicate the experiments in other less developed societies to see how robust the findings were. The sample (spanning Africa, Latin America, Papua New Guinea, and Asia) includes roughly equal numbers of hunting and gathering societies, horticultural groups, pastoralists, and small-scale sedentary agricultural populations. Those pilot studies are now complete and the results should be of great interest to fellow anthropologists (Henrich et al. n.d.). I hope to make the case in this chapter that experimental economics has much to offer anthropologists seeking to rigorously examine fundamental economic assumptions and measure the relationship among institutions, culture, and economics. Experiments offer an opportunity to add rigor to the measurement of often fuzzy phenomena such as social norms, social capital, and trust. By sharing a common method, experiments also offer a potentially great vehicle for dialog between economists and anthropologists, and a mechanism for them to talk more precisely about the impact of institutions and culture upon economic behavior. Furthermore, once we have a solid base of studies from diverse societies, we may be in a position to learn a great deal about the evolution of reciprocity, altruism, fairness, and cooperation.

In this chapter I will first outline some of the simplest economic experiments that may be appropriate for largely uneducated populations. This is followed by a rather lengthy discussion of methods that have been worked out by myself and other members of the cross-cultural project that adapt these experiments to the vagaries of the remote populations with which anthropologists often work. Finally, I discuss some of my own results from the ultimatum and dictator games that concern the relationship between market involvement and fair-mindedness. Contrary to intuition, markets seem to be correlated with more, not less, fairness. What is more, this result has been supported by the cross-cultural data from fifteen societies (Henrich et al. n.d.).

Some Basic Experiments

Economic experiments typically involve play between two or more individuals who do not know the exact identity of the partner(s) against whom they are playing. The simplest game is the dictator game, in which two partners play against each other, but never actually know each other's identity. The first player is given an endowment of cash and asked how he or she would like to divide the money with the partner. The first player is clearly the dictator in this game because their division of the money determines exactly what each player receives. This game has the potential to tell us something about norms of fairness cross-culturally. Analysis of demographic variables may also give us clues about variations in fair-mindedness based on wealth, education, sex, age, and a host of other variables.

In a slight variant of the dictator game, known as the ultimatum game, the second player has the option of rejecting the first player's offer, in which case neither player receives any money. This version of the game introduces a strategic decision by player one, who might be inclined to calculate the lowest offer that player two will find acceptable. Similarly, this game affords us the opportunity to examine punishment behavior. For example, narrow economic self-interest would predict that player two should accept any offer, however small, rather than reject and forfeit everything. But in the United States, offers of less than 25 percent are rejected about 50 percent of the time. One interpretation of these findings is that many people are prepared to pay a personal cost to enforce social norms (even anonymously) regarding what is fair. The permutations on these and other games are now well developed, and expanding rapidly; scientists have been able to examine a wide range of economic decision making and the demographic effects of variables such as sex, ethnicity, and the characteristics of the recipient upon those decisions.

Another commonly played game is the public goods game. In one version, four or five individuals are given an endowment and told that they have the option of contributing any portion of that money to a "group project." Each player then privately decides how much they wish to contribute and places that amount in an envelope. Whatever they and their fellow players contribute is placed in a common pot and doubled by the experimenter. Whatever they do not contribute to the pot is kept as a private good. Each player is then given an equal share of the common pot. This game is a test of the free rider problem, as it is in everyone's narrow economic interest to refrain from contributing to the common pot and hope that others contribute high amounts which a defector will still share equally.

The trust or investment game (see Berg, Dickhaut, and McCabe 1995) is a far less studied game, but offers the potential to test an important concept tied to the social capital literature and increasingly suggested as a variable related to economic development (Putnam 1993; Knack and Keefer 1997; Zak and Knack 1999). This game is again played with two partners who are unknown to each other. Both players are endowed with the same stake. Player one is then given the option of transferring any part of his or her stake to player two, with the understanding that anything transferred will be tripled by the experimenter. Player two then has the option of repaying player one with any part of the transfer. This game yields a measure of trust (player one's offer) and trustworthiness (player two's return).

Cross-Cultural Examples

Joe Henrich's results among the Machiguenga caught the attention of economists because they were so dramatically different from the results we have seen so often in the developed world (Camerer n.d.). Once endowed, the Machiguenga made very low offers to their partners compared to all other known studies of the ultimatum game (a mean of 26 percent versus a typical mean of 40 to 50 percent in the United States), and these offers were almost never rejected, while offers below 25 percent are rejected about half of the time in the United States. A simple interpretation of these findings concludes that the Machiguenga are less concerned with fairness, not prepared to pay a price for punishing stinginess, and more narrowly economically self-interested than Americans. In the results of the large cross-cultural project funded by the MacArthur Foundation, the Machiguenga remain the most stingy in the ultimatum game, but there is also more variation among those societies than had previously been reported for other populations.

One of the most interesting cases is that of David Tracer (n.d.), who carried out experiments with the Au and the Gnau of Papua New Guinea. Surprisingly, these populations made a lot of hyper-fair offers (greater than 50 percent). Even more curiously, these offers were as likely to be rejected as were low offers. Anthropologists will be quick to guess, correctly, that such behavior is in fact quite consistent with what one might expect from a competitive gift-giving or potlatching society, which indeed these are. This is one of the best examples we have of culture entering the context of an experiment even though it is one-shot and anonymous. It is a beautiful illustration of the way in which these experiments capture the real world coming into the laboratory, so to speak.

In another example, from my own experiments with the pastoral Orma of northeastern Kenya, we find that the Orma make rather high offers in the public goods game. They offer 58 percent, at the high end of the range (40 to 60 percent) that we commonly see in the United States. It is interesting that the Orma immediately identify the game as the *"harambee* game," a reference to a local institution which parallels the public goods game rather closely. The institution of *harambee* is widespread throughout Kenya as a mechanism for raising funds for the common good—school building and water projects, for example. Many people began referring to the public goods game as the *"harambee* game" after they had been exposed to it. This connection is all the more interesting because it turns out that different demographic variables predict offer size in the public goods game than is the case in other games played among the Orma. In the public goods game it is wealth that is a significant predictor of offer size, and wealth is a completely insignificant predictor of offer size in the ultimatum and the dictator game (see Ensminger n.d.). Interestingly, this is exactly the behavior that is expected of villagers during a genuine fundraising. The wealthy are assessed a higher percentage contribution than are poor households. While a genuine *harambee* has strict monitoring and enforcement associated with it, there was no such enforcement associated with the play in this particular version of the public goods game. Nevertheless, the presumably habituated tendency for the wealthy to contribute more spilled over into the play in this experiment.

Methods

In anticipation of the likelihood that experimental economics may catch on among anthropologists and others interested in exploring cross-cultural variation in economic behavior in the field, it is worth considering some of the methodological lessons learned from the first pilot studies carried out under the auspices of the MacArthur Foundation. While the benefits of running experiments in less developed societies is great, the problems involved in trying to replicate the controlled conditions that exist in typical laboratory studies from developed societies are immensely challenging. I suggest that standards be established early on for this kind of research, lest the reputation of such work be sullied by uninterpretable and unreplicable results due to idiosyncratic experimental method.

Aside from the advantage of adding samples from the little-studied, less developed world, experiments from typical anthropological field sites offer the added benefit of drawing samples more representative of the population at large than is often the case in laboratory studies where subjects are predominantly university undergraduates. However, this clear advantage of getting out of the university and out of the laboratory is counterbalanced by some of the problems associated with working with populations less adept at experiments, and in environments where controls are challenging. In these paragraphs I lay out the steps I followed in organizing the logistics and mechanics of the actual games I played in Kenya in 1998. Where appropriate I add notes from the experiences of other researchers from the project, who faced different logistical challenges.

The Galole Orma are cattle pastoralists living in a rather remote part of northeastern Kenya. In recent years they have begun to settle down and engage in substantial commercial exchange (largely based upon cattle trading). While their economy is still almost entirely cattle-based, many sedentary households also practice opportunistic flood-plain agriculture. Currently approximately one-third of the population is still nomadic, which also represents an attempt to live a subsistence lifestyle and resist market exchange in an effort to avoid selling productive capital through livestock sales. Two-thirds of the population is sedentary and sells livestock on a regular basis for subsistence. Outward signs of development are absent. There is no running water and no electricity, roads are scarce, and people live in grass houses with few personal possessions beyond clothing and cooking pots. Many sedentary households send their sons to primary school, a few send daughters, but relatively few children attend school for more than three years; almost all of the adult population is illiterate.

I carried out experiments with both nomadic and sedentary individuals, and I drew quite randomly from the adult population, including both men and women. The low level of education among this population raises special problems in terms of their comprehension of the experiments. Some other members of the cross-cultural group used formal quizzes of game comprehension to disqualify players who were not understanding the game. Joe Henrich (Henrich et al. n.d.) also rated his informants on the basis of his assessment of their comprehension (from one to three), though he did not find that this correlated with their offers. Some mechanism to disqualify those who are not understanding the game is highly recommended, as is the use of very simple games with those who are illiterate and possibly innumerate. Visual demonstrations with piles of coins may also be helpful.

Prior to beginning the experiments I held several large public meetings to explain the work in a few centrally located survey villages. These meetings were well attended by elders and young men, though very few women showed up, as is the norm. I explained that this work would be quite different from my previous work, and that it would involve playing "fun games for real money." I purposely said nothing in this open forum about the content of the experiments, so as not to steer behavior in any way. But I explained that these were games being carried out around the world to study economic decision making, and that they have been played many times in the United States and Europe. The discussion that ensued was one of great amusement at the "insanity" of Western ways. Most people seemed, both at this point and after the games were played, to interpret them in this light—that is, westerners "had money to throw away on such foolishness." Some seemed to have a true understanding of the nature of research and that this would somehow teach us something about human behavior. An alternative hypothesis that also floated around, perhaps never taken completely seriously, was that I wanted to provide aid to the community so I dreamt up this complicated scheme to provide an excuse to do so. One thing is certain: There was never any hesitation about accepting the money, whatever the reason assumed to explain the windfall. This appears to have been the case in most of the sites now studied by anthropologists, though one researcher working in Mongolia (see Gil-White n.d.) encountered concern among the population that they were taking money from a poor student.

I explained that I would be approaching every household in each of five villages with a household economic and demographic survey very similar to those I had administered in the past. No household was required to participate either in this survey or in the games that would follow. I promised to try to invite at least one adult from each of the survey households to play a game.

Six native-speaking Orma research assistants with Form 4 education carried out the household economic surveys with 205 households in five villages. These surveys were extremely similar to ones I had carried out in 1978 and 1987. In addition, the fact that I have lived in the community for over four years and been visiting intermittently for 20 years certainly contributed to the ease of this surveying.

Village size ranged from 13 households in one nomadic village to 36 to 69 households in the four sedentary villages, with an average of 8.1 individuals per household, totaling 1,669 individuals in all. A three-generation genealogy was drawn for each household and individual demographic statistics for all household residents were gathered on relationship to head of household, age, sex, education, work, and income by source. Household-level data on migration history, length of residence in the community, and wealth of household were also elicited. Voluntary compliance with this survey was 100%. At least one individual from almost all surveyed households played one of the 144 games (262 players). Of those who made offers in the games, the mean age was 37.7 and mean education was 1.4 years. Mean household wealth, measured in cattle equivalents, was 19.8 and individual income averaged 665 Kenyan shillings per month.

Before turning to some of the more problematic issues facing experimentalists outside the laboratory, it is worth recording a few issues that one might expect to be problems, but in fact were not for this researcher. There was no resistance by the Orma to playing the games; on the contrary, people loved them—by the end they were imploring me to make arrangements to come back as soon as possible and play more games. This was generally the experience of the other researchers in the projects as well. Of course, the participants enjoyed the remuneration component of the games, but they also for the most part actually enjoyed the play itself and were intellectually engaged to an extent that I had not previously encountered in my earlier work. I received many jovial comments such as, "I will be spending years trying to figure out what this all meant."

While I began the games with concerns about logistics, these were ill-founded. Grass houses are not at all a hindrance to running games. In fact they were the perfect size for isolating small groups from one another during the course of play, and one research assistant seated by the door and another on the opposite wall were able to keep groups from talking about the game, exiting, or chatting with visitors. "Crowd control" turned out to be relatively simple even though people sometimes had to wait three hours to finish their play. When I explained that they could not talk about the game during the play, there was remarkably disciplined compliance. It is essential, however, that groups be monitored carefully once the game has been explained, as the consequences of collusion can be extreme.

All games were run jointly by a bilingual, native-speaking research assistant (the games' master) and myself. The school teacher I chose for this purpose was amazingly patient with "slow learners," has a reputation in the village for trustworthiness, and is known to be devoutly religious. Numerous native speakers were also used as monitors, but they were not in the room with individuals at the time offers were made. Given that the games' master is known to many of the individuals playing the games, I had him turn around at the time offers were made to ensure that only I had access to that information, thus enhancing anonymity. Some people gestured for him not to bother to turn or blurted out their offers before he could turn, and seemed quite unconcerned that he knew how they played.

Considerable effort was made to control many conditions of the experimental design across sites in order to have comparable data and be in the position to make claims about cross-cultural differences. The stakes were set at approximately one day's local casual labor wage, with a show-up fee of one-third of a day's wage for all sites. In the Orma case, this translated into games played for 100 shillings or roughly the equivalent of $2; this was the local daily casual wage rate at the time. Each player received a show-up fee of 20 shillings at the very beginning of the game instructions. Limitations of small currency necessitated that I reduce the show-up fee to 20 percent of the daily wage. The show-up fee drove home the fact that they were playing for real money, and served as partial compensation to those who might not earn much in the games. Gathering sufficient small currency was a problem for a number of our researchers. It is not advisable to use IOUs, as these change the dynamic of the game and make people's pay-offs more public, as would be the case, for example, if they were exchanged in a local shop. Changing the "currency" to local goods may also change the play, as sharing norms and the visibility of pay-offs may vary, say, with payment in tobacco or tea. However, controlled experiments in which the pay-off currency is intentionally manipulated may be extremely interesting for isolating the social context of diverse norms.

Each of the game texts was back-translated; that is, one native speaker translated it from English to the local language and another one, unfamiliar with the English text and the game, translated it back into English to ensure precision and clarity of meaning. All games were one-shot with no repeat play. Some members of our project were working with extremely small populations and had to use the same individuals to play more than one game. In cases such as this there are potential learning effects and also possibilities for collusion within the community. Reversing play order and checking for these effects is one strategy for testing the impact of such factors.

I was careful to do exactly what I promised in each game to ensure that people did not distrust my intentions and to facilitate understanding of the game. Feedback from trusted participants indicates that neither distrust of the experimenters nor fear of losing anonymity was a problem. In a small community where people will certainly compare notes and talk, any deceit on the part of the experimenter is likely to have lasting and unknown effects.

Efforts were made to be as systematic as possible in sampling, but because the games had to be played en mass there were biases toward availability. Given the enthusiasm that most people had for participating, however, this was less than one might expect. Young men who herd were definitely underrepresented, but those working on their farms chose to take time out from their field preparations rather than miss the game. Undoubtedly, those who travel more and happened to be away were slightly underrepresented, though if they missed one opportunity to play they were often called a second time. A major effort was made to include at least one adult from each household, and often both a man and a woman were included. Some games were played in the evening to capture those otherwise occupied during the day.

People were notified the night before a morning game that they could show up at a certain location to play. For the ultimatum and dictator games I usually called twenty people for this purpose. In small villages the group was split in two and held in grass houses. In the largest two villages where school buildings were available I ran through the game instructions with the entire group together. No one knew at this point whether they would be player one or player two. The game master read the instructions twice (in Orma) and I then demonstrated the play with a set of ten ten-shilling coins. I ran through a randomly generated series of hypothetical possibilities of play, including rejections in the ultimatum game. Each person in the room was then individually quizzed with a hypothetical example to test for comprehension. It is advisable not to allow questions while the group is together, as these may be suggestive to the rest of the group and give others ideas about how to play the game. The group was then left with about three research assistants monitoring them with instructions that they could not discuss the game. Individual players were then brought in one by one to a separate room where only the game master and I were located. The order of play was determined publicly by drawing slips of paper from a hat with each player's name on it. This served to emphasize both the randomness in the order of play (which affected waiting time) and the assignment of roles. Once alone, we ran through the rules of the game again and all of the player's questions were answered until I was confident that the player understood the game. At this point they were told whether they were player one or player two. Player one made an offer by pushing whatever coins they wished to offer to one side of the table while the game master had his back turned. Once they had made their offer or declared their response to an offer, they were allowed to return home, but could not talk to any of those who had not already played the game. In the case of the ultimatum game, a second appointment time was set for first players to return, learn whether their offer had been accepted, and be paid if it was.

While it would be even more ideal to bring together the group of twenty and then instruct them one by one to be absolutely sure that they did not talk about the game prior to play, this method took too long for this highly illiterate population. I compensated by using a lot of highly trained monitors to ensure that there was no discussion of the game.

Four individuals had to be eliminated from play because they did not understand the game. One was blind, one was deaf, and two were rather slow mentally. Once we were in private I paid them as if they had played and no one knew that they had actually not played the game.

One of the main differences between the studies represented in this project and those most often carried out in U.S. laboratories, is that we are running them in small communities where most people know one another or at least have a high probability of having future repeat dealings. There is also a high level of interrelatedness. This characteristic may affect play in a number of different ways. People who live in small communities may habitually share more in everyday life, they may have different conceptions of privacy and anonymity, and there are more serious problems associated with contagion of the population if games are played over time.

Even though one may guarantee anonymity, in a society in which little can be kept private, people may act habitually on the assumption that anonymity does not exist. However, it may also be the case that in societies with little privacy there is less concern about anonymity.

I have a bit of anecdotal evidence that bears on the anonymity question. About a week after the play was finished in one large village, I made inquiries about what people knew about how other people had played. I was told that while some had told their close friends how they had played, others had not. They discussed the games in a general sense, but did not reveal their actual offers. A very close friend also approached me approximately a week after his wife had played the dictator game. The friend was curious how his wife had played because, "She won't tell me." Finally, three women who played the dictator game and kept the entire pot for themselves were so proud of the fact that they immediately ran into the village and told their neighbors. I also have little doubt that some Orma would not hesitate to lie about how they played, knowing full-well that there was no way anyone could challenge their assertion. Several close friends reported to me that the steps taken to ensure anonymity were obvious and that no one in the village was concerned about being found out.

I was especially concerned with the problem of contagion from the games once anyone in the village had played. People in small communities share information rapidly and freely within the community. These games raised a great deal of interest and it stands to reason that people talked about them. If one assumes that people talk, then those coming to play a game after the first round in a given village might have heard how the game was played and might also have heard discussion about the "proper way to play the game." I tried to get around these problems by calling large groups of people for a game and holding them all until the group was finished. I also moved from village to village as rapidly as possible to try to beat any news that might travel. Finally, I changed games and never announced which game people were being called for on any given day.

Despite these precautions, the problem of contagion is not to be taken lightly. When I returned in 2000 to run more games, I ran the dictator game again in one of the same villages where I had run it in 1998. While the first round of play went well, the village had clearly coordinated a strategy prior to my second round several days later. A number of young men in this village had coached the entire village to all play 50-50, and that is exactly what virtually everyone did. While this is a fascinating outcome, as there was no way to enforce this "norm," it has far different implications than it would had there been no coordinated response. The effect of this coordinated response was evident to me by the time the third player made an offer. Although these individuals had not previously played the game, none of them exhibited the usual strain associated with trying to understand a foreign task. People wished to hurriedly make their offer because they knew ahead of time exactly how they intended to play the game. Another member of our project, Abigail Barr (personal communication 2000), had an identical experience in Zimbabwe.

Some of the members of our cross-cultural project were not able to bring together large groups of players at one time and keep them isolated from one another until the play was finished. Joe Henrich (2000) for example, in the original study with the Machiguenga, had to go from house to house, given the dispersed nature of the population. This method increases the possibility that people will have been told about the game prior to playing it. However, in some situations there is no alternative. In such cases, one can test for play order effects to see if there is any effect of communication; in Henrich's case there was none.

Some Early Findings:
The Effects of Market Integration

One of the findings from our cross-cultural study of fifteen societies (Henrich et al. n.d.) is that the societies represented in the study have means and modes in the ultimatum game that are below those for developed societies. Indeed, one of the hypotheses that holds across these less developed small-scale societies is the positive relationship between market integration and offer size in the ultimatum game. While the cross-cultural evidence alone justifies a closer look at this relationship, it is also worth pursuing studies of intracultural variation in societies that have significant variation in market involvement. The Orma of East Africa is one such society.

To most people the notion that individuals in market societies might be more fair-minded seems counterintuitive. However, the argument is not without its supporters (Hirschman 1982). Nor, I would argue, is it entirely implausible. If one posits fair-mindedness as a signaling device to build reputation, it is conceivable that the pay-off for a good reputation is greater in a market economy than in a nonmarket economy. Among other things, the signaling value in a market may be higher because of the greater flow of information, which corresponds in part to the higher population density of market populations.

The Ultimatum Bargaining Game

It was Henrich's (2000) study of the ultimatum bargaining game among Machiguenga Indians that served as a pilot for this project. The Machiguenga made low offers and these were not refused. I also expected the Orma to make very low offers and for there to be almost no refusals. I was half right (see figure 3.1). Orma mean offers were a high 44 percent (exactly in line with the U.S. range), far higher than the 26 percent mean offer observed in the Amazon. Orma behavior departed from the U.S.

pattern, however, in the distribution. In the United States it is common to have low offers (below 25 percent), though there is a significant rejection rate in this range (Camerer n.d.). For the Orma the lowest offer out of 56 games was 30 percent, and there were only two refusals among the 13 who received 30-percent offers. It may be significant that the only two rejecters were both educated men from rather wealthy families. It is difficult to make much of this, but the role of such individuals as the "defenders" of social norms in society is so important that it bears further investigation. Notably, there is anecdotal evidence from a variety of the research sites reported in the larger study that rejecters in some of them also bear these characteristics (personal communication from Joseph Henrich 2000).

Figure 3.1. Distribution of offers in the ultimatum game (N=56, stake size=100 Kenyan shillings)

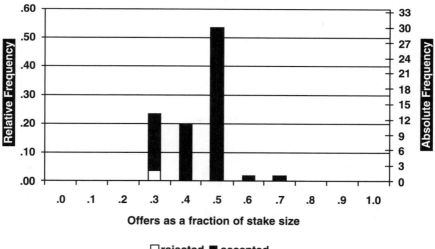

Offers as a fraction of stake size

□ rejected ■ accepted

In my post-play interviews with players, almost every player who offered 40 or 50 percent indicated that they did so because of fairness. In the formal interview immediately after the play, no one owned up to being strategic or fearing that a lesser offer would be rejected. Furthermore, virtually every responder indicated that he or she would have accepted an offer of even 10 percent, the lowest possible short of zero. While the fairness explanation was consistent with the willingness to accept low offers, I was still suspicious of proposers' motivations for giving high offers. I sought out a few reliable informants that I knew I could trust to fill me in on "the talk in the village." The "talk" revealed that people were *obsessed* with the possibility that their offer might be refused, in spite of the fact that they thought (correctly) that it was unlikely that people would refuse even a small offer. But very few wanted to take such a chance.

While we cannot differentiate fairness from strategic risk-aversion in the ultimatum bargaining game, the dictator game does facilitate this dis-aggregation.

The Dictator Game

The Orma mean offer for the dictator game was 31 percent (see figure 3.2). While this is high for comparable experiments from the developed world, which range from 20 to 30 percent, it is not far out of bounds and is significantly lower than their offers of 44 percent in the ultimatum game. What is different in the Orma case is the distribution of offers. While it is common to find 30 to 40 percent of players taking all of the pot in the United States and Canada, one finds a much smaller percentage of purely self-interested players among the Orma (9 percent). The number playing for fairness, at 40 to 50 percent, is about the same for the Orma and U.S. samples. Thus, while there are two modal strategies in the developed world—pure fairness and pure self-interest—there is less consensus among the Orma. In other words, behavior is not driven by a dominant or by two

Figure 3.2. Distribution of offers in the dictator game (N=43, stake size=100 Kenyan shillings)

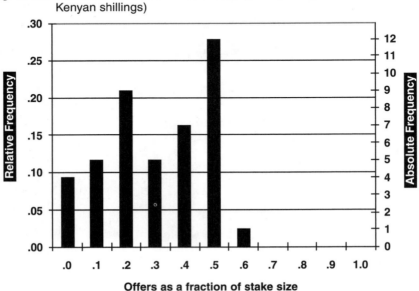

competing norms. The bulk of the distribution for the Orma falls between pure self-interest and pure fairness.

The Effects of Wage/Trade Income in the Ultimatum and Dictator Games

The most significant and potentially interesting finding to come out of this set of games has to do with differences between those who earn income other than from the sale of their own livestock and those who do not. Wage/trade income in this context includes: casual wage labor, civil service employment, profits from trade in livestock or other products that are not one's own, digging stones at a local quarry for sale to builders, or production of handicrafts for sale. The argument for excluding income from household stock sales is to better highlight the difference between those who engage directly in market exchange beyond the marketing of surplus production from their subsistence herds, and those who do not. This distinction also allows for the disaggregation of wealth and income effects. Income from livestock sales is far more closely correlated with wealth (measured in livestock) than is the income measure used here. Income, absent one's own stock sales, is not at all correlated with wealth, as many of those who are driven to market their labor do so because they cannot support themselves from subsistence livestock production or sales from their herds.

In the ultimatum and dictator games, the presence or absence of wage/trade income is a highly significant predictor of offer size. In the figures below for each game, we see that those with wage/trade income clearly favor 50-50 splits in both games. While 50 percent offer half in the dictator game, nearly 80 percent do so in the ultimatum game. These norms are in dramatic contrast to the absence of any such spike among those without such income. Indeed, what is striking about those without income is that there is clearly no normative tendency whatever, nor do we find the bi-modal pattern so typical in developed societies where both pure selfishness and pure altruism compete to form two modes. Mann-Whitney rank-sum tests were run on each of these games individually and on the sum of both games together. In the ultimatum game (N=56; no income=32, positive income=24), the Mann-Whitney is significant at the 0.022 level. In the dictator game (N=43; no income=25, positive income=18), the Mann-Whitney is significant at the 0.017 level. If one lumps together the offers in both games (N=99; no income=57, positive income=42), the Mann-Whitney is significant at the 0.001 level.

This result is certainly consistent with the notion that people are learning in the market that fair-mindedness is rewarded. I have suggested that among those selling either their labor or their goods, there may be a higher

Figure 3.3. Distribution of offers in the ultimatum game by no wage/trade income (n=32) and positive wage income (n=24), stake size=100 Kenyan shillings

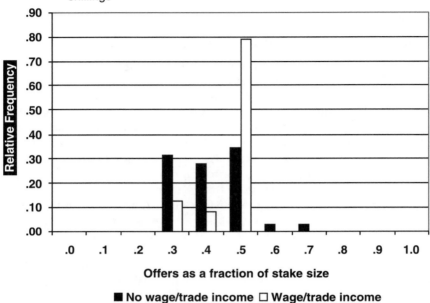

Offers as a fraction of stake size

■ **No wage/trade income** □ **Wage/trade income**

premium placed upon reputation and that one way of signaling a good reputation is to behave fair-mindedly.

While the data presented here on the relationship between market exchange and fairness are statistically strong and intriguing, they should not in any respect be accepted as definitive. Further examination of the relationship in this and other societies is warranted, and especially studies which incorporate large variation in market integration, such as that found among the Orma. We also need multiple measures of market involvement to flesh out the robustness of this phenomenon. In a new dataset I am attempting to pick apart the measure of market integration and test for information effects in the form of travel outside the village, exposure to newspapers and radios, and a variety of individual-level demographic variables. These and other big questions would greatly benefit from anthropological insight and a large number of carefully controlled experiments across the diverse societies we typically study. There is much work to be done and we are barely in the first inning of an exciting methodological frontier for anthropology. The rewards in the form of better understanding of social norms and the evolution of altruism and cooperation are arguably profound.

Figure 3.4. Distribution of offers in the dictator game by no wage/trade income (n=25) and positive wage income (n=18), stake size=100 Kenyan shillings

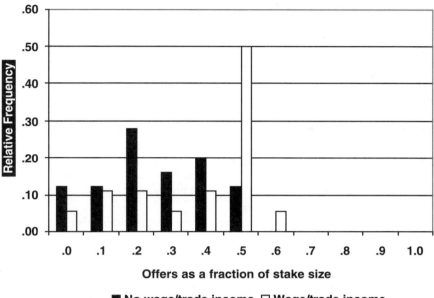

■ No wage/trade income □ Wage/trade income

Conclusions and Theoretical Applications

Many social scientists accept that human behavior is partially driven by narrow economic self-interest and partially by social norms that yield more cooperative outcomes (Ostrom 1998). But we actually know very little empirically about the circumstances that drive one over the other, or the distribution of such behaviors across human diversity—both longitudinally in an evolutionary sense and cross-sectionally in the contemporary world. We would like to know more, and preferably in a systematic fashion that translates well across the diversity of extant societies. Economic experiments offer a rigorous method to do just that. Early findings already suggest that there appears to be more fair-minded or altruistic behavior in developed societies than in less-developed small-scale societies, though this result will need to be replicated many more times. We also note, however, that "pure self-interest" is a relatively uncommon norm in small-scale societies. While it seems acceptable in some societies to take 80 percent in a dictator game, it is not at all common to take 100 percent, as has been observed in laboratory experiments with U.S. undergraduates.

The pattern of offer distribution within societies should eventually tell us a great deal about the degree of homogeneity of social norms across societies. Sometimes we see clear and strong modes, sometimes we see bimodal distributions indicating competing norms. To date, we understand very little about the nature of the differences in individuals that account for these distributions. In fact, we don't even know whether such behavior is stable across the same individuals, indicating people have "types" (such as "cooperative" or "altruistic") versus situational differences that explain behavior based upon need at the moment or even emotions.

Given the degree of attention now focused upon the role of social capital, and especially trust, in the course of development (see Knack and Keefer 1997; Putnam 1993; and Zak and Knack 1999), economic experiments have much to offer here as well. While the direction of causality may still elude us, it would be interesting to at least know whether we find higher levels of trust in societies associated with good governance rather than corrupt governance.

Economic experiments also offer a unique opportunity to measure socially beneficial "punishment" behavior such as we see in the ultimatum game. This and other experiments being developed by Fischbaker and Fehr (n.d.) offer the opportunity to identify individuals who are prepared to pay a price to support the "common good" by punishing the behavior of individuals who are perceived to have violated social norms, even if there was no personal injury to the punisher. The evolutionary trajectory of such behavior is an intriguing theoretical question with obvious relevance to the effectiveness of social cooperation and economic development.

Finally, anthropology has a great deal to contribute to the field of experimental economics. We bring a diversity of cases that cannot be matched in the developed world. We also are more likely to work with representative samples rather than university undergraduates, arguably a very poor choice for examining economic preferences that are meant to be representative of their own societies. We are also much more apt to be in a position to collect accurate and oftentimes longitudinal demographic data on the game participants. Perhaps our largest contribution will be the ethnographic context that we bring to the interpretation of the data, including background ethnographic understanding of the social norms that may underlie or explain offer distributions. In short, experimental economics in the hands of anthropologists offers great promise to a number of disciplines and theoretical investigations.

References

Barr, Abigail
  2000. Personal communication.
Berg, Joyce, John Dickhaut, and Kevin McCabe
  1995 "Trust, Reciprocity, and Social History." *Games and Economic Behavior* 10: 122–42.
Camerer, Colin F.
  n.d. "Simple Bargaining and Social Utility: Dictator, Ultimatum, and Trust Games." Chapter 3 in *Experiments in Strategic Interaction*. Unpublished book manuscript.
Camerer, Colin, and Richard Thaler
  1995 "Ultimatums, Dictators and Manners." *Journal of Economic Perspectives* 9(2): 209–19.
Cameron, L.
  1999 "Raising the Stakes in the Ultimatum Game: Experimental Evidence from Indonesia." *Economic Inquiry* 37(1): 47–59.
Davis, Douglas D., and Charles A. Holt, eds.
  1993 *Experimental Economics*. Princeton, N.J.: Princeton University Press.
Ensminger, Jean
  1992 *Making a Market: The Institutional Transformation of an African Society*. New York: Cambridge University Press.
  n.d. "Market Integration and Fairness: Evidence from Ultimatum, Dictator, and Public Goods Experiments in East Africa." In *Cooperation, Reciprocity, and Punishment: Experiments in 15 Small-Scale Societies*, J. Henrich, R. Boyd, S. Bowles, H. Gintis, R. McElreath, and E. Fehr, eds. Under review at Princeton University Press.
Fehr, Ernst, and Klaus Schmidt
  1999 "A Theory of Fairness, Competition, and Cooperation." *Quarterly Journal of Economics* 1114(3): 817–68.
Fischbacker, U., and E. Fehr
  n.d. "Third Part Punishment." Unpublished manuscript.
Friedman, Jeffrey, ed.
  1995 *The Rational Choice Controversy: Economic Models of Politics Reconsidered*. New Haven, Conn.: Yale University Press.
Gil-White, Francisco
  n.d. "Ultimatum Game with an Ethnicity Manipulation: Results from Bulgan Cum, Mongolia." In *Cooperation, Reciprocity, and Punishment: Experiments in 15 Small-Scale Societies*, J. Henrich, R. Boyd, S. Bowles, H. Gintis, R. McElreath, and E. Fehr, eds. Under review at Princeton University Press.
Green, Donald, and Ian Shapiro, eds.
  1994 *Pathologies of Rational Choice Theory: A Critique of Applications in Political Science*. New Haven, Conn.: Yale University Press.
Hagel, John H., and Alvin E. Roth, eds.
  1995 *The Handbook of Experimental Economics*. Princeton, N.J.: Princeton University Press.

Henrich, Joseph
  2000   Personal communication.
  2000   "Does Culture Matter in Economic Behavior: Ultimatum Game Bargaining among the Machiguenga." *American Economic Review* 90(4): 973–80.
Henrich, Joseph, Robert Boyd, Samuel Bowles, Herbert Gintis, Ernst Fehr, and Richard McElreath, eds.
  n.d.   *Cooperation, Reciprocity, and Punishment: Experiments in 15 Small-Scale Societies.* Under review at Princeton University Press.
Hirschman, Albert
  1982   "Rival Interpretations of Market Society: Civilizing, Destructive, or Feeble." *Journal of Economic Literature* XX: 1463–84.
Kachelmeier, S., and M. Shehata
  1997   "Internal Auditing and Voluntary Cooperation in Firms: A Cross-Cultural Experiment." *The Accounting Review* 72(3): 407–31.
Knack, Stephen, and Philip Keefer
  1997   "Does Social Capital Have an Economic Payoff? A Cross-Country Investigation." *The Quarterly Journal of Economics* (November): 1251–88.
Ostrom, Elinor
  1998   "A Behavioral Approach to the Rational Choice Theory of Collective Action." Presidential address, American Political Science Association, 1997. *American Political Science Review* 92(1): 1–22.
Putnam, Robert D.
  1993   *Making Democracy Work: Civic Traditions in Modern Italy.* Princeton, N.J.: Princeton University Press.
Roth, Alvin E., Vesna Prasnikar, Masahiro Okuno-Fujiwara, and Shmuel Zamir
  1991   "Bargaining and Market Behavior in Jerusalem, Ljubljana, Pittsburgh and Tokyo: An Experimental Study." *American Economic Review* 81: 1068–95.
Tracer, David
  n.d.   "Market Integration, Reciprocity and Fairness in Rural Papua New Guinea: Results from a Two-Village Ultimatum Game Experiment." In *Cooperation, Reciprocity, and Punishment: Experiments in 15 Small-Scale Societies*, J. Henrich, R. Boyd, S. Bowles, H. Gintis, R. McElreath, and E. Fehr, eds. Under review at Princeton University Press.
Yamagishi, T., and M. Yamagishi
  1994   "Trust and Commitment in the United States and Japan." *Motivation Emotion* 18(2): 129–66.
Zak, Paul J., and Knack, Stephen
  1999   "Trust and Growth." Paper presented at the annual meetings of the International Society for New Institutional Economics, Washington D.C. (September).

Part II

Rethinking Wealth, Exchange, and the Evolution of Social Institutions

Chapter 4

Commodity Flows and the Evolution of Complex Societies

Timothy Earle

In his 1922 ethnography *Argonauts of the Western Pacific*, Malinowski challenged scholars to understand human economies in cross-cultural perspectives. Attacking simple notions of "economic man," he emphasized that economies are highly variable both in exchange relationships and in systems of value. The role of anthropologists, as he saw it, was to document and explain cultural variability that, by observing only Western societies, was invisible to Western scholars of human nature.

Malinowski's plea for a comparative approach to economies needs renewal. Within less than a century, globalization has radically changed all economies as commodity flows from expanding capitalism have engulfed societies from the darkest forest to the most remote desert. Our views of human economies may again be distorted and limited by studying a single case—the modern interdependent world system. I draw attention to the extraordinary variation in human societies and economies that existed in the past. Based on archaeological evidence, some recent statements and broader assumptions about human economies appear to be fundamentally flawed.

How do human economies vary, and how are we to explain this variation? Much variation can be understood as outcomes of different technologies and environments. Since Adam Smith's (1937 [1776]) *The Wealth of Nations*, it has been assumed that social and political improvements required economic growth to generate the "surplus" (production beyond subsistence requirements) needed to support civilizations with their arts and culture, leisure time, and good governments. Among simpler societies, economies were thought to be involved only in making a living. With economic growth, made possible with the profits from technology, specialization, and trade, people could work less, produce more, and escape life's necessities. In one or another location, availability of raw materials such as clay, metal ore, fuel, or water determines costs of production; transport technologies, like camel caravans or boats able to carry heavy loads, lower distribution costs; and some production technologies, like pottery manufacture, create economies of scale that encourage large production volume to lower unit costs. The development of technologies was thought to increase efficiencies and require specialization. These lessons from microeconomics, so evident in the modern world, help us understand differences in the extent and volume of commodity flows from one case to another.

I, however, want to draw attention to quite a different pattern: how the extent of commodity distribution in nonmercantile and noncapitalist economies reflects the organizational character of the political economy in these societies. Specifically, I want to illustrate how, for many human societies, the volume and extent of commodity flows are determined, not by economic opportunities for profit, but by institutional demands in finance—"supply on command," as elegantly phrased by Darrell LaLone (1982).

Let us begin with Karl Polanyi's (1957) famous title: "The economy as instituted process." A human economy has two fused properties. First, it is the material process through which goods and services are produced, exchanged, and consumed. Second, the economy has form, organized by social and political relationships that arrange interpersonal interactions across space and time. Making, giving, and trading are social events that are institutionalized.

To understand variation in human economies requires us to understand variation in social institutions. With an emerging interest in agency, many anthropologists now underplay institutional analyses, but the new institutional economists (North 1990) and economic anthropologists (Acheson 1994, chap. 2 this volume; Ensminger 1994, chap. 3 this volume) have refocused attention on how institutions and economies are codependent. Based on the advantages of lower transaction costs in commodity flows, they argue that political and social institutions developed to regulate commodity flows, maintain regional peace, and guarantee contracts. Although these ideas are only beginning to be investigated in prehistory (Steinberg 1997), archaeology offers an exceptional opportunity to understand this codependency.

The key question is whether the evolution of integrating human institutions corresponds closely with the amount of commodity exchanges in human economies. The new institutional economics believe that the two developed together. Ten thousand years ago all human societies depended on hunting and gathering, population densities were comparatively low (well below 1/km^2), and groups were organized into small associations of a handful of families. The development of domestication, of settled village communities, of hierarchical societies, of cities, and eventually of states has transformed societies systematically (Harris 1977; Johnson and Earle 2000; Trigger 1998). Sociocultural evolution, not in uniform stages but in a multiplicity of parallel developments shaped by common processes, is unquestioned. According to the theories of institutional economics, exchange should expand in tandem with expanding institutional organization.

The linkage between social evolution and increasing commodity flows is logically attractive, but, as I discuss here, specialization and commodity flows do *not* increase uniformly with sociocultural evolution. Social evolution from simpler to more complex societies can be envisioned as the development of new levels of integration that organize larger polities. In world region after world region, however, the amount of exchange increases and declines episodically, not correlated to general trends of increasing scales of integration (Brumfiel and Earle 1987; Ericson and Baugh 1993; Baugh and Ericson 1994; Kirch 1991; Earle et al. 1998). Why in the evolution of social complexity is no general trend in expanding exchange observed?

Although evolutionary typologies, like Service's (1962) band-tribe-chiefdom-state, must not be seen as essentialist categories, scales of social and political integration can be recognized and variation within them studied. Chiefdoms, for example, are regional polities that organize populations in the thousands and tens of thousands (Johnson and Earle 2000). These societies are complex: Leaders are socially recognized and some own substantially more land and/or wealth than others. In this chapter, I discuss how chiefdoms vary based on their size, on the hierarchical relationships between rulers and followers, on power of the economy, warriors, and ideology, and importantly on systems of finance (Earle 1997a). My point is that the amount of exchange in chiefdoms does not correlate with the extent of political integration, as predicted by the new institutional economists, but with the nature of finance.

To begin our analysis, some terms can be defined. Two analytical distinctions help clarify how variation in commodity flows is understood within models of social evolution: subsistence vs. political economy and staple vs. wealth finance (Johnson and Earle 2000). The subsistence economy involves ways that households are maintained through everyday activities. Food is obtained by hunting, gathering, fishing, and agriculture, and tools and utensils are manufactured and used productively in everyday activities. Each household can produce much of what it wants (Sahlins 1972), but some exchange always exists because of resource availability and risk. The subsistence economy is sufficing. The political economy, in contrast, involves the ways in which surpluses are mobilized to support political activities, lifestyle, and institutional operations of an elite segment. Complex social institutions depend on an ability to finance their maintenance and operations (Earle and D'Altroy 1989). To mobilize a surplus rests on a productive economy and on practical control that derives from command over selective sectors of that economy. The political economy is competitive and maximizing.

The distinction between corporate strategies, which are based on the ownership of land and the mobilization of staples, and networked strategies, which are based on the movement of wealth, helps distinguish contrasting possibilities in emerging political economies (Blanton et al. 1996). In corporate strategies, staple finance mobilizes foods and everyday technologies to support chiefs, craftsmen, warriors, priests, managers, and commoners working on political projects. Mobilization requires control over food production through land ownership (D'Altroy and Earle 1985). Staple finance involves only local vertical transfers of goods, and commodity exchanges can be quite limited. In networked strategies, wealth finance in traditional societies involves the distribution of primitive valuables (items that have intersubjective values established in exchange) as a means of payment. Typically such objects are symbolically significant, and are used to distinguish individuals, events, or social settings. Individuals derive "prestige" from holding, displaying, and transferring wealth. Control of wealth can be maintained by restricting its manufacture, importation, distribution, or use. Wealth must, however, be convertible into other commodities and so such finance becomes linked to horizontal flows of commodities.

The evolutionary trajectories on the Hawaiian Islands and in Thy, Denmark, illustrate divergent ways that chiefdoms developed based on distinctive systems of finance. Two sets of contrasts are drawn: the first between the relatively simply organized Bronze Age chiefdoms of Denmark and the very complex contact-period Hawaiian chiefdoms; and the second between the late Neolithic Danish groups and the same region's subsequent Early Bronze Age chiefdoms.

At contact with the West (1778), Hawaiian society was organized politically into complex chiefdoms. Polities were large: in the tens of thousands of subjects with a governing hierarchy of chiefs, a religious hierarchy of priests, and a class of chiefs owning lands worked by commoners. Typically a major island and neighboring small islands were organized as a single polity. Goods were mobilized to support the chiefdom by staple finance from community irrigation and aquacultural complexes developed under chiefly supervision and farmed by commoners.

During the Early Bronze Age in Thy (1500–1000 B.C.), Danish society developed simple chiefdoms. Polities were considerably less complex than in Hawaii: perhaps only a thousand subjects organized within polities with a shallow hierarchy of chieftains, their warriors, and farmers. Chiefs dominated a pastoral sector by ownership of animals and the grassland on which they pastured. Chieftains and their warriors were a social segment, buried with their military regalia in earthen barrows that lay along the higher ridges in the landscape where pastures were best; yet, the chieftains were only modestly distinguished from normal farmers. Their houses were bigger, and they held more metal wealth (especially fine weapons), but differences were in degree and not kind. Finance derived from control over an export economy involving cattle hides and raw amber. The exports were traded for bronze ingots and objects, which were remanufactured locally into men's military regalia (swords, daggers, sword belts) and women's jewelry (fibulae, pins, and the like). Prior to the development of the long-distance commodity flows of metal that defined the chieftains' distinctiveness, the society was only modestly ranked by exchange of local prestige objects such as flint daggers (DeMarrais, Castillo, and Earle 1996).

The complex Hawaiian chiefdoms with limited exchange and the much simpler Danish chiefdoms with more extensive exchange show that the amount of exchange does not vary with institutional integration per se but with the specific nature of institutional finance. Exchange is important to understand the evolution of chiefdoms primarily in the financing role it plays in the political economy.

Archaeological Methods for Studying Commodity Flows

I am an archaeologist who studies how prehistoric economies supported the emergence of political complexity. Many people seem skeptical that an archaeologist could study an economy. How can you describe an economy with nothing but broken potsherds and lost arrowheads remaining? Documenting commodity flows (and other aspects of prehistoric economies) has long been a central endeavor for archaeologists. Descriptions of methods to study prehistoric exchange are available in several works (Earle and Ericson 1977; Ericson and Earle 1982; Renfrew and Shennan 1982; Sabloff and Lamberg-Karlovsky 1975; Wilmsen 1972).

Before 1965, exchange was documented by style. If a vessel, for example, was of an "intrusive" style, meaning that it was distinctive in decoration or form from local ceramics, it was thought to be an import from an area where the style was normal. Advances in scientific technology have transformed our ability to study exchange (Ericson and Earle 1982). Using techniques from material science and geology, researchers determine the sources of the raw materials found archaeologically. Earlier, qualitative assessments of fit between stone materials or ceramic tempers and particular geological formations permitted some conclusions on exchange (see, for example, Shepard 1956), but by the 1970s a broad suite of analytical approaches was applied to sourcing, including chemical characterization of materials by neutron activation, x-ray fluorescence, and other techniques (Harbottle 1982; Lambert 1997). The basic steps (see, for example, Ericson 1981) include: (1) samples from different raw material sources are analyzed to determine their compositional signatures; (2) artifacts from archaeological sites across a region are analyzed and identified to these sources; and (3) for each source, results are represented graphically as an array of source percentages from the different sites (source frequency on the y axis graphed against site distance from source on the x axis). The handling of such large data sets requires increasingly sophisticated statistical analyses to match chemical signatures with potential sources (Harbottle 1982).

A typical pattern is a fall off in use of a material as the distance to its source increases. The graph display of decline can then be compared to predictions of different economic and geographic models. In Renfrew's (1977) analysis, obsidian from Turkey was uniformly common near the source (the supply zone) and then became increasingly rare as distance from the source increased. Prestige goods (such as metal in Europe) also fall off in frequency away from their sources, but the rate of decline is less steep. On a general level, the decline both makes practical sense and fits well with microeconomic theories of a downward-sloping demand curve. As distance from a source increases, the expense (cost) of obtaining material from that source increases as transportation and transaction costs soar; as these costs increase, demand declines as individuals shift to lower cost alternatives. Different types of commodities have distinct rates of fall off responding to differences in transport costs (value-to-weight ratio, bulkiness, fragility) and transactions costs (exchange mechanisms) (see Hodder 1974).

As long as materials are identifiable to specific sources, archaeologists can study the extent and volume of many commodity flows in prehistory. The challenge now is for us to document how prehistoric economies develop over long time periods and correlate these changes with broad changes in economic conditions and the emergence of political organization. The new sophistication in sourcing techniques liberates us to move beyond graphic models to consider the changing contexts and roles of commodities movement in human societies.

Understanding Economic Process in Human Societies

To look at the contrasting patterns of exchange involving subsistence and finance is revealing. A common "evolutionary" interpretation is that as human populations grew and settled down into permanent village settlements, humans developed exchange in subsistence goods to adapt to contrasting availability in needed or desired resources (Fried 1967; Sanders 1956; Service 1962). It was thought that complex political institutions developed to regulate the distribution of goods either through chiefly redistribution or to guarantee the peace of marketplaces. The simple logic, repeated in many introductory courses, was that exchange developed progressively through human history in conjunction with broader patterns of social evolution.

Archaeological work in the 1970s, '80s, and '90s, however, has demonstrated that exchange in subsistence goods was not progressive; in fact it was highly variable and not correlated with political complexity (see, for example, Earle 1978, 1985; Brumfiel 1980; Hughes 1994). With few exceptions (e.g., Oceania, Kirch 1991), exchange in subsistence goods is quite limited in stateless and many state societies. A large body of archaeological studies for highland Peru (Earle 1985), North America (Baugh and Ericson 1994), and Polynesia (Weisler 1997) shows no correlation between the evolution of chiefdoms and increasing exchange in subsistence goods. This finding is counter to earlier arguments concerning the subsistence foundation of redistribution in chiefdoms. Archaeological evidence for exchange in subsistence items is quite limited and localized prior to the development of states financed by currency or currency-like payment systems. In our two contrasting historic cases (complex Hawaiian chiefdoms and simple Danish ranked societies and chiefdoms), exchange in food and technology was quite limited. If anything commodity flows were greater in the simpler Danish case, increasing as expected during the Early Bronze Age.

In Hawaii, evidence for subsistence shows no emerging specialization in food production during the emergence of complex, island-wide chiefdoms. Population densities corresponded to local subsistence potential for productive taro or sweet potato fields; local communities produced what they needed and exchanged very little (Earle 1978). Households within a community were likely differentiated to some degree by location, so that diets of coastal houses may well have had more fish, but evidence of food distribution is remarkably limited. Rather, households retained access to a broad range of resources across a community's territory from the mountain to the sea, and each household sustained a largely self-sufficient, generalized economy.

In Denmark, corresponding with the 2400–1000 B.C. transition from small-scale ranked societies to simple warrior-based chiefdoms (Late Neolithic or LN to Early Bronze Age or EBA) (Earle 1997a; Earle et al. 1998), the dietary evidence documents that, across the social transformation, the primary unit of production and consumption continued to be the self-sustaining farmstead. From the LN with its mixed-farming economy, involving various cereals and animals, the EBA economy shifted to focus much more on cattle production, although all houses in the EBA continued to maintain a similar subsistence, differentiated by status, as opposed to local specialization. Chiefly houses have evidence for special foods, such as bread wheat and even asparagus (Kelertas 1997). These chieftains may have focused agricultural production more on cattle; however, as I will argue momentarily, the emphasis on cattle did not reflect specialization for local exchange as much as an export-driven production for the political economy.

In traditional stateless societies, exchange of tools and raw materials appears to have been more widespread than food exchanges, but still quite limited and specific. Members of each household procured and manufactured for their own use the raw materials and tools used in everyday life. Certain conditions, however, encouraged households to exchange for raw materials or finished goods. Archaeologists document some exchange in both stone tools and ceramics. Andrefsky (1994), for example, has developed a model for exchange in stone tools. To minimize the costs to move heavy stone for everyday use, people consume raw materials that are immediately available to each household. When high-quality stone is rare and localized, people use low-quality local materials, with an important exception. Families trade for formal tools that have defined uses, for which additional trading costs are justified by increased life span or utility of the tool. The importance of exchange in formal tools may be illustrated by the extensive commodity flows in flint axes during the Early Neolithic when they were used to clear forests and as symbols of value (Bradley and Edmonds 1993). Long hours of grinding were needed to produce a good stone ax, and its durability was determined by how resistant its material was to shock when chopping wood. Flint with large inclusions was apparently more resistant to shock, would extend the use life of the ax, and thus lower the overall cost to the farmer clearing his fields (Steinberg 1997). Trade for axes of specific stone was understandably brisk.

From region to region, exchanges in stone tools do not increase uniformly through time, but appear to correlate with change in the use of formal tools in everyday activities. Formal-tool use can fluctuate episodically according to specific tool needs in the subsistence economy. A shift from large game to small game, from hunting to gathering, from foraging to agriculture, or from forest fallow to brush fallow may decrease the use of formal stone tools and thus decrease commodity flows in lithic materials. Oswalt (1976) emphasizes that traditional hunting (and fighting) weapons are complex and require materials that have specific properties; these are the types of items traded regularly.

For ceramics, the fairly complicated procedures for manufacturing synthetic materials with pyrotechnology create economies of scale that encourage craft specialization. Shepard's (1956) early work in the American Southwest documented considerable pottery exchange among prehistoric pueblos. Depending on geological conditions, the distribution of good clay sources may channel the rise of community specialization, especially when types require specific clay or temper properties. The amount of trade in ceramics appears related to the amount of ceramics used in households and the specific functions of their uses.

In sum, technology in traditional societies can be said to be highly variable according to quite specific situations, and no trend in developing exchange can be correlated with greater complexity. In both the Hawaiian and Danish cases, for example, despite the development of regionally integrated chiefdoms, flows of technology were limited and specific. If anything, flows of technology were more extensive in the more simply organized Danish polities where the volume of commodity flows varied episodically, rather than uniformly, with the development of more complex political forms.

In Hawaii, excavations document that, although exchange in technological items certainly took place, it was limited in both extent and volume. During the colonization of the deep Pacific by the Polynesians, ceramics ceased to be produced (an interesting example of the loss of a major technology in human history), and this loss eliminated one of the most commonly traded commodities in the subsistence economy. Only limited exchange in stone materials has been documented prehistorically for Polynesia. Basaltic glass, an obsidian-like material, has a number of local sources from which materials were procured either directly or through trade (Weisler 1990). The main evidence for exchange in Hawaii was in basalt adzes, formal tools exchanged quite broadly through Hawaii and elsewhere in Polynesia (Weisler 1997). Several important sources of high-quality basalt, such as the Mauna Kea adze quarry, are known, and other poorer quality local sources were also used (Cleghorn 1986; Lass 1994). Some level of specialization existed in the manufacture of the best-quality adzes (McCoy 1990), and some exchange in wood and mats is also described historically (Earle 1978), but the clear conclusion is that exchange in Hawaii was quite limited. Within a community's territory that stretched from the mountains to the sea, each household had access to the full range of materials needed for most technologies. In fact, despite its political complexity, the amount of exchange among Hawaiian chiefdoms was among the most limited described anywhere in the world.

In Denmark during the Late Neolithic and Early Bronze Ages, exchanges in technological items seems to have been more extensive and economically more significant than for Hawaii, but still quite limited. Our best evidence comes from formal flint tools; here I rely on the work of John Steinberg (1997). In the Danish landscape of Thy, flint occurs naturally in all fields as part of the local moraine deposits; however, the best flint is localized in seams of uplifted chalk and in exposed gravels. Using the local flints, people at each settlement knapped a variety of formal and expedient tools, and traded for a few formal tools. When specific materials were desired for the formal tools, these better flints were mined. For example, during the Early Neolithic when farming communities were expanding, the need for durable axes for forest clearance resulted in extensive shaft mining of the chalk (Becker 1959). Following clearance of the forests, however, the localized mining and distribution of axes declined. In the Late Neolithic, during a period of intense status rivalry in small-scale warrior groups, the high quality of some daggers encouraged mining at the best flint sources and some development of highly skilled craftsmen, but again this industry declined with the introduction of bronze. Although minor specialization surely existed, local stone tool production and use dominated. During the EBA, associated with the emergence of small-scale chiefdoms, specialization and regional commodity flows emerged for flint sickles. While lithic manufacture of expedient (nonformal) tools continued at all sites, individuals at some settlements began to produce large numbers of sickles for an anticipated regional demand. The development of the market in sickles appears to have been encouraged by the establishment of a regional peace and perhaps the intensification of the region's economy for export. But the important point is that the expansion and decline in exchange of flint tools follows no clear trajectory; it expands and declines with the requirements of specific technologies.

In contrast to the lithics, commodity flows in Danish ceramics appears to show a decrease from the LN to the EBA. During the LN, a high percent of the pottery is decorated and some is unusually well finished, thin, and elaborately decorated. These ceramics are stylistically related to Bell Beaker forms that represent a broad style across much of maritime Europe; most important are drinking vessels that may have been used in feasting. Although detailed analysis is not yet available, we can posit that some specialization and regional exchange in LN decorated pottery took place. Into the EBA, however, despite the development of more regionally integrated chiefdoms, the quality of ceramics declined dramatically. The ceramics were more poorly fired, highly friable, and little decorated; they were probably produced very locally, as it is hard to imagine how such friable goods could have been transported any distance. Probably the ceramics ceased to be of significance in status definition, being replaced by the use of metals for status-marking objects that became involved in the extensive, long-distance networks of prestige exchanges discussed later.

So we can conclude that little, or at least only conflicting, evidence exists for any systematic relationship between the volume and extent of commodity flows and the development of regionally organized chiefdoms. Comparatively, more complex chiefdoms, such as Hawaii, do not necessarily have more exchange in subsistence foods and technologies than do less complex chiefdoms like those in Denmark, and the expansion of political integration with the evolution of chiefdoms in Denmark did not correspond with systematic increases in subsistence exchanges. Exchange characterizes all societies, and chiefdoms are no exception. But the overall patterns of exchange in the two cases examined show low volume and extent of commodity flows, with specific exceptions such as the Hawaiian adzes or the Danish sickles and axes. A general conclusion coming out of this work and other studies (Earle 1985, 1994, 1997b; Hughes 1994) is that no trend exists for the extent and intensity of commodity flows to be associated with levels of political organization in prestate societies. Rather, we may be forced to recognize that commodity flows in traditional societies are not primarily involved in subsistence, but serve more in political rivalry and ultimately for institutional finance.

In the political economy, difference in financial strategies seems to determine how exchange functioned. The Hawaiian chiefdoms represent a particularly well-documented example of a corporately organized society using staple finance (Earle 1978). In prehistory, the subsistence economy was radically transformed with the local intensification of agriculture and the construction of irrigation and dryland facilities. The highly productive landscape, subdivided by walls and trails, was allocated to commoners in return for their *corvée* labor contribution to their chiefs (Earle 1997b). The chiefs' *konohiki* (land managers) mobilized staples by limiting the rights of access to productive facilities to those commoners who contributed labor service. Commoners worked chiefly lands on the same agricultural systems that produced staples to support managers, warriors, priests, and craftsmen. This corporate form of redistribution supported the activities of the chiefly institutions (Earle 1978). Hawaiian society was essentially nonurban, with populations distributed close to primary subsistence resources, especially agricultural land. The extent of exchange in all materials is limited to a few special items.

Special clothing and mats identified chiefs as divine personages (Earle 1987, 1990; Weiner 1992), but even with these key wealth items, distribution of these materials was very limited and carefully controlled. The feathered cloaks and helmets worn by chiefs in battle and at ceremonial events were closely held ("inalienable" in Weiner's terms), meaning that their possession or loss held key political significance. The cloaks and helmets were manufactured from rare feathers, collected as part of the annual labor tax from communities, and manufactured by specialists attached to the high chief. The cloaks were then bestowed on subchiefs in ceremonies recognizing the political hierarchy. The cloaks were only lost in battle, stripped from a defeated warrior. The important point is that the manufacture and distribution of wealth among the Hawaiian chiefdoms was not extensive and appears not to have involved extensive spheres of exchange between the islands. In a very real way, the wealth, manufactured by craftsmen and supported by the chiefly mobilization of staple goods, was an extension of the staple finance system and not linked to the creation of broader systems of commodity flows.

The use of wealth as payments/exchanges, however, can establish political strategies in a range of Big Man systems and chiefdoms (Earle 1982). The Kula exchange has been a motif for understanding differences between modern and traditional societies (Leach and Leach 1983; Malinowski 1922; Uberoi 1962; Weiner 1976, 1992), and considerable ethnographic work has been done on wealth exchange in highland New Guinea (Feil 1984; Meggitt 1972; Rappaport 1967; Strathern 1971). Value is created, prestige challenged, and convertibility between objects negotiated. The nature and importance of these exchanges are, however, quite variable, and it is my feeling (Earle 1982) that these commodity flows must be understood in their broader social and political dynamics—networks created and manipulated to obtain and maintain political positions and recognition.

In many chiefdoms, prestige goods exchanges (Friedman and Rowlands 1977) served, as a rudimentary form of wealth finance, to materialize political institutions (D'Altroy and Earle 1985). On special occasions, chiefs host feasts where wealth is displayed and exchanged. Personal success is measured by increased prestige that attracts spouses and other political alliances, and amasses social standing. Helms (1979) describes how Panamanian chiefs participated in competitive exchanges of special foreign objects. These objects were thought to embody special esoteric knowledge and power. By obtaining the foreign objects through exchange, chiefs held these powers, accessible only to the chiefs who participated in these external exchanges. In Europe, prehistorically, the networks of chiefs moved wealth translocally by what Renfrew and Cherry (1986) called "peer polity interaction." Exchanged wealth created international styles of objects that bound chiefs as a class distinguished from local commoners (Earle 1990). Chiefly control over wealth and the associated status/knowledge systems rested on control over the exchange itself or the manufacture of the wealth by specialists attached to the chiefs (Brumfiel and Earle 1987). The extensive flows of wealth objects create paths for political maneuvering that can become formally structured and transformed into systems of payment.

In Denmark from the Late Neolithic to the Early Bronze Age, the economy was intensified selectively to support the expanding exchanges in wealth across Europe (Earle et al. 1998). During the LN, population densities were low, and households practiced an agropastoralism without major facilities or evidence for land demarcation. During the EBA, population densities continued to be low, but the economy shifted to focus more on cattle raising. At this time in England and in Denmark, chiefly burial monuments may have marked a system of chieftain ownership of pasture lands that controlled cattle raising (Earle 1991).

Wealth became significant as a source of power in Bronze Age Denmark as exchange for bronze supported the chiefly hierarchy. In those monuments, the chiefs were buried with metal objects identifying their status in the political hierarchy. Swords can be distinguished between chiefly swords, with highly elaborated hilt decorations and with virtually no wear, and warrior swords, quite plain and showing extensive resharpening and damage (Kristiansen 1982). These swords of bronze required access to both copper and tin, neither of which have sources in Scandinavia. The metals had to have been imported from central Europe, manufactured into chiefly weapons and other wealth objects by highly skilled specialists attached to chieftains, and then given by chieftains as political currencies (Kristiansen 1987). Forming and reforming political relationships through exchange was evidently the political process in Bronze Age Denmark.

The Danish warrior ideology was not a product of the Bronze Age, however. Status definition using stone weapons (flint daggers and battle axes) goes back at least to the Middle Neolithic, but only when weapons were made of metal could emerging chiefs control access to them (DeMarrais, Castillo, and Earle 1996). Control appears to have been based on difficulty in procurement (as bronze came from great distances across many social boundaries) and in production (the manufacturing process was probably known initially by only a few craftsmen who could be supported by the chiefs).

But the use of metal for weapons came at a high cost. Chiefs could only access metal by gearing up the local economy for the production of exports (Earle et al. 1998). Starting in the Late Neolithic, local amber, which is gathered at the seashore following storms, ceased to be used for local jewelry; rather it was exported to the south where it was buried with elite personages in England and elsewhere in Europe (Shennan 1982). By the Early Bronze Age, raw amber was collected in fairly large amounts for export. Excavation of an EBA warrior's house in Denmark recovered a scattering of raw amber and a cache of sixty-nine pieces that had been buried in a small bag below the floor (Earle et al. 1998).

In the Early Bronze Age, economic change involved intensification of the subsistence economy to produce hides and probably plow animals for exchange southward into Europe. From that same warrior's house, preserved bone remains are almost exclusively from cattle. This contrasts to a much broader mix of cattle, sheep, goat, and pig that is described both earlier and later in the Danish sequence. The primary formal stone tools recovered from this house were flint scrapers showing a distinctive hide-working polish. Hides were an important source of wealth and the gearing up in cattle production was most probably driven by a need for export products to obtain the foreign metals.

In a large EBA chiefly hall that we excavated in Sønderhå parish Thy, cattle stalls document the first inside wintering of animals in Denmark. This may have lessened their mortality, but it would also have provided a rich (if smelly) source of manure useful to intensify agriculture. By the types of weed seeds recovered, we have been able to argue that manure was used to intensify local production during the Bronze Age (Kelertas 1997). The emerging local specialization in sickles, described earlier, may have been a direct outcome of this intensified agricultural production. Local chiefs, by asserting a system of land ownership, were able to produce hides for export and probably a surplus in food crops to feed dependents who worked for them.

The overall conclusion is that the development of significant and systematic commodity flows in prestate societies was closely linked to the political process. Exchange in the subsistence economy itself was highly variable according to local conditions and in no way corresponded to the overall patterns of developing political complexity. Rather, expanding commodity flows were focused on the accumulation of wealth and its use to materialize political hierarchies. The volume and extent of commodity flows in wealth do not relate to the degree of complexity in chiefdoms, but reflects the type of finance in the emerging political economy. In systems of staple finance, wealth exchanges could be of little significance, as seen in the Hawaiian chiefdoms or, for that matter, even in the Inka state (Earle 1985). Only with wealth finance, based on control over translocal exchanges of wealth, did commodity flows become of real significance. Such systems are, however, not generally characteristic of chiefdoms but characterize only those complex societies with fairly low intensity agriculture that depended on regional networks of wealth flows. An understanding of the variability in exchange in chiefdoms should provide a foundation for understanding the emergence of market systems in later states. My belief is that scope and volume of exchange in states will also be highly variable; following up on Liz Brumfiel's (1980) insight, the developments of markets may be understood as a response to emerging political economies and not to subsistence necessity.

Studying Prehistoric Institutions

From roots in settlement pattern studies pioneered by Julian Steward, processual archaeologists have investigated the spatial character of human societies and their evolutionary and organizational processes (see Willey and Sabloff 1974). Following on Polanyi's original insight that a basic dimension of human institutions is economic, archaeologists quickly grasped that patterns of exchange could help reconstruct prehistoric social organization. Since goods were produced, distributed, and consumed within specific social contexts, their flow patterns seen archaeologically could identify contrasting organizational forms. Renfrew (1975), for example, developed an influential typology of exchange mechanisms that would be, à la Polanyi, embedded in specific social forms. The hope was that differences in exchange relationships, identified by specific fall-off patterns, could be used to discover how prehistoric societies were organized as bands, tribes, chiefdoms, or states. For example, a simple decline in material from a source was thought to identify down-the-line exchange in which goods were exchanged reciprocally from trade partner to trade partner, and such reciprocal exchanges were thought to identify egalitarian (tribal) societies. In contrast, when the fall off showed peaks associated with ceremonial centers, it was thought that goods were exchanged in a redistributive system that characterized chiefdoms; goods were thought to be exchanged from chiefly center to chiefly center and then to be redistributed locally by the chiefs to their followers. Archaeological studies, such as Hodder (1974) and Findlow and Bolognese (1982), attempted to identify different mechanisms of commodity flows. An initial optimism was, however, soon dampened by recognizing that a specific fall-off pattern could result from different exchange mechanisms; for example, that same fall off around a center associated with chiefly redistribution could as well be produced by marketing exchange (Renfrew 1977).

Evidently archaeologists needed to understand in much more detail the institutional contexts of exchange (Ericson and Earle 1982; Hodder 1982). Part of the contextual relationship involved the way in which institutions encouraged or discouraged exchange as suggested by the new institutional economics. Based on the archaeological evidence, however, I propose that the nature of political power, rather than economic efficiency, greatly determined the extent of commodity flows in nonmercantile and noncapitalist societies.

Institutions must be built up; they are not simply imagined. Whatever the medium of their construction, the goal is to create a history of relationships that specify future contract-like activities. In our modern industrial states, institutions are built through legal contracts that specify the rights and obligations between people and are mutually recognized by participants and guaranteed by the legal process of the state. If we understand that this legal system is a product of the state, to investigate institutional formation in societies without formalized legal systems we must consider alternative media used to build institutions. I argue that institution building involves the materialization of social and institutional relationships through such events and objects as gift exchanges, ceremonies, symbolic objects, and built landscapes of walls, pathways, houses, and monuments (DeMarrais, Castillo, and Earle 1996). Ceremonies are one mechanism to formalize relationships and represent them at dramatic public events. Systems of exchange offer another.

Representing a grand tradition in anthropology from at least the pioneering work of Malinowski (1922), political and social organizations have been studied through a focus on exchange relationships. But these exchanges are not simply the movements of commodities; they are the physical embodiment of the relationships with objects. Looking at the Trobriand exchanges, individual paths through which valuables travel portray the established network that institutes political relationships among the islands of the Kula system. The political process involves the tension between the maintenance of these paths of exchanges and the attempts to redirect them. Inherent in exchanges are principles of hierarchy. Weiner (1992) describes how spheres of exchange create inalienable objects—objects that can be exchanged ("converted" in Bohannan's [1955] terminology) but only with the loss of prestige to the former owner. Control over the objects is thus the materialization of power relationships and the means to represent and redefine institutional bonds. The objects have social lives (Appadurai 1986).

Archaeological studies of exchange in wealth allow a study of long-term stability and change in the political relationships between regions. In Hawaii, evidence for the production and distribution of wealth is quite limited, but why? It might be assumed that the nature of wealth, largely in biodegradable forms (especially feathers), simply makes it poorly visible to archaeologists. Although such loss of evidence always plagues archaeology, I feel that the absence of evidence for wealth exchange in

Hawaii can be understood more directly by the fact that the polities were instituted in a different medium, namely the built landscape that characterizes staple (vs. wealth) financed polities. In Hawaii, massive changes in the landscape included religious monuments, territorial walls, and paths that materially marked and divided the social world (Earle 1998). In a staple finance system, the important relationship is between people and land with respect to rights of use and rights of mobilized surplus. Wealth was relatively unimportant in Hawaii, because the political economy depended rather on the ownership of highly productive lands. Elsewhere in the deep Pacific, decreases in long-distance interactions have been documented (Weisler 1997), involving especially objects of wealth. This decline may indicate the institutionalization of the corporate based staple-financed chiefdoms (Earle 1997b). Wealth may simply cease to have been of much political significance.

The opposite trend characterizes the Danish record. A warrior segment of society emerged, most probably tied to competition over the production and exchange of wealth. During the Late Neolithic, when the society was organized as fairly simply ranked polities, the region of Thy became connected to a translocal system of exchange. Symbolic participation in the exchange network was materialized by the possession of objects that defined a warrior's kit, including flint daggers, arrowpoints, and the elaborately decorated Bell Beaker drinking vessels. Obtaining wealth required access to exports that especially included cattle hides and amber, and so competition over access to these underlay the emergence of the region's chiefs. During the Neolithic, evidence of competition is indicated by the weaponry and by placement of settlements in defensible positions. The exported wealth, the amber and cattle products, was apparently difficult to control (easily rustled, if you will) and the materialization of status through the warrior weaponry made of local stone was also uncontrollable. Although made in imitation of metal weapons used to the south, the fine daggers and arrowpoints of Denmark were manufactured from local flint. Although the best flints were localized and some specialization in their production has been posited, the conclusion is that alternatives were always available and the accumulation and control of wealth was virtually impossible. No hierarchy emerged.

During the Early Bronze Age in northwestern Jutland, the underlying economy was very similar, but the means to materialize status was altered. Instead of flint, the weaponry was now made of bronze imported from the south. The accumulation of wealth now clearly represented an ability to control the long-distance exchanges in which local wealth was exchanged for metal. Locally attached craftsmen most probably transformed the metal into the beautiful swords characteristic of the EBA. As the basis of wealth changed from local to distant media, a political hierarchy emerged rapidly. To obtain the metal, the local economy was intensified and redirected to cattle raising, and as a result the productive base of the region was apparently degraded as too many cattle grazed fragile lands. Destabilized sand drifted inland across formerly productive fields and grasslands; degraded grasslands became heathlands. As quickly as the hierarchy emerged in northwestern Jutland, it collapsed.

Archaeologists have documented the rapid buildup of wealth and its loss. The nature of regional systems tied to the prestige goods exchanges of Europe permits us to document the nature of wealth finance and the role of valuables in political change. To explain variability in exchange through time and space, we can turn to the archaeological record of commodity flow patterns involving prestige goods. This may prove to be the historical background to the development of world systems during the periods of mercantilism and the rise of capitalism. Jane Schneider (1977) has emphasized that the broad-scale movement of wealth characterizes early world systems and may have foreshadowed the emergence of the modern world.

Anthropologists want to understand how institutions and economies are codependent, and anthropological archaeology offers both a diachronic and a truly comparative perspective that suggests that economies fuel institutional development. I suggest focusing on how wealth is generated and controlled, investigating differences between staples and wealth in emerging political economies. The long-term evolution of human societies will be linked to the particular means that mobilize and invest surplus. These are large-scale phenomena, involving broad relationships across long periods of time. I can envision a new economic anthropology in which institutional economics become placed in the comparative perspective of historical and archaeological studies and of the evolution of human societies.

References

Acheson, James
    1994   *Anthropology and Institutional Economics*. Monographs in Economic Anthropology, No. 12. Lanham, Md.: University Press of America.
Andrefsky, W.
    1994   "Raw-material Availability and the Organization of Technology." *American Antiquity* 59: 21–34.
Appadurai, A.
    1986   *The Social Life of Things*. Cambridge: Cambridge University Press.
Baugh, Timothy, and Jonathan Ericson
    1994   *Prehistoric Exchange Systems in North America*. New York: Plenum Press.

Becker, C. J.
   1959   "Flint Mining in Neolithic Denmark." *Antiquity* 33: 87–92.
Blanton, Richard, Gary Feinman, Stephen Kowalewski, and Peter Peregrine
   1996   "A Dual-Processual Theory for the Evolution of Mesoamerican Civiliza-
   tion." *Current Anthropology* 37: 1–14.
Bohannon, Paul
   1955   "Some Principles of Exchange and Investment among the Tiv." *American
   Anthropologist* 57: 60–67.
Bradley, Richard, and Mark Edmonds
   1993   *Interpreting the Axe Trade: Production and Exchange in Neolithic Britain.*
   Cambridge: Cambridge University Press.
Brumfiel, Elizabeth
   1980   "Specialization, Market Exchange, and the Aztec State: A View from
   Huexotla." *Current Anthropology* 21: 459–78.
Brumfiel, Elizabeth, and Timothy Earle
   1987   "Introduction." Pp. 1–21 in *Specialization, Exchange, and Complex Societies*,
   E. M. Brumfiel and T. K. Earle, eds. Cambridge: Cambridge University Press.
Cleghorn, P. L.
   1986   "Organizational Structure at the Mauna Kea Adze Quarry, Hawai'i." *Jour-
   nal of Archaeological Science* 13: 375–87.
D'Altroy, Terence, and Timothy Earle
   1985   "Staple Finance, Wealth Finance, and Storage in the Inca Political
   Economy." *Current Anthropology* 26: 187–206.
DeMarrais, Elizabeth, Luis Jaime Castillo, and Timothy Earle
   1996   "Ideology, Materialization, and Power Strategies." *Current Anthropology*
   37: 15–31.
Earle, Timothy
   1978   *Economic and Social Organization of a Complex Chiefdom: The Halelea District, Kaua'i, Hawaii.* University of Michigan, Anthropological Papers 63. Ann
   Arbor: University of Michigan.
   1982   "The Ecology and Politics of Primitive Valuables." Pp. 65–83 in *Culture
   and Ecology: Eclectic Perspectives*, J. Kennedy and E. Edgerton, eds. Special
   Publications 15. Washington, D.C.: American Anthropological Association.
   1985   "Commodity Exchange and Markets in the Inca State: Recent Archaeological Evidence." Pp. 369–97 in *Markets and Marketing*, S. Plattner, ed. Lanham,
   Md.: University Press of America.
   1987   "Specialization and the Production of Wealth: Hawaiian Chiefdoms and
   the Inka Empire." Pp. 64–75 in *Specialization, Exchange, and Complex Societies*,
   E. M. Brumfiel and T. K. Earle, eds. Cambridge: Cambridge University Press.
   1990   "Style and Iconography as Legitimation in Complex Chiefdoms." Pp. 73–
   81 in *The Uses of Style in Archaeology*, M. Conkey and C. Hastorf, eds. Cambridge: Cambridge University Press.
   1991   "Property Rights and the Evolution of Chiefdoms." Pp. 71–99 in *Chiefdoms:
   Power, Economy, and Ideology*, T. Earle, ed. Cambridge: Cambridge University
   Press.

1994 "Positioning Exchange in the Evolution of Human Society." Pp. 419–37 in *Prehistoric Exchange Systems in North America*, T. Baugh and. J. Ericson, eds. New York: Plenum Press.

1997a *How Chiefs Come to Power: the Political Economy in Prehistory.* Stanford, Calif.: Stanford University Press.

1997b "Exchange in Oceania: Search for Evolutionary Explanations." Pp. 224–37 in *Prehistoric Long-Distance Interaction in Oceania: An Interdisciplinary Approach*, M. Weisler, ed. New Zealand Archaeological Association Monograph 21.

1998 "Property Rights and the Evolution of Hawaiian Chiefdoms." Pp. 89–118 in *Property in Economic Context*, R. Hunt and A. Gilman, eds. Lanham, Md.: University Press of America.

Earle, Timothy, Jens-Henrik Bech, Kristian Kristiansen, Peter Aperlo, Kristina Kelertas, and John Steinberg

1998 "The Political Economy of Late Neolithic and Early Bronze Age Society: The Thy Archaeological Project." *Norwegian Archaeological Review* 31: 1–28.

Earle, Timothy, and Terence D'Altroy

1989 "The Political Economy of the Inka Empire: The Archaeology of Power and Finance." Pp. 183–204 in *Archaeological Thought in America*, C. C. Lamberg-Karlovsky, ed. Cambridge: Cambridge University Press.

Earle, Timothy, and Jonathan Ericson

1977 "Exchange Systems in Archaeological Perspective." Pp. 3–12 in *Exchange Systems in Prehistory*, T. K. Earle and J. E. Ericson, eds. New York: Academic Press.

Ensminger, Jean

1994 "Transaction Costs through Time: The Case of Orma Pastoralists in East Africa." Pp. 69–85 in *Anthropology and Institutional Economics*. Monographs in Economic Anthropology, No. 12. J. Acheson, ed. Lanham, Md.: University Press of America.

Ericson, Jonathan

1981 *Exchange and Production Systems in California Prehistory.* Oxford: British Archaeological Reports International Series 110.

Ericson, Jonathan, and Timothy Earle, eds.

1982 *Contexts for Prehistoric Exchange.* New York: Academic Press.

Ericson, Jonathan, and Timothy Baugh, eds.

1993 *The American Southwest and Mesoamerica: Systems of Prehistoric Exchange.* New York: Plenum Press.

Feil, D. K.

1984 *Ways of Exchange: The Enga Tee of Papua New Guinea.* St. Lucia: University of Queensland Press.

Findlow, F. J., and M. Bolognese

1982 "Regional Modeling of Obsidian Procurement in the American Southwest." Pp. 53–81 in *Contexts for Exchange*, J. E. Ericson and T. K. Earle, eds. New York: Academic Press.

Friedman, Jonathan, and Mike Rowlands

1977 "Notes towards an Epigenetic Model of the Evolution of 'Civilization.'" Pp. 201–76 in *The Evolution of Social Systems*, J. Friedman and M. J. Rowlands, eds. London: Duckworth.

Fried, M.
1967 *The Evolution of Political Society*. New York: Random House.

Harbottle, G.
1982 "Chemical Characterization in Archaeology." Pp. 13–51 in *Contexts for Exchange*, J. E. Ericson and T. K. Earle, eds. New York: Academic Press.

Harris, Marvin
1977 *Cannibals and Kings: The Origins of Cultures*. New York: Random House.

Helms, Mary
1979 *Ancient Panama*. Austin: University of Texas Press.

Hodder, Ian
1974 "Regression Analysis of Some Trade and Market Patterns." *World Archaeology* 6: 172–89.
1982 "Towards a Contextual Approach to Prehistoric Exchange." Pp. 199–211 in *Contexts for Prehistoric Exchange*, J. Ericson and T. Earle, eds. New York: Academic Press.

Hughes, Richard
1994 "Mosaic Patterns in Prehistoric California-Great Basin Exchange." Pp. 363–83 in *Prehistoric Exchange Systems in North America*, T. Baugh and J. Ericson, eds. New York: Plenum Press.

Johnson, Allen, and Timothy Earle
2000 *The Evolution of Human Societies: From Foraging Group to Agrarian State*. 2^d ed. Stanford, Calif.: Stanford University Press.

Kelertas, Kristina
1997 "Changing Political Economy of Thy, Denmark: The Paleobotanical Evidence." Ph.D. dissertation. Los Angeles: Archaeology Program, UCLA.

Kirch, Patrick
1991 "Prehistoric Exchange in Western Melanesia." *Annual Reviews in Anthropology* 20: 141–65.

Kristiansen, Kristian
1982 "The Formation of Tribal Systems in Later European Prehistory." Pp. 241–80 in *Theory and Explanation in Archaeology*, C. Renfrew, M. Rowlands, and B. Segrave, eds. New York: Academic Press.
1987 "From Stone to Bronze: The Evolution of Social Complexity in Northern Europe, 2300–1200 B.C." Pp. 30–51 in *Specialization, Exchange and Complex Society*, E. Brumfiel and T. Earle, eds. Cambridge: Cambridge University Press.

LaLone, Darrell
1982 "The Inca as a Nonmarket Economy: Supply on Command Versus Supply and Demand." Pp. 292–316 in *Contexts for Prehistoric Exchange*, J. Ericson and T. Earle, eds. New York: Academic Press.

Lambert, Joseph
1997 *Traces of the Past: Unraveling the Secrets of Archaeology through Chemistry*. Reading, Mass.: Addison-Wesley.

Lass, Barbara
  1994 *Hawaiian Adze Production and Distribution: Implications for the Development of Chiefdoms*. Monograph 37. Los Angeles: UCLA Institute of Archaeology.
Leach, Jerry, and Edmund Leach, eds.
  1983 *The Kula*. Cambridge: Cambridge University Press.
Malinowski, B.
  1922 *Argonauts of the Western Pacific*. New York: Dutton.
McCoy, Patrick
  1990 "Subsistence in a 'Non-subsistence' Environment: Factors of Production in a Hawaiian Alpine Desert Adze Quarry." Pp. 85–119 in *Pacific Production Systems: Approaches to Economic Prehistory*, D. Yen and. J. Mummery, eds. Canberra: Australian National University.
Meggitt, M.
  1972 "System and Subsystem: The Te Exchange Cycle among the Mae Enga." *Human Ecology* 1: 111–23.
North, Douglass
  1990 *Institutions, Institutional Change and Economic Performance*. Cambridge: Cambridge University Press.
Oswalt, Wendell
  1976 *An Anthropological Analysis of Food-Getting Technologies*. New York: John Wiley and Sons.
Polanyi, Karl
  1957 "The Economy as Instituted Process." Pp. 243–70 in *Trade and Market in the Early Empires*, C. M. Arensberg, K. Polanyi, and H. W. Pearson, eds. New York: Free Press.
Rappaport, Roy
  1967 *Pigs for the Ancestors*. New Haven: Yale University Press.
Renfrew, Colin
  1975 "Trade as Action at a Distance: Questions of Integration and Communication." Pp. 3–59 in *Ancient Civilizations and Trade*, J. Sabloff and C. C. Lamberg-Karlovsky, eds. Albuquerque: University of New Mexico Press.
  1977 "Alternative Models for Exchange and Spatial Distribution." Pp. 71–90 in *Exchange Systems in Prehistory*, T. K. Earle and J. E. Ericson, eds. New York: Academic Press.
Renfrew, Colin, and John Cherry, eds.
  1986 *Peer Polity Interaction and Socio-political Change*. Cambridge: Cambridge University Press.
Renfrew, Colin, and Steve Shennan, eds.
  1982 *Ranking, Resources, and Exchange*. Cambridge: Cambridge University Press.
Sabloff, Jerry, and C. C. Lamberg-Karlovsky, eds.
  1975 *Ancient Civilizations and Trade*. Albuquerque: University of New Mexico Press.
Sahlins, Marshall
  1972 *Stone Age Economics*. Chicago: Aldine.

Sanders, William
   1956   "The Central Mexican Symbiotic Region: A Study in Prehistoric Settle-
   ment Patterns." Pp. 115–27 in *Prehistoric Settlement Patterns in the New World*,
   G. Willey, ed. New York: Wenner-Gren Foundation.
Schneider, Jane
   1977   "Was There a Pre-capitalist World-System?" *Peasant Studies* 6: 20–29.
Service, Elman
   1962   *Primitive Social Organization*. New York: Random House.
Shennan, Stephen
   1982   "Exchange and Ranking: The Role of Amber in the Early Bronze Age of
   Europe." Pp. 27–32 in *Ranking, Resources, and Exchange*, C. Renfrew and S.
   Shennan, eds. Cambridge: Cambridge University Press.
Shepard, Anna
   1956   *Ceramics for Archaeologists*. Washington: Carnegie Institution.
Smith, Adam
   1937 [1776]   *The Wealth of Nations*. New York: Random House.
Steinberg, John
   1997   "Changing Patterns of Economic Organization in the Production, Distri-
   bution, and Use of Flint in Thy, Denmark." Ph.D. dissertation. Los Angeles:
   Anthropology Department, UCLA.
Strathern, Andrew
   1971   *The Rope of Moka*. Cambridge: Cambridge University Press.
Trigger, Bruce
   1998   *Sociocultural Evolution*. Oxford: Blackwell.
Uberoi, J. P. S.
   1962   *The Politics of the Kula Ring*. Manchester: Manchester University Press.
Weiner, Annette
   1976   *Women of Value, Men of Renown*. Austin: University of Texas.
   1992   *Inalienable Possessions: the Paradox of Keeping-while-giving*. Berkeley: University of California Press.
Weisler, Marshall
   1990   "Sources and Sourcing of Volcanic Glass in Hawai'i: Implications for
   Exchange Studies." *Archaeology in Oceania* 25: 16–25.
   1997   *Prehistoric Long-Distance Interaction in Oceania: An Interdisciplinary Approach*. New Zealand Archaeological Association Monograph 21.
Willey, Gordon, and Jerry Sabloff
   1974   *A History of American Archaeology*. San Francisco: Freeman.
Wilmsen, Edwin, ed.
   1972   *Social Exchange and Interaction*. Ann Arbor: Museum of Anthropology,
   University of Michigan, Anthropological Papers 46.

Chapter 5

Economic Transfers and Exchanges: Concepts for Describing Allocations

Robert C. Hunt

Introduction

We humans have more things than any other species, and we shift them from one organism to another more than any other species of mammal. Some humans have so many things that they might be very difficult to count. The prospect of a complete and detailed description of every object in the house of middle-class Americans is daunting at the very least. Our subdiscipline is centrally concerned with those things.

There are two major ways for us to get such things, make them, or get them from others. Economic anthropology is deeply interested in both, which we call production and allocation.[1] We have a number of terms for the allocation domain, which include distribution, allocation, and circulation. All refer to some sort of shift or movement of things/goods from one person to another.

This paper was first given at a Brandeis Anthropology colloquium in March of 1998. A version was presented to the 1998 Annual Spring Meeting of the SEA in April of 1998. I am particularly grateful to Irene J. Winter and Pearl Bartelt for close readings at that time. Two anonymous referees have made cogent comments. This paper was written at the same time as another paper on food sharing among foragers, also on transfers (Hunt 2000). Parts of the review of the literature in the two papers are similar.

Exchange Concepts

Exchange is the primary concept used in discussions of allocation. Exchange is universally found in human societies, and concepts of several types of exchange have given us a purchase on understanding much of allocation. The purpose of this chapter is to add the concept of transfers to that of exchanges.

There are three principal sets of conceptual contrasts that we often see referred to: reciprocity-redistribution-market, gift-commodity, and generalized-negative-balanced reciprocity.

Reciprocity-redistribution-market is associated originally with Karl Polanyi, and refers to three different ways of organizing exchanges. Individual exchanges can be characterized, and an economy can be integrated by, one of these principles. Bohannan's 1963 description is succinct:

> Reciprocity involves exchange of goods between people who are bound in non-market, non-hierarchical relationships with one another. The exchange does not create the relationship, but rather is part of the behavior that gives it content. (1963: 232)

> Redistribution is defined by Polanyi as a systematic movement of goods toward an administrative center and their reallotment by the authorities at the center. (1963: 231)

> Market exchange is the exchange of goods at prices determined by the law of supply and demand. Its essence is free and casual contract. (1963: 231)

Gift-commodity is another distinction, and is now more frequently used than Polanyi's. Gregory's 1982 book provides a clear summary:

> Things, land and labour assume the gift form in clan-based societies. (1982: 100)

> Gift exchange is an exchange of inalienable [sic] objects between people who are in a state of reciprocal dependence that establishes a qualitative relationship between the transactors. (1982: 101)

> Things and land assume the commodity form in class-based societies. Classes are formed when the producer loses control of his means of production. . . . Commodity exchange is an exchange of alienable objects between people who are in a state of reciprocal independence that establishes a quantitative relationship between the objects exchanged. (1982: 100)

Generalized, negative, and balanced reciprocity come from the work of Marshall Sahlins. Balanced reciprocity refers to direct and equivalent exchange without delay (Sahlins 1965, 1972: 194–95). Generalized and negative reciprocity occupy poles of a continuum. One end is generalized reciprocity, which Sahlins equates with Malinowski's "pure gift." "Altruism," "sharing," and "hospitality" are invoked (Sahlins 1972: 193–94). At the other end of the continuum is negative reciprocity, the intention to get something for nothing. Here Sahlins uses such words as "haggling," "gambling," and "theft" (Sahlins 1972: 195–96). Sahlins also discusses the social dimensions of these transactions, particularly kinship distance, and puts them in the center of his subsequent discussion.

Each of the three major sets of terms to discuss allocation has problems. There are problems of confusion, and/or problems of coverage.

One virtue of the Polanyi classification is that redistribution is part of the system (it is missing in the gift-commodity system), and redistribution is omnipresent and important in chiefdoms and states. The Polanyi classification ignores exchanges between unequals which are not redistribution. Patron-client networks are hierarchal, and may not be integrated into administrative organization. In firms a large number of within-firm transactions are neither reciprocity nor market exchanges. The pooling-sharing analysis of the domestic group, stressed by Sahlins, is an important addition to the system, which Polanyi suggested (with householding) but did not flesh out.

Much recent discussion exchange invokes the use-value/exchange-value distinction. It is central to Aristotle's discussion of exchange in his *Politics* (Aristotle 1962, Book I). It is central in Marx (in the well-known formula M -> C -> M'), and is prominent in Sahlins' discussion of reciprocity.

The distinction is of less utility than is apparent at first reading. "Exchange" takes several meanings. One is to use it to refer only to transactions which involve general-purpose money. "Exchange value" in this case would only refer to such transactions. But there are some human groups that do not have general-purpose money, and in every economy there are some exchanges that do not use money. Exchange is universally found in human groups so exchange value of those things has to be present everywhere, not just in market exchanges. The Kula valuables (off the east coast of New Guinea) are precious objects that are manufactured and exchanged. They have no utilitarian uses, and therefore the utility of these objects is found only in their exchange. In the more generalized sense of exchange, "exchange value" must be a component of every exchange. I therefore argue that the distinction between use-value and exchange-value is problematic in economic anthropology.

Gregory (1982) defined commodities as alienable, the transactors are in a state of mutual independence, and the exchange establishes relationships between objects. Gregory saw gifts as the inversion: they are inalienable,[2] there is a state of mutual dependence between transactors, and the exchange establishes relationships between the parties, not between the objects.

Alfred Gell observed about gifts that they are alienable, for the recipient gains access, and the power to donate, whereas the donor loses both. Further, he observed, commodity exchange partners can be mutually indebted, and in a relationship of mutual dependency over time (Gell 1992: 144–45).[3] As pointed out above, the gift-commodity domain does not include Polanyi's redistribution. I conclude from this that the dichotomy of gift-commodity is not well formed.

Sahlins' concepts of negative and generalized reciprocity are at least as problematic as use-value and exchange value, and as gift-commodity. Sahlins used reciprocity in at least two senses, one of which referred in general to exchange. Sahlins used "redistribution" to refer to the movement of goods from those who had them to those who did not in the context of the domestic unit, which was not the way the term was used in the Polanyi framework. One contribution of Sahlins' formulation was his focus on the domestic unit, with its principles of sharing and pooling.

A close look at negative and generalized reciprocity, however, raises the question as to why these should be seen as exchanges. If theft is the extreme pole of negative reciprocity, and the "pure gift" is the extreme pole of generalized reciprocity, neither of these is an "exchange." An exchange must involve the movement of valueds[4] in two directions. In the Sahlins cases, they move in one direction only. I conclude that as categories of exchange, negative and generalized reciprocity are not well formed. However important the events (and I will show that the events *are* important), calling them exchange is misleading.

Economic Transfers

In this chapter I argue that allocation involves what I propose we call economic transfers, and that some economic transfers take place without an economic exchange. I want to shift attention from exchange to transfer.[5]

By transfer I mean the shift of a valued (X) from one social unit (A) to another social unit (B). The valued can be tangible, a service, or knowledge. The shift can refer to changes in possession, as well as to shifts in ownership. The social units can be any locally recognized social isolate (Appell 1984) and can include individuals, corporate groups, corporations, or polities.[6]

The X being transferred has economic content.[7] It contains the efforts of production (work, skill, and experience).

Economic exchanges would be mutual transfers such that the transfer of economic valued X from A to B is matched by a transfer of economic valued Y from B to A. The identification of this double transfer as a single exchange almost certainly has to be done by the local folk culture. That two transfers have taken place is usually observable by an outsider. Their constituting a single exchange requires folk knowledge. The temporal dimension can be important. A single exchange may involve more than two transfers.

In the domain of economic allocation there are many transactions that are exchanges. But for the rest of this chapter I want to focus on transfers that are not part of exchanges. I contend that there are some transfers that are very important in economic life, and that are not part of exchange. Complete and valid descriptions of allocation in the local reality will be much improved if transfers are given their due in the ethnography. The domestic group, sharing, division of assets, donations, gifts, and theft will be briefly discussed.

Domestic Group

The human biogram ensures that every human being starts life with a prolonged period of dependency. For many years no human is able to engage in production of food, clothing, or tools. The consequence is that all of us must have received economic goods/service satisfying our needs from others. The primary locus of those transfers is the domestic group. Food is produced by being extracted from nature and then prepared, both of which involve skill, knowledge, and energy. This food is then transferred to the dependent. The same is true of clothing, and of built shelter. The tools used in extraction and processing are also the product of extraction and processing, and also involve skill, knowledge, and energy. It is often the case that there is a division of labor along age and gender lines for some of these activities.

How do we conceptualize these transfers of goods to the dependent young? I contend that in some societies some of these domestic, or pooling and sharing, transactions are pure transfers. They are part of allocation, and are not part of exchanges. In my part of middle-class America, for example, there is a strong positive value put on transfers from parents to children, and this lasts as long as the parent is alive. Parents expect to acquire assets to both support themselves and to continue support of the children, for as long as the parents live. The idea that financial assets would flow in the other direction has been anathema to several elderly people I have known very well, and it is anathema to me.[8]

Do these transfers participate in exchanges? That varies from culture to culture. In my middle-class American culture there is no exchange involved. I owe it to my descendants to be able to transfer assets to them. It is not expected, by either party, for there to be a countertransfer as part of an exchange.

In other societies these transactions are identified as exchanges, delayed by decades. Families in West Bengal, according to Sarah Lamb, explicitly mark these transfers as part of an exchange. The initial transfer is made from parents to dependent children. The return transfer (which makes it an exchange) occurs when the children are adults and the parents are dependent. These Indian parents are comfortable with the thought of receiving transfers from their children (strongly preferring that it be a son [and daughter-in-law] rather than a daughter) as they get old. It is part of a legitimate exchange (Lamb 2000: 46–58). McDowell reports similar phenomena from New Guinea (1978).

Our ethnography of economic events in the domestic arena will be much improved if transfers are identified, and if exchanges are explicitly examined from the folk point of view.

Sharing

There are social contexts other than the domestic group where assets are transferred on the basis of need, and where the existence of exchange can at least be doubted. Two social units where this occurs are work teams and small communities. One of the best-known examples is the sharing of large game in Bushmen camps. Sometimes the amount of meat is large enough so that all other members of the camp can reasonably consume a share. The process of dividing the asset is lengthy and often contested. But at the end of the day, the people who found and killed and transported the beast eat only a small portion of it, and everybody else in the camp gets a share (see Lee 1979). There is certainly a transfer involved. Whether there is exchange is more problematic (see Hunt 2000 for an extended discussion).

There are other small groups where this occurs regularly. Teams and small communities have these transfers as well. There are small communities of lobster fishermen on the coast of Maine, and they tend to fish close to home. Thus the boats on the water near them are likely to be members of their community, and in any case the boats near them, and the operators of those boats, are known to them. Lobstering is a job with some danger. The motor may quit, a person may get caught in the hydraulic machine that raises the traps, a person may have a heart attack, or a boat may start leaking in a serious way. These days all the large lobster boats have CB and VHF radio, but the marine environment is not a benign one for electronics. The fact of the matter is that everyone who is on the water on a regular basis watches all the other boats within sight. What is looked for is something out of the ordinary, and which may be a signal of trouble. If there is any sign of what might be trouble, one goes to investigate.

In the Maine boat case, there is a sense that "everybody is in this together," and help is given when and where it is needed. It is impossible to predict who will need help and when they will need it. If help is needed it is provided. There is the expectation that one will receive help if one needs it. But one does not offer help in exchange for receiving it.

I think it plausible that sharing the meat, and offering help on the water, are not exchanges. I suspect that there are considerable complexities in the sharing culture, and that detailed and sensitive ethnography will be necessary to tease the complexities out of our general background of expecting exchange.

The social units that share seem to be larger than the domestic group, to have face-to-face relationships that endure for long periods of time, and to have frequent interactions. It is probably the case that sanctions for nonperformance exist, and that disputes can disrupt at least some of the transfer activities. Moving away may be the only pacific way to solve some of these problems.

It may be the case that the model of sharing is an extension of the domestic group transfer morality. That needs investigation.

Division of Domestic Assets

In many cultures one of the strategies of married adults is to acquire economic assets, which are transferred to subsequent generations. This transfer may take place only after death, or it may take place before death. Timing of the transfers is usually connected to events in the developmental cycle of one of the parties (death of the grantor, or birth, coming of age, marriage for the grantee). These assets may be substantial and economic, as well as social and symbolic.

Many groups practice pre-mortem divisions. The pastoral Fulani, for example, disperse the milking cows to newly married children. When all the cows have been dispersed with the marriages of all the children, the aging parents no longer have assets to support themselves, and become dependents of adult children (Stenning 1958). The major assets have been transferred, not exchanged.

In some societies the assets needed for the economic viability of a marriage may not become available until the death of the senior generation, as in the case of the Irish countryman (Arensberg 1937).

In the case of middle-class Americans, it is acceptable for us to hold virtually all of our major assets until death. At that point it is normal for most of the assets to be transferred to descendants. Given the alliance of alternate generations, it is not infrequently the case that grandchildren receive substantial assets. These are transfers that are not part of economic exchanges.

Foundations

Many civilizations contain endowments, which are the result of a transfer of assets from personal ownership to a separate jural entity, usually called a foundation. There are at least two motivations for these foundations: one is to perpetuate the name and good works of the donor, and the other is to prevent the predatory state from acquiring the assets. Examples include the *waqf* in Islam, the colleges at Cambridge and Oxford, private universities in the United States, monasteries and convents in Europe, temple donations in India, and the Ford, Rockefeller, Carnegie, Getty, and other foundations in the United States.

In these cases the donors transfer specific assets (normally ownership, control, and possession, but occasionally control is, temporarily, retained by the donor) to a separate jural entity in perpetuity. The assets may include real property, equity shares in some enterprise, or the income stream from some asset (such as real property). The foundation in turn transfers some of these assets. Some go to those who may live off the foundation, and some are transferred to the poor or to students, or are transferred in sacrifices.

The transferred assets may be intended for direct use, or they may be intended for an endowment. In an endowment the asset(s) are not to be spent directly, but are to be (left) invested, and the income stream is to be transferred to others. If the transfer becomes an endowment, then some sort of organization to manage the endowment must be established and perpetuated. This suggests a study of how foundation assets are managed.

The assets donated are restricted in purpose. Normally there is a charitable or religious purpose specified in the grant (masses for the soul of the donor, education, charity, etc.). The predatory state is apparently inhibited in seizing these foundations, although Henry VIII nationalized the monasteries and convents in England, thereby changing the ownership and purpose of the assets involved.

These are transfers, not exchanges. The donor receives nothing economic in return, and the control over the assets passes (eventually) to the grantee. Some of these foundations last centuries, and others disappear in rather short order.

Another class of donation, perhaps, is charity. Whether the giving of alms to individuals, or the giving of assets to organizations which in turn give aid to individuals, these are transfers from the donor to the recipient (Benthall 1999; Huq 2000).

Whether there are exchanges involved varies from case to case. In the United States there are tax deductions for charitable contributions. For most of us these tax deductions are not the reason for the donation, many of the donations would be made without tax deductions, and the deductions are only a minor fraction of the value of the donation. If it is an exchange, the economic values of the items exchanged are very different. The feeling of satisfaction, or moral duty fulfilled which follows from a donation is not part of an exchange. Rather it is a personal result of the action, and not received as economic countertransfer.

Gifts

The term *gift* was ambiguous in natural language long before Mauss wrote a major book on the subject, and since then the situation has only gotten more complex (Kaplan 1997). In my natural English I do use the term *gift*: birthday gifts, wedding gifts, housewarming gifts, Christmas gifts, Hanukkah gifts, anniversary gifts. (In my household, transfers of money to universities, United Way, etc., are not marked as gifts, but as donations. Transfers to beggars are marked as charity, not as gifts.) The primary recipients of gifts are relatives and some friends.

The distinction between a gift and a loan (and therefore a transfer and an exchange) to one's own children may be hard to maintain. And we have (or used to have, for my mother did it often with neighbors) a category named borrow, as in "may I borrow a cup of sugar?" which almost never involved the return of the same item, and rarely involved the return transfer of the same kind of item. "Borrow" and "lend" are categories that are perhaps nearly as ambiguous as "gift," at least in the United States.

Thefts

Theft is a major means of acquiring assets in some societies. Stealing horses on the Great Plains, and stealing livestock in the pastoral societies in East Africa, are institutionalized ways for (mainly) younger men to acquire prestige, leadership, and assets. One does not legitimately steal from some categories of humans, and the sanctions for such illegitimate stealing can be severe. We are talking here of legitimate stealing.

Such stealing is transfer without exchange. The person stolen from may try to steal the goods back in a multicentric political system. But that is not exchange either. It is a subsequent transfer.[9]

Dimensions of Transfers

There are some dimensions that may be extracted from the little we know of transfers.

All exchanges must involve a social relationship of some sort. There are at least two roles, the roles are in dyadic relationships, and the rights and duties of all parties or units are generally understood, even if not always lived up to.

This applies to those transfers that are linked to exchanges. For transfers that are one-way, there can be, and probably usually is, a social relationship involved. Transfers in the context of the domestic group occur in social relationships, as do the divisions of assets of domestic groups. Most donations occur in the context of a social relationship, but there are some that occur through third parties, and a few are completely anonymous, and might involve no social relationship.

For those transfers occurring in a social relationship, one can discern differences in the locus of initiative. Sometimes it is the recipient who provides the initiative (as in begging, or a crying hungry infant). Sometimes it is the donor who provides the initiative.

Transfers can also be thought about in terms of the willingness of both parties. We can all recall instances where it was difficult to persuade the recipient to accept a transfer. We can all recall instances where it was difficult to persuade the donor to give. Theft is a case where, presumably, the donor is totally unwilling to participate, and where the initiative lies with the recipient.

There are certainly legitimate transfers in every social system. There are also transfers that are not legitimate, theft being the most visible example. There may be transfers of dubious legitimacy.[10]

The value of the objects transferred is almost certainly relevant. A gift too trivial, or a gift too luxurious, for the situation will be the wrong gift, and cause perturbation in the relationship. The gift exchange literature has focused on the social relationships more than on the objects exchanged. Whether or not the participants make judgments about the value of the gift is surely an empirical question, and one which there is no reason to speculate about. The answer lies in the folk system, and in folk judgments. Kula partners certainly make judgments about the value of the objects exchanged, for example.

Transfers and Standard Categories of Exchanges

Having sketched a new partition within the domain of allocation, namely transfer, it may be interesting to now have another look at the standard categories of exchange from the transfer point of view.

Reciprocity. Reciprocity (in the Polanyi sense) is clearly an exchange, and is clearly a double-transfer. Much of what has been called gift exchange may well belong here.

Redistribution. Redistribution in the Polanyi sense is probably an exchange. Certainly there are transfers from below to above. The goods collected at the administrative center are often transformed (money and/or labor converted into highways and schools, for example). Whether the provision of public goods is part of an exchange, or whether instead it ought to be seen as two transfers without an exchange, needs analysis. Redistribution in this sense is quite unlike reciprocity and market, for the citizens have no choice about participating.

Market. This concept is clearly an exchange.

Gift. As has been pointed out above, this is one of the more ambiguous words in our lexicon. It has been used to refer to exchanges. And it has been used to refer to transfers. It probably should be avoided as a technical term.

Commodity. Commodity has been usefully narrowed and elaborated in *The Social Life of Things.* Appadurai (1986) and his fellow authors shifted attention from the nature of the object to the nature of the transaction. It is closely allied to the concept of the market principle of exchange. There are some exchanges where the concept of commodity is useful. It is probably not useful as a description of an economy.

Conclusions

In the subdiscipline of economic anthropology our domain includes production and allocation. Within the subdomain of allocation, our field (and our civilization) have concentrated on exchange. My argument in this chapter is that there is another phenomenon in allocation that is important, and has been largely ignored—the subdomain of transfer. Transfers can and do occur without exchanges. Some important examples of transfers can be found in the domestic group, sharing, division of assets, donations, and theft. Their relative importance varies from society to society. I suspect that they are important in all economies. Our focus on exchange has obscured the transfers. They should receive more attention.

Notes

1. At the meeting in Evanston, Richard Wilk pointed out that there are transfers and exchanges within the production process itself. This is true. Wilk's point

poses a challenge for the clarity of the production/allocation division. It does not pose a challenge for the distinction between transfer and exchange.

2. Mauss' publication on gift exchange has dominated subsequent work (1925). In English and French the several words for gift (gift, present, don, cadeaux) denote both an exchange of gifts and a pure or free gift. Mauss concentrated on the exchange component, and so have virtually all anthropologists since then. As folk categories the "pure gift" exists in many societies, and this phenomenon has been largely ignored.

3. Gell went on to define gifts as "transactions in objects which occur in the contextual setting of social reproduction through marriage, affinity and alliance" (Gell 1992: 146). This was a very narrow and Melanesia-centric definition of gift.

4. *Valued* is a clumsy term. I know of no other to encompass goods, services, and knowledge, all of which can be valueds and can be transferred or exchanged.

5. It is used in the sense I use it by Frederic L. Pryor (1977), Laurel Bossen (1988), and Duran Bell (n.d.), the latter in the context of transfers accompanying marriage.

6. The role of property in this picture is not very clear. It may be the case that ownership but not possession is salient. If that is the case, then the social units must be jural isolates. See Hunt 1998.

7. I have defined it this way to try to confine our discussion to something we might all agree is economic. There is a large literature on "exchange," proceeding from Lévi-Strauss (1949), Homans (1961), and Blau (1964). There is a plausible case to be made for us exchanging insults, caresses, intimacy, psychological support, etc. I want to try to separate out the economic transfers from the (perhaps multiple) others.

8. It is also the case that other services are transferred from the adults to the elderly. Trips to the doctor, doing the taxes, arranging travel for the elderly are often needed, sometimes requested, and sometimes transferred. This is transfer in the other direction, and may cause distress on the part of the elderly.

9. There are two other topics that might yield significant understandings by looking at them in terms of economic transfers rather than exchanges: wealth transfers at marriage, and sacrifice.

10. The neighbor who borrows a tool, say, and "forgets" to return it, may be turning a loan into a one-way transfer. It is not quite stealing, and it is certainly not a gift.

References

Appadurai, Arjun, ed.
  1986 *The Social Life of Things.* Cambridge: Cambridge University Press.
Appell, George N.
  1984 "Methodological Issues in the Corporation Redux." *American Ethnologist* 11: 815–17.
Arensberg, Conrad
  1937 *The Irish Countryman.* New York: MacMillan.
Aristotle.
  1962. The *Politics.* London: Penguin.

Bell, Duran
n.d.   "Wealth Transfers Occasioned by Marriage." Manuscript.
Benthall, Jonathon
1999   "Financial Worship: The Quranic Injunction to Almsgiving." *Journal of the Royal Anthropological Institute* 5: 27–42.
Blau, Peter
1964   *Exchange and Power in Social Life*. New York: J. Wiley.
Bohannan, P. J.
1963   *Social Anthropology*. New York: Holt Rinehart and Winston.
Bossen, Laurel
1988   "Toward a Theory of Marriage: The Economic Anthropology of Marriage Transactions." *Ethnology* XXVII: 127–44.
Gell, Alfred
1992   "Inter-tribal Commodity Barter and Reproductive Gift-Exchange in Old Melanesia." Pp. 142–68 in *Barter, Exchange and Value: An Anthropological Approach*, C. Humphrey and S. Hugh-Jones, eds. Cambridge: Cambridge University Press.
Gregory, Chris
1982   *Gifts and Commodities*. London: Academic Press.
Homans, George P.
1961   *Social Behavior*. New York: Harcourt Brace.
Hunt, Robert C.
n.d.   "Apples and Oranges: Constructing Comparability in Anthropology." Manuscript.
1998   "Properties of Property." Pp. 7–27 in *Property in Economic Context*, Robert C. Hunt and Antonio Gilman, eds. Society for Economic Anthropology, Monograph 14. Lanham, Md.: University Press of America.
2000   "Forager Food Sharing Economy: Transfers and Exchanges." In *The Social Economy of Sharing: Resource Allocation and Modern Hunter-Gatherers*, George Wenzel, G. Hovelsrud-Broda, and N. Kishigumi, eds. In press, Senri Ethnological Series #53, Osaka, National Museum of Ethnology.
Huq, Samia
2000   "Zakat." Unpublished manuscript.
Kaplan, David
1997   "Gift exchange." In *Dictionary of Anthropology*, Thomas Barfield, ed. Oxford, U.K.: Blackwell Publishers.
Lamb, Sarah
2000   *White Saris and Sweet Mangoes: Aging, Gender, and Body in North India*. Berkeley: University of California Press.
Lee, Richard B.
1979   *The !Kung San: Men, Women and Work in a Foraging Society*. Cambridge: Cambridge University Press.
Lévi-Strauss, Claude
1949   *Les Structures Elementaires de la Parente*. Paris: Presses Universitaires de France.

McDowell, Nancy
1978   "The Struggle to Be Human: Exchange and Politics in Bun." *Anthropological Quarterly* 51: 17–25.
Mauss, Marcel
1925   "Essai Sur le Don." l'Annee Sociologique second serie, 1923–4, t.1. Reprinted, 1950, Presses Universitaires de France.
Pryor, Frederic L.
1977   *The Origins of the Economy: A Comparative Study of Distribution in Primitive and Peasant Economies*. New York: Academic Press.
Sahlins, Marshall
1965   "The Sociology of Primitive Exchange." Pp. 139–236 in *The Relevance of Models for Social Anthropology*, M. Banton, ed. ASA Monographs, 1. London: Tavistock.
1972   *Stone Age Economics*. Chicago: Aldine Press.
Stenning, Derek
1958   "Household Viability among the Pastoral Fulani." Pp. 92–119 in *The Developmental Cycle in Domestic Groups*, J. Goody, ed. Cambridge Papers in Social Anthropology, No. 1. Cambridge: Cambridge University Press.

Chapter 6

————◆❖◆————

Polanyi and the Definition of Capitalism

Duran Bell

It is argued, herein, that every hierarchical social formation rests on a form of wealth whose ownership is denied to many of those who are responsible for its production and augmentation. This includes societies based on wealth in female reproductivity, cattle, land, and, of course, capital. The Marxian overthrow of capital presupposes that workers have so augmented the forces of capital that its marginal valuation has fallen to zero, leading to a collapse of the system. However, Polanyi attempts to define capitalism without reference to capital and without reference to the dynamics of capitalist production.

Because of his characterization of capitalism as (in principle) an unregulated market system, Polanyi was unable to address the factors that are responsible for the dynamic properties of the system. And in his attempt to distance himself from Marxian materialism and class struggle, he falls headlong into the camp of neoliberalism, suggesting that efforts to improve the well-being of workers are necessarily counterproductive.

Introduction

Several years ago, it was my practice to assign to students in my undergraduate class in "traditional systems" a book by Polanyi called *Dahomey and the Slave Trade* (1966). Of course, I was aware of the fact that the real ethnography had been produced by Melville J. Herskovits. However, the book by Herskovits was in two thick volumes, promising to tell more about this ancient kingdom than anyone could reasonably want to know. It was only later that I realized how straightforward and readable it was (volume one would have sufficed for my purposes) and only later did I begin to develop theoretical differences with Polanyi.

What Polanyi had discovered in reading Herskovits was that Dahomey was a sophisticated and complex African kingdom, featuring a well-planned economy, an effective army including an awesome regiment of Amazons, and important elements of an exchange economy, especially in the domain of cooked food and other consumption goods. Given the prominence of market processes in Dahomey, it might appear that this "Negro" kingdom on the coast of Africa contained the beginnings of a market economy; and Polanyi's study of Dahomey is oriented toward dispelling this impression.

I would be pleased to argue with Polanyi on this point. I would delight in demonstrating that Dahomey was the original capitalist state and that, like so many things of great importance, capitalism breathed its first vibrant breath on African soil. Unfortunately, I cannot make such an argument. Indeed, I consider it to be a rather silly issue, but it is an issue nevertheless—created by Polanyi's peculiar characterization of capitalism as a "market economy."

Polanyi's Capitalism

In their preface to *Trade and Market in the Early Empires*, published in 1957, Polanyi and Arensberg said that

> [w]e asked, abstractly and analytically, what social action does the free market entail? . . . they [the economists] agreed with us upon the following tentative formulation: In the free market of supply and demand, a man can reverse roles, being supplier or demander as he can or wills. A man can go to this market or that as he sees his advantage; he is free of fixed and static obligation to one center or one partner, he may move at will and at random, or as prices beckon. He can offer to all and any comers, dole or divide among them, "corner the market" so that they all pay his price and so dance to his tune. At another turn of prices, or in a next transaction or market, formally, he is one of a similar "crowd" and dances in unison to the tune called by another who may in his turn have "cornered the market" from them all. . . .

> Where outside the recent Western world, in the ethnographic record, would we find anything resembling or parallel to this? (1957, viii–ix)

Capitalism is depicted here as a system of traders and merchants, or, some would grandly say, entrepreneurs, seeking profitable opportunity. This depiction is so focused on merchants that we are left unaware of the nature of the system of production. The production process is entirely hidden from view and relegated to the specific optimization routines of those who own the machines. Polanyi is keenly aware of workers and the need for a labor market under capitalism. A fundamental anomaly of capitalism, he claims, is that capitalism requires a market for labor and that this market cannot be a naturally occurring and freely functioning entity. In *The Great Transformation*, published in 1944, Polanyi argues with great eloquence that capitalism, defined as a purely self-regulating market system, can never exist. It must be constructed and protected by the powers of the state, because the natural processes of the market are inconsistent with the preservation of labor. The conversion of labor into a commodity is destructive in the absence of strategic state intervention that might provide protection. For the sake of capitalism, capitalism must be restrained.

The state is essential, also, to the integrity of land and money, neither of which can emerge from pure market processes, because they cannot be valued at their costs of production. For these reasons, according to Polanyi, a fully self-regulating market system is impossible; and, hence, ideal capitalism is impossible—impossible in part because labor is an unavoidable blemish on the face of a putative ideal. Nevertheless, we are told that the actually existing forms of capitalism resemble and are parallel to his picture of free and enterprising entrepreneurs; and, consequently, the blemishes created by labor, land, and money fail to destroy the essence of capitalism as a system of self-regulating markets.

Were we to follow Polanyi and define capitalism by reference to market processes, we would be unable to distinguish it from market socialism. Polanyi was familiar with the then very prominent discussion of market socialism being pursued by Oscar Lange (1938), Abba Lerner (1944), H. D. Dickinson (1939) and others, continuing with important work by Benjamin Ward (1967). Market socialism would not be a pure system of fully self-regulating markets; however, it need not be less pure than actually existing market systems. And although this debate about market socialism was at its height while Polanyi was writing *The Great Transformation*, he failed to mention it. According to Peter Rosner (1990), Polanyi contributed considerable attention to the challenge from Ludwig von Mises (1920) on the impossibility of rational resource allocation under socialism. It was the von Mises paper that had given rise to the initial debate and Polanyi had been an early participant in the fray, offering an organizational framework within which socialism might function efficiently. Yet, we do not find in *The Great Transformation* any suggestion that a socialist formation might be able to realize the advantages of unregulated markets. Had he addressed those debates, he might have been forced to consider *relations of production* as necessary factors in the characterization of social systems.

Polanyi and the Condition of Labor

In *The Great Transformation*, Polanyi focuses on the construction of the English working class and, therewith, the creation of a market for labor power. In his analysis the labor market came fully onto center stage with the abandonment of the Poor Law in 1834. The Poor Law had been established in 1795, a time of great social distress, when a group of men met in Speenhamland, just outside of Newbury, England, and

> decided that subsidies in aid of wages should be granted in accordance with a scale dependent on the price of bread, so that a minimum income can be assured to the poor *irrespective of their earnings* (his emphasis). . . . Very soon it became the law of the land over most of the countryside, and later even in a number of manufacturing districts; actually it introduced no less a social and economic innovation than the "right to live" and until abolished in 1834, it effectively prevented the establishment of a competitive labor market. Two years earlier, in 1832, the middle class had forced its way to power, partly in order to remove this obstacle to the new capitalistic economy. Indeed, nothing could be more obvious than that the wage system imperatively demanded the withdrawal of the "right to live" as proclaimed in Speenhamland. (Polanyi 1944: 78)

The "right to live" was not an innovation that came upon the scene with Speenhamland; it was the custom of the countryside and of the feudal period that members of the parish or estate would be availed the resources by which to secure a living. The parish serfdom that was installed by the Act of Settlement of 1662 had the function of binding the common folk to the village (Polanyi 1944: 78), but fortunately the village contained a variety of common resources from which life could be assured, except under the worst conditions. However, with the expulsion of village folk by the enclosures that divorced the people from their means of survival, the traditional elite sought another way to assure the right to life. Hence, Speenhamland.

Polanyi argues that the ultimate destitution of the workers of England was not the result of class exploitation. The employer offered employment and the workers accepted it voluntarily. The workers' destitution arose, he says, from the destruction of the traditional culture and groups to which they had belonged, not from meagerness of wages.

> "There is no starvation in societies living on the subsistence margin." The principle of freedom from want was equally acknowledged in the Indian village community and, we might add, under almost every and any type of social organization up to about the beginning of sixteenth century Europe, when the modern ideas on the poor put forth by the humanist Vives were argued before the Sorbonne. It is the absence of the threat of individual

starvation which makes primitive society, in a sense, more human than market economy, and at the same time less economic. (Polanyi 1944: 164)

But what, I ask, is the problem with capitalism that makes traditional rights to life so problematic? Why is it that capitalism is associated with the destruction of traditional communities both at home and abroad? Given that capitalism is associated with a massive increase in society's productive potential, is it necessary that (as Marx suggests in *Wage Labor and Capital*) the "forest of uplifted arms demanding work becomes ever thicker, while the arms themselves become ever thinner"? The answer is that capitalists are expected to pay the lowest wage consistent with securing the services of a worker, without reference to the requirements of survival for the worker and his family. It would make sense, then, to allow workers to have alternative modes of survival, such as private plots of land from which to secure certain staples. We find such structures in Latin America, where native producers seek out work on the *latifundia* only for ancillary expenditures and tax payments. The provision of family plots makes it possible to reduce wage rates to a much lower level. Yet, in the construction of the English working class, it was presumed that workers simply would not work unless threatened with starvation and driven by hunger. This partly explains Polanyi's attack on Speenhamland. His argument is that the squires of England only made things worse by attempting at Speenhamland to remove the essential foundation for labor supply.

> To later generations nothing could have been more patent that the mutual incompatibility of institutions like the wage system and the "right to live," or, in other words, than the impossibility of a functioning capitalistic order as long as wages were subsidized from public funds. (Polanyi 1944: 81)

Polanyi presumes that the industrial system *must* impose a heavy a price upon the common people; and he presumes that the labor market must be forced into existence by the state against the resistance of traditional conceptions of the right to life. Only with the removal of this traditional right could modern capitalism come into existence.

While there were certainly serious problems with Speenhamland as a form of public policy, it would be useful to reconsider capitalism *as a social formation* before addressing issues of labor regulation. Labor is a feature of capitalism. For Polanyi it is an unfortunate adhesion to the system because it is ineluctably connected to the human material that is its source. So, while it may not matter that the price of widgets goes to zero, it does matter if wages follow that course, leading to the destruction of the human community. Hence, the state must stand ready to protect labor from the ravages of free markets. One should not allow labor to be part of the self-regulating mechanism by which capitalism is defined.

The beginning of a more powerful understanding of capitalism could begin with the last paragraph of *The Grundrisse*, 1857–58, where Marx declares that

> [i]t requires no great penetration to grasp that where e.g. free labour or wage labour arising out of the dissolution of bondage as the point of departure, there machines can only arise in antithesis to living labour, as property alien to it, and as power hostile to it; i.e., that they must confront it as capital. (Marx, in Tucker 1972: 293)

With Marx the contradiction between labor and capital is not based on free versus non-free markets, but on the fact that workers, who are remunerated by wages, are thereby denied any claim on the product of their efforts. It is on the basis of this fact that in the course of capital accumulation, capital can grow relative to labor and, as the property of an alien class, become an instrument for the subjugation of labor. To the extent that workers are successful in extracting a social product from the forces of nature, to that extent also they build the power that controls and dominates them.

This argument may seem at first to be an overly dramatized and radicalized image of the worker's position. However, accepting that characterization does not entail any particular consequence or suggest any particular ethical valuation. Rather, the central thesis of this chapter is that the relationship, observed by Marx, between workers and capital is also reflected under other institutional formations that are structured hierarchically in terms of a wealth-asset. It is simply a most fundamental analytic fact that in *any system of wealth*, a class of direct producers is impressed into service by the owners of wealth in such a way as to facilitate an augmentation of the wealth held by those owners. In some systems, the strategic use of "direct producers" is only ancillary to the process of wealth accumulation, and in other cases such use is essential. The exceptional strength of capitalism arises from the fact that it most effectively extracts value from direct producers.

If we agree that labor is an essential factor in capitalist accumulation, we can go forward to ask to which extent is the "right to life" incompatible with this process of accumulation. Moreover, the same question can be posed in relation to direct producers within other systems of accumulation. We shall, not surprisingly, find that decreasing the resources to be received by such producers is to the advantage of those who make use of them, increasing the rate at which the wealth-asset can be accumulated. However, we cannot find support for the notion that the right to life is incompatible with accumulation, per se. The issue of labor regulation is reduced to the determination of shares of economic resources that are to accrue to labor and the owners of capital. A social policy that aims to maximize the rate of accumulation on the backs of dehumanized workers may be politically unstoppable, but it is not logically necessary.

The Exigencies of Wealth Accumulation in other Social Formations

Wealth is defined herein as a resource that possesses four essential properties:

(a) it provides a flow of benefits (consumption goods) to some set of individuals;

(b) under effective management, it has the capacity of growth (at a nonnegative rate) in magnitude or quantity over time;

(c) the resource does not achieve redundancy in magnitude, so that additional units of the asset possess positive valuation; and

(d) there exists a mechanism by which the benefits of this asset devolve indefinitely across generations.

Consider wealth in the form of female fertility. This form of wealth is the asset around which matrilineal groups are formed within both human and nonhuman societies (satisfying characteristic "d"). Any group that can capture the reproductivity of women will be able to experience an increasing quantity of that asset, as women produce additional women in an indefinite sequence of reproduction (characteristic "b"); and in any generation the women and men who are the product of women are directly the sources of various benefits and are useful in the production of consumption goods (characteristic "a"). Finally, if ecological factors have not induced a demographic transition and if food sources are adequate to a growing population, additional children will have positive social value (satisfying characteristic "c").

In order for fertility to be maintained as a wealth-asset, it is necessary that the biological capacities of women be expressible without the critical economic intervention of men. If men are primarily responsible for food, for example, then the number of men available for food acquisition would become the limiting factor for population growth, not the number of women; and it would be men who can gain the advantages associated with possessing an essential wealth-asset.[1]

Over the course of human existence, the more common social ecologies were, arguably, those in which women were fully capable of supporting themselves through the gathering of wild foods or by simple horticultural methods or by other methods that were not monopolized by men; and it is plausible that the power of female fertility was more directly a function of the number of women and not particularly affected by the number of men. Under these conditions social organization may be structured around female fertility and men may be forced to abandon their natal domestic groups in search of sexual and other domestic satisfactions. A most pitiable example comes from Africa, where a man of the Cewa tribe submits to a life of agricultural work on the land of his wife's people.

> Mitchell says that unsuitable husbands are dismissed with compensation and sent away. He adds that the husbands of the women of a village are often away visiting and are definitely not reckoned as members of the community. Stannus states that a widower is usually given a present with the suggestion that he go elsewhere since he no longer has any standing in his wife's village. Marwick indicates that Cewa marriage ties sit loose and speaks of a man and his sister and "her current husband."

> The Cewa talk of the father as a stranger. "He is a beggar; he has simply followed his wife." At divorce he leaves his wife's village with his hoe, his axe, and his sleeping-mat and has no right to any of the children of the marriage, even if he may have begotten as may as seven children. (Richards 1950, 233–34)

A similar story can be told about men in Rembau, one of the nine states of Negri Sembilam, Malaysia. Here we find not only matriliny but matriarchy, where all clan land is inherited by women only. The position of men in marriage is predictably low:

> But if the responsibility for a husband's welfare rests with his wife, his relative position is one of inferiority. He is at the beck and call of his relations by marriage; his mother-in-law boasts that she can find some use for any sort of son—the clever may be cajoled, and the fool bullied; the blind man can be put to pound the rice; the cripple to mind the *padi* drying in the sun; the deaf to fire the cannon and the braggart to take the hard knocks.

> The mother's dominance in the home is patent to her children and has prevented the growth of a sincere filial affection for the father. (Parr and Mackray 1910: 87)

In matriarchal Rembau most marriages are arranged by the dominant women of the group, who give their sons away in the hope of a fruitful affinal alliance. However, some men obtain wives "by storm" whereby they gain entrance into a woman's house, grab hold of her, and refuse to budge. The woman's kin fly into the house, bludgeoning him in an effort to force him from the house. If they fail, if he hangs on, bruised and bloody, he is able (after an appropriate monetary penalty) to claim the woman as his bride. We see here the kind of indignity to which men will fall in the absence of wealth-assets with which to demand the transfer of women.

It is reasonable to argue that the circulation of men and their competitive attempts to gain entry into groups containing the resources of women have been predominant over the course of hominid and human existence. In this event, men *in their roles as husbands-fathers* have been induced to contribute to the growth of alien matrilateral groups as a condition for sexual access to women in those groups—*structurally indistinguishable from the position of labor under capital.*

The enormous power of female fertility has been denied by some feminists, since the conditions of contemporary capitalism are not conducive to it. The "demographic transition" that accompanies industrialization announces the death knell of fertility as an asset around which people can organize as corporate groups. While fertility continues to be essential to the continuation of the society, there emerges a redundancy in its availability; and the actual number of births could be produced by a smaller number of women, implying that the *marginal social value* of women's fertility has fallen to zero.

While female fertility is no longer a source of power, neither is it the source of female subordination, as some have argued. The subordination of women arises from the fact that men have gained access to forms of wealth that overwhelm fertility as a basis of power. The most elementary form of wealth that men have claimed is animal stock. By "elementary" I do not suggest that animal stock was the historically original form of wealth (other than fertility); rather, it is elementary because the forms of social organization that are required to accommodate the growth of animal stock are comparatively simple; other forms of wealth cannot grow except with the development of relatively complicated social structures and the imposition of a host of social rules. Yet, the exploitation of this natural process is revolutionary for social organization. In order to manage and gain the advantages of animal stock, men organize themselves around it in patrilateral organization; and by standing on a platform made possible by animals, men are able to make claim on the fertility of women.

We encountered this issue initially in relation to characteristics of cattle used as bridewealth in certain African societies. In the course of studying this issue, we noticed that if cattle are to be employed as bridewealth, it is necessary that the rate of growth of herds exceeds the rate of growth of the human population. Stated differently, cattle can be used as bridewealth only because the fertility rate of cattle exceeds that of women. It is this fact that confers power on those who own cattle, relative to those who have daughters; and it is fundamentally for this reason that cattle-holding, patrilineal organization can generally overwhelm the matrilineal, whose basis of power is female fertility. For most readers, this fact must come as a surprise. Certainly, it is not a fact that can be established by ethnographic observation; we can see it clearly, however, in structured simulations of bridewealth regimes (see Bell and Song, 1990, 1992–93, 1995). These findings strongly contradict the economistic notion that bridewealth is a market valuation of women's contributions. Indeed, we show that if one attempts that form of evaluation, wives are worth much less that the cattle expended on them![2] On the other hand, since cattle possess a higher rate of growth than the human population (much like a higher rate of interest on money), it can be a source of greater power for those who possess it, and this power is greater when the level of bridewealth is lower.[3]

When men are able to join together in corporate ownership of cattle, they are able to induce the transfer of women to their group and use those women as instruments for the growth of their patrilineage, a patrilineage with which women are associated but to which they cannot belong. It is a classic case of direct reproducers being alienated from their product and contributing to the power of the group that controls them. And as the patrilineage grows stronger, its power grows over those groups who must accept a net outflow of women in order to accumulate cattle.

Hence, with re-productivity as a wealth asset, men are often exploited as instruments in the growth of alien matrilineages; on the other hand when cattle are the wealth-asset, women are exploited as instruments of alien patrilineages. Both processes are parallel to use of wages as mechanisms for excluding workers from rights to capital whose growth depends on their work efforts.

Land is potentially a wealth-asset. However, the fertility of land is measured in products different from land itself. The husbanding of land does not generally produce more land. In any case, having more land is of great value only when one can force other people to work on it. By working the land yourself, you secure your subsistence; by exploiting the work of others, you have the potential of converting land into an effective wealth-asset. The technology of land accumulation is a process by which some people seize the land of others, creating a class of landless individuals who will work for others in return for a share of the harvest. However, this hierarchical structure is feasible only with the construction of a set of institutions, the raising of an army, and the legitimation of the rules that allow the collection of surplus. It is only by means of a rather complex set of social mechanisms that land becomes a source of additional land for an elite minority. Once again, we find that the efforts of direct producers are essential to the strengthening of the overlords. In China and Egypt men could be forced into "corvee labor" for the construction of canals and other infrastructure projects that facilitated an expansion of the arable. This is a case of land supporting labor which could be used to create land by means of "an indirect process re-production" and the state, emperor, king or pharaoh claimed ownership of the land and took a direct interest in its expansion.

It is only with great difficulty that the owners of land are able to generate a continuing growth of power and wealth. This difficulty is demonstrated by the overrunning of a powerful and sophisticated Chinese empire by herding peoples, the Mongols in the thirteenth century and by the Manchus in the seventeenth. Let me say, emphatically, that the Chinese were technically capable of vanquishing any of their adversaries. However, an almost effete culture had developed that disparaged military activity and China sought to hide behind a Great Wall. This was a culture that found the control of military leaders to be quite difficult, finding that they were sometimes a source of attack, rather than defense. In other words, the institutions of China were not articulated in a fashion that would maximize the growth of the imperial domain. Only a more militaristic (and a culturally less sophisticated) culture would have accomplished this. Moreover, the efforts of the state were generally oriented toward preventing the growth of landlordism and the attendant danger of warlordism. Not only did accumulation of land by elites tend to reduce peasants to desperation and perhaps rebellion, but it gave rise to an elite that could not be trusted by the state.

Land is a powerful wealth-asset only to the degree that it is embedded in a social mechanism that promotes growth of the asset and protects it from attack. Social mechanisms of various forms are essential for any form of wealth, including wealth in women or animal stock. However, in these latter cases, the wealth-asset has a natural process of growth; and the institutions that can be elaborated for augmenting the accumulation of these wealth-assets appear to be relatively uncomplicated.

Characteristics of Capitalism

Which brings us back to capitalism. The industrial means of production is not like cattle; it has no natural tendency to reproduce and become wealth. In order for the means of production to become capital it must be embedded in a set of social institutions and rules that allow it to grow thereby becoming a wealth-asset. We cannot begin to understand capitalism as a general form of social organization unless we focus on capital as a form of wealth and hence on capital accumulation. Capitalism is *one of the sets* of institutions that facilitates the growth of industrial capital; and wages (rather than shares of the product) are central to its effectiveness. During the period of its embryonic development, during the period of "primitive accumulation," it would appear that no system of social organization can compete with capitalism as a mode of accumulation. Surely, the grinding down of the worker's living standards that one finds in that period is not consistent with worker control.

Historically, the state has been the organized collectivity within which the growth of capital is articulated. Land as wealth has also required a state formation; but in the case of land, subsidiary corporate structures are common and strongly encouraged, especially patrilateral structures. Capital, however, greets traditional wealth-holding groups with hostility, while accepting the state as an ideologically illegitimate but functionally necessary entity. Indeed, Polanyi's conception of capitalism as a self-regulating market implies the irrelevance of the state. His discussion is directed, then, to explaining why a state is necessary for the regulation of money, land, and labor in an otherwise unregulated terrain.

All too often, scholars are able to recognize the cultural context of behavior in other societies, while denying culture as an arbiter of their own behavior. *They* have culture, while we are rational. *They* are embedded in social relations, while we are free to act. *They* have duties, while we have freedom of choice. And by accepting the ideology of an ascendant European bourgeoisie one can be led to believe that "free enterprise" has no need for superordinate authority. Perhaps labor, the weak, and the poor have a need for government, but not free enterprise. This, of course, is the argument of Polanyi, who does not notice that for every line of legal code produced in support of labor there are one thousand written in support of some section of capital. It is these many lines of legal code and public administration that are the foundation of "free enterprise." And given the fact that the industrial means of production cannot grow by intrinsic or natural forces, state machinery provides the necessary context for growth. Capitalism is necessarily embedded in a nest of rules, defined at the level of the state (and increasingly at the transnational level). So, while capitalism systematically destroys most forms of social relation common to precapitalist formations, such as lineages, village communities, and a wide range of other associations, it remains embedded in social relations. *The state is to capital as the patrilineage is to cattle and as the matrilineage is to female re-productivity.* In a world system of capitalism, with many state systems in competition, conflict, and cooperation, it is precisely the state, whose role Polanyi believes to be extrinsic, that acts as the manager of systems of capital accumulation.

There is a multiplicity of institutional frameworks for the management of capital, but "self-regulating markets" is not one of them.

Which brings us back to Speenhamland. What was Polanyi's point in attacking this policy? He argues that capitalism is inconsistent with the right to life, so that the steady movement toward free markets is met by a countermovement of restrictions by the state for the protection of labor. Polanyi would have us believe that the capitalist state exists for the benefit of workers; and in the last pages of *The Great Transformation*, in an appendix on Speenhamland, he joins with the enemies of labor in an attack on social policy in general:

> The utter incompatibility of Speenhamland with the wage system was permanently remembered only in the tradition of the economic liberals. They alone realized that, in a broad sense, every form of the protection of labor implied something of the Speenhamland principle in interventionism. (Polanyi 1944: 301)

An astounding statement: "Every form of the protection of labor" is, by implication, misguided and counterproductive. Capitalism is a tragedy for workers, but Speenhamland proves that it is better to leave them to their fate.

Yet, on closer inspection any policy analyst would see immediately that the problem with Speenhamland was specific to the details of its provisions and implied nothing about "every form of the protection." In particular, it was an income subsidy that guaranteed a specific minimum level of income, *with a 100-percent tax on increased earnings below this minimum!* If you earned less than a stipulated amount, the state would raise your income to the standard, removing the relationship between income and work. This is simply bad public policy; but by focusing on Speenhamland and suggesting that its failure implies a much broader fault of policy, Polanyi falls into the camp of brain-dead neoliberalism. Of course, he is exceptional in that he enters that camp with heavy heart, in horror, with tears; but he enters nevertheless with a seemingly rational acceptance of the awful necessities of human progress.

Polanyi and Marx

The characterization that we have provided of Polanyi is not the common one. More common is the perception of Rhoda Halperin (1998). In this view, Polanyi was a socialist whose ideas are largely derived from Marx; and it is suggested by some observers that Polanyi's apparent differences with Marx were the result of a strategic use of terms that promised to be less problematic and more influential during a time of right-wing McCarthyism. However, our discussion has relied almost entirely on *The Great Transformation* for insight into his views; and that book was published in 1944. In that book Polanyi makes a number of references to Marx, most of which dismiss him as a follower of David Ricardo.

Professor Halperin's version of Polanyi is derived from his papers on "the early empires." In various chapters that he contributed to the *Trade and Market in the Early Empires* (Polanyi 1957) and especially in his "the economy as instituted process," Polanyi presents reciprocity, redistribution, householding, and exchange as features of those early empires; and he argues that these processes of resource allocation are embedded in social institutions. Unfortunately, Polanyi does not carry these valuable insights over into his understanding of capitalism. Under capitalism, he argues, the market overwhelms these institutional forms, replacing human relations with the strictly economic. However, Professor Halperin has applied Polanyi's model of early empires to an analysis of capitalism, in contradiction to Polanyi's very explicit position on the matter, and she has suggested that Polanyi's early empires model was derived from Marx's model of capitalism. As much as I wish that it were so, it is not so.

As I have argued herein, Marx's model of capitalism is a model of accumulation and power at the micro level and of an increasing concentration of capital at the macro level. Workers are victims in this process, but so are the many capitalists who bite the dust of atomistic competition. This process can come to an inglorious end only when capital becomes abundant. And, much like the overthrow of fertility by the demographic transition, we would have the overthrow of capital by socialist revolution.

While labor is the source of capital and the force behind its continued accumulation in Marxian analysis, workers enter only negatively in the Polanyi model. The struggles of workers are oriented toward securing the "right to life," even when the promotion of that right can only retard the evolution of fully unregulated markets. There seems to be no dynamic in Polanyi, other than the back-and-forth movement and countermovement between free markets and restriction. The movement toward the free market ideal will never be realized (unfortunately!) because of worker resistance. Some have complained (e.g., Block 1997) that Polanyi appears at times to suggest that the ideal of unregulated markets has been (nearly) realized. My own view is that he does not presume that any major progress toward complete (capitalist) freedom is feasible; there is only a stalemate in which workers seek a better life, even though no better life can be found.

Notes

1. One possibility is that the technology of food acquisition favors the capacities of men, as among the Inuit; another possibility is that food can be obtained effectively by violent attacks upon those who have it. And a final possibility is that men may be essential to the protection of women and the product of their fertility from external attack and decimation. These are cases where the biological capacities of men provide for them an advantage. Under these circumstances, matrilineal forms are unlikely to survive. They fail because the underlying asset, female fertility, is without autonomous power.

2. Since women are exchangeable for cattle, the value of a woman's fertility can be measured in terms of the cattle gained from the marriage of her daughters, her daughters' daughters, etc., discounted to the present. We can then compare the cattle value of a woman's reproductivity against the cattle value of a cow's reproductivity. This is the basis of a "benefit-cost" calculation that we show to be inappropriate for the analysis of bridewealth regimes.

3. It is clear that cattle growth, and human growth, can be affected by famine, disease, and other calamities. Indeed, at some point the growth of herds can be expected to encounter limiting resource conditions. Our discussion of relative rates of growth neglects these complications.

References

Bell, Duran, and Shunfeng Song

1990 "Growth and Process in a Lineage-based Social Technology." *Journal of Quantitative Anthropology* 2(1): 17–45.

1992–93 "Sacrificing Reproductive Success for the Primitive Accumulation of Cattle." *Journal of Quantitative Anthropology* 4(2): 175–84.

1995 "Explaining the Level of Bridewealth." *Current Anthropology* 35(3): 311–16.

Block, Fred

1997 "Polanyi and the Concept of Capitalism." Paper presented at the meetings of the Social Science History Association, November.

Dickinson, Henry D.

1939 *Economics of Socialism*. London: Oxford University Press.

Halperin, Rhoda

1998 "Reading Karl Polanyi: The Institutional Paradigm in the Context of Contemporary Culture Theory and Practice." Unpublished manuscript.

Lange, Oscar, and Fred Taylor

1938 *On the Economic Theory of Socialism*. Minneapolis: University of Minnesota Press.

Lerner, Abba P.

1944 *The Economics of Control*. New York: Macmillan.

Parr, C. W. C., and W. H. Mackray

1910 "Rembau, One of the Nine States." *Journal of the Straits Branch of the Royal Asiatic Society*. N. 56.

Polanyi, Karl

1944 *The Great Transformation*. Boston: Beacon Press.

1957 *Trade and Market in the Early Empires*. Glencoe, Ill.: The Free Press.

1966 *Dahomey and the Slave Trade*. Conrad M. Arensberg, Harry W. Pearson, and Karl Polanyi, eds. Seattle: University of Washington Press.

Richards, A. I.

1950 "Some Types of Family Structure amongst the Central Bantu." Pp. 207–51 in *African Systems of Kinship and Marriage*, A. R. Radcliffe-Brown and Daryll Forde, eds. London: Oxford University Press.

Rosner, Peter
   1990   "Karl Polanyi and Socialist Accounting." Pp. 55–65 in *The Life and Work of Karl Polanyi*, Karai Polanyi-Levitt, ed. New York: Black Rose Books.
Tucker, Robert C., ed.
   1972   *The Marx-Engels Reader*, 2ᵈ ed. New York: W. W. Norton.
von Mises, Ludwig
   1920   "Die Wirtshaftsrechnung und sozialistischen Gemeinwesen." *Archiv für Sozialwissenschaften und Sozialpolitik* Bd. 47: 86–121.
Ward, Benjamin
   1967   *The Socialist Economy.* New York: Random House.

Part III

Small Producers Interacting with the Wider World

Chapter 7

Chayanov and Theory in Economic Anthropology

E. Paul Durrenberger
and
Nicola Tannenbaum

Theory

Since theory plays such an important role in postmodern discourse, mathematics, economics, anthropology, and science, and because it is amenable to correspondingly different formulations that relate abstract ideas, concrete events, aesthetics, and judgments of adequacy, it behooves us to take a moment to explore what it might mean.

One use of the term refers to abstract statements people use to state the assumptions they employ to understand or to elaborate stories. The abstractions relate to experience via stories or anecdotes that establish their credibility, often in terms of a plausibility criterion—"because of this story, it is imaginable that . . ." They are amenable less to proof than to various interpretations—"readings," in fashionable parlance (Durrenberger 2000). The canons of judgment are the aesthetic of joke recognition—as Geertz (1973) put it, you have to "get" it. If you don't, you don't. The chief criterion of quality seems to be fashionability. Such theories often carry the name of the imaginative thinker who gained credence and an audience for the opinions: Freudian, Foucaultian, Lacanian, Jungian. A self-referencing group centered on a closed body of texts can achieve quasireligious status for such a doctrine and earn an "ism": Freudianism, Marxism. Sometimes the word "theory" is appended to a label for the range of phenomena to which the assumptions are held to be relevant: reception theory, translation theory, performance theory. Confined to the academy, these are the stuff of harmless and fast-moving fads; backed with the machinery of think tanks and the power of media, they can become the stuff of political doctrine to justify various policies: e.g., trickle down or supply side economics. In today's academic fashion marketplace, the more inaccessible, abstract, and opaque, the better. These are the marks of the intellectual property of a highly trained and incredibly gifted elite to which most of us can but aspire.

Opposite to the first orientation in its approach to experience is a refusal to consider theorizing or, at best, to put it off until there is adequate empirical data to speak sufficiently well for itself to state its own theory. In this practice experience is valued over assumption. The ritualized forms of science are more valued than its operational philosophy and practice. Outsiders are likely to call such practices "scientistic," while insiders value them as inductive or empiricist to emphasize their fascination with the collection and classification of data rather than its interpretation. Practitioners of this form are likely to pride themselves in quantification and statistical manipulations.

Another use of the term "theory," as abstract as the first but disciplined, is a practice that follows customs of reasoning for relating assumptions (axioms) to their logical consequences (theorems). These include consistency (no contradictions), completeness (all of the theorems are related to the axioms), and economy (there are no unnecessary axioms, axioms that can be derived from other axioms). The aesthetic of judgment is mathematical. The truth of a statement is self-contained and apparent to the followers of this custom—guaranteed by adherence to customary rules. The game is to explore all possible implications of inherited sets of assumptions, to investigate the range of possible assumptions, and imagine new ones to explore. Examples include group theory, ring theory, number theory, topographic theory, graph theory, automata theory, and economic theory. To the tribes that practice this art, any connection to experience is serendipitous and inconsequential. Experience is as irrelevant to these theorists as assumptions are to the scientistic folk. Perhaps it is the irrelevance of the connection with experience of this kind of theory that makes purveyors of the first and undisciplined sort—the storytellers—think of their opinions as theory.

A fourth usage considers theory to be sets of assumptions that are connected to experience through critical observation to determine to what extent the assumptions are useful for understanding experience. The connection between assumptions and experience is the critical observation or testable hypothesis. This is called operational philosophy and holds something to be true if it can be formulated as an assertion that can conceivably be connected by a critical observation to experience (else it is meaningless), if someone has done the observations in a disciplined way that others can replicate (else it is indeterminate), and if the observations match the expectations (else it is false). This is what we call science. There is a strong interplay between abstractions and concrete experience, each defining the other in a continual process of self-correction, critical appraisal, and revolution (Kuznar 1997). This is the mode we favor, and we discuss the place of Chayanov's ideas in developing such an approach for some dimensions of economic anthropology.

Like mathematics and interpretive theory, science derives its meanings and practices from the communities that practice it. The definition of a scientific community would be close to Durkheim's definition of a "church" as all those who hold a common set of values and practices join into a community, though perhaps not a moral one. Like other cultural constructs, scientific theory requires a community of practice (see Lave 1988) to define and practice it.

Few if any of the storytellers have had anything to say about Chayanov since the '70s (Durrenberger and Tannenbaum 1979), and Chayanov has not been discussed in any serious political arena since Stalin purged him (Durrenberger 1984a). Some of the inductive empiricists have framed statistical summaries in terms of some of Chayanov's ideas (Tannenbaum 1984a). Perhaps because he returned to tables of numbers that represented peasant households, their budgets, their scheduling of work, their organization of production and consumption, Chayanov has not been attractive to the mathematical theorists. Such realities are not inviting sources of theorems.

We discuss Chayanov's ideas as a theory in the fourth, or operationalist, sense, as a set of assumptions about the categories appropriate for understanding household economies and related to experience through critical observation and useful for understanding a wide range of economies. Because they do not contribute to the operational sense of theory that we favor and because we have treated them in detail elsewhere (Durrenberger and Tannenbaum 1979, Tannenbaum 1984a), we do not discuss the other uses of Chayanov's ideas. In conclusion we return to the questions of theory, Chayanov, and the future of economic anthropology.

Chayanov's Theory

Though Chayanov's work was first introduced to American academic audiences in 1931, his concepts were neither incorporated into American thinking about agriculture nor independently developed. There was some movement in that direction that was quashed by a powerful institutional structure (Durrenberger 1984a). While Wolf (1966: 15) quoted with approval Chayanov's 1931 article to the effect that the peasant farm economy is a family economy, that profit cannot be computed as for a capitalist firm, that the yearly budget is important rather than daily wages, and that peasants will work for a small remuneration as long as family requirements remain unsatisfied, there is no evidence that Chayanov's analytical scheme influenced Wolf's. American anthropologists' general introduction to Chayanov came through Sahlins (1971, 1972, in Durrenberger 1998). Gudeman (1978: 353) indicates that some confused Sahlins with Chayanov and wonders why Chayanov's marginalist analysis appealed to the anti-marginalist Sahlins.

Sahlins extracted his "Chayanov's Rule," which he stated as "the greater the relative working capacity of the household the less its members work" (1972: 87). "Chayanov's Rule" describes an ideal, abstract case where households are independent production and consumption units. Sahlins compares the theoretically ideal level of production, based on this rule, to what households actually produced. The differences between the theoretically expected ideal and the empirical, Sahlins argued, is a measure of the impact of the social system on the economic system. Sahlins's Chayanov's Rule draws on one aspect of Chayanov's analysis but does not represent Chayanov's general theory. This broader theory is only rarely incorporated into American anthropological works (see Durrenberger 1980b,1984b; Durrenberger and Tannenbaum 1990; Tannenbaum 1984a), although it was recognized in peasant studies where it often served as a straw man to frame more orthodox arguments (see below).

Chayanov, at least rhetorically, argued that the data led him to his theory. He and others in the organization of production school of Russian agriculture were faced with anomalous data that did not make sense in either the standard capitalist or Marxist analyses. Chayanov lists a number of these in his introduction: households would not accept the threshing machine although it made sense in bookkeeping terms; they paid rents higher than the profit of the land; and they grew labor-intensive crops that were less profitable than other crops (1966: 38–41). Rather than deciding the peasants were irrational, a favorite choice for development workers and government officials, Chayanov argued that peasants operated rationally within a different economic system:

> [W]e take the motivation of the peasant's economic activity not as that of an entrepreneur who as a result of investment of his capital receives the difference between gross income and production overheads, but rather as the motivation of the worker on a peculiar piece-rate system which allows him alone to determine the time and intensity of his work. (1966: 42)

Here the household is the unit of production and consumption. Household production decisions do not entail the standard categories of capitalist firms—wages, profits, return to capital—but are based on the satisfaction of household consumption desires mediated by the noxiousness (the inverse of productivity) of the work necessary to produce the goods to do so. This is not a universal economy that characterizes all times and places, but rather one where households are the units of production and consumption.

Rather than the expanding logic of capitalist production, household economic production is one of limited goals derived from the balance between what people would like to have versus the difficulty of the labor entailed in achieving those consumption goals. Chayanov began his determination of household need with the number of people they must support and the workers available to do so—this is the basis of Sahlins's Chayanov's Rule. However, for Chayanov, unlike Sahlins's statement of Chayanov's Rule, the relationship between the number of consumers to support and the amount each worker needs to produce is not linear. Factors that affect household need include taxes, rents (Wolf's [1966: 5–6] rent fund), and prices of products they need but cannot produce while those affecting productivity include prices for their products, access to markets, soil condition, and technology (Durrenberger 1980b: 137–39). In addition to external demands, households also had to produce enough to maintain and replace production equipment (Wolf's [1966: 5–6] replacement fund). The dependency ratio was but one among many factors in Chayanov's writing (see below).

Chayanov's theory does not rest on any assumptions about market involvement or access to land. In fact, he discusses the role of alternatives to agriculture such as wage work and craft production. Chayanov argued that peasants will follow alternatives to agriculture if they result in a more favorable balance of labor and need (1966: 108–9; Durrenberger 1984a). In no sense is Chayanov's theory limited either to the particular empirical conditions of Russia from the freeing of the serfs to the New Economic Program or even to agriculture. Chayanov's goal was a general theory of household economics (Tannenbaum 1984b).

Chayanov, Household Economies, and the Explanation of Economic Systems

Durrenberger was led to Chayanov's original argument from Sahlins's Chayanov's Rule when his analysis of the economic systems of Lisu, an upland group in Northern Thailand, in terms of Sahlins's Chayanov's Rule produced anomalies (Durrenberger 1998). The profiles of domestic production for four nearby Lisu villages differed considerably. If the deviations of the actual allocations of labor from the expected allocations are a measure of the "economic coefficient of a given social system," how could villages of the same region, the same culture, the same political and social institutions exhibit such very different empirical lines? Why?

The answer was ecological. In constructing these profiles, Durrenberger had looked only at rice production, not the full subsistence pattern, which included opium production as an important element. As a village stayed in an area longer, the people exhausted its capacity to produce rice by swidden agriculture, and turned increasingly to the more sustainable opium production to supply the wherewithal to purchase rice from the lowlands. Durrenberger needed a more realistic conceptualization of household production, that would account for such variation through the incorporation of the full range of production rather than relying on a single subsistence crop as Sahlins did (1971, 1972).

To gain that, Durrenberger went backwards from Sahlins to Chayanov and worked out the algebra of the intersection of the curves of drudgery and usefulness that Chayanov discussed as the determinants that put the ceiling on domestic production. Durrenberger then computed how much each Lisu household should produce if what they did was consistent with Chayanov's logic (1980b: 140–43; 1984b: 40–46). The theoretically derived production targets were highly correlated with each household's actual days of labor or the area of land they used or the amount of rice and opium they produced (see Durrenberger 1980b: 143; 1984b: 46).

Durrenberger took Sahlins at his word when he wrote in the operational mode (1972: 102) that "to avoid a sustained discourse on generalities, to give some promise of applicability and verification, it is necessary first to attempt some measure of the impact of concrete social systems upon domestic production." Having operationalized Chayanov's production targets, it is possible to ask what affects them *aside* from the ratio of consumers to workers. Answering this question gives a very precise answer to the economic consequences of any social or political system by showing just what the consequences are and how people bear them in their work.

Tannenbaum had begun to work with Durrenberger and they needed quantitative data to test and develop these theoretical ideas but could find no other published data that were comparable in detail to the Lisu material. Some authors aggregated data in ways that made it tantalizingly suggestive, but not useful. There were some unpublished data. To test hypotheses he had developed and further develop what seemed to be a promising economic theory, Durrenberger returned to Thailand in 1976 to study the economic system of a lowland Shan village in an area he had first visited in 1967. Tannenbaum joined him in the field toward the end of that study, and in 1979 following a research strategy and problem that were quite different from Durrenberger's, Tannenbaum collected the same kinds of data for another year so we had comparable material on the same households for two points in time as well as corresponding data for two different social orders—the egalitarian Lisu and the stratified Shan. In 1990 we collaborated to write *Analytical Perspectives on Shan Agriculture and Village Economics* where we could see and specify the relations among production, exchange, political system, and ideology for Shan and Lisu household production.

Shan production targets computed in Chayanov's terms were correlated with and reasonable predictors of harvests (Durrenberger 1979a, 1979b, 1984b) but Tannenbaum (1982, 1984a), like Donham (1981), found that the apparent homogeneity of the community masked considerable diversity. Tannenbaum showed that Shan farmers operate in one of three production levels: intensified, normal, or minimal. She analyzed not only rice, the major subsistence crop, but all other crops whether produced for sale or not, as well as all sources of income of any kind, and suggested ways of incorporating these differences into the computations of production goals. A comparison of Lisu and the three Shan production levels shows that each Lisu worker's intensity of labor is close to that of the normal production group of Shan.

Chayanov's analysis accounted for the limits to production, how the ceiling on what a household was willing to produce was calculated. The comparison of Shan and Lisu show that the political and social systems also affect the limits on production. We found that the formula that best predicts production for highlanders underpredicts for Shan, while the formula that best characterizes Shan overpredicts for highlanders. As Sahlins suggests, and Dove (1984) points out for Kantu' swiddeners, Lisu operate in a system in which the highest levels of production (per household) and levels of marginal utility are reserved to those in the worst consumer/worker ratio positions. Other households, with lower consumer/worker ratios, having less urgent curves of marginal utility that decline faster, engage in lower levels of production. Why do households in more favorable positions, those with low consumer/worker ratios, work less than possible? The standard for work is not based on what households in the *most* favorable position *could* do but rather on what households in the *worst* position are *able* to do. This standard makes it possible for all households to participate at approximately the same level in the system of reciprocal exchanges. This is possible only because low ratio households do not produce at their capacity.

Not only are Lisu production levels constrained by the same factors as constrain Shan production, but the households in the best positions to produce more, having less urgent utility curves, do not overproduce. Shan operate only in terms of the single constraint of the equilibrium between drudgery and utility. Why are there different Chayanovian equations for computing production levels for Lisu and Shan so that Lisu underproduce relative to Shan while Shan overproduce relative to Lisu?

Over- and underproduction have different consequences in different political-economic systems. In rank societies, prestige aspirations motivate overproduction to create wealth to exchange for prestige. In egalitarian societies, overproduction is a threat to balanced reciprocity. If households overproduce, they can give more away to obligate others to a degree which the recipients cannot repay. In state systems, controlled access to productive resources and power reinforces unequal access and separates a class of nonproducers who have political and economic power from a class of producers without power. As McGough (1984) pointed out, in states those without power overproduce to support those with power.

The acceptable range of variation in production is narrower for Lisu than Shan. Lisu households need to produce enough to feed their households and participate in reciprocal exchanges—not much more and not much less. There are powerful incentives such as ostracism, migration, and assassination that limit overproduction for the egalitarian Lisu, but for Shan, with their nonreciprocal exchange, there are none (Durrenberger 1976a, 1979a, 1979b, 1981). Shan try to produce enough to meet their goals, whether of sufficiency, of meeting the community's standard of living, or of accumulation beyond consumption and social needs to establish the basis for normal production in the future. A household producing intensely that does not succeed in meeting these increased goals will have to continue to work hard for another year. A household producing at the normal level that fails to meet its production goals will either intensify production or slip into the minimal level. Minimal households that fail remain in the minimal level and increase their dependency on other households. Failing to meet the community's standard of living or temporarily overproducing does not affect the household's status in the community. Continued failure to meet the community's standards does affect the household's status. Nevertheless, as members of relatively poor communities embedded in a state political system, Shan villagers have limited political power and there are no political implications to either under- or overproduction.

The major difference between the upland and lowland systems is the different political-economic systems. The egalitarian form of social relations defines the limits to Lisu production. There are no such limits for Shan and, therefore, no political consequences for different production levels. The differences in the Chayanovian equations reflect this. The basic logic of the Chayanovian calculations remains the same—the level of production is given by the intersection of the drudgery and utility curves. Score one for the marginalists. However, the factors that affect the utility curves differ given the different political and economic settings. The social relations of production and the ideology that inform production goals must be incorporated into the drudgery and utility analysis. Score one for the substantivists.

We used Chayanov's theoretical constructs, along with those of Sahlins and others, to develop understandings of the dynamics of individual households. We have also shown, via the arguments necessary to develop those understandings, that one must understand the political economy, which provides the context for household operation. We have shown that these two endeavors provide a foundation for answering the questions anthropologists typically ask of ideology, culture, custom, ritual, symbolism, and their relationships with the concrete realities of economic life.

Sloganeers may wonder whether this is production oriented or circulationist. Clearly, if the forms of production change—as between swidden and irrigated agriculture in these examples—the political economy changes, with all of the implications for ideology, practice, and religion. Equally clearly, if there is limited access to lowland markets in the highlands, production is based on coalitions built around prestigious or chiefly households, but if there is unlimited access to lowland markets, households are the units of production and the political system is relatively egalitarian.

Chayanov, Sahlins, and Chayanov's Rule

Cook (1985) points out that before Sahlins formulated "Chayanov's rule" many students of peasants knew of Chayanov from the 1966 translation of Chayanov's works. Still, it was Sahlins (1971, 1972) who first made theoretical use of Chayanov's concepts in economic anthropology. A review of citations in the *Annual Review of Anthropology* from its inception in 1972 suggests that most anthropologists appreciate Chayanov's work in terms of Sahlins's uses of it.

Sahlins wanted to explore the impact of social and political relationships on production. To determine this, he developed "Chayanov's Rule" to describe an ideal case where each household produced only for itself and there were no social or political relationships that would affect production. To review, Chayanov's Rule states that the "greater the relative working capacity of the household the less its members work" (Sahlins 1972: 87) or "the intensity of labor per worker will increase in direct relation to the domestic ratio of consumers to workers" (1972: 102). By taking this abstraction, translating it into local terms, calculating the difference between the ideal production levels and what people actually produced, one could see the impact of social and political relationships on production.

Sahlins argued that we can locate each household on a graph, first along a horizontal line that specifies the ratio of consumers to workers, then along another vertical axis that specifies how hard people work. There should be a straight line from a minimum where each worker supports only himself or herself to the heavy work demands of whatever the maximum dependency ratio might be. Return to the graph and locate each household on the vertical axis that indicates labor according to how much each worker *actually* works. Then construct the line that best fits the points for all the households and compute its difference from the theoretical line. The extent that the two lines are dissimilar is the measure of the economic consequences of the sociopolitical system in place and illustrates to what extent other things are not equal in fact. The deviations of the actual allocations of labor from the expected allocations are a measure of the "economic coefficient of a given social system." The location of the points relative to the Chayanov line shows who bears those costs (see Evans 1974 for significance tests of the difference between the ideal abstract line and what people actually do; see Durrenberger 1976b for a computer program to calculate the lines and determine whether the lines are significantly different).

Sahlins argued that we could construct a profile for the amount of work we should expect each worker to do with "a few statistical data not difficult to collect in the field" (1972: 103). Whatever else Sahlins was right about, he was wrong about the data being easy to collect in the field. We suspect that is why there is so little of it, even today. The brilliance of Sahlins's work is in its promise of a quantifiable and comparative economic anthropology; an economic anthropology that can move beyond the overly theorized maximizers of the formalists and the hyperrelativism of the substantivists to conceptualize economies as social processes with political causes as well as consequences for world views, religions, and policies.

Others have followed Sahlins's lead and used departures from the Chayanov line as a way of posing questions about and analyzing social, historical, and political relations of single communities. Lewis (1981) located the production per worker of each social unit relative to a Chayanov line for sorghum and millet farmers in central Mali. He used both the indicated underproduction and overproduction to formulate an analysis of labor availability and the organization of production and show the importance of lineages in controlling "two key elements of social reproduction—food production and marriage" (70).

Donham (1981) developed a similar approach to Malle in Ethiopia to frame an ethnographic description of the control of labor in local politics. Saul (1986: 763) asked whether such a procedure is a rather roundabout way to observe these differences, but Donham suggests that Sahlins's way of framing the questions forces a rigorous analysis of an apparently egalitarian and uncomplicated organization of production. Donham concludes that neoclassical analyses *assume* answers to questions of history, power, and ideology which a Marxist or any other alternative approach must *comprehend* (Donham 1981: 538). It was in just this sense that Tannenbaum (1984b) meant that "together, Chayanov and Marx provide a full account of the peasant economy." Marx provides an account of political economy within which to contextualize an understanding of the organization and process of production. It was this position that Durrenberger summarized in his (1996) HRAF article on economic anthropology.

Dove (1984) analyzed the economy of Kantu' of western Kalimantan in similar terms. While the slope of the empirical least squares regression line for intensity of labor and consumer/worker ratio is almost identical with the Chayanov line computed as Sahlins does, there are remarkable departures which Dove explains in terms of the organization of production and uses of labor. High ratio houses hire labor to intensify their labor and low ratio households which need to deintensify their labor sell their labor to even out fluctuations in their domestic economies (1984: 113).

McGough (1984) explained nonstandard forms of Chinese marriage and adoption as ways to adjust household composition to fixed areas of land available to households. He argues for a more detailed understanding of power relations within the household. Instead of understanding households as units, we should examine, for instance, the exploitation of females by males. Moving beyond the typical interest in the consumer/ worker ratio, McGough points out that states force household production beyond internal needs and such demands as the payment of taxes and rents must be converted into parts of a "consumer" in the calculation of consumer/worker ratio as sources of demand.

While they do not develop an analysis of political economy, Munroe et al. (1984) show that the work of children in four societies (Logoli in Kenya, Garifuna in Belize, Newars in Nepal, and Samoans in American Samoa) is related to the consumer/worker ratios of their households in accordance with Chayanov's Rule (371). Their definition of labor includes domestic chores and "all instrumental activities judged to contribute to the maintenance of the household or to the well-being of its members" (369). Neither the mothers' nor fathers' work is correlated with consumer/ worker ratios, perhaps because children do the work necessitated by higher ratios, which is suggested by the negative correlation between the level of children's work and that of their parents. The authors suggest that counting children as potential workers in the computation of the consumer/ worker ratio might affect the correlations, but they had data for work of children between three and nine years of age only. This study is one of few that makes theoretical use of Chayanov's insights and brings empirical evidence to bear on them. It expands the questions to include considerations of definitions of work, the actual contribution of children to households, and the details of the organization of production.

Conclusions

Maclachlan (1987: 4) attributes the "near immediate popularity among economic anthropologists" of Chayanov's work after it was translated to two practices which American anthropologists enjoy: the revelation of reasons behind seemingly irrational behavior, and the criticism of conventional economics. It is perhaps ironic that Maclachlan's is one of three papers to cite Chayanov in a volume from the Society for Economic Anthropology entitled *Household Economies and Their Transformations*. In spite of Chayanov's anthropologist-pleasing approach, economic anthropologists have not embraced Chayanov's theory. At best most, in the empiricist mode, have flirted with correlations of the consumer/worker ratio with production per worker that do not test Chayanov's analysis.

One possible reason is the data requirement for Chayanovian analyses. While the data is not difficult to collect in principle, in practice it requires detailed economic surveys to track labor inputs, income, and expenditures for at least one complete agricultural cycle. Anthropologists may be unwilling to commit themselves to both the time and detail this requires. Such detailed long-term surveys demand either a fair level of native language skills or an assistant interpreter to help with it. This may be difficult when anthropologists must learn the language in the field and where funding agencies are not willing to support assistants.

Chayanov's theory may not fit what economic anthropologists consider appropriate theory. Theoretical debates in economic anthropology tend toward arguments about the appropriate application of broader theories—standard economics, Marxist, cultural ecology, development. One argument was the formalist-substantivist debate and whether economies could be understood in marginalist economic terms or were so embedded in other aspects of the society so it was impossible to study the economy as a separate system. Other arguments in economic anthropology are about data and such issues as testing Chayanov's Rule. There is little middle-level theory dealing with one kind of economy and linking this theory to particular cases.

We think that Chayanov is a truly appropriate middle-level theory with a clearly developed set of assumptions about the relationship of production to other social and economic variables that are capable of being defined in appropriate cultural, ecological, and historical terms. While we do not presume to suggest that all economic anthropologists embrace it, we do wish that they would embrace this level of theorizing.

Richard Wilk (1996) suggests that the theoretical trends he discusses—maximizing individuals, sociological conformity, and cultural—may be folk models, explanations people offer to rationalize their own behavior. As he puts it: "I did it to help others; I did it for myself; I did it because it was right and proper" (1996: 147). He argues that we should question human motives rather than assume them. He suggests that we find out what makes human nature rational—that we not force diverse motives into discrete boxes but admit mixed, multiple, and ambiguous motives (1996: 147)—and distinguishes conflicting rationalities for the intersections of different time scales from the immediate to the infinite graphed with the size of the social group from the individual to all of humanity. Whatever the merits of his solution, the definition of the problem calls attention to the possibility that some of our analytic categories and approaches are projections of our own proclivities, just as they are in the study of religion when we project the concept of belief from state religions onto the practices of nonstate social orders (Durrenberger 1980a). Similarly, it is plausible that anthropologists, embedded in the institutional structure for the certification, creation, and recreation of the middle class, the University, with it's ideology if not practice of meritocratic individualism (Newman 1988, 1993) for both students and faculty, project that ideology onto the rest of the world as "agency" (Durrenberger and Erem 1997) and subscribe to the abstractionist assumptions of methodological individualism that Halperin (1994) inveighs against.

The antimarginalist Sahlins was a vehicle to introduce the marginalist Chayanov to anthropologists in the United States. Some have used Sahlins's formulation of Chayanov's concepts as he suggested, to develop evidence of the material consequences of social and political relationships and then have used this evidence as the basis of analyses of the social and political order. We have taken Chayanov's concept of the on-farm balance as central and developed descriptions of household production in such terms. These descriptions provide evidence for the way households fit into the material realities of their economic, social, and political systems, as evidence of the impact of such arrangements on households. To paraphrase McGough (1984), a household in the Chinese state system has an invisible consumer, perhaps more demanding than most, which census takers are unlikely to enumerate. We have shown where this consumer is and how it affects households. This, we think, is the theoretical potential of Chayanov.

George Dalton (1974) asked how, exactly, peasants were exploited. William Roseberry answered that they are exploited by nonproducers' appropriations of a portion of their product (1976). Both Sahlins's Chayanov's Rule and the calculation of the on-farm equilibrium point show not only precisely how peasants are exploited, but just how much and how that relates to other sources of demand. In his 1973 synthesis, Scott Cook suggested that "the discipline of economic anthropology has not yet reached a stage in its development conducive to a concise, integrated, and uniformly accepted definition of its scope" but in spite of disagreement about many issues, he saw unifying themes and proposed "that economic anthropology is rapidly approaching the threshold of scientific unity" (801). In his studies of domestic production among Oaxacan metate producers and their relationships to an embracing capitalist system, Cook (1982: 4) came to appreciate a number of limitations of the substantivist and formalist approaches in economic anthropology. He summarized them as:

1. a tendency to reduce explanations of complex processes involving interrelated and contradictory variables to descriptions of isolated events;

2. a tendency to explain economic process at the empirical level and a failure to develop any conceptual framework to expose underlying social dynamics;

3. a pervasive focus on individual agents; and

4. an almost completely "circulationist" view of the economy.

He also discusses the inability of economic anthropologists in the United States to understand and use theoretical propositions (Cook 1982: 349–51). Tannenbaum's (1984a) study of anthropologists' use of Chayanov's concepts in the United States underscored Cook's conclusion. She concluded (1984a: 940) that misuses of Chayanov's ideas are part of a more general trend of conceptual distortion, preference for method over theoretical reflection, and an empiricist outlook that equates statistical summaries with theory and attempts to develop theories from "data."

It is perhaps ironic that in this review of Chayanov's reception and use in the United States we find ourselves in agreement with Cook (1973, 1984), who at times seems to disagree with the whole Chayanovian enterprise, at times cites him with approval, and at times uses some of his ideas to frame a Marxist analysis. He has adduced detailed ethnographic data and interpreted them in theoretical terms, always trying to bring the concrete to bear on the abstract and bring the abstract down to earth. He is using a complex set of theoretical concepts in an intellectual environment that does not appreciate them. While he may not relish being cited in this context, we think his appreciation of economic anthropology in the United States is appropriate if for no other reason than that Tannenbaum (1984a) reached similar conclusions when she analyzed the misunderstandings and misuses of Chayanov's ideas.

Some will continue to stumble on citations to Chayanov in computer searches of literature and cite him in a generic way to show their thoroughness. Supposing they are evaluating Chayanov's theory, some will

ιe consumer/worker ratio and
ιisinterpret his concepts. Some
ing the economic consequences
Sahlins and Chayanov. Some
γanov's and contextualize them

ιic anthropologists may do to
Wilk (1996) that the real hope
ldress key problems and issues
with global corporations to the
to the connections a system of
)ur scholarship is engaged with
real uses, not just for thinking
but for thinking about a wired
th millions of destitute ex-farm-
ifference (Wilk 1996, 153).
tion of eclectic observation. In
. When we see them producing
we want to know how they re-
itical, and economic systems,
ʔe source of ideas and insights.

rner, B. Kerblay, and R. E. F. Smith,
c Association.

in Theory, Method and Analysis."
ral Anthropology, J. Honigmann, ed.
Chicago: Rand McNally.
1982   *Zapotec Stone Workers: The Dynamics of Rural Simple Commodity Production
in Modern Mexico.* Washington, D.C.: University Press of America.
1984   "Peasant Economy, Rural Industry, and Capitalist Development in the
Oaxaca Valley, Mexico." *Journal of Peasant Studies* 12(1): 3–40.
1985   Review of *Chayanov, Peasants and Economic Anthropology*, E. Paul
Durrenberger, ed. *American Ethnologist* 12(1): 157–58.
Dalton, George
1974   "How Exactly are Peasants 'Exploited'?" *American Anthropologist* 76: 553–
61.
Donham, Donald
1981   "Beyond the Domestic Mode of Production." *Man* 16(4): 515–41.
Dove, Michael
1984   "The Chayanov Slope in a Swidden Society: Household Demography and
Extensive Agriculture in West Kalimantan." Pp. 97–132 in *Chayanov, Peasants,*

and *Economic Anthropology*, E. Paul Durrenberger, ed. San Francisco: Academic Press.

Durrenberger, E. Paul

1976a "The Economy of a Lisu Village." *American Ethnologist* 3: 633–44.

1976b "A Program for Computing Sahlins's Social Profile of Domestic Production and Related Statistics." *Behavior Science Research* 11(1): 19–23.

1979a "Rice Production in a Lisu Village." *Journal of Southeast Asian Studies* 10: 139–45.

1979b "An Analysis of Shan Household Production Decisions." *Journal of Anthropological Research* 35: 447–58.

1980a "Belief and the Logic of Lisu Spirits." *Bijdragen tot de taal-, Land-en Volkenkunde* 136: 21–40.

1980b "Chayanov's Economic Analysis in Anthropology." *Journal of Anthropological Research* 36: 133–48.

1981 "The Economy of a Shan Village." *Ethnos* 46: 64–79.

1984a "Introduction." Pp. 1–25 in *Chayanov, Peasants, and Economic Anthropology*, E. Paul Durrenberger, ed. San Francisco: Academic Press.

1984b "Operationalizing Chayanov." Pp. 39–50 in *Chayanov, Peasants, and Economic Anthropology*, E. Paul Durrenberger, ed. San Francisco: Academic Press.

1996 "Economic Anthropology." Pp. 365–71 in *Encyclopedia of Cultural Anthropology*, David Levinson and Melvin Ember, eds. Human Relations Area Files. Lakeville, Conn.: American Reference Publishing Co.

1998 "A Shower of Rain: Marshall Sahlins's Stone Age Economics Twenty-five Years Later." *Culture and Agriculture* 20(2/3): 102–6.

2000 "Power, Culture, and Knowledge: Comparative Studies of Corporate Structures." *Anthropology of Work Review* 20(2): 35–39.

Durrenberger, E. Paul, and S. Erem

1997 "The Dance of Power: Ritual and Agency among Unionized American Health Care Workers." *American Anthropologist* 99(3): 489–94.

Durrenberger, E. Paul, and N. Tannenbaum

1979 "A Reassessment of Chayanov and His Recent Critics." *Peasant Studies* 8: 48–63.

1990 *Analytical Perspectives on Shan Agriculture and Village Economics*. Southeast Asia Monograph Series. New Haven, Conn.: Yale University Press.

Evans, Martin

1974 "A Note on the Measurement of Sahlins' Social Profile of Domestic Production." *American Ethnologist* 1: 269–79.

Geertz, Clifford

1973 *Interpretation of Cultures*. New York: Basic Books.

Gudeman, Stephen

1978 *The Demise of a Rural Economy: From Subsistence to Capitalism in a Latin American Village*. London: Routledge & Kegan Paul.

Halperin, Rhoda

1994 *Cultural Economies: Past and Present*. Austin: University of Texas Press.

Kuznar, Lawrence

1997 *Reclaiming a Scientific Anthropology*. Walnut Creek, Calif.: AltaMira Press.

Lave, Jean
  1988   *Cognition in Practice.* Cambridge: Cambridge University Press.
Lewis, John Van D.
  1981   "Domestic Labor Intensity and the Incorporation of Malian Peasant Farmers into Localized Descent Groups." *American Ethnologist* 8(1): 53–73.
Maclachlan, Morgan D.
  1987   "From Intensification to Proletarianization." Pp. 1–27 in *Household Economies and Their Transformations,* Morgan D. Maclachlan, ed. Lanham, Md.: University Press of America.
McGough, James P.
  1984   "The Domestic Mode of Production and Peasant Social Organization: The Chinese Case." Pp. 183–201 in *Chayanov, Peasants, and Economic Anthropology,* E. Paul Durrenberger, ed. San Francisco: Academic Press.
Munroe, Ruth H., Robert L. Munroe, and Harold S. Shimmin
  1984   "Children's Work in Four Cultures: Determinants and Consequences." *American Anthropologist* 86(2): 369–79.
Newman, Katherine S.
  1988   *Falling from Grace: Experience of Downward Mobility in the American Middle Class.* New York: The Free Press.
  1993   *Declining Fortunes: The Withering of the American Dream.* New York: Basic Books.
Roseberry, William
  1976   "Rent, Differentiation, and the Development of Capitalism among Peasants." *American Anthropologist* 78(1): 45–58.
Sahlins, Marshall
  1971   "The Intensity of Domestic Production in Primitive Societies: Societal Inflections of the Chayanov Slope." Pp. 30–51 in *Studies in Economic Anthropology,* G. Dalton ed. Washington D. C.: American Anthropological Association.
  1972   *Stone Age Economics.* Chicago: Aldine.
Saul, Mahir
  1986   Review of *Chayanov, Peasants, and Economic Anthropology,* E. Paul Durrenberger, ed. *American Anthropologist* 88(3): 762–63.
Tannenbaum, Nicola
  1982   "Agricultural Decision Making among the Shan of Maehongson Province, Northwestern Thailand." Ph.D. dissertation, University of Iowa.
  1984a   "The Misuse of Chayanov: 'Chayanov's Rule' and Empiricist Bias in Anthropology." *American Anthropologist* 86: 927–42.
  1984b   "Chayanov and Economic Anthropology." Pp. 27–38 in *Chayanov, Peasants, and Economic Anthropology,* E. Paul Durrenberger, ed. San Francisco: Academic Press.
Wilk, Richard
  1996   *Economies and Cultures.* Boulder: Westview Press.
Wolf, Eric R.
  1966   *Peasants.* Englewood Cliffs, N.J.: Prentice-Hall.

Chapter 8

Space, Place, and Economic Anthropology: Locating Potters in a Sri Lankan Landscape

Deborah Winslow

Over the past two decades, the literature on space and place has mush-roomed impressively. This expanding field now encompasses an extensive, interdisciplinary gamut that runs from photographers to sociologists study-ing street gangs to retail marketing specialists, while still including the more predictable geographers, anthropologists, archaeologists, and histo-rians. Theoretically as varied as the questions they ask, space and place writers include those who emphasize postmodernist fragmentation and deterritorializations (Appadurai 1996; Clifford 1997); others who insist that grand theory (particularly that of Marx and Gramsci) remains crucial for understanding the changing territoriality of the contemporary world of flexible accumulation (Harvey 1990); as well as those concerned with more immediate materialities of built environments, political geographies, and other aspects of the spatial realization of human social and cultural life (Blanton 1994; Feld and Basso 1996; Hayden 1995; Mitchell 1988; Sack 1986).

As I have tried to connect these studies with my own research into world and national influences on economic change among rural pottery makers in Sri Lanka, I have found landscape studies, a subgenre of the space and place field, particularly and rather unexpectedly useful. As it turns out, landscape studies have developed far beyond the regional ge-ographies with which I long had associated the term, to include a variety of cultural, social, and political, as well as geographic, positionings. Un-derstanding how the potters are situated in multidimensional local, regional, and national landscapes helps us to understand why they have prospered in recent years and why they have made the choices they have

155

about what to do with their new wealth. This has led me to disagree with Geertz for his suggestion that place theorists should concentrate on local studies. "Place," Geertz once wrote, "makes a poor abstraction. Separated from its materializations, it has little meaning" (Geertz 1996: 259). Certainly it is important to know, as he puts it, "what it means to be here rather than there" (Geertz 1996: 262), but part of being here is a sense of there, that is, a sense of how one's place fits within larger systems of places. Furthermore, it frequently is this larger system on which, or in relation to which, the people we are studying, such as the Sri Lankan potters, want to act.

Thus, one virtue of landscape studies is that they incorporate simultaneously both *here* and *there*. For economic anthropologists in particular, they can complement the regional systems (Skinner 1964; Smith 1976) and capitalist world systems (Wallerstein 1974) approaches with which many of us first framed our studies of the extralocal. By connecting economic patterns with social and cultural ones, as well as clarifying the ways in which people actively locate and relocate themselves, albeit in landscapes only partially of their own making, the landscape approach provides an integrating way of bridging local and larger frames of analysis. However, different landscape theorists tend to focus on either the material *or* the cultural *or* the social aspects of landscape practice. Here, I argue that the real potential of this approach lies in the ways in which these different aspects can be integrated.

The importance of such integration was brought home to me when I first presented the results of my studies of rural Sri Lankan potters to a group of Sri Lankan scholars. They immediately were skeptical of my tales of rising potter incomes and educational achievements. When I mentioned where the potters lived, in the far reaches of the Kurunegala district, they were downright amused. "Those [Kurunegala] people," one archaeologist said, "they are *pre-modern*." A historian added, "They might even be *Indians* [that is, recent immigrants], you can't say." Clearly, elite preconceptions of potters in rural Kurunegala were hard to get around: In the elite landscape, the potters are preplaced—where they live is who they have to be; if they do not conform, then perhaps they are another sort of people altogether. Remoteness, ruralness, low casteness, and low classness all work together as a single cultural construction. While the elite evince admiration for the cultural authenticity of such places and the people in them, it is as idealized representatives of a glorified, precolonial national past (Woost 1990), not as localities inhabited by cultural contemporaries. A change in class position was unfathomable given where they lived and what they did for a living. Therefore, it should have come as no surprise to me that at least some of the potters believe that to translate their substantial economic gains into social ones, they have to reposition themselves in their local cultural geography in ways that others will interpret as the potters' wish.

Space, Place, and Landscape

Landscape observations are not new to anthropologists, but until lately there were few who incorporated landscape as an active analytical variable. More typically, ethnographers made introductory references to surroundings to engage readers and to locate themselves convincingly in the scene (Hirsch 1995: 1–2; Geertz 1988: 4–5): "Imagine yourself set down . . . ," as Malinowski so famously began; and "Hiking down from the forests and scattered swiddens of the Meratus Mountains . . . I came," as Tsing opens a more recent book (Malinowski 1961 [1922]: 4; Tsing 1993: 5).[1] The term landscape has the disadvantage that it has already at least two conventional meanings: (1) "a painterly way of seeing the world that creates a picturesque view" (Duncan 1995: 414) or just the paintings of such views, in which sense landscape has a specific European and class history (Hirsch 1995: 2–3); and (2) "a portion of a natural and cultural environment" (Duncan 1995: 414), as in the phrase, "landscape gardener." These common usages do not integrate local and larger spatial systems because they imply a distanced viewer, who might, for example, pause to admire the old fishing shack on the Maine coast or draw up a "landscaping" plan.[2]

But recently a number of scholars concerned with theorizing place have argued for a more inclusive sense of landscape, what Ingold calls a "dwelling perspective," in which place is not just constructed, politically, culturally, and otherwise, but also is inhabited (Ingold 1993: 152; also, Werlen 1993). Ingold observes:

> The landscape, in short, is not a totality that you or anyone else can look at, it is rather the world *in* which we stand in taking up a point of view on our surroundings. (Ingold 1993: 171, his emphasis)

Ingold argues that human actions always are undertaken in relation to other actions—perhaps steps in a procedure or parts of a regular cycle, all involving movement over time and through space. This people-centered sense of landscape is thus inherently active and temporal, an ongoing process rather than a static "thing." Ingold's formulation opens up the possibility of different sizes and levels of spatial systems: the daily round at home versus periodic marketing trips, bride-scouting visits, or pilgrimages elsewhere, for example. Because it is holistic, historical, and relative, the dwelling perspective helps to bring together local, regional, and extralocal systems while still retaining a human viewpoint.

Eric Hirsch, in his introduction to a collection of articles on the anthropology of landscape, adds one more aspect to this lived-in world: the dimension of possibility, what is not actually present in the landscape but potentially could or even should be. For example, the potters whom I study in Sri Lanka recently planted in their village a sapling from the Great Bo Tree at Anuradhapura, itself allegedly grown from a sapling of the Bo Tree under which Buddha achieved enlightenment. The potters' scrawny tree is unimpressive in itself, but to those who understand its significance, it manifests in the village the power of both distant trees, connecting these local potters in time and space to two levels of a larger Buddhist system as well as a Sri Lankan discourse of Buddhist nationalism (Nissan 1988). Hirsch describes this phenomenon as the relationship between a foreground and a background:

> Landscape is a process in so far as men and women attempt to realize in the foreground what can only be a potentiality and for the most part in the background. Foreground actuality and background potentiality exist in a process of mutual implication. (Hirsch 1995: 22–23)

Hirsch's sense of the dynamism of landscape is different than Ingold's, but the two appear complementary. Ingold's landscape is a consequence of the movement of people over and through the terrain and all it contains. As they move in work and other human social and cultural activities, they relate to other people and other places, other times that were and will be, here and there. Although Ingold does not say so specifically, it seems obvious that these understandings and movements will vary with age, gender, class, and other social distinctions. Hirsch tends, I think, to distance people from their landscapes a bit more (and perhaps too much, in that they emerge sometimes as very conscious landscape constructors), yet his emphasis on background potentiality brings out an important dimension. Like the Sri Lankan potters who wrote careful letters to the authorities to obtain their Bo Tree sapling, people act not only habitually but also innovatively through changing senses of possibility—I do not think the potters consciously entertained even the desire for this tree in the 1970s, when I began my research—in ways that both reflect and change their lived-in worlds.

A recent book by Tilley brings together some of these considerations (Tilley 1994). Tilley writes within a contemporary school of archaeology sometimes labeled "post-processual" (Fleming 1995), although Tilley himself does not use the term here. He does argue that archaeologists should pay more attention to meaning and agency and not simply collect spatial data, map it, and then look for a "spatial process" to explain it (Tilley 1994: 9). Some critics deplore what they see as Tilley's rejection of science, of any possibility of really knowing the past (Lekson 1996: 890), but this study, which is simultaneously systematic, materially focused, *and* interpretive, seems to me a compelling attempt to do just that.

In *A Phenomenology of Landscape*, Tilley contends that landscape perception needs to be taken into account in order to understand how Neolithic people chose sites to construct megaliths in Wales and southern England. He observes that when we approach the monuments on foot in open country, as Neolithic people must have done, we can appreciate the degree to which these enormous constructions alter the landscape by their very presence. Therefore, even if we cannot actually know what they perceived, we can be certain that Neolithic people lived in a different landscape than did the Mesolithic foragers who came before them and who left behind little but footpaths and stone tool flakes. Tilley suggests that this changed perception may even have been the point. He notes that many of the megaliths have quite small internal chambers (so would have had only a minor role as burial sites) and are not centrally located in important territories (that they might thus claim). But by their location and orientation they point to significant natural features that differentiate one piece of territory from another. Over time, as the monuments became more standardized, they also seem increasingly to have been constructed in relation to each other.[3]

Tilley underlines the fact that Neolithic monument builders were working in a previously encultured landscape. Their world was, as the phenomenologist Edward Casey put it, "bedecked in places; . . . a place-world to begin with" (Casey 1996: 43). Neolithic tombs and long barrows are found in the same places where the Mesolithic flint scatters are found, and when one is missing, so is the other (Tilley 1994: 205). But the Neolithic people, who herded cattle, required secure access to grazing lands as they moved seasonally along paths made permanent by the passing of hooves and, presumably engaged in more complex social relationships, transformed the face and the meaning of this long-inhabited landscape through their different activities, including the building of megaliths (Tilley 1994, esp. 202–8).

Fashioning the landscape, indirectly as they followed their herds and more directly as they built their monuments (like the potters and their Bo Tree), Neolithic people slowly changed the encultured landscape they received. As Ingold suggested, the landscape is not a world "looked at," but a world "lived in," as people moved between specific places within it. Some of the changes were produced simply by these movements, particularly, Tilley suggests, the permanent trails cut by cattle hooves, which created divisions where none had been before; other changes were produced deliberately by the construction of monoliths, which would have required repeated strategizing and acting on a sense of landscape potential, not unlike the potters and their Bo Tree.

Given Tilley's interpretive approach, it is interesting that the causality underlying his analysis is largely economic: a change in subsistence from foraging to herding. The economy plays itself out in an encultured physical world, a landscape in all its dimensions, but the motor force of landscape change is the conversion of one sort of movement in space to another sort because of the subsistence shift. It is not simply that Neolithic people "had a different culture," but that they actively experienced (and fashioned) the world in a different way. This is not to say that their particular response was predetermined: Neolithic herders in the southern Sudan did not construct megaliths (they could not: they had no stone); and Zafimaniry agriculturalists in Madagascar erect megaliths but do not herd (Evans-Pritchard 1940; Bloch 1995). But from Tilley's account we can see megalith construction as both an outcome and a cause of spatially realized social and cultural changes that resulted from subsistence change in a particular context.

The landscape approach tracks people's experiences of space, both physically and conceptually, to define and understand space as an important, universal cultural process.[4] This does not mean that spatial worlds have to be composed solely of landscapes experienced directly. For example, both the anthropologist Arjun Appadurai (1996) and the geographer David Harvey (1990) have developed spatially specific theories of global, postmodern capitalist panoramas that extend far beyond the immediate worlds in which daily life is conducted. Appadurai's approach is more cultural in emphasis, while Harvey's is more economic, but both are of interest to economic anthropologists.

Appadurai begins with the assertion that since the mid-1970s, electronic media and worldwide migration have created transforming "ruptures in the imagination" (1996: 3) and produced new "globalized landscapes." The landscapes have multiple dimensions—people, media, technology, finance, and ideology—each of which Appadurai calls a *-scape* (ethnoscape, mediascape, financescape, technoscape, and ideoscape, respectively). Scapes make up the "building blocks" of "imagined worlds" that tie individuals in relationships beyond the neighborhoods and nation-states in which they reside (Appadurai 1996: 33). This world is fragmented, discontinuous, and heterogeneous: or, in a word, *postmodern*. In it, people are pulled both by various global forces and by the states in which they live, which are increasingly intrusive as they struggle to retain control despite competition from other global entities. But, Appadurai contends, people do not just go with the flow, abandoning their own places and the feelings of connection that come with them. Because locality, as a sense of social immediacy, is a fundamental human quality, people fight to maintain the local neighborhoods and landscapes that produce it (1996: 178ff). Nevertheless, Appadurai's own analytical focus is more on local response to larger-scale forces than on truly local processes (such as those described by Ingold, Hirsch, and Tilley) of locality production. Appadurai writes:

> The capability of neighborhoods to produce contexts . . . and to produce local subjects is profoundly affected by the locality-producing capabilities of larger-scale social formations (nation-states, kingdoms, missionary empires, and trading cartels) to determine the general shape of all the neighborhoods within the reach of their powers. (Appadurai 1996: 187)

We need, I think, to keep in mind that locality production under these conditions is never finished but is rather an ongoing struggle whose outcome may be determined as much by local priorities as by external ones.

Like Appadurai, the geographer Harvey agrees that fragmentation and constant change characterize the modern world, although he asserts that there is "more continuity than difference between the broad history of modernism and the movement called postmodernism" (Harvey 1990: 117; also, Kahn 1997). In contrast to Appadurai, however, Harvey's analysis focuses on the economic roots of the observed changes. Previously, Fordist capitalism emphasized stability, mass production, mass consumption, and intimate management of workers in the work place and at home. In contrast, flexible capitalism, which has held increasing sway since the 1970s, turns on the ability to quickly change products, workers, markets, and tastes, producing the celebration of flexibility that characterizes what Harvey calls the condition of postmodernity (Harvey 1990: 284ff; 1991). Thus Harvey connects the way capitalism has been reinvented since the depression of the 1970s with changes in the way space and time are experienced, arguing that:

> The breaking down and reorganization of spatial barriers has been one of the chief means whereby capitalism has sustained itself in the 20th century. But the shifting social construction of space and time as a result of the restless search for profit creates severe problems of identity: To what space do I as an individual belong? Do I express my idea of citizenship in my neighborhood, city, region, nation, or world? These are the sorts of questions that are being at least partially addressed within the postmodern rhetoric, even when the answers (the passive acceptance of fragmentation, for example) are patently false. (Harvey 1991: 76–77)

Appadurai and Harvey provide different frameworks for a larger landscape analysis of contemporary life. Appadurai's scapes—building blocks of imagined worlds—involve local connection to larger forces. Still, they may be less useful as practical models because they evoke interconnections that they do not specify, even when they relate to such material processes as migration. In contrast, Harvey is so particular and inclusive as to be overwhelming. He strives to encompass both the global reach and technologies of modern capitalism and the spatial realization of daily life (Harvey 1990: 220–21). In this complex approach, imagined spaces (landscapes, fictions, poetics, consumer desires) are complemented by material spatial practices (flows of goods, money, people, transport) and spatial representations (maps, understanding of distances, communications; and personal, community, and national religious spaces). It is a perspective easier to admire than to operationalize and the temptation is always to oversimplify (by evoking an all-powerful globalization, for example).

Therefore, I think that the more localized perspectives of Ingold, Hirsch, and Tilley can be useful as complements to Appadurai and Harvey. And without this correction, Appadurai and Harvey might cause us to see local people as *only* responding to larger forces, as *only* taking their relatively powerless places on the globalized landscape, although I do not think that is what either author intends. Contemporary people, such as the Sri Lankan potters, do move in a world with larger horizons, but they are under no less pressure than Tilley's Neolithic herders to imagine their own landscapes in relation to all the material and social practices and representations in which they participate. Some of these they control, and some, they do not. Nevertheless, the potters confront the spatial representations and localizing practices of larger-scale social formations creatively and in keeping with their own agendas, revealing themselves as more than mere respondents to an external postmodern or post-Fordist world.

Walangama, Sri Lanka

Intermittently over the past twenty-five years, I have been following the lives of people in a small village (current population about 650 people) in central Sri Lanka (map 1). The village's residents are Buddhist, speak the Sinhalese language, and are potters by caste and primary occupation. They produce a wide variety of the terra-cotta cooking and storage vessels used in kitchens throughout rural Sri Lanka. My original 1970s investigation of this village was part of a regional systems analysis that included regional social and cultural systems of deities (Winslow 1984), marriage (Winslow 1994), and weekly markets (Winslow Jackson 1977). One conclusion of this first study was that economic opportunity in Walangama was shaped primarily by its peripheral and disadvantageous regional position (Winslow 1982).

When in 1989, after a thirteen-year hiatus, I visited Walangama briefly to plan future research, I expected their situation to have worsened. Major economic changes, including structural adjustment programs, had been undertaken in Sri Lanka in 1977, just after the conclusion of my first study,

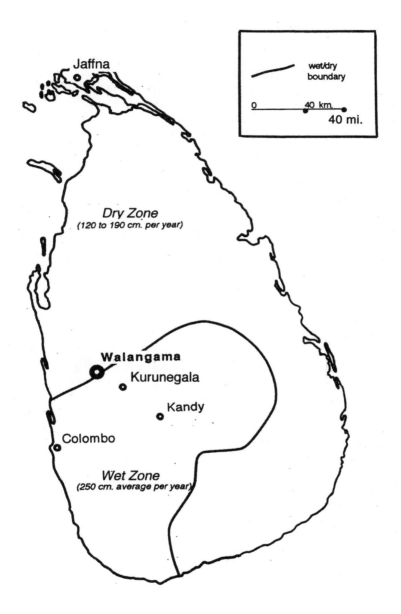

Map 1. Walangama in relation to climate zones of Sri Lanka.

and several subsequent studies (e.g., Sahn 1987) had criticized the new policies for their impact on the poor. Thankfully, my fears were not realized; instead, I was surprised by the village's prosperous appearance: Large new houses abounded and people avidly described how their lives were improving. My sense of Walangama as a struggling, lower-caste artisan village with limited opportunities now seemed irrelevant.

My 1992 restudy confirmed that 1989 impression. Walangama potters are prospering and for four principle reasons: their advantageous location in relation to supplies of clay, fuel, and customers; previous government development programs that taught them to mass produce and market their wares; new government programs that have increased the availability of transport and opportunities for pottery sales; and their own ambitions (Winslow 1996). The result has been that most household incomes have been able to more than keep ahead of the persistent inflation that troubled Sri Lanka through the 1980s and 1990s, and which is so characteristic of newly "opened" economies.

In 1992, the national poverty line was a household income of Rs.750 per month. While I always have found it difficult to get complete household income data, I am certain that, except for elderly women living alone and subsisting in large part on hand-outs from kin, not even the poorest Walangama household had less than Rs.1000 per month and the most industrious made ten times that, incomes exceeding those of school teachers, policemen, and white collar office workers. Such incomes have allowed them to build houses valued upwards of Rs.100,000;[5] to encourage talented children to stay in school through the advanced-level ("A-level") exams; to acquire agricultural land, although fewer and fewer are making this traditional investment choice; and to provide labor and funds in support of community programs such as the construction of a Montessori preschool, the founding of a Buddhist temple, and the expansion of the funeral insurance society. Walangama people today have choices that they did not have in 1975. These choices reveal how they see their futures and what they value, but they also indicate a changed dwelling perspective. As this world has been transformed economically, they, like Tilley's foragers-become-herders, appear to be redefining their local "scapes" and their connections to the nation.[6]

One of the most important choices that village families ever make is the selection of marriage partners for their children. In Walangama, marriages usually are arranged by parents but only after considerable input from the young people involved. Historically, there has been a requirement of caste endogamy and a preference for cross-cousin alliances. Most marriages are patrilocal, with the new couple building their own house in the husband's village, although a matrilocal variant is followed 5 to 10 percent of the time. In practice, couples may move several times over the course of their marriages between husband's and wife's villages, following shifts in family relations and the availability of housing, land, and employment. As might be expected from the convergence of cross-cousin marriage, caste endogamy, and repeated exchanges between the same villages, in 1975, over three-fifths of all marriages were highly localized, about one-fifth endogamous to Walangama and another two-fifths involving a limited number of nearby communities.

However, in 1992, this pattern seemed to be shifting. I found that over the intervening seventeen years there had been a 20-percent decline in local marriages, that marriages were being undertaken with partners from more villages, and that marriages also were more geographically diffuse. That is, at least some people in Walangama were inhabiting their landscape in different ways. Understanding the reasons for that change begins, I think, with an appreciation of the Walangama landscape: the potters' "place" within it.

Walangama's Landscape

Many Walangama people speak of their local area as one to which they have historical claims and connections. A long time ago, perhaps 300 years, people told me, a man named Jayakody Mutha (Great Grandfather Jayakody) came by sea to Sri Lanka. He landed on the coast thirty miles southwest from Walangama and proceeded inland with his followers, into the territory of the old Kandyan kingdom, the Up Country.[7] There, he marked off village boundaries where his people should settle. These settlements became the potter villages of today: Walangama and the ones where Walangama people now marry, all lying between two rivers, the Deduru Oya to the north and the Maha Oya to the south (map 2).

This sense of belonging in and to a particular piece of territory is reinforced by the belief that the deities, too, are localized. Walangama's local area deity is a goddess named Vellani Amma, whose temple is a few miles away at the base of a large rock, an inherently supernatural sort of place. Like many local area gods (Winslow 1984), Vellani Amma is a euhemerized deity, a deified mortal, a girl believed to have actually lived and visited the spot where her temple now is. As such, Vellani Amma is both unique—this is her only temple—and quintessentially local. People in her area give Vellani Amma the first rice from each harvest and make vows to gain her help with illnesses, childbirths, and other family matters. When they cross the Deduru Oya and enter the territory of another deity, the god Ayyanayaka, they stop and offer a coconut at his shrine to ensure that he will take up where Vellani Amma leaves off. To the south, the border is less marked and the identity of the deity less clear, but there are numerous coconut smashing places along the Maha Oya River where offerings are

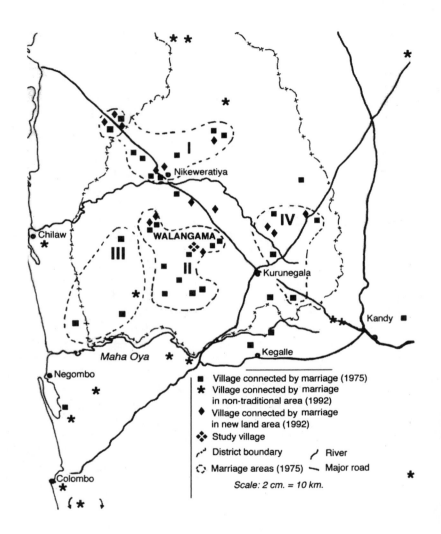

Map 2. Walangama in relation to marriage areas.

made to whomever the area deity may be, his identity less important than his right to homage.[8]

As potters,[9] of course, Walangama people have their own intimate ties to the land around them because they depend on its resources to practice their trade: clay from natural local deposits, palm branches and coconut husks from nearby estates to fuel their kilns, and the uncrowded space around their homes to work. Visitors to the village and even casual passers-by know immediately that it is inhabited by potters: potsherds line the paths, outdoor pit kilns are prominent, and stacks of pots surround every house. Until the creation of a pottery marketing cooperative in the 1950s, Walangama potters sold their wares by carrying them to and from their local weekly market and by hawking them door-to-door in surrounding nonpotter villages. Twice a year, at harvest time, men would take cartloads north to trade pots for rice. The potter caste is a lower caste and selling pottery in this way meant that people were also showcasing their inferior status. Older potters described for me how women used to not be allowed to wear blouses and could only cover their breasts by bringing up an end of their long waist cloths, while men had to go bare-chested altogether. Potters were (and sometimes still are) expected to sit on the ground if others of higher castes are on chairs and to sit at the outer edge of the circle in a temple crowd. Adults still remember taunts in schools and, even in 1992, strangers on the road passing through the village could be heard making demeaning comments about the potters as they went by.

Therefore, the creation of the pottery marketing cooperative by the government Department of Cooperatives was a social as well as an economic blessing. It also began a shift in the economic landscape, structured by the opportunities presented by the cooperative. Beginning in the 1950s, pottery was sold directly to the cooperative which then resold it to traders who came to the village to buy. By the 1960s, sales had climbed to the point where only the wares that did not meet co-op standards were taken to markets and then only by the poorest families. In the 1980s, the government expanded an irrigation project about fifty miles to the north of Walangama and pottery demand soared, both from the thousands of poor colonists who settled in the area and from the related expansion of dairy farms, which used the pots for buffalo milk yogurt (Winslow 1996). In 1992, the village was sending out over 100,000 pots a month.

As their incomes rose, the change in the economic landscape was matched by a change in the landscape of identity, initiated by the potters but within the nationalist discourse of Buddhism. At first, the potters used their new discretionary incomes to increase donations to the nearby temple they always had supported, but their feelings of being second-class citizens became increasingly irksome as their larger donations did not buy them greater respect. So, in the late 1980s, they started their own temple:

They acquired the Bo Tree sapling, constructed a small shrine at its base, and financed the building of a large airy house nearby for a resident monk. Since then, they have added a roofed platform where people can meditate and hear sermons, and have begun work on a large image house. They also have given up the frequent demon exorcisms (widely perceived as "un-Buddhist") that I observed in the 1970s, investing instead in the Buddhist temple and its rituals and increasing their participation in pilgrimages to religious sites of national importance.

Over the past thirty years, Sri Lankan politicians increasingly have used Buddhism as a symbol of Sinhalese nationalism. It has become a required part of the school curriculum for children of Buddhist families; Buddhist sermons are broadcast on the radio; and politicians regularly visit and make donations to national shrines. In abandoning exorcisms and developing their own Buddhist institutions, Walangama villagers are participating in and allying themselves with a national movement, giving up lower status and caste-specific religious practices and adopting high status and caste-neutral ones.

Together, the pottery marketing and religious changes have had the effect of changing the potters' interactions with other people (both potter and nonpotter) in their local area and beyond. They have, first of all, been able to withdraw from certain interactions that they deemed undesirable: direct sales of their pottery to consumers and second-class participation in the ceremonial and fund-raising activities in the temple in the neighboring village. Both of these changes had the effect of pulling them back to the village, decreasing their contacts outside of it. At the same time, some within the village have left the village more frequently to rent trucks to transport pots and to take selling trips to other parts of the island; and others, to meet with religious and civil officials to plan Buddhist activities and consult about building the temple, acquiring the sapling, and locating a priest. Still others make trips away to find suitable medical treatments, to attend a wider range of schools, and to shop for goods and services that increasing numbers can afford and feel are necessary. The landscape of their lives has shifted in small but significant ways, even though the place where they live has not changed.

Interestingly, not only has the potters' relative prosperity allowed them to change their relationships in ways they see as positive, it also seems to have given them the means to avoid other economic and geographic shifts that might have engulfed them. While tens of thousands of Sri Lankan village women have sought employment as housemaids in the Middle East (Gamburd 2000) or work in the hundreds of garment factories that have sprung up all over the island (Lynch 1999), almost no one from Walangama has chosen to do either. In addition, very few young men from Walangama have taken up military service, despite campaigns by a government whose need for soldiers seems infinite as it struggles to survive a civil war against separatist forces (Gamburd 1997).

This is not to say that Walangama people are insulated from the global economy. The irrigation project that increased demand for their pottery is itself the result of the national turn to export agriculture and industrial production (the irrigation was meant to produce electricity) for the world market; deregulation of vehicle imports, called for by the open economy, has increased the availability of trucks to transport their pots; and immersion in global systems of credit and exchange has increased cash flow in the island, even in rural areas. Newspaper and television advertising keeps them abreast of the latest consumer trends. Cell phones make it possible for village entrepreneurs to stay in contact with buyers, despite the limitations of the national electric and telephone grids (the village still is not fully served by electricity). In multiple ways, Walangama people are fully fledged members of all of Appadurai's 'scapes and the globalized landscape they compose.

Yet while Appadurai would have us focus on the limitations of local power to "produce contexts," in small ways Walangama villagers seem to be actively, even confidently, seeking out ways to transform and improve the contexts they inherited. Harvey raises the spectacle of identity crisis, but the potters seem to be seeking out the possibility of a change in identity, an identity *opportunity*, albeit in such small, fine-textured ways that we easily could miss or dismiss them as unimportant, focused, as we have become, on the grander changes of colonialism and global capitalism. Yet it is in such choices among alternatives that social life takes place and change happens (cf. Rosaldo 1980: 17, 27). As I suggested above, one arena in which the microactivities that comprise this sort of landscape negotiation in Walangama can be perceived is in the area of marriage connections.

Marriage Changes in Walangama

In the 1970s, as part of my original regional-systems study, I surveyed marriage connections to find out if marriage ties between communities simply networked their way across the countryside in a series of more or less infinite links, or if they turned back on themselves to form distinct marriage regions, as the Jayakody myth and the potters themselves suggested. I censused households and recorded genealogies for all the potters in Walangama and in the thirty-four villages connected to Walangama by marriage. As is typical of Sinhalese villages more generally, Walangama is essentially a single-caste community, with only a few households of other castes. I found this to be true generally of the thirty-four named places that showed up in tracing out marriage connections, although a few turned out to be simply small hamlets at the edges of larger villages instead.

Overall, however, the multi-caste community considered stereotypical of India is not common is Sinhalese Sri Lanka. The census provided data on marriages extant at the time; the genealogies allowed me to look at changes in marriage patterns over time.[10]

Three findings in particular emerged in my analysis (map 2):

1. there appeared to be distinct marriage regions—geographic subareas of higher endogamy;

2. Walangama's primary region (II), the area with which it had the most marriages ties, emerged as a group of eleven (including Walangama) potter communities located between the Deduru Oya and Maha Oya Rivers; and

3. there were and long had been regular flows of spouses between regions.

I was not surprised to find that Walangama marriages were localized. The localization of family names, the fiction that village coresidents are patrilineal descendants of a founding ancestor, and, as noted earlier, caste endogamy and cross-cousin marriage, all work together to produce localized in-marrying groups (Moore 1981, Obeyesekere 1967, Tambiah 1958). It also was not unanticipated that the marriage areas were not perfectly discrete. As Adams and Kasakoff noted a quarter-century ago in their cross-cultural review of marriage regions, endogamy regions commonly are only semi-closed so that "there are going to be at least two marriage patterns in every society: marriage within the group and marriage outside of it" (Adams and Kasakoff 1976: 168). Potter marriages in central Sri Lanka proved to be no exception.

I found four marriage areas, shown as I, II, III, and IV on map 2.[11] Altogether, about 58.5 percent of all marriages took place within each of the four areas (table 8.1). A preliminary historical analysis, which looked at five periods over one hundred years, for some of the villages, suggested that the basic areas persisted over time (except for area III, which disappears before 1960 in my data).

In 1992, I updated the Walangama census and recorded 132 marriages that had taken place since 1975. Table 8.2 summarizes and compares marriage spatial patterns in the two time periods.

Table 8.2 reveals that three major changes took place during the eighteen years between the two surveys. First, the number of different villages with which Walangama is connected by marriage increased dramatically from around 34 in 1975 to approximately 59 in 1992. Divided by the total number of marriages involved, it gives a measure of dispersion: in 1975, this number was 0.17, meaning that each additional marriage brought in a connection to 0.17 other villages on average; while in 1992, this figure had almost tripled, so that each marriage brought in a connection to 0.45 villages.[12]

Table 8.1. Rates of marriage endogamy by region (all potter marriages)

Marriage Area	Endogamy Rate
Area I	56.8%
Area II*	61.7%
Area III	66.9%
Area IV#	48.5%

* = Walangama's own area; # = Area known to be incompletely surveyed

Table 8.2. Spatial analysis of Walangama marriages,1975 and 1992

	Marriages extant in 1975	Marriages made 1976–1992
Total number of marriages	201	132
Endogamous marriages (both spouses from Walangama)	40 (19.9%)	29 (22.2%)
With spouses from Area I	29 (14.4%)	24 (18.1%)
With spouses from Area II*	86 (42.8%)	37 (28.0%)
With spouses from Area III	10 (5.0%)	7 (5.3%)
With spouses from Area IV	22 (10.9%)	15 (11.4%)
Other/unknown	14 (7.0%)	9 (6.8%)
With spouses from new regions	___	11 (8.3%)
Villages/marriage#	34/201 = .17	59/132 = .45

* = Walangama's own area   # = measure of marriage dispersion

The second change is that local marriage (marriages within Walangama plus those in Area II, Walangama's marriage area) declined from 62.7 percent in 1975 to 50.0 percent in the 1976–1992 period, a decrease of over 20 percent. The third change can be seen by noting the location of the eleven marriages that connect Walangama with new areas, noted as "stars" on map 2. These villages represent totally new marriage connections, outside and in some cases quite distant from the 1975 regions. There are only eleven such marriages altogether, but in conjunction with the other two observations about greater numbers of villages involved in marriages and the decreasing proportion of local marriages, this shows fairly convincingly that, overall, individual decision by individual decision, there is a clear pattern of Walangama people seeking spouses in a greater variety of places and increasingly far from home.

However, it does not appear to me that the way in which marriages are arranged has changed significantly; at most, there has been an increase in tendencies that were clearly evident even in the 1970s. Young people then, both males and females, had a great deal of say about whom they would marry. It was considered more acceptable for the groom's family to locate and propose to him various possible brides, but both of the young people had the right to refuse their families' choices, and they quite often did. They might also select a mate themselves, usually someone they had met at school or through connections via peers who had moved outside the village at marriage. Unlike the practice in much of Hindu India, Walangama girls were never expected to be married before puberty.

Overall, I would characterize Walangama marriages as arranged by parents at the behest of their children, with the amount of initiative from parents or children varying from family to family. It does appear and villagers allege, however, that children are relying less on family arrangements than they used to, although this is hard to be sure about because families normally finalize the undertaking no matter who made the initial contacts. But on the whole, it is not *who* is arranging marriages that has changed, but *where* they are being arranged. Instead of being confined to a few nearby communities, carefully repeating marriage ties to families and places where marriage ties already existed, more and more Walangama young people are seeking to connect to new families and new communities, some nearby and some quite far away.

We should note, however, that spatial change is not characteristic of all recent marriages. The rate of village endogamy has been quite stable at about one in five marriages (19.9 percent in 1975, 22.0 percent in 1992). Also, Walangama always has had a few marriages outside its local area and that has continued at pretty much the old rate of about one in every three. Area I was connected to Walangama through about 14.5 percent of marriages in 1975 and about 18.1 percent in 1992; Area III was 5 percent in 1975 and 5.3 percent in 1992; Area IV was 11 percent in 1975 and 11.4 percent in 1992. Altogether about 30.4 percent of Walangama marriages were neither endogamous nor in their local area in 1975, and about 34.8 percent in 1992. Adding up the relatively stable rates of endogamous marriages and marriages into other areas we find that they total 50.3 percent in 1975 and 56.8 percent in 1992, so that overall we can conclude that about half of the 1992 marriages were reproducing 1975 patterns.

What has changed is that the rate of marriage within what I call Walangama's local area (Area II on map 2) has declined from 42.5 percent in 1975 to only 28.0 percent among the more recent marriages. Furthermore, eleven (8.3 percent) of the recent marriages connect Walangama villagers with widely dispersed communities (indicated with stars on map 2) with which they were not connected before. Finally, even the marriages that are *within* old areas are often with different villages, so that although they appear to be reproducing the old geography, they in fact are not. Taken altogether, I think it is reasonable to describe these changes as a dispersal of marriage that, if it persists, seems likely to break down the old areas of endogamy.

Sinhalese Sri Lankans are well known in the anthropological literature for using marriage strategically, often for economic ends. They have been observed to make genealogy a "charter" for land rights (Obeyesekere 1967); to forsake local marriage if either poverty or wealth meant that their best opportunities lay elsewhere (Tambiah 1958); and even to abandon cross-cousin marriage when households became economically competitive with each other (Stirrat 1977). My findings, too, might be construed as the seeking of economic opportunities, because the farthest flung of the new marriages almost always involve the pursuit of non-pottery-making employment opportunities for men: agricultural lands (or, in one case, work in a sugar mill) to the far north or jobs as cobblers, policemen, soldiers, teachers, and civil servants to the south and west.

However, because pottery making is relatively lucrative, these new jobs, which do require investment in the form on longer periods in school, do not necessarily result in higher incomes. Marriage into Area I, the region north of the Deduru Oya, was attractive even in the 1970s because decades of government irrigation schemes in the region have resulted in good opportunities to acquire farm land. Yet when I visited women who had married there, they clearly had lower standards of living than they would have had in Walangama, whose relatively luxurious lifestyle they said they missed. Similarly, in 1992, a young man who had gone into the police and married a nonpotter caste girl, still depended on his potter parents for financial assistance, because their income (which combined pottery making with good landholdings) exceeded his low police pay (even combined with his wife's salary, since she, too, was in the police). Even the pension benefits of formal sector employment, when combined with a relatively early retirement age (fifty-five years), pale beside the economic potential of pottery making.

But if farming and policing far from home do not provide immediate economic rewards, they do seem to be at least a step toward leaving behind pottery as a stigmatized profession. On those visits north, I would be warned not to ask about pottery making. The young policeman's mother confessed to me that while she had met and was fond of her higher-caste daughter-in-law, she still had not met the daughter-in-law's parents, who were as yet unaware of the low caste status of their son-in-law. Now that her son's little daughter was old enough to talk, she sadly was no longer brought to Walangama to visit, for fear she might report back revealing details to her other grandparents. Another woman told me that her own father, who had become successful as a carpenter instead of as a potter, encouraged his children to seek nonpotter-caste spouses, to improve themselves, she said. In Walangama, being a potter is more of a social problem than an economic one. It is as much for this reason, I think, as for economic opportunizing, that some in Walangama are using the opportunity of marriage to connect themselves to different places, hoping in that way to gain access to new social spaces.

Conclusion

I do not want to overstate my case. Pottery making is very difficult physical work, which brings no pension and leads frequently to repetitive stress injuries at the end of a lifetime. No one in the village romanticizes its attractions, nor is it marked with traditional rituals or cultural cachet. These potters rarely even decorate the pots they produce by the hundreds. Yet as one walks around the village, the economic case in favor of pottery appears abundantly clear: large, light, and well-furnished new houses; a beautiful new temple; and a schoolhouse packed to overflowing. There also is what one does not see: the young women who have not joined the rush of others like themselves in pursuit of jobs as domestics in the Middle East or as garment workers in the factories being built all over the island because, they say, they can plan their own days at the wheel and make more money besides; the young men who have not sought military careers, as have their counterparts in poorer regions. There even is the spectacle of land not being planted because the time can be more profitably put into pottery.

This economic success has changed Walangama potters' movements in the landscape. They do not hawk pots door-to-door, demeaning themselves before high caste neighbors. They do not stay up all night to exorcise demons. And an increasing number do not marry nearby. They sit at home, selling their pots to the traders who now maneuver their trucks down the narrow lanes, bypassing even the co-op in their eagerness to acquire Walangama wares. When not working, the potters stroll to their own temple to meditate at the phases of the moon, to make offerings, or to listen to their monk's sermons. They teach their older children to take the bus to town schools, hoping they will get better educations; and they pack them into rented cars to see the sacred sites of national Buddhism. When it comes time for the children to marry, they support and sometimes encourage even their unconventional choices,[13] clearly seeing social as well as economic advantages to the new marriage geography.

In their excellent study of demographic change in southern India, John Caldwell, P. H. Reddy, and Pat Caldwell observed both "rising village exogamy" and "expanding geographical borders" of marriage (1988: 239). They attributed this to the fact that "[i]n a society increasingly heterogeneous in terms of education and occupation, parents have to look further afield for suitable marriage partners for their children" (1988: 239). The situation in Walangama appears somewhat different. As we have seen, village exogamy rates have *not* increased, which is understandable in that the improving village economy has its ongoing attractions: young village women know that if they stay in Walangama, they will probably not have to go abroad or to the garment factories to support their families, and young men know that village wives will have the willingness and skills to make pottery. But even if the rate of endogamy has remained steady at about 20 percent, the 80 percent of marriages that always have been outside the village are today expanding the "geographical borders" of Walangama marriage, just as reported for southern India. However, in India, the spatial patterns of marriage apparently are a *consequence* of increasing social differentiation; in Walangama, where parents have less input into marriage choices in any case, the more dispersed marriage choices do not appear to reflect differences within Walangama so much as a deliberate attempt to, if not create social differentiation, at least become socially different in the eyes of the world.

Like Tilley's Neolithic herders, the potters of Walangama have experienced economic change in part through spatial reorientations of a previously encultured space. As their economic interactions in space have changed, some actively are seeking to transform their social interactions to follow suit, to bring to the foreground what once was only background possibility. The few hours of television now available each day also show the potters new possessions and possibilities that may affect their choices as they renegotiate the traditional "ethnoscape" of caste and class. The tales brought by migrants returning from abroad tell them of even wider worlds, albeit in the limited and sometimes negative terms of housemaids' experiences. The continued profitability of pottery making has given them the ability to pick their way carefully across this new terrain. They can alter their identities as they want, molding their social and cultural land-scapes to suit themselves, even if not in discourses of their own making. This may not always be the case, of course; the continued and increasing demand for terra-cotta pottery has surprised even the potters. But given this opportunity, they are making of it what they can, and paying atten-tion to the shifting geography of their lives helps us to see how.

Notes

The field research described in this paper was conducted in Sri Lanka (formerly, Ceylon) from 1973-1976; and in 1992, with a brief planning trip in 1989, and fol-low-up visits in 1993 and 1997. Research was funded by the National Institute of Health, the National Science Foundation (Grant DBS-9108196), the College of Lib-eral Arts Faculty Research Fund of the University of New Hampshire, and the UNH Vice-President for Research Discretionary Grant Fund, all of which I acknowledge with gratitude. Writing time has been supported by the National Endowment for the Humanities and the University of New Hampshire Humanities Center, with additional assistance from the James Fund of the College of Liberal Arts. I also thank my friend and field assistant, Mrs. Shirani Potuhera for her skill and patience; the International Centre for Ethnic Studies (Kandy) for sponsoring my 1992 research; Michael D. Woost for both tact and insight in his comments on early drafts; and the very helpful anonymous reviewers of this volume for their diligence.

1 . It is interesting to me that E. E. Evans-Pritchard did not open *The Nuer* with this usual *mise-en-scene*, even though it is one of the most landscape-grounded eth-nographies ever written. Instead Evans-Pritchard began with maps and aerial photographs, letting the reader know from the start that in his analysis the envi-ronment would be put to more substantive use than as a scene-setting device.

2. Geographers such as Duncan, however, do use landscape in this sense when they talk of it as fashioned for political ends.

3 . One critical reviewer of this apparently controversial book notes that the rocky outcrops to which some of the monuments "point" also provided their build-ing material. He suggests that this might have been an "instructive" basis for a comparative analysis (Fleming 1995: 1040–41; also, Lekson 1996). While I find "in-structive" a rather vague criticism, it seems to me quite possible that in developing one mode of analysis, Tilley has neglected others. Nevertheless, Tilley's book is a refreshingly straightforward attempt to explore a particular approach, remarkably free of jargon and arrogance.

4 . This sounds similar to but actually is profoundly different from the "com-modity orientation" methodology once suggested by Roseberry to deal with the problem of integrating local and larger systems of analysis (also, Obukhova and Guyer, this volume). Roseberry suggested that by tracking a particular commod-ity (he chose coffee) in time and space, anthropologists can "move beyond the spatial and layer cake metaphors" that have restricted anthropological studies of

peasant societies in the past (Roseberry 1989: 120). Current landscape studies, however, assume that space is more than a metaphor and that it would be misleading to isolate a single area of social life on any level. Roseberry was, however, quite aware that his methodological suggestion would produce insights only at the expense of partiality, noting that "[s]uch choices . . . are basic to anthropological fieldwork" (1989: 120).

5. Several government shelter programs provide inexpensive construction loans to income-qualified Sri Lankans. However, these programs gave considerably less than Walangama villagers spent on their houses. The government loans were Rs.5000 for remodeling and Rs.7500 for new construction while new houses in Walangama, far more elaborate than the basic structures envisioned by government planners with apparently conventional notions of villager aspirations, regularly cost upwards of Rs.50,000.

6. There is considerable variation in how different households have responded to prosperity. Here I am talking about general patterns in Walangama, but the future character of the community is as likely to derive from the heterogeneity of these choices as from their commonalities.

7. The old kingdom boundaries roughly define a contemporary cultural divide between the Low Country, under colonial domination from 1503 until independence in 1948, and the Up Country, which was not conquered by Europeans until the British took it over in 1815. Although Walangama is located well out of the mountainous center of the Up Country, Walangama villagers consider themselves Up Country people, wear Up Country dress, and practice Up Country rituals.

8. It is often assumed to be Suniyam Deviyo, a semi-demonic being whose powers for sorcery are sought after increasingly. There is an important Suniyam shrine in the area, but it is not actually on the Maha Oya.

9. Walangama villagers also grow rice, but the village's land base of forty-five acres is inadequate for its population. Less than half of the households own any rice land at all and only a handful have enough to supply their annual rice needs. Virtually all households make pottery.

10. The genealogies were analyzed for only a portion of the villages, so the data used for this chapter are primarily drawn from the census. To determine marriage areas, I first developed a measure that I called "marriage connectivity," which equals the total number of marriages between any two communities divided by the total number of exogamous marriages in which those two communities are involved. I then analyzed connectivity figures (as a measure of shared features) using standard cluster analysis techniques to arrive at marriage areas. For the villages whose genealogies I did analyze, I repeated the analysis after subdividing the data into periods, which allowed me to examine changes over time.

11. Area III is undoubtedly incomplete because its villages had marriage connections to many villages not in the survey. Walangama marriages into Area III began only after 1960 and even then they were few in number, but there was enough evidence to suggest another marriage area in that direction. There also was a group of villages that suggested another area of potter marriage around Kandy, but it was too vague from my information even to be considered an incomplete area, so those few marriages are included in the Other category in table 8.2.

12. Many villages have multiple names, so it is very difficult to be precise about these figures. However, the direction of change is clear.

13. The question of intercaste marriage is still an uneasy one. Intercaste marriages do occur sometimes. They are rare, but, I think, increasing in frequency, although I do not have systematic data, particularly about earlier periods. When the potter caste spouse marries up, it is considered less of a problem than if he or she marries down in the caste hierarchy; I know of no cases of women marrying men who are considered definitely lower than they are. But marriage up is said to present its own problems, as evidenced in the case of the young policemen. Parents do not, as they say, feel free to "come and go," as they do when their children marry someone of their own caste.

References

Adams, John W., and Alice Bee Kasakoff
  1976   "Factors Underlying Endogamous Group Size." Pp. 149–73 in *Regional Analysis, Vol. II: Social Systems*, C. A. Smith, ed. New York: Academic Press.
Appadurai, Arjun
  1996   *Modernity at Large: Cultural Dimensions of Globalization*. Minneapolis: University of Minnesota Press.
Blanton, Richard E.
  1994   *Houses and Households: A Comparative Study*. New York: Plenum Press.
Bloch, Maurice
  1995   "People into Places: Zafimaniry Concepts of Clarity." Pp. 63–77 in *The Anthropology of Landscape*, E. Hirsch and M. O'Hanlon, eds. Oxford: Oxford University Press.
Caldwell, John C., P. H. Reddy, and Pat Caldwell
  1988   *The Causes of Demographic Change: Experimental Research in South India*. Madison: University of Wisconsin Press.
Casey, Edward S.
  1996   "How to Get from Space to Place in a Fairly Short Stretch of Time: Phenomenological Prolegomena." Pp. 13–52 in *Senses of Place*, S. Feld and K. H. Basso, eds. Santa Fe: School of American Research.
Clifford, James
  1997   *Routes: Travel and Translation in the Late Twentieth Century*. Cambridge: Harvard University Press.
Duncan, James S.
  1995   "Landscape Geography, 1993–94." *Progress in Human Geography Research* 19(3): 414–22.
Evans-Pritchard, E. E.
  1940   *The Nuer: A Description of the Modes of Livelihood and Political Institutions of a Nilotic People*. Oxford: Clarendon Press.
Feld, Steven and Keith H. Basso, eds.
  1996   *Senses of Place*. Santa Fe: School of American Research Press.
Fleming, Andrew
  1995   "A Tomb with a View." *Antiquity* 69: 1040–42.

Gamburd, Michele Ruth
   1997   "Wearing a Dead Man's Jacket: State Symbols in Troubled Places." *South Asia: Journal of South Asian Studies* XX: 181–94.
   2000   *The Kitchen Spoon's Handle: Transnationalism and Sri Lanka's Migrant House-maids.* Ithaca: Cornell University Press.
Geertz, Clifford
   1988   *Works and Lives: The Anthropologist as Author.* Stanford, Calif.: Stanford University Press.
   1996   "Afterword." Pp. 259–62 in *Senses of Place*, S. Feld and K. H. Basso, eds. Santa Fe: School of American Research Press.
Harvey, David
   1990   *The Condition of Postmodernity: An Enquiry into the Origins of Cultural Change.* Cambridge: Blackwell Publishers, Inc.
   1991   "Flexibility: Threat or Opportunity?" *Socialist Review* 21(1): 65–77.
Hayden, Dolores
   1995   *The Power of Place: Urban Landscapes as Public History.* Cambridge: Massachusetts Institute of Technology Press.
Hirsch, Eric
   1995   "Landscape: Between Place and Space." Pp. 1–30 in *The Anthropology of Landscape: Perspectives on Place and Space*, E. Hirsch and M. O'Hanlon, eds. Oxford: Oxford University Press.
Ingold, Tim
   1993   "The Temporality of Landscape." *World Archaeology* 25(2): 152–74.
Kahn, Joel S.
   1997   "Demons, Commodities and the History of Anthropology." Pp. 69–98 in *Meanings of the Market: The Free Market in Western Culture*, J. G. Carrier, ed. Oxford: Berg.
Lekson, Stephen H.
   1996   "Landscape with Ruins: Archaeological Approaches to Built and Unbuilt Environments." *Current Anthropology* 37(5): 886–92.
Lynch, Caitrin
   1999   "Good Girls or Juki Girls? Learning and Identity in Garment Factories." *Anthropology of Work Review* XIX(3): 18–22.
Malinowski, Bronislaw
   1961 [1922]   *Argonauts of the Western Pacific.* New York: E.P. Dutton.
Mitchell, Timothy
   1988   *Colonising Egypt.* Cambridge: Cambridge University Press.
Moore, M. P.
   1981   "The Ideological Function of Kinship: The Sinhalese and the Merina." *Man* (N.S.) 16(4): 579–92.
Nissan, Elizabeth
   1988   "Polity and Pilgrimage Centres in Sri Lanka." *Man* (N.S.) 23(3): 253–74.
Obeyesekere, Gananath
   1967   *Land Tenure in Village Ceylon: A Sociological and Historical Study.* Cambridge: Cambridge University Press.

Rosaldo, Renato
    1980 *Ilongot Headhunting, 1883–1974: A Study in Society and History.* Stanford: Stanford University Press.
Roseberry, William
    1989 "Peasants and the World." Pp. 108–26 in *Economic Anthropology,* S. Plattner, ed. Stanford: Stanford University Press.
Sack, Robert David
    1986 *Human Territoriality: Its Theory and History.* Cambridge: Cambridge University Press.
Sahn, David E.
    1987 "Changes in the Living Standards of the Poor in Sri Lanka during a Period of Macroeconomic Restructuring." *World Development* 15(6): 811–21.
Skinner, G. William
    1964 "Marketing and Social Structure in Rural China, Part I." *Journal of Asian Studies* 24(1): 3–43.
Smith, Carol A., ed.
    1976 *Regional Analysis. Vol. I: Economic Systems* and *Vol. II: Social Systems.* New York: Academic Press.
Stirrat, R. L.
    1977 "Dravidian and Non-Dravidian Kinship Terminologies in Sri Lanka." *Contributions to Indian Sociology* (N.S.) 11: 271–93.
Tambiah, Stanley J.
    1958 "The Structure of Kinship and its Relationship to Land Possession and Residence in Pata Dumbara, Central Ceylon." *Journal of the Royal Anthropological Institute* 88(1): 21–44.
Tilley, Christopher
    1994 *A Phenomenology of Landscape: Places, Paths, and Monuments.* Oxford: Berg.
Tsing, Anna Lowenhaupt
    1993 *In the Realm of the Diamond Queen: Marginality in an Out-of-the-Way Place.* Princeton: Princeton University Press.
Wallerstein, Immanuel
    1974 *The Modern World System: Capitalist Agriculture and the Origins of the European World-Economy in the Sixteenth Century.* New York: Academic Press.
Werlen, Benno
    1993 *Society, Action and Space: An Alternative Human Geography.* London: Routledge.
Winslow, Deborah
    1982 "Pantheon Politics: A Regional Analysis of Buddhism in Sri Lanka." Ph.D. dissertation, Department of Anthropology, Stanford University.
    1984 "A Political Geography of Deities: Space and the Pantheon in Sinhalese Buddhism." *Journal of Asian Studies* XLIII(2): 273–91.
    1994 "Person and Place in a Changing Sri Lankan Geography." Paper presented at the Annual Meeting of the American Anthropological Association. Atlanta.
    1996 "Pottery, Progress, and Structural Adjustments in a Sri Lankan Village." *Economic Development and Cultural Change* 44(4): 701–33.

Winslow Jackson, Deborah
　　1977　"Polas in Central Sri Lanka: Some Preliminary Remarks on the Development and Functioning of Periodic Markets." Pp. 56–86 in *Agriculture in the Peasant Sector of Sri Lanka*, S. W. R. de A. Samarasinghe, ed. Peradeniya: Ceylon Studies Seminar.
Woost, Michael D.
　　1990　"Rural Awakenings: Grassroots Development and the Cultivation of a National Past in Rural Sri Lanka." Pp. 164–83 in *Sri Lanka: History and the Roots of Conflict*, J. Spencer, ed. London: Routledge.

Chapter 9

Indians, Markets, and Transnational Studies
in Mesoamerican Anthropology:
Predicaments and Opportunities

Jeffrey H. Cohen

The members of the little community define themselves as a group partly
by contrast with less well-known people who are "out there," and who are
not quite like themselves.
— Robert Redfield (1960a: 113)

Abstract

Much energy and thought in anthropology has been invested in the discussion of things transnational, yet there is little agreement over the meaning or importance of the term (see, for example, Appadurai 1990; Basch et al. 1994; García Canclini 1993; Gledhill 1995; Hannerz 1992; Kearney 1995). Common to many definitions of things transnational is an inherent sense of interconnectedness rooted in shared economic, cultural, social, and/or communicative practices. There is simultaneously a sense that transnational processes create social, cultural, economic, and political disjuncture. In other words, while societies grow more interconnected through communicative, economic, and practical social processes, local identities disappear due to the inequalities inherent to the new global order (Appadurai 1990). A further complication is the lack of agreement over how we measure the contradictory processes that are assumed to define transnational space. What are we to make of the alternative definitions of transnationalism? How might we gain a handle or measure on the vari- ous positive and negative connotations implicated in its use?

This chapter is rooted in the belief that to understand the current usage of the term we should first examine our field's history for signs of its development. My goal is to illustrate ways in which transnationalism reinvents earlier theoretical constructions in anthropology. Specifically, I examine three phases of research in Latin America: the psychological functionalism of Robert Redfield, the dependency theory of Cardoso and Faletto (1979), and the articulationist, political economy of Eric Wolf. I argue the criticisms of functional and dependency approaches are equally applicable to transnationalism. As an alternative, I offer a political economy that is focused on the social organization of and the power structures that characterize local/global relationships (see Wolf 1966, 1982, 1986). Think- ing through the ways in which we decide to approach and measure the bundle of economic formations that we call *transnational* is crucial to pre- vent the creation of elaborate codes that sound erudite but are in the analysis little more than repetitions of the past mistakes.

Transnationalism, Economy, and Social Change among Mesoamerica's Indians and Peasants

Basch, Schiller, and Blanc introduce the concept of transnationalism as a framework for talking about the encounter between societies stripped of geographical continuity and existing in weak nation-states that are char- acterized by fluid boundaries, expanding economies, and growing bureaucracies. New identities are formed to gain a voice in this cacophony of contrasting social, cultural, economic, and political systems (1994: 7). Thus, transnationalism is really a framework to talk about social encoun- ters and culture change (fundamental issues in anthropology) in a world that seems far removed economically and politically from the one in which our field was born.

Does a transnational approach move us beyond the shortcomings of earlier models in the field? In this section, I will argue it does not. It reca- pitulates the mistakes of earlier work and leaves a transnational world marked by functional shortcomings and dependent dualisms (see critiques in Kearney 1996; Wilk 1996).

Robert Redfield's psychological functionalism, discussion of the "little community," and his development of the folk-urban continuum are prob- ably not approached as concepts that have much to offer transnational studies. For Redfield, the little community was a bounded entity, demar- cated by its group consciousness, scale, homogeneity, and self-sufficiency

(Redfield 1960a: 4) and therefore of little use in discussions of social hybridity, economic fluidity, and cultural disjuncture. Yet, as we describe transnational processes the goal is to explain the kinds of changes that fascinated Redfield and mark much of his writing.

In a similar manner, we cannot discount dependency models in our quest to understand transnational processes. The dependistas examine the place of proletariat, peasant, and Indian societies in broader systems of exploitation and abuse. All of the political, economic, and ethnic inequalities and contradictions that mark transnational space are present in the dependency model. The economy (in the guise of markets), society (education and communication), and culture (the arts) are forces through which natives are assimilated into new social universes (for Mesoamerica see Bonfil Batalla 1987, Dennis 1981, Knight 1990).

Redfield has been criticized for his psychological functionalism (see Hewitt de Alcántara 1984), the dependistas for creating dualistic systems where the native (read Indian, peasant, or proletariat) remains largely powerless in relation to the state and larger economy (Kearney 1996). But what if transnationalism makes the same mistakes? The solution to some of these problems may also lurk in past work.

It is in the articulationist, political economy of Eric Wolf and others that we can construct a transnationalism that is rooted in the local (microlevel strategies and decision making) collective practices and traditional beliefs and yet never loses sight of macrolevel processes and history. Thus, "esteemed (but largely meaningless) ancestors" might not be the best way to describe Redfield, Frank, and others, and we should not be so quick to discount their work. Rather, we need to look at their work, and understand their mistakes in the effort to build a useful transnational model.

Functionalism and Transnationalism

The tone of functionalist anthropology in Mesoamerica was set by researchers early in this century including Redfield, Tax, and Foster working from the United States and Gamio, de la Fuente, and Beltrán in Mexico. The resulting models defined what was perceived to be culturally distinct and geographically isolated ethnic populations, organized into independent and self-sufficient communities. There were a few exceptions to these models, particularly in the realization of ways in which alternative systems of production articulated (or acculturated, to use the terminology of the period) and the recognition of economic rationality and strategic decision making within the market itself (Malinowski and de la Fuente 1982; Parsons 1936; Tax 1953). Unfortunately, Redfieldian models which situated economic action in community types that were held together by powerful collective mentalities (Redfield 1960b: 105) overshadowed the limited economic integration noted by Parsons (1936) and the place of entrepreneurial activism in market relationships as noted in the Oaxacan market system by Malinowski and de la Fuente (1982) and in Guatemala by Tax (1953).

Redfield's model of the folk community was conducive to the systematic comparative exploration of indigenous Mesoamerica. It was also limited by an overemphasis on the motivations for collective action (termed "ancient mentalities" by Redfield); a functionally circumscribed and geographically isolated conception of community; and an assumption of communalism rooted in sociocultural homogeneity and harmony (see Hewitt de Alcántara 1984: 22).

The essential quality and romantic vision of peasant and Indian cultures constructed by the functionalists made it difficult to talk about sociocultural change in a nonjudgmental way. As noted by Kearney (1996: 52), change (often fomented through markets) for the functionalists came at a high cost to local cultural systems and ancient mentalities. In response to the impacts of new market systems, local communities grow increasingly disorganized, individualized, and secular in nature. It is not that Redfield assumed Chan Kom and Tepoztlán were free of change; rather, that he feared much of the change that would occur would be by definition negative and destructive of local traditional systems.

Contemporary research, while recognizing that change is given, often makes functional mistakes (particularly in terms of transnational processes) that have much in common with Redfield's fears of local chaos. Annis (1987) reproduces a fairly traditional functionalism in his analysis of the rise of Protestantism in Guatemala. The author recognizes local economic differences, the impact of national politics on community identity, and the growing presence of global economics in native life. However, his discussion is rooted in the contrast between Indians who practice "milpa logic" and Protestant converts who practice commercial rationality. Milpa logic is "an expression of the Indian's place in Guatemalan colonial society" (Annis 1987: 10); it defines production for self-consumption, not for profit or marketing. Guatemalans who have converted to Protestantism embody entrepreneurialism and organize for the market and profit making. The difference, rooted in opposing psychologies, is not far from Redfield's suggestion that Tepoztlán's barrios become unified social units through the centralizing influence of the chapel and Santo (Redfield 1928: 291). These systems only break down when the villagers throw themselves into the market and forsake the traditions with which they were born (Redfield 1950).

A second problem of functionalism arises from the arguments of moral economists interested in the practice and creation of social structures within communities that stand apart from capitalist-based relations (even when those communities are part of wider economic systems; see essays in Halperin and Dow 1977). The moral economists describe Indian and peasant society as having a sense of shared morality and communal identity (based upon ritual and gift exchange—see Crumrine 1969) that limits the impact and effect of market relations and the dehumanizing effects of capitalism. And while the approach often illustrates important ways in which native peoples resist the "onslaught" of capitalism, woe be to the native who chooses to participate in the "global ecumene" (see critique in Hannerz 1992). Rather than describing the native as a person with choices to make, the moral economist endows him with an alternative economy that exists in a social realm apart from markets and competition that characterize capitalism. Thus, the approach forces the native into a different set of essential categories (defined by resistance to the world system rather than simply the dedication to a set of traditions) whose actions are still circumscribed, although they may be circumscribed by history, social practice, and so forth (see Guttmann 1993; Watanabe 1992). We are left then with an untenable situation where the choice is to be a native or not:

> Many Indian communities in modern Latin America find themselves caught in a dilemma. If they continue their traditional agricultural, landholding, and marriage practices, their internal economics will stagnate, and they will have to export many of their young people or relegate them to increasing poverty. If they encourage integration into national market economies, however, over time their populations are likely to lose their ethnic uniformity, and their societies their cultural integrity. Either choice is unpleasant, but in the modern world the need to make such a choice seems unavoidable. (Kicza 1993: xxvi)

The critiques of functionalism and moral economy offer important insights for the construction of transnational models. First, transnational scholars inadvertently shroud the time before transnational processes appear in romantic and homogeneous terms and give the pre-transnational a timeless quality. Thus, in discussions of transnational migration, for example, movement across international borders becomes a destructive and destabilizing force for assimilation (Guidi 1993). There is also a sense that transnational societies, once rooted in their new homelands (whether New York or Mexico City), are largely homogeneous (see critique in Conway 2000) and undergo a process of disidentification (Barabas 1995). Second, where the moral economist constructs an alternative social system defined by cultural beliefs rather than (or parallel to) market systems, the transnational scholar often overstates the "resistance" and counterhegemonic force that transnationals (migrants, activists, etc.) hold (see Basch et al. 1994: 272). Of this final point, Conway remarks, "transnational concept is of little use when it comes to understanding the daily material realities of transmigrant lives" (2000: 212). The point is not to belittle the process of change. Migration and the impact of global economics can undermine social systems (see Rubenstein 1982). Nevertheless, to moralize about change rather than trying to get a handle on its real effect (that is, in terms of economic outcomes for household, for example) treats transnationalism as a general threat to indigenous and peasant communities and gives little space to the native to construct a response. Thus, transnationalism reduces native peoples (no matter where) to poor, homogeneous, suffering souls, unable to understand or defend their position (poster children for paradise lost) or as too confrontational in their response to global capitalism (recruiters for the coming revolution, my point in Cohen 1997, and see critique in Wilk 1996).

Dependency and Transnationalism

Dependency theories are a critical response to functionalism, modernization theory (see Rostow 1960), and the increasing economic inequality that characterized the relationship of rural communities and urban centers, particularly in Latin America. The work of the dependistas injected a much-needed dose of history and critical thinking about political economy into the debate over the place and meaning of proletarian, peasants, and Indians in the Third World (see Cardoso and Faletto 1979). Rather than assuming that the poverty and inequality of peasant and indigenous communities would be developed away (or was part of some great and static schema), the dependistas saw the growth of poverty as a historical process. The relationship of Indian communities to urban centers was a necessary outcome of a system characterized by inequality and socioeconomic domination rooted in the colonial encounter between Indian and Spanish following the conquest (Bonfil Batalla 1987; Stavenhagen 1978). Hewitt de Alcántara describes the dependistas' position clearly; "the Indian community became a creation of the wider society, not a subtraction from it" (1984: 75).

The dependista position, that the Indian or peasant community is a creation of the encounter between indigenous and Spanish systems, also highlights a persistent problem; the tendency to posit the indigenous or peasant community in a minor role in relation to the state, market, or world system. To define the nature of Indian society today as largely the outcome of the pressures of the Crown, the Church, and later the state brought to bear on indigenous culture and society allows for little active response by the locals.

Nevertheless, dependency theory shifted the debate concerning the structure of indigenous and peasant society away from models based upon shared psychology, geography, and morality. It replaced the assumption of indigenous community as isolate or semi-isolate (as a gauge of more or less "Indianness") with a model rooted in political economy, history, and exploitation. Finally, the dependistas broke the world into a dynamic system of powerful core nations (the West) and weak underdeveloped peripheries (the rest) rooted in the maintenance of economic, political, and social inequality (Stavenhagen 1978).

Given such a model, one that recognizes the history, linkages, and inequalities that exist between local (indigenous) societies and global (economic) systems, dependency theory would seem a useful precursor to talking about transnational processes, and yet it creates a set of problems that, while different from those of the psychological functionalists, still characterizes indigenous and peasant communities as unique.

Chief among the problems as noted by Kearney (1996: 81) is that dependency theory "is only a partial deconstruction of dualist anthropology, for its 'core' and 'periphery' are but permutations of the polar ends of the folk-urban continuum, a spatial opposition that also corresponds to the temporal distinction between anthropology Self and ethnographic Other—the one 'traditional,' the other 'modern.'" In other words, the peasant or Indian is an outcome of the encounter, not an active participant in the construction of society (local, global, or otherwise) and is therefore marked as unique and separate from the surrounding system and at the mercy of an economy it can neither respond to nor understand.

Articulationalists and Transnationalists

Articulationalists' models of the relationship of Indian and peasant society to national and global processes are rooted in what Mintz describes as "comparative emporeatics—not a study of the marketplace nor even a system of market places, nor is it simply a study of class structure of a region. It is rather, a composite, synthetic overview of the ecology and economy of a region . . . which transcends both individual communities and particular classes" (1976: xii). Articulation models move beyond the limits of geographic determinism and cultural essentialism to identify broadly based systems of socioeconomic interaction. Like dependency research, articulation models note history and economic inequality (see Smith 1984). They also go well beyond the dependistas in their awareness of regional, national, and international economic ties that are capitalistic and nondualistic (Alvarez 1994; Sheridan 1988); local variability in the status and class of study communities (Cohen 1998; Cook and Binford

1990; Littlefield 1978; Stephen 1991); and an emphasis on household-level production and decision making as part of broader national and global market systems (Acheson 1996; Cancian 1992; Miller 1997; Wilk 1991). Approaching transnationalism from an articulation perspective offers the possibilities of a "people first" approach (Conway and Cohen 1998) that recognizes individual agency and household decision making (microlevel strategies) and the relationship of these microlevel strategies to macrolevel social, political, and economic processes. For example, Gledhill (1995) notes the ways in which national and international politics influences local agrarian policy and the practices of peasant producers in rural Mexico. He goes on to create a refined model of peasant society that is characterized as neither dependent nor overwhelmingly resistant. Rather, we follow the development of the relationship of peasant producers to the state in terms of local decision making that is itself rife with both conflict and coordination. In a similar fashion, Nangengast and Kearney (1990) outline the ways in which international economics, ethnic identity, migrant associations, and national politics come together to foster reforms within the Mexican state. What makes their discussion important is the way in which the Mixtec "transcommunity" comes to exist in the United States but exercise power in Mexico. Here, rather than a distilled transnational outcome (an Americanized version of Mixtec cultural practices) we find a unique and fluid blending of traditions in an effort to maintain community and society. Finally, Hendrickson (1995) places indigenous craft production into broad global networks and explores global/local economic processes, including the influence of tourism on small-scale producers, but also focuses on the positive and negative gendered outcomes of these processes. Thus, Mayan women (in Hendrickson's example) struggle not only in a global market, but with changing community processes that include religious conversion, alcoholism, and new economics.

One of the most important of current trends in transnational studies are those involved with the ongoing discussion of Maya identity and society in Chiapas and the Yucatan peninsula of Mexico and the western highlands of Guatemala. Much of this work follows how the most essentialized of Mesoamerica's Indians (in other words, a group described as traditional due to language, dress, and practice) purposefully manipulate international media in service to local battles over agrarian, political, and economic reform (Díaz Polanco 1997; Gossen 1994; Nash 1996). Guatemalan Maya have begun to organize socially and politically around a shared conception of Mayanism that is rooted in local leadership informed by anthropological reporting and theory, *not* the local practice of traditions (Fisher and Brown 1996). What is more interesting is that many practices that have come to represent this "new wave" of Mayan activism may have few if any roots in "real" practices (Watanabe 1995). In this sense the Maya are adapting (or, to build on the theme of this chapter, transculturizing) an academic definition of "their" identity. In other words, Maya leaders have taken anthropological theories of identity and ethnographic descriptions of native culture and reformulated those descriptions and discussions as a foundation for an ongoing social revival (Nash 1996).

Given the shift toward a new identity based upon ethnographic reporting, anthropological analysis, and historical description rather than indigenous practices and meanings, the question for some researchers becomes, What is or is not authentic in the construction or reproduction of this new pan-Mayan identity (see the review by Watanabe 1995). The search for authenticity among specialists, in turn, is one signal of the creative force with which the Maya are adapting to our postmodern, destabilized world, and doing it perhaps better than the anthropologists (Nash 1996).

The recreation of Maya identity and the response of researchers to this process signals an interesting imbalance of power. Those people who were formally defined by anthropologists are finding it difficult to use that very information in their renaissance. The situation plays out in what Clifford (1997: 201) describes as the "zero-sum game of acculturation": Europeans using native cultures to model ethnographic information and describe human society are described as inclusive and modern. On the other hand, natives, and we can add the peasants or underclass of any society, who use European systems (or the descriptions written by Europeans of themselves) are imitative and threatened with a loss of tradition. Thus, in this last example, the most creative application of transnationalism we find—the reconstruction of Maya identity around data collected by anthropologists—becomes just another threat to the kinds of psychologically determinative, geographically specific, and ethnographically essential models of culture we would have hoped to have left behind.

Discussion

Why is it important to think about the connections between theories in anthropology, studies of the market, definitions of the Indian, and transnationalism? Raymond Williams makes a strong argument for understanding the processes from which our theories and terminologies arise in *Marxism and Literature*. He reminds us that signs and symbols do not exist in nature nor are they very often "natural." Instead, signs and symbols "reflect and refract" reality and realities (1977: 38). In other words, signs and symbols duplicate meaning, but also bend that meaning over time and space.

Transnationalism is one of the more seductive signs of the moment in anthropology, literary studies, geography, and sociology. Yet, the various and multiple meanings used to talk about transnational processes are treacherous and there is little agreement between competing definitions. More important, we often look toward such terms in the hope that they will explain the unexplainable to us—or at least that they will begin to order the disordered and chaotic world of human practice. The problem we run into is when we overburden terms like transnationalism in the hope that they will decipher human social action, forgetting that the transnational is, in itself, nothing more than the outcome of the actions of humans involved in the production of society. Once we forget the constructed nature of transnationalism we fetishize it as a symbol and imbue it with mystical powers to order and explain.

There is a welter of ways to define transnationalism, and none are neutral in their effect. Cosmopolitanism, creolization, Diaspora studies, "McDonaldization," and "Disneyification" carry very different moral weights and set rather different tones for discussion. These terms can contribute to the "othering" (to borrow a favorite term of many transnational scholars) of the very social groups and societies we, as anthropologists, hope to explain through transnational models. Thus, it is crucial to remember how words bound and limit explanations. Economic anthropology is well positioned for the continued studies of transnationalism and the analysis of transnational processes. Our subfield is built around materialist logic and positivist methods, but it also recognizes the integral importance of cultural beliefs and social practices as well as the symbolic basis of human communication (see Wilk 1996). Because we often study economic processes rooted in cultural beliefs and social practices, we have moved beyond geographically limited models of social interaction characteristic of the functionalists and the dualism common to the dependistas. Finally, because we are involved with the study of exchange we are ready to embrace transnationalism, not as a discrete event going from the West to the rest, but as a two-way street (a new kind of exchange, if you will) in which we are all involved (although never forgetting that the involvement is unequal for very specific reasons) in ever more complex interrelationships.

References

Acheson, James M.
   1996   "Household Organization and Budget Structures in a Purepecha Pueblo." *American Ethnologist* 23(2): 331–51.

Alvarez, Robert R.
1994   "Changing Ideology in a Transnational Market: Chile and Chileros in Mexico and the U.S." *Human Organization* 53(3): 255–62.
Annis, Sheldon
1987   *God and Production in a Guatemalan Town*. Austin: University of Texas Press.
Appadurai, Arjun
1990   "Disjuncture and Difference in the Global Cultural Economy." *Public Culture* 2(2): 1–24.
Barabas, Alicia M.
1995   "El Proceso de Desidentificación Etnica de los Chochos de Oaxaca." Pp. 127–49 in *Primer Anuario de la Dirección de Etnología y Antropología Social del INAH*. México: Instituto Nacional de Antropología e Historia.
Basch, Linda G., Nina G. Schiller, and Cristina S. Blanc
1994   *Nations Unbound: Transnational Projects, Postcolonial Predicaments, and Deterritorialized Nation-States*. Amsterdam: Gordon and Breach Science Publishers, S.A.
Bonfil Batalla, Guillermo
1987   *Mexico Profundo: Una Civilización Negada*. Mexico, D.F.: Secretaria de Educación Publica: CIESAS.
Cancian, Frank
1992   *The Decline of Community in Zinacantan: Economy, Public Life and Social Stratification, 1960–1987*. Stanford, Calif.: Stanford University Press.
Cardoso, Fernando H., and E. Faletto
1979   *Dependency and Development in Latin America*, M. M. Urquidi, trans. Berkeley: University of California Press.
Clifford, James
1997   *Routes: Travel and Translation in the Late Twentieth Century*. Cambridge, Mass.: Harvard University Press.
Cohen, Jeffrey H.
1997   "In the Shadow of the Unknown." *Anthropology Newsletter* (March): 52.
1998   "Craft Production and the Challenge of the Global Market: An Artisans' Cooperative in Oaxaca, Mexico." *Human Organization* 57(1): 74–82.
Conway, Dennis
2000   "Notions Unbound: A critical (re)reading of transnationalism suggests that U.S.-Caribbean circuits tell the story better." Pp. 203–26 in *Theoretical and Methodological Issues in Migration Research: Interdisciplinary, Intergenerational and International Perspectives*. B. Agozino, ed. Aldershot: Ashgate.
Conway, Dennis, and Jeffrey H. Cohen
1998   "Consequences of Return Migration and Remittances for Mexican Transnational Communities." *Economic Geography* 74(1): 26–44.
Cook, Scott, and Leigh Binford
1990   *Obliging Need: Rural Petty Industry in Mexican Capitalism*. Austin: University of Texas Press.
Crumrine, N. Ross
1969   *Ceremonial Exchange as a Mechanism in Tribal Integration among the Mayos of Northwest Mexico*. Tucson: University of Arizona Press.

Dennis, Philip A.
1981 *Utopía y Revolución: el Pensamiento Político Contempráneo de los Indios en América Latina*. Mexico: Nueva Imagen.
Díaz Polanco, Héctor
1997 *Indigenous Peoples in Latin America: The Quest for Self-Determination*, L. Rayas, trans. Boulder, Colo.: Westview Press.
Fisher, Edward R., and R. McKenna Brown, eds.
1996 *Maya Cultural Activism in Guatemala*. Austin: University of Texas Press.
García Canclini, Nestor
1993 *Transforming Modernity: Popular Culture in Mexico*. Lidia Lozano, trans. Austin: University of Texas Press.
Gledhill, John
1995 *Neoliberalism, Transnationalization and Rural Poverty: A Case Study of Michoacán, Mexico*. Boulder, Colo.: Westview Press.
Gossen, Gary H.
1994 "From Olmecs to Zapatistas: A Once and Future History of Souls." *American Anthropologist* 96(3): 553–70.
Guidi, Marta
1993 "¿Es Realmente la Migración una Estrategia de Supervivencia? Un ejemplo en la Mixteca Alta Oaxaqueña." *Revista Internacional de Sociología Tercera Epoca* (5): 89–109.
Guttmann, Matthew C.
1993 "Rituals of Resistance: A Critique of the Theory of Everyday Forms of Resistance." *Latin American Perspectives* 20(2): 74–92.
Halperin, Rhoda, and James Dow, eds.
1977 *Peasant Livelihood*. New York: St. Martin's Press.
Hannerz, Ulf
1992 "The Global Ecumene as a Network of Networks." Pp. 34–56 in *Conceptualizing Society*, A. Kuper, ed. New York: Routledge.
Hendrickson, Carol
1995 *Weaving Identities: Construction of Dress and Self in a Highland Guatemala Town*. Austin: University of Texas Press.
Hewitt de Alcántara, Cynthia
1984 *Anthropological Perspectives on Rural Mexico*. Boston: Routledge and Kegan Paul.
Kearney, Michael
1995 "The Effects of Transnational Culture, Economy, and Migration on Mixtec Identity in Oaxacalifornia." Pp. 226–43 in *The Bubbling Cauldron: Race, Ethnicity, and the Urban Crisis*, M.P. Smith and J. R. Feagin, eds. Minneapolis: University of Minnesota Press.
1996 *Reconceptualizing the Peasantry: Anthropology in Global Perspective*. Boulder, Colo.: Westview Press.
Kicza, John
1993 "Introduction." Pp. xi–xxvi in *The Indian in Modern Latin America*, J. Kicza, ed. Wilmington, Del.: Scholarly Resources.

Knight, Alan
  1990 "Racism, Revolution, and Indigenismo: Mexico 1910–1940." Pp. 71–114 in *The Idea of Race in Latin America, 1870–1940*, R. Graham, ed. Austin: University of Texas Press.
Littlefield, Alice
  1978 "Exploitation and the Expansion of Capitalism: The Case of the Hammock Industry of Yucatan." *American Ethnologist* 5(3): 495–508.
Malinowski, Bronislaw, and Julio de la Fuente
  1982 *Malinowski in Mexico: The Economics of a Mexican Market System.* Boston: Routledge and Kegan Paul.
Miller, Daniel
  1997 *Capitalism: an Ethnographic Account.* Oxford: Berg.
Mintz, Sidney
  1976 "Preface." Pp. xi–xv in *Markets in Oaxaca*, S. Cook and M. Diskin, eds. Austin: University of Texas Press.
Nangengast, Carole, and M. Kearney
  1990 "Mixtec Ethnicity: Social Identity, Political Consciousness, and Political Activism." *Latin American Research Review* 25(1): 61–91.
Nash, June
  1996 "The Reassertion of Indigenous Identity: Mayan Responses to State Intervention in Chiapas." *Latin American Research Review* 30(3): 7–41.
Parsons, Elsie Clews
  1936 *Mitla: Town of the Souls.* Chicago: University of Chicago Press.
Redfield, Robert
  1928 "The Calpolli-Barrio in a Present-day Mexican Pueblo." *American Anthropology* 30(2): 282–94.
  1950 *A Village That Chose Progress: Chan Kom Revisited.* Chicago: University of Chicago Press.
  1960a *The Little Community.* Chicago: Chicago University Press.
  1960b *Peasant Society and Culture.* Chicago: Chicago University Press.
Rostow, Walt W.
  1960 *The Stages of Economic Growth.* Cambridge: Cambridge University Press.
Rubenstein, Hymie
  1982 "The Impact of Remittances in the Rural English-Speaking Caribbean: Notes on the Literature." Pp. 237–66 in *Return Migration and Remittances: Developing a Caribbean Perspective*, W. F. Stinner, K. De Albuquerque, and R. S. Bryce-Laporte, eds. RIIES Occasional Papers #3. Washington, D.C.: Research Institute on Immigration and Ethnic Studies, Smithsonian Institution.
Sheridan, Thomas E.
  1988 *Where the Dove Calls: The Political Ecology of a Peasant Corporate Community in Northwestern Mexico.* Tucson: University of Arizona Press.
Smith, Carol A.
  1984 "Does a Commodity Economy Enrich the Few While Ruining the Masses? Differentiation among Petty Commodity Producers in Guatemala." *Journal of Peasant Studies* 11(3): 60–95.

Stavenhagen, Rudolfo
1978 "Capitalism and the Peasantry in Mexico." *Latin American Perspectives* 5(3): 27–37.
Stephen, Lynn
1991 *Zapotec Women.* Austin: University of Texas Press.
Tax, Sol
1953 *Penny Capitalism: A Guatemalan Indian Economy.* Publication no. 16. Washington, D.C.: Smithsonian Institute for Social Anthropology.
Watanabe, John M.
1992 *Maya Saints and Souls in a Changing World.* Austin: University of Texas Press.
1995 "Unimagining the Maya: Anthropologists, Others, and the Inescapable Hubris of Authorship." *Bulletin of Latin American Research* 14(1): 25–45.
Wilk, Richard
1991 *Household Ecology: Economic Change and Domestic Life Among the Kekchi Maya in Belize.* Tucson: University of Arizona Press.
1996 *Economies and Cultures: Foundations of Economic Anthropology.* Boulder, Colo.: Westview Press.
Williams, Raymond
1977 *Marxism and Literature.* New York: Oxford University Press.
Wolf, Eric
1966 *Peasants.* Englewood Cliffs, N.J.: Prentice-Hall.
1982 *Europe and the People without History.* Berkeley: University of California Press.
1986 "The Viccisitudes of the Closed Corporate Peasant Community." Pp. 211–19 in *Directions in the Anthropological Study of Latin America: A Reassessment,* J. Rollwagen, ed. Monographs of the Society for Latin American Anthropology, no. 8. Washington, D.C.: American Anthropological Association.

Part IV

Commodity Chains and the Formal/Informal Sector Distinction

Chapter 10

Transcending the Formal/Informal Distinction:
Commercial Relations in Africa and Russia
in the Post-1989 World

Elena Obukhova and Jane I. Guyer

Introduction

In much of the world, the ten years since that fall of the Berlin Wall have seen an advance in the formal structuring of economic transactions in the international sphere but a decline in the reach of the state at the national level. The "informal sector" that has increasingly clearly accounted for provisioning, employment, and enrichment within regional economies can range in power from a comprehensive "shadow state" of distributive patronage networks that is dependent on formal sector access (as in Sierra Leone, Reno 1995), to key sector control (as in Zaire, MacGaffey 1991), and down to what are often quite resilient provisioning systems that have great historical longevity. Due to the complexity of commodity chains— in and out of formal institutions, through and around formal sector regulations—any overall systemic understanding can no longer oppose formal and informal sectors, but rather compares their interactions in varied contexts. Castells (1996) focuses on network organization, information management, and a radical "logic of timelessness" in which rapid change—in ideas, images, and conditions of inclusion in financial flows— becomes the norm. He predicts the differentiation of the world economy into major sectors on the basis of their linkage to finance capital, most of them subject to rapid shifts and therefore "structural" only as categories and not as actual places or real populations. By his logic, at the outer extreme are whole regions of the world and categories of the population that fall into what he refers to as "redundant workers" (1996: 147), who are hardly linked in at all. This vision of shifting and variable relationships between the dynamics of capital and a differentiated global population, with key points managed by powerful gatekeepers, has largely supplanted the incrementalist development model of past decades.

And yet neither the world nor the scholarship can be quite that neatly divided between pre- and post-1989, between the useful and the redundant, the progressive and the regressive, the ordered and the chaotic. In some places, similar dynamics have been at play for a very long time, as Guyer (1995) has argued in the case of currency instability in Africa. The post-1989 world may seem far more similar to the more distant past from some vantage points than others. Because of local continuities as well as shifts, our task in anthropology is in some senses more difficult than that of national and global theorists because we are faced with less obvious transformations, either of the situation "out there" or of our concepts to understand it. Many of the places we study have been living under conditions of contingency and volatility for such a long time that we might even suspect that concepts and relationships that predict or counter volatility—for example in prices—might have been already institutionalized, long before the current era of structural adjustment and financial crisis. All our thinking has to include the possibility of a long-term experience of the modern economy, a specifically modern tradition of economic relations, a commercial morality that has grown up over—in some places—centuries of engagement with an expanding world trade and financial system. If so, dealing with "redundancy" on a world scale in a new world order may draw on older social and cultural resources. On the other hand, we are not sure how adequate or apposite these resources might be to increased rates of change, new macro power relations, or simply a new generation of young people, trying to create careers and self-respect at a moment when health and education structures are in disarray and world culture provides new aspirations and idioms for self-expression. Their own experience of redundancy in the 1990s may have a different political implication and cultural idiom than in the 1890s or the 1930s.

A strategy for encompassing both formal and informal sectors, and the theoretical and conceptual repertoire that comes from the study of each, is to focus ethnographic attention precisely on the points themselves at which the institutions of state and finance meet the emergent orders of commercial life. We choose commodity chains that cross these thresholds, vodka in Russia and newspapers in Nigeria, and that also have a much longer history than the hectic decade of the 1990s. One has to start with specific cases; as Hart points out: "Whereas states and markets may plausibly be described in terms of abstract social principles, membership in bodies between the two extremes is always specific and concrete" (1992: 222). There is necessarily something arbitrary, or rather, idiosyncratic to the authors' research locations and languages, that determines the choice of such apparently divergent cases. But much can be illuminated by stepping outside conventional categorizations of place. The interest in comparing these two cases arises from the following common characteristics: They are national commodities, in regular demand long before the rise of new global markets in the 1990s, of continuing political importance, and produced and traded through chains that link the formal and informal sectors. Such commodities are likely to be managed through important institutions that have been created, validated, and operated in relation to, but not necessarily subject to, the disciplines of taxation and regulation or to the precise temporal frames of the massively elaborate credit system that underlies capitalism. We can expect them, therefore, to work through repertoires of routinized practices whose changes over time continually elaborate the formal-informal interface that is at the center of our interest.

Our focus is less on the social organization of the commodity chain per se than on the forms of institution that respond to instabilities over time: in the delivery of goods, development of payment schemes, terms of access to labor services of various kinds, sanctions on breach of contract, and so on. Heterogeneous and probably surprisingly innovative and even powerful, this kind of institution must be central to the terms of coexistence and mutual influence over time between a globalized financial capital and the vast majority of the world's population. People link to the moving targets of shifting state capacities, fluctuating world prices, and corporations that declare bankruptcy in part through their own social and cultural constructions. Our cases cannot yet offer a sound basis for generalization about what these are at present, but they can offer insights into certain key processes and they provide the opportunity to examine analytical challenges. Ethnographic method has consistently proved its capacity to identify and address originality in society and culture (Burawoy 1991; Guyer 1998); the formal-informal interface demands nothing short of classic anthropological study.

So we return here to a social history and ethnography of the literal interface, of the points at which "formal" and "informal" sectors meet and transact, where each is reaching to transcend the formal-informal divide. Doing so requires that instead of assuming two different structures that are articulated with each other we work from a concept of analogical processes and interface institutions. In the present exploration we work from four related propositions to guide documentation and analysis: (1) for any topic, ethnographic research needs to encompass the dynamics across the entire *continuum* from state measures to social constructions, and the history of their intersection; the study of networks lends itself well to this endeavor; (2) the process of *regularization* is central to people's creation of predictability, and it can be studied along the entire continuum, with formal regulation at one end and the emergent creation of regularity at the other; (3) *volatility* appears to be a chronic condition in economies that are not protected by very powerful formal sector measures such as the U.S. Federal Reserve and the Securities and Exchange Commission, so history and experience become central to analysis of the interface; (4) the study of key *commodities*[1] offers one way of describing all these processes—the complex formal/informal linkage, regularization as a process, and volatility as a historical condition—in a rigorous but flexible multimethod fashion.

Our case studies analyze dynamics that have a long history in their respective economies and have certain other features in common, even though we do not try to treat them in a directly comparative way. Vodka in Russia and newspaper production and distribution in Nigeria are both national markets, with local nodes, and both are of political relevance. Otherwise, vodka has a centuries-long engagement with the Russian state while Nigerian newspaper history is about one century, and, in its dealings with the independent state, about forty years. Conversely, the Nigerian present is more fully known than the current Russian situation. For Russia we draw on secondary sources, the media and on interviews by Obukhova in the summer of 1998 because we have no recent detailed ethnographic studies, whereas for Nigeria Obukhova carried out two summers of field research in 1996 and 1997.[2] The central theme of both cases is volatility and emergent regularizations along commodity chains that cross the continuum between formal and informal sectors.

Russia's "Commodity Number One"

When people think about vodka at the holiday table, they are sitting there in a good mood. But when they are seated at the official's desk, and in the Kremlin, that means that there is a black hole in the budget.
—Levin and Vagrov (1996)

So long-standing is the place of vodka in Russian state revenue[3] that this quotation could describe the sixteenth century, as well as the twentieth. It actually refers to 1996, but we think it captures well the persistence and opportunistic change in regulation of the vodka commodity chain. The Russian state has advanced and retreated, experimenting with different regulatory forms, all with different political and social implications. These oscillations in state policy partially reflect the fact that the state itself is an arena of competitive social alliances and ideological models. The oscillations also represent the state's response to particular constellations of informal processes engendered by and specific to each regulatory framework.

Since the fifteenth and sixteenth centuries when successful experiments with distillation were made,[4] the development of the vodka commodity chain has occurred in a symbiotic relationship with the development of the Russian state. Unlike other drinks of the Slavs,[5] vodka demands relatively low value inputs in comparison with the price that the market would bear for the final product. Value added was potentially very high, which invited controls and taxation by the Russian and later Soviet state. This special relationship between the state's interests and vodka was expressed in a now famous quote by E. F. Kankrin, a nineteenth-century Minister of Finance: "one must wish that the moderate use of spirits among the simple people should increase, for after the extreme contraction of the overseas grain trade in a country where agriculture is the main activity and cities are few, grain can only find use by transformation into spirits" (cited in Pinter 1967: 78).

Liquor revenues from 1763, when the earliest figures are available, to the beginning of Soviet times were no less than 20 percent of total state revenue (Christian 1990: appendix I). Indeed, after 1840 liquor taxes were the major source of state revenue, averaging 30 percent of ordinary revenue throughout the nineteenth century (Smith and Christian 1984: 301–2). The situation did not change much after the Revolution: By 1927–28 revenues from vodka were equal to 11 percent of total revenues (Christian 1995: 97), and turnover taxes on alcohol constituted 9 percent of all revenue in 1979 (Treml 1982: 31). Taxes on alcohol in 1979 were 29 percent of the entire taxes paid by the Soviet population (Treml 1982: 30). Only under Yeltsin did alcohol taxes decline to only 2 percent of state revenue.[6] Thus, throughout vodka's history the state had an important fiscal interest in regulation of the vodka commodity chain.

At the same time other social alliances and ideologies shaped the regulatory environment. The state was subject to and a source of paternalistic "popular morality" ideologies.[7] The state also had a concrete interest in maintaining public order, as, for example, during the mobilization for World War I when prohibition was introduced (Christian 1995: 91–92). In addition, other parties participated in the creation of regulatory frameworks: trade interests, such as producers and various middlemen, consumers, various sobriety movements, and churches which opposed unchristian rituals that were part of drinking customs. Actual frameworks at any one time were the result of a complex interplay of all these considerations and social forces. Certain characteristic configurations mark the historical periods; identifying them would allow us to deduce the kinds of enterprise that moved into economic opportunities opened up by the selective presence of the state.

The Pre-Soviet Period

As early as the 1540s the state asserted its control over a lucrative commodity chain that had previously been subsumed in the domestic economy by introducing Imperial *kabaks* (tavern-distilleries). Over the next two hundred years the state switched between directly administering *kabaks* and farming them out, depending on changing needs for revenue and emerging constellations of informal activities such as illegal production, corruption, and adulteration of products.[8] These informal activities not only deprived the state of revenue and eroded the authority of the government (Christian 1987), but also aggravated the consumers, leading to a peasant sobriety movement and vodka riots of 1858–61 (Christian 1990: chaps. 10 and 11).

As part of Alexander II's Great Reforms,[9] the excise system of alcohol trade was established in 1864. Under the excise system distillers paid a tax, while retailers paid a license fee; otherwise the market was unregulated. State revenue was boosted, for now the state had better access to taverns' profits. Prices declined, and the number of retail outlets increased. Abuses continued, but mostly at the retail level, where vodka continued to be diluted and toxic substances added to it. Overall, under the excise system drinking did not seem to decrease, and a crisis of perpetual underpayment of taxes was developing.

The state monopoly was established in 1895 as part of the reforms of S. Yu. Witte, then a Minister of Finance (1892–1903). Under the new system, private distillers, who purchased raw materials from the Treasury, sold unpurified alcohol to the state, which refined it and sold it to Treasury-operated stores (Witte 1921: 55). In his memoirs, Witte attributed the idea of state monopoly to Alexander III, who "confided in me that the heavy drinking prevailing among the people was a matter of great concern to him" (Witte 1921: 54). However benign Witte's intentions were, he also desperately needed money for his projects, and especially for construction of the trans-Siberian railroad.[10] The promonopoly position was also advocated by the producers, who felt that by not being subject to quality control, the retailers unjustly benefited from the excise system (Von Laue 1963: 103).

The Soviet Period

The Bolsheviks inherited from the previous regime almost complete prohibition, imposed during World War I. The next ten years witnessed

two interrelated developments in alcohol policy: One was a gradual retreat from the initial prohibition, another a campaign against illegal
distilling, which picked up in 1922–23 and 1928. At first, in 1920, restrictions were lifted on state sale of wines not exceeding 12 percent alcoholic
content, and by 1925 production of vodka at 40 percent alcoholic content
was allowed. By 1927–1928 production of alcoholic beverages by volume
reached more than half of the 1913 figure (Christian 1995: table 1). Rein-
troduction of the state monopoly on alcohol was motivated less by concern
for the drinking public than by fiscal and political considerations. Since
prohibition led to increased production of *samogon* (or moonshine), it
poured profit into the coffers of presumed "antisocialist" elements in
peasant/domestic production, sabotaging the new state's agricultural
policy.[11]

Acknowledging both the peasants' propensity to produce moonshine
and the state's needs for revenue in the mid-1920s, Stalin argued that the
victory of the proletariat and peasantry could not be achieved without
getting a little dirty and reinvesting in alcohol (Stalin 1948–52: 1948 [1927]:
192; 1949 [1927]: 232). Imposing an alcohol monopoly to bring in state
revenues was the only alternative to receiving foreign loans on Western
terms, which included the politically and ideologically unacceptable return of nationalized industries and repayment of the prerevolutionary debt.
In addition Stalin calculated that the state monopoly would not endanger
grain reserves, since production could be based on potatoes (Weissman
1986: 362).

The state monopoly regulatory framework provided for the most
comprehensive regulation by the state of an entire commodity chain in
Russian history. However, even this regulatory framework was surrounded
by a host of "informal" activities. Illegally produced alcohol entered the
state distribution system, while officially produced alcoholic beverages
entered into unofficial distribution channels (Feldbrugge 1989: 328). Officially made vodka entered unofficial channels through "spillage
allowance." Allowances of this sort for a specified amount of allowable
loss during production or distribution made sure that the product did
indeed get lost, or entered the black market.[12] Moonshining seems to have
continued through the entire Soviet period.[13] In the 1960s and 1970s the
government admitted that production of *samogon* was often of
semiindustrial character and intended for sale in unofficial markets (White
1996: 122–23). Particular regulations restricting retail sales of alcohol engendered a host of informal activities. For example, prohibitions on the
sale of alcohol during morning and evening hours in state stores bred
their own informal dynamics in speculative trade in products bought from
the store during legal hours (Katsenelinbogen 1977: 83).

Gorbachev's anti-alcohol campaign (1985–88) dramatically curtailed production and distribution of "official" alcohol and initiated new measures against production of unofficial alcohol. The campaign was an outcome of an objective growth in alcohol consumption during the socialist years, and broadening of social scientific research on alcoholism and its economic and social cost, coupled with the ascetic bent of new leadership in response to the extravagance of the Brezhnev years (Tarschys 1993). Thus, between 1985 and 1987 production of "official" alcohol declined to less than half (Levin 1997: 103) and consumption from 8.8 liters to 3.9 liters of 100-percent ethanol per year per person (Nemtzov 1997: 114). However, according to the State Statistical Bureau's study of family budgets and purchases of sugar by the population (cited in Nemtzov 1997: 114), simultaneously the proportion of "official" alcohol consumed out of total alcohol consumption declined from 72 to 39 percent. It is said that even at an Antarctica station officials confiscated fourteen distillation devices (Romanov 1998: 285). The campaign was recognized as a widespread failure. Clearly, unofficial production and distribution not only formed an alternative system, but probably interdigitated with the official system in complex ways, as it had in the past: supplying inputs, transporting, making sales, and so on. One can imagine from other cases that bottles were probably recycled and relabeled from one system to the other, and that official outlets might include vodka from both sources.

The Post-Soviet Period: Once-a-Year Monopoly and Fakes

In 1992 by presidential decree the sixty-eight-year-long monopoly on one aspect or another of production and sale, and the fifth declared monopoly in the history of the Russian state, was abandoned. The result was that the country "drowned in a sea of vodka" (Romanov 1998: 297). Fakes flooded the market: "Stolichnaya" sold in kiosks was fake half the time (Romanov 1998: 300). The following year, in June 1993, in an attempt to regulate the anarchic market, the "monopoly" was reinstated.[14] Production, sale, and distribution were supposed to be licensed.[15] According to Russian journalists, the regulations were on paper only: "The only person who did not get a license was a lazy one."[16] Even so, in 1994 it was still estimated that consumption of illegal domestic alcohol and illegal foreign exports was two-thirds of the consumption of legal alcohol. Between 1994 and 1996 the state security organs closed down 6,000 illegal alcohol production facilities (Zaigraev 1997). Smuggling was rampant; borders with Belorus and Ukraine are particularly permeable. While legal imports of alcohol from Belorussia were supposedly declining, "410 times more vodka, 46 times more ethyl alcohol and 31 times more beer were imported into Belorus from far abroad in the first six months of 1996 compared with the corresponding period of last year."[17] At the same time, alcohol production became a leader in the nonpayment and evasion of taxes,[18] in particular through bogus exporting which gained the enterprise an exemption from VAT and excise taxes.[19]

At the very end of 1996 the state was making another attempt to establish control over the alcohol commodity chain. It planned to install tax services at all distilleries in 1997, providing taxpaying producers with excise stamps.[20] Thus the burden of taxes was shifted to distilleries, the point at which it is easiest for the state to control how much is being actually produced. Import stamps were sold illegally in Poland almost as soon as they were sold in Russia.[21] However, production of illegal, adulterated, and fake alcohol continues, as is manifested in the title of a recent newspaper article giving a whole new meaning to a line from a Russian fairy tale: "Do not drink from a puddle, or you will become a goat." The best defense for consumers and producers alike is still fancy bottles and disposable caps. The difficulty of central state control is exacerbated by a general tendency toward regionalization in Russia and other post-socialist countries (Humphrey 1991; Verdery 1996); lucrative commodity chains take on specific regional characteristics, the nature of whose antecedents would greatly repay study.[22]

In this situation, when in 1997 the production of *samogon* was legalized, the book markets started selling numerous pamphlets and books full of recipes for production of *samogon* or purifying store-bought vodka. One book (Mishin 1998) contains thirty-four "folk recipes for regular *samogon*" alone! Authors of another book hope that their recipes will help people to save their stomachs from surrogates and store-bought vodka, as well as to spend more on their children's food (Korefanov and Strokova 1998).

The shifting pressure and accumulation points exerted by the Russian and Soviet states are one part of the social history of the vodka commodity chain. In the present volatile global economy, where states' policies are deeply affected by international bond markets and fluctuating prices for the goods on whose taxation they depend for revenue, we should expect to see much more of this continual reshaping of regulatory schemes. Another major part of the story is the continuing alacrity with which operators have moved into the vodka market, depending on the actual frameworks in place, which then deeply affects what state policies can be. A final aspect, and the one that must interest anthropologists the most, can only be inferred here: namely that there are organizations and interests poised to take advantage of opportunities that shifting state policies open up. There is long experience in Russia in dealing with, and probably creating, the profitable interstices that different regulation regimes present. Whether these forms have generated characteristic institutions of trust and financial management, networks of relationships, alliances across the for-mal/informal sector interface and modes of apprenticeship, or, conversely, whether there is a constantly shifting army of atomistic participants, re-main questions for detailed ethnographic and historical work.

Also suspected but not verified is our sense that vodka has been used as an asset and not just a consumption item in times of volatility in the value of currency. The role of vodka and samogen as an exchange instru-ment in rural nineteenth-century Russia has been documented (Herlihy 1991: 137–40; Stone 1986: 369–70) and is supported by anecdotal evidence for the Soviet period. Quite recently, due to widespread shortage of cash, people have turned to IOUs and barter in the post-Soviet economy, and there are reports of, for example, teachers being paid in herring and vodka.[23] Market purchase is a function of both dynamics: consumer demand and hedging against financial fluctuations. Thus the type of commodity, and its insertion into local repertoires, must come to the fore.

The probable dual importance of vodka supports the commodity chain approach as a first step to constituting a basic ethnography of emergent commercial systems, functioning under conditions of volatility, beyond the state but deeply conditioned by its policies. The following case ex-plores how such a sector works for the case of newspaper production and distribution in Nigeria.

The Nigerian Newspaper and Periodicals Industry

In this case study we want to illustrate how, under conditions of state and market-induced volatility, regularity is created in economic transactions that are sparsely regulated by the state. The research for this paper was carried out during the summers of 1996 and 1997. It included a survey of 183 agents and vendors, collecting information about their demographic and business characteristics (in the text referred to as survey); semistructured interviews about credit relations with fifteen media repre-sentatives and ten agents (in the text referred to as contract enforcement interviews); and about one hundred informal interviews.

In Nigeria, newspapers and periodicals are produced by formal sec-tor firms, but are distributed only through informal sector actors; thus the commodity chain crosses the entire formal/informal continuum. As com-modities, newspapers, and magazines have certain characteristics that influence the organization of the commodity chain.[24] The first peculiarity is that newspapers and periodicals are produced for political purposes, to control information and influence public opinion, and are therefore only slowly responsive to shifts in demand that are entirely economically based while being very vulnerable to major interventions by the state. Owners try to survive intervention and may even expect to subsidize production. This mutes to some degree the susceptibility of the commodity chain to relative price fluctuations in the economy as a whole, although we do see effects of low consumer demand on the lower levels of the distribution system. Newspapers are also a highly perishable commodity. Accumulation by the consumer cannot function as asset formation in any meaningful sense, so the organization of distribution has to be particularly coordinated with respect to time and place. These commodity characteristics make it likely that the commodity chain differs in some important respects from, for example, the chain for goods that might well operate as longer-term assets (such as vehicles and appliances, or foreign exchange currencies) and—at the other extreme—goods in which no symbolic or financial interests are embedded at all.

The study shows that the critical node in the commodity chain, or the node that creates regularity backwards and forwards from itself, is powerful agents or distributors, who mediate between the formal sector media representatives, on the one hand, and the informal sector agents and vendors, on the other. Distributors are located at the intersection of three institutional forms through which commercial relations are regularized: the union, the sole distributorship, and the association. We argue that whatever regularity distributors create in the newspaper and periodicals commodity chain, they achieve by their occupational longevity and expertise in finance, management, sales, and policing. Furthermore, we suggest as a tentative hypothesis that while the presence and likely location of a regularizing node is a function of commodity characteristics and commodity-specific volatility, the particular forms emerging represent distributors' creative adoption and use of locally valid institutional forms (the union and the association) that cross commodity forms, as well as being a function of their privileged attachment to the formal sector (through sole distributorship).

In the morning the representatives of the formal-sector media houses (the circulation personnel) distribute the products of their media house to the agents and vendors. Agents aggregate products from different media houses and distribute them to vendors. Vendors, who receive the products from agents or directly from media houses, sell the products on the street throughout the day. The agents and vendors keep the commission on the sales, while the circulation staff is paid salaries by the media house. The whole distribution system is based on recurrent short-term credit transaction. Vendors receive their consignment from agents or from media representatives with an understanding that after selling it (that is, the following day in the case of newspapers or week in the case of weeklies) vendors will subtract their own commission and turn the proceeds of the sale over to the person from whom they collected the consignment. Agents receive consignments on credit from the media representatives and distribute them on credit to vendors.

The commodity chain is formally regulated by the media houses and by the Newspaper Proprietors Association of Nigeria (NPAN). Media houses with NPAN guidelines determine the size of the commission from the sale of each copy that will go to those who receive the product directly from the media house and to those who receive it indirectly. NPAN certifies agents and vendors before they are allowed to receive the product directly from the media houses, and some media houses attempt to control to whom their circulation personnel distribute the product. But their control is incomplete. Circulation personnel often distribute the product to people with whom they develop personal trust, disregarding registration and directions from the top. For example, based on the survey, the media house representative at the bestselling paper in Ibadan distributed the paper directly to more than a quarter of forty-six unregistered agents and vendors. In this way, agents and vendors are only subject to indirect media house regulation. In sum, large parts of the distribution of newspapers and magazines are not regulated by the formal structure of the media houses.

The newspaper and periodicals industry has been subject to both state- and market-induced volatility. State-induced volatility is a result of the political and symbolic significance of the product more than of any state economic policy toward the informal sector in general. The state's major concern is not with regulating the production and distribution of newspapers and magazines, but with their content. The state "regulates" content through censorship, official harassment, persecution, and proscription (i.e., legal closure) of media houses. Most of these measures are temporary and occasioned by major political events or particular exposures of the opposition press.

The major volatility affecting the newspaper and periodicals commodity chain during the period of research was produced by the market. Since the early 1980s the Nigerian economy has been in decline. Shrinking consumer incomes took the newspapers and periodicals out of ordinary buyers' reach. Currently, few newspapers have print runs of more than 50,000 copies.[25] Decline in demand coupled with raising prices of inputs put a squeeze on the industry. Lowered profitability affected vendors whose commission between 1982 and 1992 has declined from 25 percent of the cover price to 15 percent (Fatokun 1992). Agents' commission remained relatively stable at around 5 percent, possibly reflecting distributors' critical location in the commodity chain and greater potential for mobilization to preserve their own interests (see below).

One of the challenges of doing business in a volatile economy is the emergence of an economy of debt, which is characterized by liquidity preference, widespread indebtedness, debt and default chains, preferences for what Nigerians call "cash 'n carry" transactions, and the distress of the banking system (Guyer 1997; Obukhova n.d.). The newspaper and periodicals business, which functions on credit basis, did not escape the economy of debt. In contract enforcement interviews, 80 percent of circulation personnel and 100 percent of agents mentioned nonpayment as a problem they experience with their customers, or those to whom they distribute on credit.

Furthermore, there is a lack of formal means for enforcement of contracts, as well as little evidence for social embeddedness playing a major role in discouraging malfeasance (Obukhova n.d.). In the contract enforcement interviews only 31 percent of media representatives and 10 percent of agents mentioned resorting to legal means in case of repayment problems, for the law is considered to be a very ineffective means of enforcing contract performance. Only 23 percent of media personnel attempt to revoke agents' or vendors' NPAN registration in case of nonpayment. Thus, formal processes do not play a major role in contract enforcement.

At the same time, based on the survey, agents and vendors have only a slight preference for business partners of the same ethnicity or religion. Most business relations are simply about business: With 56 percent of business contacts the respondents had only business relations. Only 5 and 26 percent of contacts were described as "friends" and "friends and neighbors," respectively; only 6 and 2 percent as "relative" and "relative and neighbor." Thus formal processes or social embeddedness do not appear to be major sources of regularization in this case, forcing us to look elsewhere for economic forms creating predictability and ways in which these forms are given efficiency and longevity.

The Union: Agents and Vendors

One means through which economic relations are regularized is through customer ties[26] between agents and vendors. Agents develop relatively stable and exclusive relationships with their vendors who become known as an agent's union. Vendors belonging to unions of powerful agents are rewarded with end-of-the-year parties or dashes. In cases of hardship for the vendor, vendor loyalty is rewarded with extension of payment deadlines in exceptional circumstances, which is a form of insurance.[27] This relationship of loyalty is particularly important during periods of political crisis,[28] when, due to skyrocketing demand for product, some vendors are willing to pay cash in order to receive larger consignments and agents are tempted to switch from credit, with its attendant dangers of default, to demanding cash 'n carry transactions. Here the existence of long-term relationships between agents and vendors guarantees the vendors access to at least some copies on a credit basis. In exchange for vendor loyalty, some agents sacrifice short-term gain in potentially lucrative periods of political crisis.

Sole Distributorship: Circulation Personnel and Agents

Media representatives often do not have at their disposal effective sanctions to discipline agents and vendors who do not pay up. Thus, to the formal sector circulation personnel, agents represent an opportunity to shift the risk. One way to shift risk is the sole distributorship system, in which an agent has exclusive access to the products of the media house and, in turn, distributes them to other agents and vendors. The sole distributor then enforces contractual compliance from other agents and vendors. A sole distributor comes to have a loosely organized group of agents and vendors who depend on him alone for one particular product. Thus, a sole distributor of desirable products has considerable power over numerous agents and vendors.

The Associations

A third means of regularization of economic life is occupational associations. Associations often serve as intermediaries between vendors, agents, and the media houses. Vendor and agent associations play a role in maintaining what agents and vendors consider as fair distribution of commission from sales. Associations in Ibadan in the past protested against late arrival of certain publications, introduction of the sole distributorship system, particular fraudulent media personnel, and even progovernment content of publications that made them hard to sell in times of general popular disaffection. We suggest that the fact that agents' commissions appeared to stay relatively unchanged throughout the current period is due to the present domination of the associations by agents, and particularly by sole distributors. Another way that associations regularize economic life is through mobilizing agent and vendor protests in cases of state's prosecution of the press and particularly prosecution of the agents and vendors themselves. Lastly, associations play a role in contract enforcement. On the one hand, they disseminate information among agents about vendors and help agents to extract debts from vendors. On the other hand, circulation personnel sometimes turn to associations for information and enforcement.

The Distributors

The final factor in regularization is less explicitly recognized and identified. Among agents the study found that there is a group of distributors with large volumes of product and great occupational longevity. Eight percent of 183 vendors and agents surveyed sold more than 200 copies of their three best-selling publications.[29] These 8 percent on average sold 425 copies, while 92 percent at or below this mark sold on average only 61 copies. Also, these 8 percent had spent on average twice as long in distribution business as those at or below this mark (18.3 versus 9.5 years respectively).[30] We suggest that it is this group which is able to draw on the already culturally legitimized forms and formal-sector sanctioned forms to directly control and indirectly regularize a high proportion of transactions.

Powerful distributors manage to head large unions, become leaders of associations, and win sole distributorship. These three organizational forms tend to interact giving each other added effectiveness. A sole distributor who, by distributing to many agents and vendors, has some degree of power might eventually organize an association and become its head. The association will help serve the goals of the membership as well as of the leader. In other words, powerful distributors, those who possess sole distributorship, leadership of an association and large unions, are in a better position than any other node to create regularity along the entire commodity chain for they can influence the behavior of vendors and agents as well as of media houses.

It would go beyond the preliminary nature of this study to infer very large conclusions, but the social forms of the newspaper distribution chain in Ibadan do show how a patronage/big man element coexists with, and is framed by, the existing forms of Yoruba associational life that apply to all crafts. At the same time, one sees—in the large number of vendors who sell very few newspapers and have spent very little time in the business— how an atomistic and floating population may move from one commodity to another, their conditions of work being set by a regularized set of institutions ensured by long-time participants. We suggest, from answers to the "embeddedness" questions, that leadership in this particular market may not emanate (at least, not only) from preexisting advantages of social connection that have nothing to do with skill on the job. In fact, there may well be a premium in new and emergent local and regional markets on the personal capacities such as business acumen and social skill, patience and experience, that seem to characterize the major distributors, and for which the floating population of vendors may effectively be an applicant pool and vending an apprenticeship. In studying these markets, then, one should not be too quick to categorize them by known sociological concepts without examining the operation of the entire chain, which may include and integrate a variety of elements—personal skill and network manipulation and classic associational form, longevity and extreme ephemerality—in some locally understood model of operation or an emergent innovation from it.

Conclusion

These two commodity distribution systems have existed for much longer than the current scramble over the great financial flows and raw material sources that the post-1989 globalization forces set in motion. Like a very large number of products, both of these are produced locally and are largely oriented to a domestic market, so both include local populations in various roles across the entire chain from production to consumption. Both also deal in a commodity whose demand is broadly distributed both socially and geographically, a national commodity of some importance to the state, that sells retail at low enough prices to be part of the consumer bundle of large segments of the population. This kind of market is very large and very important in the employment and basic welfare of populations that are otherwise only indirectly affected by the capital flows and networks for minerals and other major world commodities. Neither distribution system appears to be dominated by mafias or new kinds of patronage networks although both involve activities beyond state regulation or escaping from it.

Our studies suggest that there are characteristic sector-specific dilemmas and institutions that have grown up over long periods of time. In Russia, there is a continuous history of domestic-level production and distribution, and a repertoire of already tried organizational frameworks, each offering its own opportunities for working the loopholes. If we had the chance to do ethnographic research we would certainly look for nodes with longevity: central places where the level of expertise in the vodka business was particularly high, families whose business had included vodka over more than one generation, cultures of vodka as an asset in times of currency instability. All of these would give some predictability to the terms of employment, management, and consumption in the vodka industry. In Nigeria we found that certain roles embodied and managed the intersections not only between formal and informal sectors, but between different nonformal rubrics for organizing commercial relations under volatile conditions. The fact that such stabilizing existed is perfectly consonant with an extreme situation of ephemerality at the bottom of the industry; neither view summarizes the chain in its entirety.

By studying commodity chains historically and ethnographically, and particularly commodity chains that employ and provision local and regional populations rather than global markets, we can identify key processes in the formation of livelihoods and economic orders in varying contingent relationships to global forces. Within their own geographical reach these processes can shape the entire economy of employment, provisioning, wealth generation, and skill acquisition. Aggregated and linked across the globe, they may have more influence on economic dynamics than any view of globalization from the great financial centers and focused on capital circulation can account for.

Notes

This chapter as a whole benefited from LaRay Denzer's expertise on the Ibadan local economy and her patience with the authors' intermittent demands on her. Research in Nigeria was carried out by Elena Obukhova under the auspices of a larger project organized by Jane I. Guyer and LaRay Denzer, entitled "Money Morals: The Decline of the Naira in the Social Life and Popular Culture of Nigeria, 1985–1995," funded by the John D. and Catherine T. MacArthur Foundation. Obukhova's participation was funded by a Hans Panofsky Award, Program of African Studies, Northwestern. Data collection was made possible by assistance from Akindayo A. Sowunmi, Soji Olasoko, Akinyemi Olufemi Ogunkeyede, Taiwo O. Aikulola, Rotimi Adeyemo, and Anthony Okiwelu.

1. We draw here on Gereffi, Korzeniewicz, and Korzeniewicz (1994).

2. Undertaken under the auspices of a project on the popular economy under devaluation: Jane I. Guyer and LaRay Denzer: "Money Morals: The Decline of the Naira in the Social Life and Popular Culture of Nigeria 1985–95," funded by the John D. and Katherine T. MacArthur Foundation.

3. The term "commodity number one" was first used by a Soviet dissident, A. Krasikov (real name Mikhail Baitalsky, 1903–78), who attempted to calculate real consumption of alcohol in the U.S.S.R. (see White 1996: 36–37).

4. See Pokhlebkin (1992: 86) for the fifteenth century and Smith and Christian (1984: 102) for the sixteenth century.

5. *Kvas* (a drink of varied strength similar to beer), mead (made from honey), and birchwood wine (made from fermented sap of birchwood) were drunk in communal drinking houses (*korchmas*). Their production was tied to the agricultural cycle, festivals and communal functions (Pokhlebkin 1992).

6. "Kto I Skol'ko Zarabatyival na "P'yanyih Den'gah" ("Who and How Much Made on 'Drunk Money'"), *Komsomol'skaya Pravda*, 2 July 1998, p. 3.

7. See for example Krukones' (1991) analysis of how the problem of alcoholism was discussed in government newspapers (1881–1917) directed at rural populations.

8. See Christian (1987) for description of corruption in vodka trade in 1850s and '60s.

9. The most noted achievements of the Great Reforms were abolition of serfdom, reform of the legal system, and creation of *zemstvost'* and town *dumas*, both elected bodies of local self-government.

10. The trend toward increased taxation during his ministership was clear. In addition, Witte frantically borrowed abroad, especially in France (Von Laue 1963).

11. On grain policies see Stone (1986). On distorted low prices for agricultural products, including grain, and high prices for industrial and mass consumer goods during NEP, see particularly Weissman (1986). Christian (1995: 96) adds that the first retreat by the Soviets from Prohibition was also aimed at preservation of supplies of industrial alcohol, used for the making of explosives and transportation (after oil supplies from the Caucasus were cut off). For the political implications of moonshining, see particularly Stone (1986).

12. O'Hearn also writes about the "spillage allowance" that "under the present law in most republics, a driver can 'lose' up to 9r. 99 k. of his load without accounting for the loss. A loss of over 10 rubles must be accounted for . . . and the only penalty awaiting the driver is to repay the *wholesale volume* of the loss. Meanwhile, he sells the goods on the black market at three times the official cost" (1980: 230).

13. See Connor (1971: 572–73) for a description of a study from the 1950s which found that 78.5 percent of offenders used "special apparatus" for illegal distilling.

14. B. Fedorov critiques the government's inability to enforce monopolies which are "introduced at least once a year" in FBISSOV97001, Daily Report, 31 Dec. 1996.

15. B. Fedorov in FBISSOV97001, Daily Report, 31 Dec. 1996.

16. Levin, K., and A. Vagrov in *FBISSOV97042S*, Daily Report, 27 Dec. 1996.

17. Zhokov, S. In FBIS-SOV-(&-)%*-S, Daily Report, 26 Dec. 1996.

18. Pismennaya, Ye. in FBISSOV97016, Daily Report, 31 Dec. 1996.

19. Kozlov A. in FBISTDD97002L, FBIS Report, 18 Dec. 1996.

20. ITARTAS in FBISSOV97009, Daily Report, 13 Jan. 1997.

21. CSO in FBISSOV97050, Daily Report, 14 Mar. 1997.

22. For alcohol we think that this continues a tradition of city-level regulation of retail trade (Connor 1971: 586), but on a wider scale. For example, Taterstan limited vodka imports and implemented new regulatory structures. In Omsk, the mayor instituted regulations that require any alcohol sales firm to "discuss" the assortment of their beverages with the mayor and city administration, and to produce, at inspection, their registration, product quality certificates, and documentation on purchases and transportation. See "Kontrol' sa Torgovley Spirtnim Uzhestochaet'cya" in *Segodnya*, 10 Dec. 1994: 4).

23. "Krasnoyarsk Kray Plight Viewed" FBIS-SOV-97-041-S Daily Report, 10 Dec. 1996.

24. Similar points about the link between commodity characteristics and commodity chain structure have been made for coffee (Talbot 1997) and fresh produce (Buck et al. 1997).

25. "Stormy Weather Buffets the Press," *The Guardian*, June 24, 1996, p. 29.

26. See Trager (1981) on customer ties in a Yoruba context.

27. See Udry (1990) on credit as a form of insurance in the rural Nigeria.

28. Obukhova is grateful to Sola Olorunyomi who suggested investigation of this topic.

29. This is not an indigenously defined category. Empirically, the survey showed a larger group of agents, about 10 percent of the total number.

30. For the entire sample, the correlation between years in business and natural logarithm of proxy for income is 0.23. The regression results, available from

the author, suggest that people with a longer time in business tend to earn more (the dependent variable is natural logarithm of sold, "years in business" has a regression coefficient of 0.05 that is significant at p=0.01 level).

References

Buck, Daniel, Christina Getz, and Julie Guthman
   1997 "From Farm to Table: The Organic Vegetable Commodity Chain of Northern California." *Sociologia Ruralis* 37(1): 3–20.
Burawoy, Michael, ed.
   1991 *Ethnography Unbound: Power and Resistance in the Modern Metropolis*. Berkeley: University of California Press.
Castells, Manuel
   1996 *The Rise of the Network Society*. Malden, Mass.: Blackwell.
Christian, David
   1987 "Vodka and Corruption in Russia on the Eve of Emancipation." *Slavic Review* 46(3/4): 471–88.
   1990 *"Living Water": Vodka and Russian Society on the Eve of Emancipation*. Oxford: Clarendon Press.
   1995 "Prohibition in Russia 1914–1925." *Australian Slavonic and East European Studies* 9(2): 89–108.
Connor, Walter D.
   1971 "Alcohol and Soviet Society." *Slavic Review* 30(3): 570–88.
Fatokun, Olukemi Stella
   1992 "Newspaper Price Increases and Its Impact on Buying and Readership Patterns: A Study of Two Widely Read Newspapers." Long essay (bachelor's thesis), University of Ibadan.
Fedorov, B.
   1996 FBISSOV97001, *Daily Report*, 31 December.
Feldbrugge, F. J. M.
   1989 "The Soviet Second Economy in a Political and Legal Perspective." Pp. 297–338 in *The Underground Economies: Tax Evasion and Information Distortion*, E. L. Feige, ed. Cambridge: Cambridge University Press.
Gereffi, Gary, Miguel Korzeniewicz, and Roberto Korzeniewicz
   1994 "Introduction: Global Commodity Chains." Pp. 1–14 in *Commodity Chains and Global Capitalism*, G. Gereffi and M. Korzeniewicz, eds. Westport, Conn.: Greenwood Press.
Guyer, Jane I.
   1997 "Popular Reactions to Currency Instability." Paper presented at the Program of African Studies, Northwestern University (November).
   1998 "Anthropology: The Study of Social and Cultural Originality." Paper prepared for the symposium on Social Sciences and the Challenge of Globalization in Africa. Council for the Development of Social and Economic Research in Africa (CODESRIA), Johannesburg.

Guyer, Jane I., ed.
    1995   *Money Matters: Instability, Values and Social Payments in the Modern History of West African Communities.* Portsmouth, N.H.: Heinemann.
Hart, Keith
    1992   "Market and State after the Cold War." Pp. 214–27 in *Contesting Markets: Analyses of Ideology, Discourse and Practice,* R. Dilley, ed. Edinburgh: Edinburgh University Press.
Herlihy, Patricia
    1991   "Joy of the Rus': Rites and Rituals of Russian Drinking." *The Russian Review* 50: 131–47.
Humphrey, Caroline
    1991   "Icebergs, Barter, and the Mafia in Provincial Russia." *Anthropology Today* 7: 8–13.
Katsenelinbogen, A.
    1977   "Coloured Markets in the Soviet Union." *Soviet Studies* 29: 62–85.
Korefanov, Yu., and L. Strokova
    1998   *Prigotovleniye Napitkov v Domashnih Usloviyah: Ot Vodki do Chaya (Preparation of Drinks at Home: From Vodka to Tea).* Moscow: Ripol Classic.
Krukones, James H.
    1991   "Satan's Blood, Tsar's Ink: Rural Alcoholism in an Official 'Publication for the People,' 1881–1917." *Russian History/Histoire Russe* 18(4): 435–56.
Levin, B. M.
    1997   "Glavnyie Factoryi Alkogolizatzii Obshchestva v Usloviyah Sottzial'nyih Peremen (Main Factors in the Alcoholization of Society during Social Changes)." *Sotziologicheskie Isledovania* 4: 102–8.
Levin, K., and A. Vagrov
    1996   "The Monopoly on Vodka is Returning." FBISSOV97042S, Daily Report, 27 December, electronic version.
MacGaffey, Janet
    1991   *The Real Economy of Zaire: The Contribution of Smuggling and Other Unofficial Activities to the National Wealth.* Philadelphia: University of Pennsylvania Press.
Mishin, S.
    1998   *Samogon Domashniyi (Homemade Samogon).* St. Petersburg: Litera.
Nemtzov, A. V.
    1997   "Potreblenie Alkogolia I Smertnost v Rossii (Alcohol Consumption and Death Rate in Russia)." *Sotziologicheskie Isledovania* (9): 1997.
Obukhova, Elena
    n.d.   "Living and Trusting in the Economy of Debt: Nigerian Newspaper Distribution." To appear in *Money Struggles and City Life: Devaluation and the Popular Economy in Southern Nigeria, 1986–96,* J. Guyer, L. Denzer, and A. A. B. Agbaje, eds.
O'Hearn, Dennis
    1980   "The Consumer Second Economy: Size and Effects." *Soviet Studies* 32(2): 218–34.

Pinter, Walter McKenzie
    1967   *Russian Economic Policy Under Nicholas I.* Ithaca, N.Y.: Cornell University Press.
Pismennaya, Ye
    1996   FBISSOV97016. *Daily Report,* 31 December.
Pokhlebkin, William
    1992   *History of Vodka.* New York: Verso.
Reno, William
    1995   *Corruption and State Politics in Sierra Leone.* Cambridge: Cambridge University Press.
Romanov, Sergei
    1998 *Istoriya Russkoyi Vodki (History of Russian Vodka).* Moscow: Veche.
Smith, R. E. F., and David Christian
    1984   *Bread and Salt: A Social and Economic History of Food and Drink in Russia.* Cambridge: Cambridge: Cambridge University Press.
Stalin, I. V.
    1948–1952   *Sochineniia.* Moscow: Gosudarstvenoe Izdatelstvo Politicheskoyi Literaturyi.
Stone, Helena
    1986   "The Soviet Government and Moonshine, 1917–1929." *Cahiers du Monde Sovietique* 27(3/4): 359–80.
Talbot, John M.
    1997   "The Struggle for Control of a Commodity Chain: Instant Coffee from Latin America." *Latin American Research Review* 32(2): 117–35.
Tarschys, Daniel
    1993   "The Success of a Failure: Gorbachev's Alcohol Policy, 1985–88." *EuropeAsia Studies* 45(1): 7–27.
Trager, Lillian
    1981   "Customers and Creditors: Variations in Economic Personalism in Nigerian Marketing System." *Ethnology* 20(2): 133–46.
Treml, Vladimir G.
    1982   *Alcohol in the U.S.S.R.: A Statistical Study.* Durham, N.C.: Duke University Press.
Udry, Christopher
    1990   "Credit Markets in Northern Nigeria: Credit as Insurance in a Rural Economy." *World Bank Economic Review* 4(3): 251–69.
Verdery, Katherine
    1996   *What Was Socialism and What Comes Next?* Princeton, N.J.: Princeton University Press.
Von Laue, Theodore H.
    1963   *Sergei Witte and the Industrialization of Russia.* New York: Columbia University Press.
Weissman, Neil
    1986   "Prohibition and Alcohol Control in the U.S.S.R.: The 1920s Campaign Against Illegal Spirits." *Soviet Studies* 38(3) (July): 349–68.

White, Stephen
  1996   *Russia Goes Dry: Alcohol, State and Society.* Cambridge: Cambridge University Press.
Witte, Sergei
  1921   *The Memoirs of Count Witte*, Abraham Yarmolinsky, trans. Garden City, N.Y.: Doubleday, Page.
Zaigraev, G. G.
  1997   "Gosudarstvenaya Politica kak Faktor Alkogolizatsii Naseleniya (State Policy as a Factor in the Alcoholization of Population)." *Sotziologicheskie Isledovania* 4: 109–16.

Chapter 11

Commodity Chains and the International Secondhand Clothing Trade: *Salaula* and the Work of Consumption in Zambia

Karen Tranberg Hansen

The recommodification of the West's used clothing into what since the mid-1980s in Zambia has been referred to as *salaula* comprises a gray area both empirically and conceptually. In empirical terms, the extent and scope of the expanding commodity chain that results from the international secondhand clothing trade is hazy, as are the economics of the relationship between the charitable organizations and commercial clothing recyclers who are the single largest source of this expanding and profitable business. In conceptual terms, the designation *salaula* reconstructs the West's cast-off clothing into a desirable commodity without making reference to its origin or provenience, in effect obliterating the history of sourcing and production, once retailers place secondhand clothing bales for sale at the end of the chain in Zambia. Consumers here explain the presence of salaula as a result of "donations" from the West, as is the case with so much else in Zambia. The term means, in the Bemba language, to select from a pile in the manner of rummaging. In effect, salaula describes the selection process that takes place once a bale of secondhand clothing has been opened and consumers select garments to satisfy both their clothing needs and desires.

From the supply side at the point of sourcing in the West through all intervening stages to the point of consumption in poor countries like Zambia, the secondhand clothing trade is shrouded in a charitable guise. The mapping of its history in my larger work remains preliminary.

Perhaps the most striking difficulty has been the lack of scholarly interest in considering secondhand clothing consumption as anything other than the flip side of Western fashion and mere satisfaction of basic clothing needs. But clothing consumption has complex bearings on how people organize their livelihoods, and the manner in which they conduct their everyday lives touches on the production and distribution relations that are available to them.

This chapter concerns consumption and, in particular, what we may make of Zambian preoccupations with clothing, both used and new for of course they implicate one another. On the pages that follow, I first briefly discuss the relevance of the paradigmatic shift toward consumption to explanations of the salaula phenomenon in Zambia. I suggest that the relevance of this shift depends on what type of commodity we examine in relationship to which consumers, when, and where. Secondhand clothing is not just any commodity, but a rather special one, because of the way in which it, as dress, mediates both individual and collective identities and desires, and because of the way it, as an imported commodity, offers a special exposure on interactions between the local and the West. Turning to salaula in Zambia, I suggest that the work of production does not end in consumption, but that in fact it begins there. For in dealings with salaula, consumption has complicated ramifications in the realm of production.

Explaining the salaula phenomenon challenges the conventional division between production, distribution/exchange, and consumption in economic anthropology. In effect, the divide obscures the complex character of people's dealings with clothing. As an approach to capture such complex interactions I use Fine and Leopold's (1993) notion of commodity-specific systems of provision. The bulk of the chapter delineates the processes involved in a sketch of the secondhand clothing system of provision that includes the West and Zambia. In conclusion, I briefly reflect on the implications of this case for economic anthropology, for development research, and above all for a serious reckoning with why and how consumption practices matter to the people we are studying.

The Turn toward Consumption

Once upon a time, but really not so long ago, economic anthropology comprised the study of production, distribution/exchange, and consumption in pre-industrial societies. The economic inventory of *Man and His Work*, Melville Herskovits' (1948) first excursion into the economic realm, included all of these processes plus the people and things that produced and consumed. The pots and pans approach to economic anthropology did not have a long life. Substantivist economic anthropologists turned their interests toward separate exchange spheres, different types of money, and marketplaces without markets, while the formalists saw the market principle at work in societies everywhere. The Marxist engagement in economic anthropology considered production as the driving force of the economy and paid special attention to articulations of variously labeled productive systems with capitalist relations of production in the former "primitive" world. In all these paradigms, consumption was an epiphenomenon, relegated to the margins of production and distribution.

Within the last ten years, some anthropologists concerned with economic issues have turned toward consumption both at home and abroad, highlighting the cultural nature of this process (Appadurai 1986; Friedman 1994; Miller 1987, 1994, 1995, 1997; Rutz and Orlove 1989; Wilk 1990). There are many contending genealogies behind this shift, and my account is merely one. At its most obvious, historical and analytical issues intersect. The historical turn in anthropology, combined with growing concerns with globalization and transnationalism, makes us grapple with a variety of not-so-local processes that are affecting the livelihoods of the people we study and their cultural conceptions of being in the world on changing terms. And ongoing transformations of the world economy are recasting the roles of production and consumption as engines of growth, challenging conventional accounts of empirical development trajectories.

Part of the impetus behind the recent preoccupations with consumption has come to us from history. The questioning of accounts of the birth of consumer society as a product of late capitalism is revealing that consumption has a longer and more complex history that does not stretch back unchanged to the sixteenth century. In short, the history of consumption in the West lends itself to a different periodization than the conventional one (Campbell 1987; de Grazia et al. 1996; Goldthwaite 1992; Thirsk 1978; Weatherill 1988). For research on developing countries, these insights not only invite a rethinking of local and external production/consumption dynamics, they also raise the possibility that we may in fact be exploring consumption sensibilities that differ from those we have long taken for granted.

By neglecting the early history of consumption, reigning explanatory frameworks have contributed to impede our grasp of the broader significance of consumption (Bermingham 1995: 3). When consumption was seen as the end point of the economic circuit, what is consumed is no longer a commodity but a use value and when it has been realized in the final act of consumption, there is nothing left to explore (Narotzky 1997: 103). But the explanatory scope has now shifted as questions about culture and agency are brought to bear on explanations of how people shape and create conceptions about themselves and their world through consumption

(Miller 1987). Because consumption concerns what people do with things and how things fit into their lives, the issue of agency rather than the relentless hand of the market comes to the fore. In this view, consumption is not only about how people use things and how cultural beliefs and practices shape their appropriation of such things, but also about the consequences of such appropriations for the wider contexts of their lives.

As with all turns of the explanatory pendulum, this one has begun to shift (Carrier and Heyman 1997; Fine and Leopold 1993; Miller 1997; Narotzky 1997; Roseberry 1996). Pointing to the lack of political economy in much of the new anthropological work on consumption, James Carrier and Josiah Heyman remark on the "ironic" timing of the boom in work on this subject. "It has occurred," they note, "while the practice of consumption has been threatened . . . [when] real incomes have decayed in many countries peripheral to Western capitalism" (1997: 356). To insert concerns with class and inequality into the study of consumption, they suggest that we situate it in the reproduction of households, as does Susana Narotzky with her means of livelihood approach (1997: 209–11). But while Carrier and Heyman are turning the timing of the boom in consumption studies into an extraordinary fact, they do not reckon with the ramifications of their own observations for our understanding of the relationship between consumption and development, of the importance of specific commodities subjectively and collectively to people's efforts of making a living in "peripheral countries." Indeed, in Zambia, as I demonstrate below, salaula makes a difference that matters. Secondhand clothing not only mediates desires, but it also satisfies basic needs by dressing bodies. Wearing clothes rather than rags gives dignity to persons with few means and this is an important reason why clothing constitutes a major dimension of well-being in Zambia.

Clothing: A Special Commodity

Commodities differ and have distinct production, distribution, and consumption regimes in relationship to specific consumers, when, and where. Clothing is not just any commodity but one that mediates between self and society in a very special way (Elias 1978: 78; Turner 1993). The point is not that clothing possesses this power inherently, but that it enables it in an interactive process through which the self is expressed/presented in possession (Miller 1987). But if the power of the dressed body derives in part from the special nature of clothing as a commodity, its significance in particular cases has to do with the historical circumstances that have made it appear so. We cannot explain the social and cultural significance of clothing consumption unless we examine how this commodity has been delivered and how it has entered people's lives. As I demonstrate in my larger work, cloth and clothing were key commodities in the long-term transformations that brought the market to this part of Africa and gradually made local people dependent on it as consumers (Hansen 2000).

During the opening decades of the twentieth century, clothing access depended on location in relationship to the shifting centers of economic activity, and on the building of roads and railways. Anthropologists who worked during the colonial period in what is now Zambia were struck by the active interest local people took in clothing (Mitchell 1956; Mitchell and Epstein 1959; Richards 1969: 16–18; Wilson 1942: 18). The clothing consumption practices that emerged were thoroughly gendered. Women caught on more slowly than men, who eagerly acquired clothing as labor migrants in contrast to women whom colonial authorities attempted to keep back in the rural areas. When women came to towns in larger numbers during and after the post-World War II period, they went for the new fashions with abandon (Parpart 1994: 250–54). Because cultural norms continue to hold that husbands, fathers, or guardians should provide women and children with clothing at regular intervals, women who dress expensively, particularly stylishly or extravagantly, easily lend themselves to suspicion. In the popular mind, women's bodies dressed either "too well" or "too shabbily" are a barometer for extramarital relations or conjugal neglect.

Clothing goes to the heart of widespread understandings of well-being in Zambia.[1] In terms of too many indicators, among them education, health, longevity, child mortality and nutrition, formal employment, and wages, people in Zambia in the first half of the 1990s were worse off than they had been in the mid-1970s (GRZ and UN 1996). When Zambians speak about development, they construe the modern through its objective attributes: education, occupation, and wealth. At the very least, they want satisfaction of basic needs such as food, schooling, work, housing, health services, and transportation.

People in Zambia also want well-dressed bodies. Unlike the scholarly literature which is having a hard time with the normative aspect of the relationship between consumption and development (James 1992: vii), many Zambians keenly express their subjective interpretations and desires. And clothing is at the dead center of widespread understandings of well-being. That much of this clothing in recent years has consisted of imported secondhand garments from the West does not reduce the power of this commodity to mediate modern sensibilities but has rather accentuated the role it plays in externalizing identity in everyday life. For not only does salaula give people what they need, namely clothing they can afford, it also gives them what they want: the ability to dress rather than wearing rags. Secondhand clothing consumption traverses a wide field of social practice across class and between rural and urban areas that both gives effect to cultural normative values and helps to transform them.

Because clothing consumption is a cultural force to be reckoned with, the salaula phenomenon mobilizes public opinion at many levels of society. For example, it has spurred a public debate about production vs. consumption in Zambia in which manufacturers' associations have taken a lead, arguing that the growth of salaula imports is destroying the domestic textile and clothing industry. At issue in the anticonsumption criticism is an implicit distinction between primary or basic ends/needs versus secondary or social wants/desires that are frivolous. The operative logic is a needs/wants distinction that construes as "natural," rather than historical and social, the conditions of production, distribution, and consumption that have brought about the salaula phenomenon and help to reproduce its significance. Such a model runs into trouble when it is called upon to explain the popularity of salaula, the workings of the consumer practices that are arising around it, and ultimately people's desires for clothes.

While salaula consumption satisfies basic needs, it also mediates social and cultural desires that have important material and economic implications. The process is perhaps more adequately accounted for, as I attempt below, when we reckon with the entire chain of activities that embed the consumption of this particular commodity.

A Salaula System of Provision

How do we account for the preoccupation with clothing in Zambia and, in particular, the rise in consumption of secondhand clothing imported from the West in recent years? The salaula phenomenon in Zambia may be explained in terms of an analytical framework that recognizes both economic and social factors, including the cultural meanings people attribute to clothing. Pointing out the limitations of scholarship that approaches consumption "horizontally," that is to say, without recognizing differences which distinct commodities help to bring about, Ben Fine and Ellen Leopold have suggested a "vertical approach" that entails a "comprehensive chain of activities between the two extremes of production and consumption, each link of which plays a potentially significant role in the social construction of the commodity both in its material and cultural aspects" (1993: 33). Their idea of a "system of provision" sets the role of consumption in a perspective that "views it as determined both historically—and therefore varying over time in strength and influence—and jointly with other variables within separate systems of provision which are themselves subject to significant long-term change, achieved at different rates and with different consequences" (1993: 23).

The secondhand clothing phenomenon can be viewed as a subsystem of provision in its own right, distinct from the system of provision of new garments with which it articulates in complex ways. Very briefly, historically changing supply and demand forces for new clothing on a global scale shaped by both cultural notions about bodies and dress and by income source and distribution have created a vast supply of secondhand clothing in the West. The growing demand for secondhand clothing in the Third World, and Africa in particular, in the period after World War II is influenced by the production and distribution of new clothes, both imports and local manufacture, and by consumer income. To place the salaula phenomenon in Zambia in that context requires an outline of the system of provision within which it is lodged as well as some reference to the economic and cultural practices that comprise the production, distribution/ exchange, and consumption circuit through which this commodity travels.

Production

I take the production of salaula to be comprised of the activities involved in the sourcing of secondhand clothing in the West. The history of this process has complex links to global changes of capital and labor, textile and garment production, and it requires attention to international trade regulations, state policies on manufacturing, trade, commerce, and retail regulations that I won't go into here. It also concerns the growth, or lack thereof, of disposable income and above all changing cultural and social norms about bodies and dress. These are among the preconditions for the emergence of a vast surplus of still wearable clothing in the West that have helped give rise to the secondhand clothing system of provision.

The secondhand clothing system of provision begins in our homes. Its largest single source is the garments we donate to charitable organizations such as Goodwill Industries and the Salvation Army in the United States and Humana in Europe, to mention just a few. Our clothing donations produce an enormous yield, about half, or less, of which reaches the racks of the charity retail stores. The charitable organizations sell the rest in bulk to textile recyclers, today's version of a previous era's rag dealers, who comprise a network of recyclers, rag makers, wholesalers, brokers, and used clothing exporters.[2]

"Used clothing" includes not only garments but also shoes, handbags, hats, belts, draperies, towels, and sheets. Because every piece of clothing has many potential future lives, textile recycling is a lucrative business. In their factories, the textile recyclers sort clothing into many categories, some intended for industrial use as rag and fiber, the domestic "vintage" clothing market, and others for export. Some wool garments are exported to Italy which has the world's largest wool recycling industry in Prato near Florence. Blue jeans, especially Levi Strauss 501, are popular in many European countries and find a huge market in Japan. The remainder of the used garments intended for export is sorted by fabric and garment type. Depending on legislation in the receiving country, the clothes may or may not be disinfected and fumigated. The lowest grade goes to African and Asian countries. Most recyclers compress the garments into 50 kilogram bales while some press bales weighing as much as 300 kilograms. Then the bales are wrapped in waterproof plastic, bound with metal or plastic straps, placed in containers, and shipped to Third World locations and, increasingly, eastern Europe.

Because the secondhand clothing trade is a potentially very profitable export business, it is surrounded by a variety of not-so-legal activities from the point of sourcing to the point of overseas retailing. Charitable organizations and dealers alike look for wider access to the valuable supply of our clothing donations. Many charitable organizations contract out the collection of clothing to commercial firms which in turn vie with one another for this access and/or lobby municipal governments for permission to collect in their own right. In the process, some firms use names that invoke charitable and welfare work, but are purely commercial. At the point of sorting, commercial dealers have been criticized for employing illegal, underpaid, overworked, and environmentally unprotected workers. Deception enters the process of declaring the export value of this commodity with widespread underinvoicing of both volume and value. In some cases shippers have been taken to court in African ports because the dealer had underinvoiced the cargo. The complications of African bureaucracy at the port encourage corruption in the transfer of port storage and port clearing fees. There is corruption as well in the payment of customs and tariff fees at the point of entry to Zambia. Fraud and deceit do not stop here but extend into wholesale and retail.

Processes such as these are part of an immense, profitable, but barely examined worldwide trading network that ships millions of dollars' worth of used clothing in an international trade which, according to news accounts, has quadrupled in scale worldwide over the last decade, and it keeps on growing. Some charitable organizations and nongovernmental organizations also ship secondhand clothes overseas, for example in crisis situations and as direct donations to needy people. In fact some, for instance Development Aid from People to People (DAPP), which is part of a nongovernmental organization headquartered in Scandinavia operating under the name Humana in many European countries, sells used clothing directly to Third World consumers, especially in southern Africa, using the revenue to finance local development projects. Overall, charitable donations as opposed to commercially sourced clothing form but a fraction of the total export. Even then, there is no doubt that charitably donated clothing, for example to refugees, often is commercially marketed.

Although the international secondhand clothing trade has a long history in which Zambia has participated since the early decades of the twentieth century if not before, markets selling commercially imported used clothing in this part of Africa began growing noticeably in the mid-1980s. They saw enormous expansion and proliferation in the early 1990s, becoming more important retailing sites than ever before in a vast worldwide commodity trade that involves many countries in Africa, other parts of the Third World, the former Soviet Republics, and eastern European countries. Although this trade does not exclusively target Third World countries, sub-Saharan African countries are among the world's largest importers of secondhand clothing, exceeding the imports of all other developing regions. Some reports estimate that one-third of the people in that region are wearing cast-off European and American clothing. These proportions have risen in recent years along with the economic decline experienced across the African continent. Although the available statistics underestimate the extent and real scope of this trade because of widespread illegal practices throughout the process, they certainly capture its rapid growth. According to United Nations documentation, for example, worldwide exports of secondhand clothes from the United States grew almost 50 percent between 1990 and 1994, from a value of U.S. $174,269,000 to $290,335,000. Total export to Africa from all sources increased by about the same rate over this period, from $177,022,000 to $311,166,000. Turning to Zambia, the total import of secondhand clothes, worth $1,181,000 in 1990, grew to $6,393,000 in 1994. And in 1994, the United States supplied around half of the value of Zambia's import of this commodity, namely U.S. $3,596,000 (UN 1995: 60).

Wholesale, Retail, and Distribution

Container loads of secondhand clothing purchased by wholesalers in Zambia are shipped from North America and Europe to the ports of Durban in South Africa, Beira in Mozambique, and Dar es Salaam in Tanzania. They then travel by truck to warehouses, mostly in Lusaka, although one of the largest dealers in this trade in recent years was based in Chipata, a provincial headquarters on the border of Malawi. Most large firms use clearing agents to handle customs procedures on the arrival of the containers to Zambia's official border entry points, including Lusaka's dry port. The customs charges have increased steadily since the late 1980s, as have attempts to regulate this import by the Zambian Revenue Authority

(ZRA). While the ZRA occasionally does impound secondhand clothing consignments and impose fines for noncompliance with tariffs, there is no doubt that large volumes of secondhand clothing enter the country without payment of fees. In addition, there is widespread smuggling across the border to Zimbabwe both by dealers and individuals who find a growing market in that country where secondhand clothing imports were banned in 1994.

Most of the secondhand clothing currently retailed in Zambia is imported by twenty to thirty firms, many of them general wholesalers who have added salaula to their inventory. The oldest of the firms I met in Lusaka began importing secondhand clothing between 1986 and 1987, first through contacts in the Democratic Republic of the Congo (formerly Zaire) which since the early 1900s was the main entrepot for the secondhand clothing that reached Zambia. Between 1989 and 1992, the direction in the flow of merchandise into Zambia changed due to upheavals within the former Zaire and the change in Zambia in 1991 to a political regime set on economic liberalization. Traders from the Democratic Republic of the Congo now cross the border to purchase secondhand clothing on the Zambian side of the Copperbelt or travel all the way to Lusaka for that purpose.

At the warehouse, bales of secondhand clothing are purchased by marketeers and private individuals of both sexes, who in turn distribute and sell their goods in urban and rural markets, hawk them in the countryside, and transfer them in rural exchanges in return for produce, goats, chickens, and fish. Secondhand clothing finds wide use in the rural areas as remuneration for piecework instead of cash. Tailors and rural shops selling new clothes are few and far between, and modest clothing expenditures are closely linked to very low levels of income. In fact, rural areas are the main destination for much of the salaula in fabrics, colors, and styles that do not appeal to urban consumers. In cities and towns secondhand clothing has spilled from the markets onto main streets. In medium-to high-income residential areas salaula is also sold from private homes and brought by traders into downtown offices and institutions for sale on credit arrangements to employees who receive monthly paychecks.

The relations that structure secondhand clothing retailing and circulation at the local level are both economic and social. Salaula retailing has created work for many people without jobs in Zambia's declining economy, including young people out of school and persons laid off in the ongoing employment retrenchment in the private and public sectors, and as I noted, it has provided gainful work for some people on a long-term basis. It has given rise to many ancillary activities as well that put people to work and help to support households. It is also a sideline activity for many who need to make extra money to stretch declining household incomes. In short, salaula traders are not merely economic agents who operate in a market that responds to basic clothing needs and clothing desires. They bring to this work their individual and household backgrounds which affect their work priorities and make claims on their time and attention. In short, success and failure in this trade are not only the results of how this specific market works in economic terms, but also, and significantly so, of the ways this particular activity accommodates personal agendas for making a living.

The meanings of clothes in the Zambian world of consumption in which secondhand clothing circulates are not given on the arrival of this commodity to the wholesaler's warehouse. Rather, unhinged from its origin, the decommissioned use value of the West's discarded clothing is charged anew in a process that actively involves Zambian consumers whose term *salaula* has effaced many references to the source of this commodity and to its previous life. This process of recommodification involves several phases during which the West's used clothes are transformed into new objects, beginning in transactions between external suppliers and local importers. Subsequent transformations of used garments into new clothes are achieved by a variety of processes that begin at the point of resale and are made public by how clothing is put to use. Transformations that involve recycling are obvious while others have to be teased out of interactions. The meanings produced by these transformations become evident in a variety of informal practices that have evolved around the selling and buying of salaula and which I have described elsewhere (Hansen 1994).

Briefly explained, some of these meanings hinge on the implication of the term *salaula*: selecting from a pile in the manner of rummaging. Some of the informal practices that express this meaning become evident in the process of purchasing and opening a bale. At the wholesaler's, customers scrutinize the plastic wrap and the metal straps to ensure that the bale has not been tampered with. The customers' scrutiny reflects their preference for bales whose contents are "fresh" from their western source, untouched by dealer interference, thus offering a range of what consumers of this commodity consider to be "new" items.

The concern with "newness" is evident, for example, on "opening day," when a bale is broken open for resale. At this point, it is important that garments have not been meddled with. Both traders and customers prefer to open a bale publicly, enabling customers to select on the spot. A bale that is opened in the market is considered to contain "new" clothes. If it is opened privately the trader might put aside choice items, causing customers to suspect that they are being presented with a second cut and not new clothing. This desire for "newness" is also evident in the "boutique" section where traders piece together outfits from garments they carefully select when bales are opened. In recent years the garments displayed in the salaula market's boutique section are hung up "fresh" from the bale— that is, with wrinkles and folds, without the benefit of ironing and washing. Prewashed and ironed clothing, in the opinion of traders and customers alike, leave the suspicion that the clothes are "third-hand" (their term), meaning previously owned and worn by Zambians.

The most obvious transformations of the West's used clothing involve recycling and alteration. Because both traders and consumers are concerned with quality and style, items made of fabrics that do not sell easily are turned into a variety of garments. The small-scale tailors who repair and alter salaula take in or extend garments of the wrong size for Zambian bodies, restyle jackets and trousers, and make colorful sweat suits from contrastive colored pieces they cut up from ill-matched salaula sweat suits. Tailors also add or remove a variety of trim, from buttons, zippers, and pockets to pleats to approximate what customers consider as "the latest." These and many more transformations offer rich evidence of both traders and customers working hard at giving new lives to the West's discarded garments, making salaula into their own creation.

Consumption

Consumption is hard work, a kind of invisible production, according to Michel de Certeau (1988: 30–31), that is not revealed in numerical tabulations of household expenditures. Instead it may be understood through the practices and meanings consumers bring to bear on how they use things.

The specific imperatives that people bring to salaula consumption derive from the socioeconomic, cultural, and personal contexts in which they live their lives rather than from clothing notions imposed from the outside. Background information the importers of secondhand clothing in Zambia gain from the retail trade about what consumers will and will not buy flows to the overseas dealers, some of whom undertake site visits to learn about clothing preferences and the local market. Taste and style preferences in clothing are not to any great extent the results of advertisements since Zambian media do not pay much attention to clothing. Still, syndicated television shows, CNN, MTV, and BBC, films and music videos, foreign magazines, and old pattern books do offer fragments of Western clothing styles to sections of society much broader than the now-limited television-viewing and magazine-subscribing public. Consumers combine these clothing fragments and refashion them into ensembles that achieve the effect of "the latest" in ongoing interaction. Evidence of this dynamic is found on streets, in social gatherings, at work, and during special events, in what people wear and how, and in their commentary about other people's dress and the scrutiny with which they examine styling.

The work of salaula consumption includes shopping in the market where customers gather information on the availability of specific garments/styles, screen, and sort products while they skillfully work their way through the piles of salaula checking for both quality and style. They turn garments inside out to examine if the sewing is neat and whether there are rips or other flaws in the fabric. But the work of consumption extends far beyond the market. A well-dressed person is well kempt herself and her clothing is well kept. Producing the smooth, tidy clothing profile that adult Zambians of both sexes prefer involves processes that easily escape the gaze of the casual observer or traveler who sees salaula only as the West's cast-offs. The desire to be well turned-out, even if the garments are secondhand, makes clothes-conscious Zambians insist on immaculate ensembles whose elements are carefully laundered and ironed. For this reason, the faded and torn jeans that are part of salaula bales from the United States are particularly unpopular. The desire to look spick-and-span prompts careful scrutiny of fabric quality to ascertain that colors of printed fabrics will not run in washing. Fading in sunlight is an issue as well. Most households do their laundry in cold water using strong detergents containing bleach and clothes are usually hung up in the sunlight to dry. This is why colorfastness and fabric quality are important issues in identifying clothes that are durable and will keep their good look.

Working their way through the salaula markets, consumers in Zambia display extensive clothing competence in matters of quality and style. Because it involves both needs and desires, the work of salaula consumption has important material and economic implications for the entire system of provision that embeds this commodity. Above all, the consumption of salaula is influenced by and has complex effects on household activities and welfare. These effects flow into the domains of distribution and production, which is why consumption does not constitute the end point of the economic process but helps to fuel its beginnings.

Conclusion

Distinct commodities have different consumption histories in which their significance to and in people's lives have varied. When the West's used garments emerge as salaula at the end of the chain in this clothing provision system, they have become redefined. The social and material practices that surround Zambian dealings with this particular commodity are shaped both by needs and wants—that is, by the distribution of available income and by normative ideas about bodies and dress that comprise local notions of taste. These notions are never static. The meaning and significance of secondhand clothing in and to people's lives have changed between the colonial period and the present, they shift across the life cycle of specific individuals, and they vary by gender, generation, class, and urban and rural residence.

In Zambia, clothing, both new and old, continues to have a powerful hold on people's imagination because the self and society articulate through the dressed body in ways unlike those of most other commodities. By situating the salaula phenomenon and the hard work it involves in its broader social and cultural context I have attempted to demonstrate that questions about what people consume and why can be examined with good effect from within a systems of provision approach. Such an approach captures the articulation of economic and social factors that influence both the extent and nature of salaula consumption and the meanings that give this process particular welfare significance in Zambia. There is a lesson for development research to be drawn from this concerning widespread assumptions about basic needs fulfillment which is not the only, or necessarily the most important, barometer of local well-being.

Notes

This chapter was written while I was in residence at the Rockefeller Foundation's Bellagio Center in Italy in February 1998 during my 1997/98 academic year fellowship at the National Humanities Center in North Carolina, through an award from the National Endowment for the Humanities. It draws on preliminary work carried out in Zambia during the summers of 1992 and 1993, extensive field research and archival work conducted in Zambia, the southern African region, and Europe during the calendar year of 1995, on continued work in Europe during the summer of 1996, spring and summer of 1997, and a return to Zambia during the summer of 1997. My research has been supported by faculty grants from Northwestern University and awards from the Social Science Research Council (U.S.A.) and the Wenner Gren Foundation for Anthropological Research. I wish to recognize Jane Guyer's stimulus of my thinking on consumption.

1. In a recent assessment of poverty, rural respondents were asked to describe a poor person. Wearing rags played a major role in characterizations of poverty, and more so for women than for men. These perceptions were drawn from a combination of household survey and participatory data in the analysis of which gender profiles of poverty were constructed, attributing proportional weight to specific aspects of poverty. Both women and men referred to lack of food and clothing as the most important characteristics of a poor person, with women giving emphatically more weight to these basic items than men. In their composite poverty profile women weighted "wearing rags/no clothing" as 21 percent and "having no food/does not eat well" as 20 percent. Men assigned 14 percent to "wearing rags/no clothing" and 15 percent to "having no food/does not eat well." Although the overall poverty assessment was conducted in both urban and rural settings, the published report does not include any urban poverty profiles (World Bank 1994: 30–31).

2. There are hardly any conventional social science or economic studies of this process. My richest source of insights has been newswires. While journalistic reports are often sensationalist, they do identify important issues.

References

Appadurai, Arjun, ed.
1986   *The Social Life of Things: Commodities in Cultural Perspective.* Cambridge: Cambridge University Press.
Bermingham, Ann
1995   "Introduction: The Consumption of Culture: Image, Object, Text." Pp. 1–20 in *The Consumption of Culture 1600–1800: Image, Object, Text,* Ann Bermingham, ed. New York: Routledge.
Carrier, James G., and Josiah McC. Heyman
1997   "Consumption and Political Economy." *Journal of the Royal Anthropological Institute* 3(2): 355–73.
Campbell, Colin
1987   *The Romantic Ethic and the Spirit of Modern Consumerism.* Oxford: Blackwell.
de Certeau, Michel
1988   *The Practice of Everyday Life,* Steven Kendall, trans. Berkeley: University of California Press.
de Grazia, Margreta, Maureen Quilligan, and Peter Stallybrass, eds.
1996   *Subject and Object in Renaissance Culture.* Cambridge: Cambridge University Press.
Elias, Norbert
1978   *The Civilizing Process: The History of Manners.* New York: Urizen.
Fine, Ben, and Ellen Leopold
1993   *The World of Consumption.* London: Routledge.
Friedman, Jonathan
1994   *Cultural Identity and Global Process.* Thousand Oaks, Calif.: Sage.
Goldthwaite, Richard A.
1992   "Identity and Consumerism in Renaissance Florence." Transcript of twelfth annual Phi Alpha Theta distinguished lecture on history at the University of Albany, State University of New York (March 16). GRZ and UN (Government of the Republic of Zambia and the United Nations System in Zambia).
1996   *Prospects for Sustainable Human Development in Zambia: More Choices for Our People.* Lusaka: Pilcher Graphics.
Hansen, Karen T.
1994   "Dealing with Used Clothing: *Salaula* and the Construction of Identity in Zambia's Third Republic." *Public Culture* 6(3): 503–23.
2000   *Salaula: The World of Secondhand Clothing and Zambia.* Chicago: University of Chicago Press.
Herskovits, Melville J.
1948   *Man and His Works: The Science of Cultural Anthropology.* New York: Knopf.
James, Jeffrey
1992   *Consumption and Development.* New York: St. Martin's Press.

Miller, Daniel
1987   *Material Culture and Mass Consumption*. Oxford: Blackwell.
1994   *Modernity: An Ethnographic Approach*. New York: Berg.
1995   "Consumption Studies as the Transformation of Anthropology." Pp. 264–95 in *Acknowledging Consumption*, Daniel Miller, ed. New York: Routledge.
1997   *Capitalism: An Ethnographic Approach*. New York: Berg.
Mitchell, J. Clyde
1956   *The Kalela Dance*. Rhodes-Livingstone Papers no. 27.
Mitchell, J. C., and Arnold L. Epstein
1959   "Occupational Prestige and Social Status among Urban Africans in Northern Rhodesia." *Africa* 19: 22–40.
Narotzky, Susana
1997   *New Directions in Economic Anthropology*. London: Pluto Press.
Parpart, Jane L.
1994   "'Where is Your Mother?': Gender, Urban Marriage, and Colonial Discourse on the Zambian Copperbelt, 1924–1945." *The International Journal of African Historical Studies* 27(2): 241–71.
Roseberry, William
1996   "The Rise of Yuppie Coffees and the Reimagination of Class in the United States." *American Anthropologist* 98(4): 762–75.
Richards, Audrey I.
1969 [1939]   *Land, Labour and Diet in Northern Rhodesia*. Oxford: Oxford University Press.
Rutz, Henry, and Benjamin Orlove, eds.
1989   *The Social Economy of Consumption*. Lanham, Md.: University Press of America.
Thirsk, Joan
1978   *Economic Policy and Projects: The Development of a Consumer Society in Early Modern England*. Oxford: Clarendon.
Turner, Terence S.
1993 [1979]   "The Social Skin." Pp. 15–39 in *Reading the Social Body*, Catherine B. Burroughs and Jeffrey Ehrenreich, eds. Iowa City: University of Iowa Press.
UN (United Nations)
1995   *1994 International Trade Statistics Yearbook. Vol. II: Trade by Commodity*. New York: United Nations.
Weatherill, Lorna
1988   *Consumer Behavior and Material Culture in Britain 1660–1760*. London: Routledge.
Wilk, Richard
1990   "Consumer Goods as Dialogue about Development." *Culture and History* 7: 79–100.
Wilson, Godfrey
1942   *An Essay on the Economics of Detribalization in Northern Rhodesia. Vol. II*. Rhodes-Livingstone Papers no. 6.
World Bank
1994   *Zambia Poverty Assessment. Vol. I: Main Report (no. 12985-ZA)*. Human Resources Division. Southern Africa Development: Africa Regional Office.

Part V

The Role for "Big Theory" in Economic Anthropology

Chapter 12

When Good Theories Go Bad: Theory in Economic Anthropology and Consumer Research

Richard Wilk

Abstract

How important is high-level theory in economic anthropology? This chapter contrasts the approaches of practicing social scientists in consumer research and marketing (which could be defined as a sort of applied economic anthropology), with those of current economic anthropologists. I discuss the role of elite "high theorists" in both disciplines, and the contrasting ways that theory informs practice. In marketing and consumer research, much of what passes for theory is really just taxonomy, and low-level generalization. Yet the empirical work actively engages those propositions, and is sometimes used to invalidate them. In anthropological work on consumption, there is a great deal of quite high-level and abstract theory, but fieldwork and research rarely challenge or reflect upon these theoretical premises. The gulf between observations and the theories that drive and inform them sometimes threatens to swallow the whole enterprise.

Introduction

The goal of this chapter is to compare the ways two disciplines, consumer research and anthropology, go about using theory to understand a single form of behavior, which both fields label "consumption."[1] My intent in this quick survey is to suggest that theoretical sophistication is not necessarily a good thing in the daily conduct of empirical research, especially when that sophistication provokes loyalty to a pure version of a particular theory. Not surprisingly, I will reiterate some points made by Rutz and Orlove in their introduction to the SEA volume on the Social Economy of Consumption, surely one of the best collections published by the society (1989).

Some years ago I was standing with a Belizean farmer, a clever man who had the misfortune to live very close to an agricultural experiment station. We were watching three Ph.D. agronomists struggling to get through a barbwire fence, just twenty feet from a perfectly good gate. He asked me, in all innocence, why it was that the smarter people get, the stupider they behave. That's something similar to the point I want to make about theory; like a pair of binoculars it can help us see some things very clearly, but often at the expense of tunnel vision that excludes essential background. And used the wrong way, it ruins our perspective on everything and makes important things look insignificant.

This is not meant as an attack on cultural or socioeconomic theory. The problem is how theory is used, and how it is brought into engagement with empirical data. When theory informs research activity, and the results of research are used to question and modify theory, no matter how distant and indirect the connections between theorizing and research practice, I think the situation is healthy. But when theory becomes a domain where small elite groups can strut the latest hot French fashion down the runway, or a matter of faith founded on moral convictions about the state of the world, we have problems. Fieldwork then becomes a search for confirmation, illustrations for stories we have already written. In general, I think economic anthropologists are much more sensible than most anthropologists in their use of theory, so this is not a blanket indictment of our subdiscipline. (A broad theoretical overview also gives me an opportunity to be cranky in a sweeping and generic way; forgive me if I paint a bleak picture, for I will end up arguing that there is light at the end of the tunnel.)

Consumer Research: Midlevel and Proud

One way to understand the role of theory in the anthropology of consumption is through contrast with another discipline that goes about its work in a very different way. Over the last twenty years consumer research has emerged from marketing departments, growing gradually into a separate discipline, centered on the Association for Consumer Research (ACR) and the *Journal of Consumer Research (JCR)*. The membership of the

ACR and the readership of *JCR* still overlap with the more traditionally applied American Marketing Association, but ACR is much more academic and research-oriented. At recent meetings a bit more than half of the papers had a directly applied point, aimed at helping advertisers and retailers sell their goods, while the other half were theoretical, or could be classed as "pure" empirical research.

The disciplinary roots of consumer research are complex. The founders of the Association were mainly social and behavioral psychologists, but early members included people trained in economics, organization studies, management, and sociology. The last ten years have seen a rapid rise in the influence of anthropologists in the ACR. John Sherry, an anthropologist at Northwestern, was recently president, and Eric Arnould, my contemporary in graduate school at Arizona, has been an editor of *JCR* and program chair for the annual ACR meeting. Ethnography and other qualitative research methods have become commonplace, and there is now even a textbook in "postmodern marketing," laden with the obligatory French theorists and thick prose (Brown 1995; see also Firat et al. 1987).

I have a general sense of the role of theory in consumer research from attending three ACR annual meetings, reviewing papers for the *JCR*, attending several smaller workshops organized by consumer researchers, and from a brief stay as a visiting lecturer in a marketing department. For this chapter I also reviewed all the papers in the 1997 volume of the *JCR*.

These articles reference an extraordinary range of sources in many disciplines, including some I had never heard of before like "Psychonomics" and "Chronobiology." Psychology journals are numerically predominant, and there was not a single reference to classic social scientists like Weber, Durkheim, or Marx. There were also no references to recent high theorists of consumption, like Baudrillard, Foucault, and Benjamin, whose names have seeded bibliographies in the humanities and social sciences like caraway in rye bread. In a whole year, only one reference was made to Bourdieu.[2]

Instead of grand theory, consumer researchers are prolific users of heuristic simplifications and midlevel theories. These are often relatively simple propositions about the way people think, communicate, or evaluate information, which can be directly challenged by research findings. Midlevel models are treated as provisional, are made fully explicit, and produce easily measurable consequences. A good example is a paper on reference prices—the ideas that people have about what something should cost, which they bring to every transaction (Briesch et al. 1997). The authors test five different models of how reference prices are formed, based on combinations of memory, communication, and cues from the product characteristics, or from the transaction itself.

In the *JCR*, graphic depictions of causal models in the form of structural equations are fairly common. A typical example uses multiple boxes and a spaghetti of arrows to model the connections between when a delay occurs, and the type of delay, in predicting how angry consumers get while waiting for service (Hui et al. 1998, figure 2).

Of course, this kind of model strikes most anthropologists as hopelessly culture bound, mechanistic, and worse, lacking an underlying theory of culture or human behavior. They seem to be highly quantified versions of ethnocentric ad-hoc commonsense explanations. The social psychological obsession with measurement and correlation analysis is often more concerned with replicability than with theoretical coherence. The analytical categories are usually commonsense middle-class concepts that may work with the usual research population of Business 101 students, but they are of questionable universal validity. Besides, the research problems and results often seem limited and trivial, as in one study of why prices that end in the digit "9" are more attractive to consumers (Schindler and Kirby 1997).

When you take this kind of work to other countries and other cultures, many of these shortcomings become obvious—as in abundant new cross-cultural studies of "materialism," which could easily be seen as the imposition of Western categories of thought and knowledge onto other cultures (e.g., Rudmin and Richins 1992). The real theoretical premises of this kind of work hover above, rarely questioned, something absorbed in graduate school as a set of commonsense premises about human beings as goal-seeking partially rational thinkers, and hardly worth repeating or making explicit in research papers.

Yet, at the same time, within this empirical and relatively untheorized research tradition, people are asking some very important questions. There is growing interest in cross-cultural research, and in consumption that has direct and dramatic environmental effects. More importantly, the lack of theory makes consumer researchers unusually open to new ideas, models, and methodologies. Their research practice is guided more by what works than by theoretical parsimony, which means that they actually reject models on the basis of empirical data, and they have few qualms about poaching good intermediate models from any place they can find usable ones, whether it's in psychophysics or garbology.

Anthropology and Consumption: The Role of High Theory

Can we say any of these things about the study of consumption in anthropology? I don't think so. I can't claim to have read more than a sample of the current flood of research, though I struggle to keep up with the help of an annual graduate seminar. In anthropology, I find, consumption has been overtheorized, to the point where fieldwork and theory rarely make contact, except when one is explicitly driving the other. In anthropology in general, and especially in economic anthropology, we have very different theoretical propositions about the causes of individual and group behavior, and to a large extent consumption is just another of the arenas where theorists perform their magic for the crowd.

In *Economies and Cultures* (1996) I argue that theories of human nature are founded ultimately on unquestioned propositions about who we are, and what makes us uniquely human. I divide theories into three groups: the social, the cultural, and those based on individual, rational choice. It's not hard to find good, clear examples in the anthropology of consumption of each kind of theory put into practice.

Many archaeologists looking at ancient material culture use a relatively simple utilitarian theory of consumption as economizing behavior, positing, for example, that people adopt new technologies because they save labor or increase output. The idea of consumption as an expression of individual rationality can also be found in cultural ecology, for example in the work of Dan Gross and collaborators among four South American forest cultivating groups. They argue that it is perfectly rational for the Bororo and Kanela to engage in cash cropping and wage labor to get money to buy wristwatches, handguns, household goods, and tools. By engaging with the market they produce more efficiently, and the goods they buy are effective ways to store value for the long term, in an environment that offers few such options (Gross et al. 1979: 1046–47). A more socioeconomic approach to consumption rescues the idea of rationality by including status and prestige among the values that consumers seek to maximize.

Social theories of consumption in anthropology are generally drawn from Thorstein Veblen or from Marx. They depict consumption as driven by class competition and striving for social advantage, and/or from the alienation of workers from the products of their own labor, the breaking of the organic unity of a primordial economic cycle based on use-values. Consumption holds groups together and divides them from each other, and modes of consumption are the products of types of economic formation. A classic example is Mintz' work on sugar in Britain and the Caribbean (1979, 1985); a more recent version, also historical, is Burke's study of soap in Zimbabwe (1997). He argues that the British colonial regime used issues of hygiene to divide and control their subjects and soap therefore became an important way of making class, ethnic, and gender distinctions for both the colonists and the colonized. Social theorists have lately concentrated almost exclusively on the theme of consumption as either domination or resistance, to an extreme point where we are rooting out the hidden power relations that lie behind each bite of a meal, and the lather on every bar of soap.

Cultural theories, in contrast or in concert, focus on the meaning of consumer goods, the ways they create similarity and difference among and between people, and the way that they create personal identity. A cultural theory argues that wants and desires are products of ideology and identity, not rational choice, class, power, or group membership. The purest version of a cultural theory is presented by Sahlins in *Culture and Practical Reason* (1976), where he argues that consumption is no more than the surface reflection of underlying structural oppositions and binary categories of cultural order. North Americans don't eat horses because they are "bad to think with"; they are taboo because they cross boundaries between nature and culture. In *Stone Age Economics* (1972) Sahlins tells us that in band-level societies consumption is extremely limited, the consequence of a cultural economy based on generalized reciprocity that decreases everyone's incentive to produce.

It makes sense that anthropologists have concentrated their efforts on cultural models of consumption, since cultural difference is fundamental to our discipline. The vast majority of anthropological work on consumption takes this approach, from Annette Weiner (1992) on the Trobriands, to the recent book *Golden Arches East*, edited by James Watson (1997). We tell everyone that each culture is different, and therefore each consumes in its own way. When the Chinese eat McDonalds hamburgers, they do it in a uniquely Chinese way that only an anthropologist can adequately interpret. As the articles in Tobin's *Re-made in Japan* (1992) tell it, when the Japanese take up the tango, or play baseball, or visit Disneyworld, their consumption is still uniquely Japanese, and has to be read as part of a local and unique Japanese cultural reality. Yet these reassuring tales of the survival of local difference and the continuing cultural embeddedness of all consumption seem a bit unreal in a world where billions aspire to own motorbikes and satellite dishes.

We offer the uniqueness of culture at the expense of the general and comparative analysis of processes of change, which were once carried out under the now discredited rubric of "acculturation." If today we have any general comparative models of consumption to offer, they consist of weak evolutionary linkages of types of consumption with the conventional levels of social organization; in bands people give gifts, in chiefdoms they redistribute staples, in early states elites amass fine crafts for mortuary ritual.

In a perceptive article on theory in anthropology, Ulf Hannerz (1986) argues that both evolutionary historical arguments about society, *and* the idea of radical cultural difference between types of societies, constitute what he calls the "anthropology of the Other," which thrives in the small-scale local communities that are today largely extinct. This style of anthropology shrinks from engagement with complex, hybrid, urban society. As he says, "It flirts with them, in occasionally expounding on the view from Bongo Bongo towards modern society, but this seldom results in serious engagement" (1986: 364).

The immediate result of this emphasis on cultural difference in consumption has been a kind of tribal isolation of each case study from all others. We have no well-grounded theory that does not begin with radical cultural difference, or the subsumption of all modes of consumption into an all-encompassing capitalism, a theory that does start off with an essential division between gift and commodity economies (even if we later admit that they are often combined in the modern world). In the meantime, other disciplines, notably history and cultural studies, have been producing masses of fascinating material on consumption, creative and heterogeneous, and largely free of attempts to fit consumption into overarching theories of human nature (e.g., Slater 1997; Mackay 1997).

Conclusions:
Theoretical Purity and Theoretical Practice

The three models of human nature I have just used are no more than heuristic devices. In practice most anthropologists mix them in some way, and economic anthropologists tend to be less purist than most. But they are not mixed in equal proportions. I was struck, at the 1997 SEA meetings in Guadalajara, by a remark made during one of the discussion periods, after Ron Waterbury's paper on the first day. I don't recall exactly who said it, but it went roughly like this: "I only use a cultural explanation after all the economic ones had failed." I think a lot of theory, when put into practice, works exactly like this. Clifford Geertz (1984), discussing the controversy generated by his 1963 book *Agricultural Involution*, expressed almost the opposite sentiment, that he would never use an economic explanation until all the cultural and historical ones had failed! In figure 12.1 I have sketched some variations on this "default option" model of the use of theory. We use our favorite, and use a backup theory to deal with the things that don't fit. This leaves us free to reject the third option as just plain wrong. The alternation between number one and number two provides some illusion of dynamism.

This begs the question of where our theoretical preferences come from in the first place. In the standard philosophy of science models it comes from our training, from books, influential thinkers, and scholarly communities like the SEA. The social constructionists also tell us it comes from our own social context, from our class and gender position, and from the

Figure 12.1. Stepwise "Default Option" model of theory use.

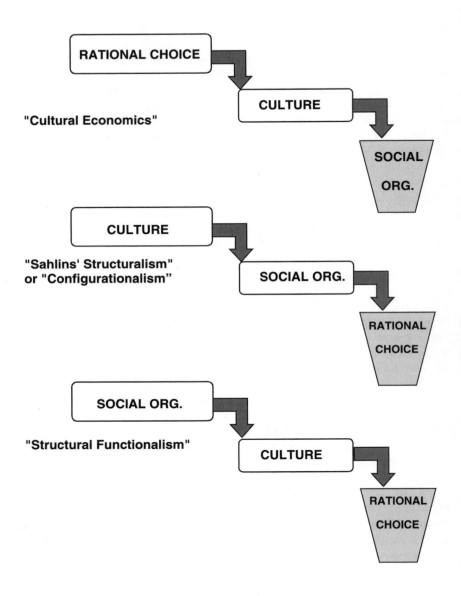

theorists' geopolitical position (Latouche 1996; also Wilk 1985). There is also a personal level at which we choose theories that make sense, for us, out of our own experience, because they offer insight and provide a basis for our political commitments and passions. Some proponents of postmodernism even argue that there is no difference between theory and personal engagement, between what we say about others and what we think about ourselves (cf. Moore 1994: 107–28). Theory is deeply engaged in all these things. The degree to which our own personal worldview is consonant with our theoretical perspective is always in question, but it is not a unique issue to anthropologists. Some research suggests that academic training in a particular discipline (the example was economics) actually changes the political opinions and worldview of students (Scott and Rothman 1975).

Theory and status are also intertwined in interesting ways in the discipline of anthropology. As a class project in 1998, my graduate proseminar students surveyed the topics of articles in major and minor anthropology journals over the previous thirty years. They found that higher-status journals consistently print articles with more theoretical focus. Of course, theoretical work may just be intrinsically of interest to the broader readership of the elite journals. But one could argue the same for methodological papers, which rarely appear in mainstream journals anymore. Instead I think we are looking at a status and reward system which favors high theory over empirical work, which rewards people who clearly state widely shared suppositions, instead of challenging them.

For all of these reasons, our theoretical commitments run very deep. And this affects the choices we make of what to study, and how to study it. But it also means that our work is often chosen to bolster, rather than challenge, our theoretical beliefs. The three paradigms of social theory I've outlined then become almost religious matters of faith, instead of provisional generalizations, subject to modification. It follows that when theory and faith are so closely intertwined, challenges to theory and orthodoxy are more likely to raise strong emotion, because they are more than theoretical arguments—they are personal and political. This emotional and political content attaches especially strongly to theories of consumption because the practice of consumption is itself so often cast as a moral issue. Almost every study of consumption is in some way enmeshed in making moral judgments about consumption as socially positive or destructive, as false, or dominated, unequal, addictive, or unhealthy.

This is a tremendous amount of baggage for theories to carry, and also maintain their internal consistency and external validity. When we search for consistency, theoretical arguments tend to be more encompassing than they should be—they are totalizing, in the sense that we want them to explain everything, instead of having limits. I have argued elsewhere that our major theories in economic anthropology are each partial representations of human nature, that all humans have the capacity for acting rationally, socially, and culturally, that beliefs, calculations, and group identity all make a difference. Instead of blotting this complexity away in the interest of theoretical purity, we would do better to pay more attention to the kinds of things that don't fit any theory, that fall between the cracks and disappear.

There is also a serious practical problem with the kinds of theoretical purification we see in anthropology today. Most of us are familiar with economists who are so single-minded in their devotion to rational choice theory that they are blind to the absurdities it produces in practice. Thus we get "structural adjustment" programs that punish the poor and destabilize the governments that are supposed to implement them.

But when it comes to giving useful advice on problems of consumption, at least economists have practical recommendations: raise or lower the prices, taxes, or subsidies. Anthropologists who have only a cultural theory of consumption are generally helpless when faced with policy problems. If our answer to every question is that consumption is embedded in history and culture, and we have no recommendation for change, then people will simply conclude that we are useless and stop listening. In applied work, theoretical purity is often self-destructive.

Of course any theory has its place, if only in the classroom to provoke students or to inspire creative thinking. But when our theories are too high, too abstract, and too pure, they will not produce directly testable statements about the world. Instead they provoke reductionism, and consistency at the expense of reality, and this is the point where—to return to my title—good theories go bad. This is not to say that I suggest we take consumer research as a model to emulate. I am not recommending that we become psychologists and adopt more path-model flow charts and go back to testing banal hypotheses with correlation analysis. But given the rate at which we are consuming the resources of the planet, and the urgency of figuring out ways to change consumption practices, I don't think we can afford the luxury of high theory anymore.

Notes

1. This chapter is the result of numerous conversations with my graduate students in introductory and advanced classes on theory in sociocultural anthropology and economic anthropology, and I wish to thank them all for being a fair and critical audience, and for always asking the tough questions. Many thanks to Anne Pyburn, whose ideas and interests continue to inspire me to think things through. Daniel Miller, Elizabeth Shove, and Alan Warde contributed key insights, though

they cannot be held responsible for what I did with them. Nathalie Arnold, my brilliant research assistant, did much of the primary research in the Journal of Consumer Research, with her usual thoroughness and intelligence. Finally I would like to thank Rhoda Halperin, whose misreading and misunderstanding of my work made me angry enough to write this chapter in the first place.

2. The most frequently cited anthropologists are Grant McCracken, Mary Douglas, Daniel Miller, and Eric Arnould.

References

Briesch, Richard, Lakshaman Krishnamurthi, Tridib Mazumdar, and S. P. Raj
    1997   "A Comparative Analysis of Reference Price Models." *Journal of Consumer Research* 24: 202–14.
Brown, Stephen
    1995   *Postmodern Marketing.* New York: Routledge.
Burke, T.
    1997   *Lifebuoy Men, Lux Women.* Duke University Press.
Firat, Fuat, Nikhilesh Dholakia, and Richard Bagozzi
    1987   *Philosophical and Radical Thought in Marketing.* Lexington: Lexington Books.
Geertz, Clifford
    1963   *Agricultural Involution.* Berkeley: University of California Press.
    1984   "Culture and Social Change: The Indonesian Case." *Man* 19: 511–32.
Gross, Daniel, George Eiten, Nancy Flowers, Francisca Leoi, Madeline Ritter, and Dennis Werner
    1979   "Ecology and Acculturation among Native Peoples of Central Brazil." *Science* 206(30): 1043–50.
Hannerz, Ulf
    1986   "Theory in Anthropology: Small is Beautiful? The Problem of Complex Cultures." *Comparative Studies in Society and History* 28: 362–67.
Hui, Michael, Mrugank Thakor, Ravi Gill
    1998   "The Effect of Delay Type and Service Stage on Consumers' Reactions to Waiting." *Journal of Consumer Research* 24: 469–79.
Latouche, Serge
    1996   *The Westernization of the World.* Cambridge, U.K.: Polity Press.
Mackay, Hugh
    1997   *Consumption and Everyday Life.* London: Sage.
McCracken, G.
    1988   *Culture and Consumption.* Bloomington: Indiana University Press.
Mintz, Sidney
    1979   "Time, Sugar and Sweetness." *Marxist Perspectives* 2: 56–73.
    1985   *Sweetness and Power: The Place of Sugar in Modern History.* New York: Penguin.
Moore, Henrietta
    1994   *A Passion for Difference.* Bloomington: Indiana University Press.

Rudmin, Floyd, and Marsha Richins
   1992   *Meaning, Measure and Morality of Materialism.* Provo, Ut.: Association for Consumer Research.
Rutz, Henry, and Benjamin Orlove
   1989   *The Social Economy of Consumption.* Lanham, Md.: University Press of America.
Sahlins, Marshal
   1976   *Culture and Practical Reason.* Chicago: University of Chicago Press.
   1972   *Stone Age Economics.* Chicago: Aldine-Atherton.
Schindler, Robert, and Patrick Kirby
   1997   "Patterns of Rightmost Digits Used in Advertising Prices: Implications for Nine-Ending Effects." *Journal of Consumer Research* 24: 192–201.
Scott, James, and Mitchell Rothman
   1975   "The Effect of an Introductory Economics Course on Student Political Attitudes." *The Journal of Economic Education* 6(2).
Slater, Don
   1997   *Consumer Culture and Modernity.* Cambridge, U.K.: Polity Press.
Tobin, J., ed.
   1992   *Re-Made in Japan.* New Haven, Conn.: Yale.
Watson, James
   1997   *Golden Arches East: McDonalds in East Asia.* Stanford: Stanford University Press.
Weiner, Annette B.
   1992   *Inalienable Possessions: The Paradox of Keeping-While-Giving.* Berkeley: University of California Press.
Wilk, Richard R.
   1985   "The Ancient Maya and the Political Present." *Journal of Anthropological Research* 41(3): 307–26.
   1996   *Economies and Cultures: An Introduction to Economic Anthropology.* Boulder, Colo.: Westview Press.

Chapter 13

---·──✕◉✕·──---

Decision Making, Cultural Transmission, and Adaptation in Economic Anthropology

Joseph Henrich

It's our custom. —Bartolo Gallardo, a Mapuche farmer in Chile who was replying to a question about why his neighbors only plant winter wheat (1998)

Custom, then, is the great guide of human life. —David Hume (1748)

With the exception of the instinct of self-preservation, the propensity for emulation is probably the strongest and most alert and persistent of the economic motives proper. —Thorstein Veblen (1899)

Abstract

This chapter argues that economic anthropologists need to reduce their reliance on cost-benefit decision making, and incorporate a cognitively informed understanding of social learning, cultural transmission, and information processing. Human behavioral patterns are unlikely to be primarily a product of cost-benefit decision making because: (1) laboratory data show that human information processing is so fraught with errors,

---

The author would like to thank Allen Johnson, Natalie Smith, Robert Boyd, Jean Ensminger, Pete Richerson, Nick Blurton-Jones, and three anonymous reviewers for their helpful comments and criticisms of earlier versions of this manuscript.

biases, and miscalibrations that, if this is our primary mode of adaptation or of achieving individual goals, we should observe systematic patterns of maladaptation or of goal-averting behavior; and (2) ethnographic data show that individuals often lack the kinds of information required by typical cost-benefit models. As a theoretical alternative, I argue that humans rely heavily on biased cultural transmission. By *selectively* copying certain individuals or ideas, biased cultural transmission can (over time) generate the well-integrated, adaptive behavioral patterns that we observe ethnographically.

Introduction

Most research in economic anthropology relies heavy on the assumption that economic behavior and behavioral change can be understood as the product of individuals making decisions based on the costs and benefits of alternative options. From this perspective, the key to explaining widespread behavioral patterns, or the direction of change, resides in understanding how individuals evaluate information about specific problems (their perceptions) and integrate this with their preferences, beliefs and expectations. Depending on the researcher, "culture" may be invoked to account for all, some, or none of these perceptions, preferences, beliefs, and expectations. In this chapter I argue that researchers should reduce their reliance on these cost-benefit decision models and incorporate cognitively based models of social learning and cultural transmission processes. By understanding more of how individuals acquire cultural information from the minds of other individuals (in the form of ideas, behaviors, beliefs, values, and worldviews), we can provide both alternative and complimentary explanations for behavioral patterns, adaptation (and maladaptation), change, tradition, and cultural evolution.

The issue debated here is not whether individuals or groups are well adapted to their environmental, socioeconomic, and/or political circumstances. Rather, the question is one of *process*: how or why do individuals or groups alter their behaviors or behavioral strategies to adapt, and sometimes maladapt, to their circumstances. Numerous anthropological studies from many different societies have convincingly shown that individuals and groups possess behavioral practices that are well suited to their environments or quite "sensible" given the socioeconomic situation and cultural world. However, from a cognitive perspective, it remains unclear whether humans can perform the information processing necessary to generate the kinds of adaptation (and maladaption) that we observe. In many cases, human behavior and culture—with its intricately integrated, well-adapted, and often subtle rules, decision-heuristics, and scripts—

seems too well adapted, given what we know about our decision-making abilities. In others cases, static cultures or traditions seem incredibly resistant to new information that, at least to outsiders, seems to indicate a need for behavioral adjustments.

It's easy to misunderstand my characterization of *cost-benefit decision making* as a simple relabeling of the infamous rational actor model that continues to pervade much of economics and political science. However, criticizing mainstream economic anthropology for adhering to rational models would be a big mistake, as most anthropologists have long abandoned the simplistic maximization models typically associated with the rational actor approach. Indeed, the classic rational actor represents a subcategory of cost-benefit decision makers, but the overall cost-benefit category is much more general. Looking at the core assumptions, what both economics and economic anthropology have inherited, perhaps from Renaissance philosophy, is the intuitively pleasing notion that people are best understood as goal-driven strategists who deploy their reasoning abilities (however meager) in pursuit of their goals. This is what I mean by *cost-benefit decision making*. Decision makers may have limited information, limited ability to process that information, multiple goals, and a constraining social structure, but if they are evaluating information about alternative behaviors, then they're still doing cost-benefit decision making. The cost-benefit category says nothing about where individuals' goals come from, only that individuals have goals, and that they evaluate information relevant to achieving those goals—and make behavioral choices based on those evaluations. I am not arguing that people never do cost-benefit decision making, but that this approach leaves out nonstrategic cognition mechanisms, such as cultural learning that may substantially affect the evolution of behavioral patterns.

Most forms of cultural transmission create cultural evolution—i.e., a change in the frequency or distribution of behaviors, ideas, beliefs, and values—under a wide range of conditions *without any cost-benefit decisions being made by anyone*. To demonstrate this, imagine human cognition has the learning rule "preferentially imitate the person with the most children." With such a rule, individuals of all ages will count the offspring of each person in the group and attempt to copy the behaviors, ideas, beliefs, and practices of the most fecund person(s). In a foraging society, this will cause things such as tracking techniques, food preferences, child-rearing practices, private rituals, prey choice, and arrow manufacturing procedures of the most fecund individual to spread through the group. And, to whatever degree this individual's behaviors and ideas initially differed from other members of the group, we will observe a shift in the distribution of ideas and behaviors in the group (i.e., cultural evolution). This occurs without anyone considering the costs and benefits of different foods, types of arrows, or prey choice. If, in a few years, as a different person emerges as the most fecund, the current cultural configuration will shift to incorporate whatever idiosyncratic ideas and behaviors this individual possesses. If we call a culture "well adapted" when its configuration of ideas and behaviors promotes the efficient production and maintenance of offspring, then the process described above will produce a "well-adapted" culture over several generations, without any cost-benefit decisions.[1]

My point is that cultural learning rules (or transmission mechanisms) do not necessarily pass beliefs and behaviors from one generation to the next in stable traditions. Under some conditions, cultural transmission mechanisms can create stable traditions that endure for long periods. If, in the above example, the idiosyncratic differences possessed by the most fecund individuals are never systemically (causally) related to the individual's fecundity, then the distributions of behaviors in the group will fluctuate through time without showing any directional evolutionary change or stable adaptive pattern. Or, if people don't vary in the number of offspring they produce, then such a learning rule will not drive any cultural change. Under other conditions, however, cultural transmission mechanisms will produce rapid cultural change and drastic behavioral shifts. Note that the above example is only meant to illustrate a theoretical point, and is not intended to be a claim about human psychology.

The word *culture* always creates some confusion. By *culture* I refer to those ideas, beliefs, behaviors, and values that *can* be transmitted from one individual to another via some form of direct social learning. From this perspective, animals are *cultural* if they possess the cognitive ability to acquire information (i.e., behaviors, ideas, etc.) by observing or interacting with others. Humans, sea otters, songbirds, and perhaps chimpanzees demonstrate at least some cultural abilities. This approach to culture allows us to make a clear distinction between *social* and *cultural* things. Humans, baboons, and wolves (for example) are all social animals, meaning they frequently interact with one other and prefer to live in groups. However, of these three, only humans are cultural, because only humans possess the cognitive capacities for observation learning, imitation, and other forms of direct social learning. In contrast, both songbirds and humans have cultural abilities, but songbirds are not very social. Consequently, we may talk of baboons' behavior being influenced by social factors (e.g., social structure, coalitions, or dominance hierarchies), but baboons cannot be influenced by the culture of their group—as best we know, baboons have no ability to acquire behaviors by direct social learning. For my goals in this paper, it's important to distinguish social from cultural forces—and I will focus on cultural forces.

Economic anthropologists invoke "culture" in a variety of ways. Some staunchly avoid it, maintaining that "culture" is not an explanation, but the thing to be explained. Others explain everything as cultural, and see that as sufficient. Most economic anthropologists, however, fall somewhere between these two extremes. In these instances, "culture" may provide individuals with certain preferences, perspectives, or context-specific heuristic rules. Unfortunately, labeling a belief, preference, or heuristic as "cultural" halts further inquiry into why people possess that particular belief, preference, or heuristic. For example, explaining the Mapuche's practice of planting only one major cereal crop (wheat) as a consequence of their belief that their god will bless only one crop requires explaining why they have that belief, and how it's maintained in the face of alternative beliefs (why not believe that god will bless three crops?). In what's to come, I show how understanding the cognition of cultural transmission allows us to crash through the imaginary bulwark erected by the label "cultural" to explain how certain things come to be widely shared, and why they change through time.

Cost-Benefit Decision Making and "Culture" in Economic Anthropology

In this section I provide examples from recent work in economic anthropology to demonstrate two things. First, I show that economic anthropologists model individuals as cost-benefit decision makers. Where appropriate, I detail the types of information and calculations necessary for the required cost-benefit decisions in order to emphasize the difficulty of such cognitive feats, given what we know about human cognitive abilities (which is subsequently discussed). Second, I illustrate how economic anthropologists invoke "culture" and how this invocation halts further analysis.

Wilk's (1996) excellent introductory text on economic anthropology illustrates how tightly cost-benefit decision making is interwoven into the fabric of economic anthropology—as well as into social and economic theory more generally. Wilk astutely divides the wide variety of approaches that have influenced economic anthropology into three categories according to their underlying assumptions about human nature. These three categories alternatively assume humans are rational, social, and moral/cultural. Wilk's description of these three approaches can be simplified as follows: (1) *rational* models assume humans are motivated by narrow self-interest; (2) *social* models assume that humans give important weight to the well-being of others, their social group, or society; and (3) *moral* models assume humans' decisions are guided by a set of culturally learned principles that distinguish right from wrong.

All three of these categories are actually subcategories of the cost-benefit approach. *Rational* actors make choices and plan strategies based on their own self-interest—the goal being to maximize self-interest. *Social* actors make choices and plan strategies aimed at benefiting others, or their social group—so their goal, or at least one of them, is to help others or their social group. Moral actors make choices and plan strategies according to their principles—with the goal of living up to, or at least not violating, these principles. Underlying all of these models is the assumption that individuals are goal-driven strategists who weigh choices according to their own ends (i.e., they are cost-benefit decision makers). Wilk's final chapter presents an interesting effort to construct a framework for incorporating all three models on varying temporal and social scales. His synthetic framework encompasses a vast range of cost-benefit models, but does not seriously consider that cultural evolution might (sometimes) be driven by nonstrategic cognitive processes, such as selective imitation (also see Rocha 1996).

Many economic anthropologists believe that cultural evolution, behavioral change, and adaptation result from individuals making cost-benefit decisions *and* transmitting these decisions, or their behavioral outputs, via social learning to their progeny. So, although most see "culture" or "tradition" as part of the process, the actual cultural transmission among individuals (or generations) plays no dynamic role. In this view, cultural transmission simply replicates the existing distribution of behaviors, beliefs, etc. without substantially altering their distribution or form. I term this particular type of cultural learning *static transmission*. From this perspective, the driver of changes lies in the decision-making process, not in the transmission process. Gladwin and Butler (1984: 210), following Chibnik (1981), articulate this approach in three steps: (1) individuals evaluate alternatives using low-cost experiments to gather information; (2) these decisions become codified in cultural rules; and (3) these rules are *statically* transmitted to the next generation. For Gladwin, Butler, and Chibnik, the driver of change lies in the cost-benefit evaluation of alternatives based on low-cost experimentation, not in the intergenerational transmission of this information. Similarly, while Harris maintains that "[a]s a species we have been selected" for our ability to acquire elaborate repertories of socially learned responses" (1979: 62), he believes that sociocultural evolution is driven by individuals opportunistically selecting among cultural/behavioral variants according to their benefit/cost ratios. Throughout the rest of my discussion I term this combination of static transmission plus cost-benefit decision making the *standard model*. In the standard model, cost-benefit decision making can only be the primary driver of change if the interpersonal or inter-generational transmission does not substantially alter the distribution ideas, rules, and behaviors through time. To the contrary, I will show that there's good reason to believe cultural transmission is heavily biased in ways that have substantial, and often adaptive, consequences.

In a more concrete example, Stonich (1993: 109) uses a cost-benefit approach to explain why farmers in the town of Oroquina (Honduras) rely on a system of intercropping of corn and sorghum:

> This farming system is a compromise between the clear cultural preference for corn, the staple of the peasant diet, and the need for the less desirable but climatically better adapted and more reliably yielding sorghum. . . . The function of the more drought tolerant sorghum as a risk reduction crop is illustrated.

Stonich has modeled these farmers as maximizing a benefit/cost function containing both a "cultural" preference for corn and a preference for "bet-ter adapted and more reliably yielding" crops (sorghum in this case). To accomplish this farmers must calculate the proper amount of sorghum to cultivate, given the strength of their cultural preference, their desired degree of risk reduction, the average yields of corn and sorghum, and the variance in those yields (the variance is required to assess the risk involved). All this requires an accurate recall of crop production from previous years, the ability to calculate expected yields and variances, and some capacity to integrate and process all this information. As we'll see in the next sec-tion, this is no easy task for our meager primate brains.

Another question arises from considering the information required for this cost-benefit analysis: How do Oroquinan farmers know *not* to plant crops that they don't routinely plant (and thus have no information on)? That is, why don't these farmers plant rice, millet, or manioc? Do they somehow know the expected yields and yield variances for each of these, and can thus eliminate them? One might argue that such crops are not well suited to the local environment, but how do farmers *know* this?[2]

Regarding culture, corn is invoked as a "cultural preference" when it doesn't seem to make good adaptive sense. The implication is that farm-ers should plant all sorghum, but don't because a cultural preference gets in the way. If this is true, why is such a preference maintained in the face of cost-benefit decision making that favors sorghum? Why don't people have a sorghum preference? How do we explain the stability of the corn preference? If a corn preference is essential to explaining the behavior of these farmers, then the real key is to understand the process that spread and now maintains this corn preference.

Stonich also mentions risk reduction as a factor in farmers' computations. How do farmers compute or acquire their risk preferences? We know individuals and groups vary in their risk preferences (Henrich and McElreath forthcoming). Thus, a more complete explanation should explain where this risk preference comes from—that is, why do they want to reduce risk by this amount. Presumably, if they desired even *less* risk, they would plant even more sorghum. Why aren't they more risk-averse? Is their risk aversion a cultural preference? How do well-suited risk preferences arise?

In another example, Eduardo Garland tries to explain why Andean colonists migrating into the Upper Huallaga region of the Peruvian Amazon employ extensive agricultural practices instead of more intensive agricultural methods:

> Their subsistence strategies are structured around very restrictive patterns of maximization. . . . Colonists combine a strategy of reducing the requirements for labor [by cutting new land to avoid weeding] with that of minimizing risk [intensive agriculture is more productive, but requires risky expenditures]. Such an approach leads to a pattern of extensive land management and continuing deforestation. (1995: 224; brackets are mine)

In this approach, individuals seem to be maximizing a utility function containing a preference for little work, a preference for low risk, and a desire for greater production/profit (implicit). To arrive at this behavior, individual farmers must be able to calculate the difference in the average amount of labor required to cut a new garden vs. that necessary to continue weeding an older field, and the difference between the expected crop yields from each garden. This requires sufficient experience in both continuing to weed older gardens and in cutting new gardens, as well as an accurate memory of the labor requirements and yields of each. Farmers must also be able to integrate the probability of catastrophic failure (the yield falling below a subsistence minimum) with the probability of generating greater income with higher crop yields, given environmental and market fluctuations. Such calculations require the accurate assessment of expected yields, yield variances, environmental conditions, and market prices, as well as the ability to weigh and process this information. Given that these are new *immigrants*, who have little or no experience with local markets, regional price fluctuations, or the effectiveness of modern inputs under local conditions, it is difficult to see how farmers could acquire the necessary information, let alone process it.

Interestingly, Garland goes on to use this cost-benefit approach to analyze the differing rates of deforestation among five swidden agricultural groups in Peru: the Amarakaeris of the Madre de Dios, the Machiguenga of the Urubamba, the Ashaninka of Satipo, colonists of the

Upper Huallga, and colonists of Satipo (see table 13.1). In standard fashion, Garland attempts to explain these differences by first examining how factors such as land pressure, wage labor, and resource availability affect individual economic decisions. However, these situational differences seem small relative to the large differences in deforestation rates between indigenous peoples and colonists (note, for example, the difference between the colonists of Satipo and the Ashaninka of Satipo). In response, his analysis moves to focus on group-level differences in such things as resource management strategies, resource diversification, and conservation ethics—things that vary, not as a consequence of individual cost-benefit decisions, but as a consequence of individuals having been reared in certain social groups. "Culture" is used to label beliefs and practices that vary among groups. Unfortunately, due to the lack of any *theory of culture*, the analysis stops once something is designated as "cultural." The next question should be, Why do beliefs and management practices differ between these groups, and how can such beliefs be maintained through time under changing economic and environmental circumstances, and in the face of opposing individual-level cost-benefit analysis? Static transmission processes will *not* maintain such a pattern in the face of even small amounts of migration or interaction. Garland's analysis suggests that the key to understanding the differences in deforestation rates lies not in cost-benefit decision making, but in the cultural processes that create and maintain differences in resource management strategies and conservation ethics among groups.

Table 13.1. Estimated deforestation rates for five Peruvian groups

Group	Estimated Deforestation Rate
Amarakaeris of the Madre de	0.31
Machiguenga of the Urubamba	0.68
Ashaninka of Satipo	0.76 or 0.81*
Colonists of the Upper Huallga	1.47
Colonists of Satipo	2.13

*Depends on the assumptions about cropping cycle

Source: Garland, Eduardo Bedoya. 1995. "The Social and Economic Causes of Deforestation in the Peruvian Amazon Basin: Natives and Colonists." In *The Social Cause of Environmental Destruction in Latin America*, Michael Painter and William Durham, eds. Ann Arbor: University of Michigan Press.

Humans Are Not Very Good
Cost-Benefit Decision Makers

In this section I review evidence from cognitive psychology, experimental economics, and ethnographic research to show two things. First, laboratory evidence indicates that humans lack the computational abilities to behave according to typical cost-benefit models (as illustrated in the above examples from Garland and Stonich). Of course, the fact that people are systematically inaccurate at analyzing information does not, in and of itself, mean that we don't rely on cost-benefit decision making. It does means that people should *systematically* select alternatives that *do not best facilitate* their goals—that is, even if people are trying to make strategic decisions according to some set of goals, their cognition will cause them to systematically (and obstinately) make "wrong" or goal-averting choices. Thus, any effort to explain human behavioral pattern as a consequence of informational analysis should account for these, and thus expect to observe systematic "errors" or maladaptation. However, only rarely are these cognitive findings mentioned (e.g., Quinn 1978), let alone incorporated into explanations for persistent behavioral patterns. Second, field evidence further suggests that humans, whether peasants or MBAs, do not rely on cost-benefit models because people lack much of the information required by such models.

Because this experimental literature on decision making has grown rapidly in both psychology and economics, many of these results are aimed at disputing or confirming specific theories within their respective disciplines. In this section however, I've tried to distill all this into a brief summary of the robust findings, and unfortunately have space only to detail a few studies as illustrative examples. Interested readers should begin with some of the excellent review papers: see Camerer (1995), Rabin (1998), Abelson and Levi (1985), and Thaler (1987).

Memory Bias

Experimental work suggests that human memories are biased by what psychologists call *availability* (Tversky and Kahneman 1973). In assessing the probability of events or frequency of items, people search or sample from their memory. Events involving recent examples and personal experiences are more available and overweighed (judged more likely). For example, a comparison of married couples indicates that individuals overweigh their responsibility and contribution toward household activities, including their contributions to negative items like starting arguments and making messes (Ross and Sicoly 1982). Similarly, in judging the likelihood of the next earthquake, individuals who have recently experienced an earthquake greatly overestimate the short-term chances of another (Camerer 1995).[3]

In memory, some items are more "retrievable" or salient than others. For example, given a list of names of men and women, in which there are more men but more famous women, subjects remember the list as containing more women's names. Similarly, if asked which is more common, words that start with an "r" or words that have "r" as the third letter, most people reply that it's words that start with an "r", despite the great predominance of words with "r" as the third letter (Tversky and Kahneman 1973).

When assessing the probability of a rare event or the risks involved in a novel task, people reveal an *imaginability bias*. When events or tasks have no precedents stored in memory, individuals judge the likelihood of risks associated with them according to the ease with which they can be imagined. In assessing the risks of a new practice or a dangerous journey, people disproportionately rely on imagining vivid potential contingencies without incorporating the probabilities of more-difficult-to-imagine scenarios. Our capacity to evaluate such things depends on our ability to imagine different scenarios, but our ability to imagine different things does not seem to covary strongly with the occurrence of actual events (Tversky and Kahneman 1990).

If people cannot accurately store and retrieve the relevant information (see Kahneman et al. 1982 for more biases), how can we expect them to properly compare crop yields from previous years, notice recurrent patterns in the environment, or accurately assess what past events tell them about the present? Now, from a cognitive/evolutionary perspective, memory should not be thought of as a monolithic information storage device, but rather a space differentially allocated and organized to meet the fitness challenges of life in our ancestral environment. Humans should be best at acquiring, storing and accurately recalling information that would best assist them in survival and reproduction.[4] For our purposes however, it does not matter if humans excel at remembering fitness-enhancing items and forgetting other information. What matters is whether people possess sufficient memories of events and items, which were *never* encountered or selected for in the ancestral environment, in order to perform the computations required by most benefit/cost approaches. Can people, for example, remember a sufficient number of crop yields, rainfalls, labor allocations, and market prices to make economic decisions in the way many economic anthropologists think that they do? This evidence suggests that they cannot.

Data Processing Biases

In addition to biases in their recall of information, people also have difficulty processing information. They often make systematic errors in processing information and making judgments. In this section, I review a small fraction of this data from four areas: sample sizes and the gambler's fallacy, regression to the mean, covariation detection, and forecasting.

Sample size and the gambler's fallacy

Humans often underweigh or sometimes even ignore the effect of sample size when using data, depending on the type of problem. People reason as if they assume that samples of any size will be representative of the distribution or underlying process from which they arise (the *representativeness heuristic*). Small samples are often weighed as heavily as large samples. This means that individuals gather too little data and overgeneralize from these small samples to distributions, processes, and decisions (Tversky and Kahneman 1993; Kahneman et al. 1982).

For example, Kahneman and Tversky (from Nisbett and Ross 1980: 78) posed the following question to students at the University of Michigan:

The average heights of adult males and females in the U.S. are, respectively, 5 ft. 10 in. and 5 ft. 4 in. Both distributions are approximately normal with a standard deviation of about 2.5 in. An investigator has selected one population by chance and has drawn from it a random sample. What do you think are the odds that he has selected the male population if:

i   The sample consists of a single person whose height is 5 ft. 10 in.?
ii The sample consists of 6 persons whose average height is 5 ft. 8 in.?

As you might guess, a substantial majority of subjects estimated odds that favored the sample of one (choice i) over the sample of six (choice ii). The median odds estimated by the subjects favoring the male population for the one-person sample were 8:1, while their odds favoring the male population for the six-person sample were 2.5:1. The actual odds of 16:1 and 29:1, respectively, demonstrate that subjects misperceive the effect of sample size *in the opposite direction*—they favor the information provided by the small sample over a sample six times the size.

More recently, scholars have begun to refine the conditions under which humans (i.e., university students) properly weigh, underweigh, and ignore sample size information. In a meta-analysis of this body of work, Sedlmeier and Gigerenzer (1997) have shown that people almost entirely ignore sample size when they are analyzing one kind of sample size problem (which they term "sample distributions"—a distribution of sample means), but that many people (70 percent) will use sample size information, in some fashion, to guide their judgments when analyzing problems involving standard frequency distributions—however, it remains unclear how well they use the information.

Although this distinction is an important refinement of the existing literature, and potentially related to the evolutionary origins of human brains, it does *not* help the cost-benefit decision makers that inhabit the minds and models of economic anthropologists. Lots of real economic problems, to which anthropological peoples have well-adapted solutions, would require cost-benefit analysts to compare sample distributions. Many people need to "choose" among different gathering patches, fishing spots, crops, cropping techniques, domesticated animals, and hunting techniques. For example, if farmers relied on their individual informational processing abilities, they would incorrectly switch to new crops and practices based on small-scale experiments, limited information, and one-time trials because they (being only human) would overweight small samples—notably, this is not what we generally observe among farmers. This research also indicates that if people relied primarily on cognitive data-processing algorithms that evaluate pay-off relevant information (crop yields, hunting yields, etc.), then people would not possess very stable, nor very adaptive, behavioral patterns.

This insensitivity to sample size may cause a phenomenon termed the "gambler's fallacy" in which individuals perceive events in the world as occurring in swings or streaks. Basketball players and fans, for example, possess an unshakeable belief that certain players get "the hothand"— meaning they're on a scoring streak (i.e., field goals are positively autocorrelated).[5] In reality, however, actual hits and misses by players are remarkably close to independent (Gilovich et al. 1985). When presented with this information, basketball coaches refuse to accept it and don't alter their strategy. Instead, they continue trying to get the ball to the player with "the hothand." Similarly, a mistaken belief in winning streaks creates systematic errors in betting odds on professional basketball games (Camerer 1989). People also consistently see streaks and patterns in random data (Bar-Hillel and Wagenaar 1993)—such data does not "look" random. Consequently, farmers, herders, and foragers should falsely perceive relationships between random events in the world, and as cost-benefit decision makers, they should unintentionally make goal-averting decisions based on these believed patterns—just as basketball coaches do because of their belief in the "hothand."

Regression to the mean

This insensitivity to sample size, or perhaps a tendency to assume any sample is representative of its underlying distribution or generative process, causes people to misperceive a statistical phenomenon termed *regression to the mean*. I'll explain regression to the mean with an example. Pilot instructors, among many others, have "learned" from experience that negative reinforcement (scolding and criticism of trainees) after a poor landing performance works better than positive reinforcement after a better-than-average landing. Unfortunately for trainees, pilot instructors are mistaken. If student pilots have an average quality of landing, then some landings will be better than average and some landings will be worse than average. A particularly poor landing is likely to be followed by a better-than-average landing, and quite likely to be followed by at least some improvement. Good landings are likely (as a statistical fact) to be followed by worse landings, and often worse-than-average landings. Pilot instructors recognize this, but rather than seeing it as a statistical phenomenon, they falsely assume that their negative reinforcement on bad landings had a positive effect on their students and their positive reinforcement after good landings had a negative effect. Psychologists exploring the influence of both positive and negative reinforcement on performance have accounted for this statistical tendency, and actually found that positive reinforcement improves average future performances, while negative reinforcement retards improvement! So, in many situations, human teachers do exactly the wrong thing.

Covariation detection and illusory correlation

In general, evidence from psychology shows that people are poor detectors of covariation and correlation, except under very specific conditions. For example, after reviewing the data, Nisbett and Ross (1980: 111) conclude the following:

> The evidence shows that people are poor at detecting many sorts of covariation. . . . Perception of covariation in the social domain is largely a function of preexisting theories and only very secondarily a function of true covariation. In the absence of theories, people's covariation detection capacities are extremely limited. . . . Though the conditioning literature shows that both animals and humans are extremely accurate covariation detectors under some circumstances, these circumstances are very limited and constrained.

People often miss subjectively important strong covariations when the interval between the stimuli and the reinforcement, or the interval between successive sets of stimuli and reinforcements, is too long. For example, few insomniacs understand how temperature, the presence of an odd smell, exercise before bed, or mental concentration prior to retiring influence their ability to get to sleep. Freedman and Papsdorf (1976) demonstrated that insomniacs, whose sleep onset was delayed by a pre-bedtime exercise program, nevertheless reported that the program *reduced* their insomnia.

Besides missing strong covariations, people also frequently see correlations where none exist—a phenomenon termed *illusory correlation*. Chapman and Chapman (1982) found that scientifically sophisticated clinicians insist that projective tests like the "draw-a-person" and Rorschach tests are important diagnostic tools, despite the *fact* that empirical validation tests consistently show that most of these associations have little or no real correlation. The Chapmans argue that clinicians have some preexisting notions that connect specific test results to certain diagnoses, and that these notions cause them to perceive correlations where none exist.

If people solve complex solutions in the manner suggested by many cost-benefit approaches, then individuals need the ability to detect a wide variety of correlations in environmental and economic information. For example, calculating when to stop investing labor in some activity by analyzing the diminishing marginal rate of return to labor input (the point of "diminishing returns") in a stochastic environment (every real environment) requires the cost-benefit analyst to observe correlations between labor input and productive returns. Unfortunately, humans are terrible at observing such correlations, at least in laboratory settings, so it seems unlikely that individual-level computation is responsible for the subtle and intricate ways in which humans have adapted to various environments.[6]

Forecasting

In studies intended to explore our ability to incorporate multiple predictor variables in a forecast of another dependent variable, psychologists have shown that learning is very difficult in simple deterministic situations and extremely difficult in stochastic situations (Castellan 1977; Brehmer 1980). Even experts perform worse than simple linearly weighted combinations of observable variables. In over 100 careful studies of repeated judgments about stochastic outcomes in natural settings by medical doctors, psychiatrists, and other experts, researchers have consistently shown that a weighted linear combination of observable variables outperforms these "experts" under most circumstances (Dawes et al. 1989). For example, Dawes (1971, 1982) discovered that the success of doctoral students could be better predicted by an equally weighted linear sum of three measures—GRE scores, undergraduate school ratings, and undergraduate grades—than by the rating of the faculty admissions committee.

Effect of Training, Practice, and Expertise

Some might think that many of the biases and decision-making patterns I have discussed result from a lack of training, practice, or familiarity with these abstract tests. This is not the case. For example, the objection does not apply to evidence such as the basketball coaches' belief in the "hothand," or the systematic mistakes by odds makers, not to mention the repeated market games used by experimental economists. Outside the laboratory, actuaries and stockbrokers consistently reveal many of the same mistakes that freshmen do in the laboratory. Under some conditions, with well-structured feedback in repeated tasks, subjects can learn to avoid some of these mistakes, or at least diminish the strength of their biases, but extensive investigations demonstrate that these acquired abilities do not transfer well from task to task, across time or even when the parameters of the same task are altered (Camerer 1995). In short, there's no reason to believe that experience in the stochastic, poorly organized world of real life eliminates or even significantly reduces these errors and biases.[7]

Throughout the literature on judgment and data processing, humans place much greater weight on preexisting theories, expectations, and suspicions than they do on data.[8] Most covariation remains quite invisible to human cognition without a preexisting theory or expectation. The unfortunate consequence of this is that we often see correlations where none exist, just as we see patterns where only randomness exists. Perhaps researchers need to begin asking: From where do people get their preexisting theories, expectations, and suspicions? In the next section, I argue that individuals acquire such things from other people via biased cultural transmission.

Ethnographic Data

During my fieldwork among Mapuche farmers in south-central Chile, I explicitly addressed the question of whether economic behavioral patterns can be explained by cost-benefit decision making. This research, based on extensive observational, experimental, and interview data from sixty-three farmers, shows that many of the broad patterns of Mapuche economic behavior, although often quite "sensible" given their socioeconomic situation, do not result from typical cost-benefit decision-making models because people lack the required informational input for such models.

Before digging into the details of particular economic behavior patterns, I will briefly sketch the ethnographic context. The description derives from my work in the rural communities of Carrarreñi, Cautinche, and Huentelar around the town of Chol-Chol.[9] In this cool, wet Mediterranean climate (similar to San Francisco), the Mapuche live in widely scattered farming households that range in size from two to thirty-eight hectares, with an average size of approximately ten hectares. All practice a form of three-field cereal agriculture using steel plows and two-oxen teams. Most households subsist primarily on wheat (consumed in the form of bread), but many also produce oats—which are used only as animal feed. Households supplement their diets with vegetables, legumes, and livestock, as well as some store-bought foods. Cash income to buy these foods and other goods such as cooking oil, chemical fertilizers, and school supplies derives from a number of other sources, including (listed in decreasing degree of importance): livestock, lumber (fast-growing pines and eucalyptus trees), wage labor, the sale of vegetables, and cottage crafts.

My analysis examines the broad patterns of economic behavior among three Mapuche communities. The goal is to find theories (cost-benefit or otherwise) that explain the general patterns found in these data. Often the particularistic or idiosyncratic explanations of informants may seem to explain the behavior of one or two farmers, but the essential question is, Can these explanations elucidate the overall pattern? Often candidate models can be eliminated from competition if it's clear that individual farmers do not possess the requisite information or knowledge to make the required calculation. For example, if price is considered a key decision-making factor used by farmers, yet nobody has even a vague idea of a product's market price, then models that incorporate price as a decision variable can be eliminated.

Here I analyze one of the most important decisions of farmers anywhere: which crop to plant. Among the 63 farmers, 100 percent always plant wheat, while 95 percent have never planted barley. Why not plant at least some barley? How can we explain this strong pattern of "barley aversion"? This aversion seems particularly strange considering that, from everything I have found *including* the testimony of some Mapuche farmers, barley seems to be a fine crop for the local conditions, perhaps better than wheat. Local agronomists, working in the region's agricultural extensions, believe barley is an excellent crop for the climate and soil, and claim that regional breweries will subsidize the purchase of seeds and fertilizers. They frequently recommend barley to Mapuche farmers, and are willing to supply "start-up" seeds. Similarly, crop ecologists have shown that barley sustains its yields in the face of drought much better than wheat (Loomis and Connor 1992: 374). Interestingly, the number-one farming concern of many Mapuche farmers is insufficient rainfall, and they often cite persistent droughts as the cause of their low wheat yields, yet most never plant barley.

As an economic anthropologist, my initial instincts were that the Mapuche's long experience with their land, climate, social structure, economic position, and lifestyle must have revealed something to them that the agricultural extension agents and I were missing. This certainly would not have been an unusual occurrence in an anthropological inquiry. To address this, I asked sixty-three farmers why they (and their neighbors) do not plant barley. Table 13.2 summarizes their responses.

Table 13.2. Why don't you plant barley?

Why don't you plant barley?	# of responses	Percentage
Nobody here plants that	16	19.5
Good yield/good rotation w/wheat	10	12.2
Poor yield	9	11.0
Don't know why	8	9.8
No seeds	8	9.8
Not enough land	6	7.3
Don't like it	6	7.3
Needs lots of care/fertilizer	5	6.1
Low market price	4	4.9
Tough to cut with sickle	2	2.4
It's not our custom	1	1.2
Birds eat it	1	1.2
No transport to market	1	1.2
No good land	1	1.2
Hills are good for barley	1	1.2
Good market price	1	1.2
Don't like to eat it	1	1.2
Type of seed is gone now	1	1.2
Total number of responses	82	100.0

Data compiled by author.

Methodologically, all interviews were done with farmers I knew well and had interacted with over several months. In this simple table, I have greatly reduced and summarized the data. It was extracted from long and repeated discussions about crops, farming practices, and economic decisions. My method involves cross-checking responses from repeated discussions about the same topics with the same informants (separated by at least one month), and from data gathered from those same informants by local Mapuche assistants (who independently asked the same questions, but in my absence). On average, every informant was asked the same question twice. If answers from the same informant did not substantively match, I returned to the informant for further clarification. Often nonmatching responses provided additional information rather than revealing contradictions or misunderstandings. Table 13.2 includes all eighty-two different responses given by sixty-three different informants/ farmers—several guys gave more than one (noncontradictory) response to our probes. Whenever possible, interview data were checked against actual behavioral data. In this case, it's difficult to conceal what one sows in his field, especially around harvest time.

To understand this data, first compare the behavioral pattern (95 percent of farmers have never planted barley) to the informants' eighteen different reasons for their behavior. Notably, of the 5 percent (three out of sixty-three) who have planted barley, two have just recently experimented with it, and the other one remembers planting it over thirty years ago. Here we have a strong behavioral pattern (avoiding barley), yet farmers fail to articulate any consistent reasons that could explain the prevalence of this *pattern*. The most common response (one in five informants) was "nobody here plants that," as if the low frequency of this behavior justified avoiding any further consideration of the idea (which suggests *conformist transmission*—see my later discussion).

I wanted to know if this pattern of cropping behavior could result from some kind of cost-benefit cognitive processing. Almost any economically oriented, cost-benefit model of barley analysis would have to involve one or more of the following factors: barley yields (per unit of land), market price, labor requirements, and processing difficulties/costs. I asked around, and none of my anthropological or economics colleagues could suggest a sensible model that did not incorporate at least two of these factors. Admittedly, the pattern could be a product of cost-benefit decisions not involving these factors.

Factor 1: Can knowledge or beliefs about barley yields (as compared to wheat) account for the observed pattern? The second and third most popular responses to my inquiry about barley begin to illuminate this question. These two answers mostly arose from my secondary probes. After initially asking, Why don't you plant barley? I would wait patiently and record any responses. After the informant(s) had said all they wanted, I would probe a bit further by suggesting, "Perhaps barley gives a poor yield." This leading question produced an interesting result: Ten farmers *disagreed* with my suggestion and claimed that barley probably produces just fine, while nine agreed that perhaps its yields are a bit low (compared to wheat). This disagreement among farmers about the productivity of barley suggests that the *strong* pattern of barley aversion does *not* result from a pervasive belief about the productive potential of barley (accurate or otherwise). Farmers who think barley grows just fine (producing as much as wheat or more) don't generally plant barley. Similarly, those who think its yields might be low also don't generally plant barley. Further, ethnographic experience tells me that, if anything, the answers to my leading question may have biased the answers toward a "low yield" response, as some might have though it more diplomatic to simply agree with me, especially if they were uncertain about the real yields of barley. This suggests that, perhaps, more than ten of nineteen believe barley yields are equal to or better than wheat—which means beliefs about barley yields are even less likely to account for barley aversion.

Further, almost no one has any experience with barley (60 out of 63 have never planted it), or even knows anybody who does have experience with cropping barley (57 out of 63). When I asked people, What's the yield of barley? they would typically answer *"no tengo idea"* ("I have no idea"). In contrast, *everyone* knows the yield of wheat. Of the ten who claim that barley has a good yield, eight have never planted it and don't plan to in the near future; one has recently experimented with it and plans to plant more; and one has not planted it, but plans to next year. Of the nine who think its yields are low, one has just recently experimented with it *and* plans to try it again, while eight have never planted it and don't plan to in the near future.

This indicates that cost-benefit models, which require knowledge about the yield of barley relative to alternative crops, cannot explain the pattern of cropping among the Mapuche. There's no reason to believe that individual farmers possess experimental information or any accurate knowledge of barley's performance against other cereal crops. Further, there's no correlation between beliefs about barley yields (good or bad) and actual planting behavior. Most people admit they have no idea about barley yields, and those who do indicate a belief seem evenly divided on the issue. Meanwhile, the empirical pattern remains: Almost no one plants barley or plans to plant it.

Factor 2: Any cost-benefit model that includes the price of barley cannot explain the pattern of Mapuche behavior. I asked 61 farmers about the market price of barley and 57 of 61 had no knowledge of price—yet everyone knew the market price of wheat. Of those four who ventured a guess on the price, three were in the ballpark, and one was way off (three times the actual price). All four of these farmers believed the price of barley was equal to, or higher than, wheat. In case people were not able to give the price numerically, I also asked if they thought the price was higher than, about equal to, or lower than the price of wheat. Only one additional person felt they had some sense of this, and guessed correctly that barley had a somewhat higher price per sack than wheat. So, not only do most people not know the price of barley, but those few who do believe its price is higher than wheat. Consequently, cost-benefit models that include price as an important variable cannot explain the observed pattern of barley aversion.

Factor 3: It's possible that some aspect of the planting, harvesting or processing of barley makes it less desirable by increasing labor or processing costs relative to alternatives. To address this, I asked a subsample of twenty farmers about these aspects directly. I found that no one thought barley producing and processing would be any more difficult than wheat. They also felt it would not be any trouble to make into bread. Of course, only three of these twenty had ever grown barley before, and only two of those three had ever milled it—the other farmer sold his barley after threshing. Therefore, even if it is true that barley is more difficult to process than wheat, nobody knows that, so that cannot be the reason for the strong pattern.

This analysis indicates that any cost-benefit model of crop selection, which includes prices, yields, or labor/processing costs, cannot account for the pattern of Mapuche behavior. Other researchers have made similar observations. For example, Ortiz (1980) has argued that Colombian farmers lack sufficient knowledge of weather and price dynamics to make decisions based on this information (also see Quinn 1978).

Evidence from interviews with older farmers combined with past ethnographic work (Latcham 1909; Stuchlik 1976; Titiev 1951) among the Mapuche, sometimes in the same communities, suggests that somewhere between thirty and fifty years ago these Mapuche farmers abandoned planting barley. Ten out of sixty-three interviewees mentioned that they (only one case), their fathers, or their grandfathers cultivated barley. Four of these accounts noted that there was a problem with *polvillo* (a symptom of a crop disease where the seeds crumble). This indicates that in the past Mapuche farmers did include barley in their planting strategy, but dropped the practice a generation or two ago as a crop disease spread. Nowadays, such crop diseases are not a serious problem as most farmers (over 90 percent) routinely disinfect their wheat seeds with commercially available chemicals (the same technique could be applied to barley). Thus, memories of a crop disease in barley are not the reason why so few people plant barley now. Plus, no one suggested that a fear of *polvillo* was the reason why they were not presently cultivating barley.

Finally, some preliminary evidence suggests that the practice of planting barley may be gradually reentering the farmers' repertoire. The pattern of readoption suggests, not individual-level cost-benefit decision making, but biased cultural transmission. Two farmers have recently experimented with barley and another plans to plant it in the coming year. Of the two, Martín claims he got the idea while working in a local *fundo* (a large-scale, managed farm). The other guy, Domingo, says he got the idea from a local agricultural extension agent who is also a friend. The farmer who intends to plant it, José, got the idea and all his information from his neighbor, Domingo. So, the practice was transmitted from one individual to another, and perhaps from higher-status individuals, or at least through social networks.[10]

Machiguenga Slash and Burn Agriculture

It's my view that cultures are often too well adapted, given what we know about human information processing abilities and about what people actually know. The Machiguenga's approach to tropical forest agriculture provides an example. Many anthropologists and agronomists agree that swidden agriculture is adaptive in the infertile tropical soils of the Amazon (Moran 1993; Johnson 1983). Cutting and burning trees, bushes, and other plants release a range of important nutrients into the soil and slows the invasion of weeds (although it also sublimates valuable nitrogen). This nutrient boost helps for a couple of years, but soil quality soon declines. When this occurs, swidden agriculturalists like the Machiguenga typically cut new gardens—sometimes every year or every other year (Johnson 1983; Baksh 1984; Henrich 1997). This practice creates an agroecological cycle in which farmers can always plant in richer soil, while avoiding the labor of weeding older gardens. Further, the small size of these gardens and their rapid turnover rate allows forest regrowth to fill in fairly rapidly. Meanwhile, these fallow plots continue to supply supplemental foods to families.

The Machiguenga of Camisea live at the confluence of the Urubamba and Camisea Rivers and farm on soils much more fertile than typical Amazonian soils. In fact, many of the soils around Camisea are even more fertile than interfuvial parts of the same region (ERM 1996). As a result, government agents have attempted to convince the Machiguenga to switch to an alternative method of *slash and mulch* agriculture, but farmers have been entirely uninterested in this suggestion and continue to use fairly traditional swidden techniques. This led me to ask: Do swidden agriculturalists like the Machiguenga practice slash and burn agriculture because they understand the soil-enhancing and agroecological benefits of slash and burn agriculture, or is it part of a culturally transmitted agricultural script (see Alcorn 1989)? As part of my investigation, I asked Machiguenga farmers three questions: (1) Why do you burn after you cut a new garden? (2) Does burning or the ash affect the soil? and (3) If you had a machine to clear your garden, would you continue to burn? Table 13.3 summarizes their responses.

This research indicates that the Machiguenga do not understand the adaptive connection between the burning of forest biomass in swidden agriculture and the temporary infusion of nutrients and organic matter into the soil. The Machiguenga clearly believe that, given their present agricultural system, not burning would make planting and moving about the garden too difficult (table 13.3A). However, they recognize no general connection between burning and improving soil quality (table 13.3B). And, if given the ability to clear the garden without burning, they would discontinue burning entirely (table 13.3C).[11] Because no Machiguenga farmers in the region practice methods of slash and mulch agriculture, the Machiguenga of Camisea haven't had any exposure to alternative agricultural systems that deal with the difficulties of infertile Amazonian soils. Consequently, they have no way to comparatively *evaluate* the relative costs of systems that involve burning with those that do not—and no one has experimented with not burning. In this particular section of Machiguenga territory, slash and mulch *may* be superior (in terms of long-term yields per unit land), but the Machiguenga maintain an agroecological system adapted to more typical regional environments and lower population densities—only recently (in the last thirty years) did Machiguenga begin living in communities along major rivers near more fertile soil. Thus, the generally adaptive pattern of tropical forest agriculture (averaged across environments and time) used by the Machiguenga cannot be a product of cost-benefit decisions related to ecological or productive advantages because they lack the necessary comparative information, as well as the impetus to obtain the information via experimentation. Instead, it appears consistent with the patterns created by cultural transmission mechanisms adapting agricultural practices to more traditional Machiguenga environments—which were not along the fertile ground of the Lower Urubamba. This finding is similar to that of Alcorn (1989) for Bora and Huastec farmers, and of Wilken (1987) for Mexican farmers. If individuals' adaptation results from an adherence to such agricultural scripts, and not cost-benefit decision making, then explaining adaptation relies on understanding the cultural transmission processes that assemble adaptive scripts, or spread particularly useful rules of thumb. It's also worth emphasizing that static transmission will not maintain practices in the face of opposing cost-benefit decision making. Only biased transmission can subvert the

Table 13.3. Machiguenga farmers in Camisea use of slash and burn agriculture

A. Why do you burn?

Responses	Number of responses	Percent of total
To clear thorns and stickers	1	90.5
No response§	3	—
Clear out snakes	1	4.76
Custom	1*	4.76
Total	24	100.00

B. Does burning or the ash affect the soil?

Responses	Number of responses	Percent of total
No	12	85.7
No response§	2	—
Yes (improves it)	1*	7.1
Affects a little (damages it)	1	7.1
Total	16	100.00

C. If you had a machine to clear your garden, would you continue to burn?

Responses	Number of responses	Percent of total
No	10	100
No	6	—
Total	16	100.00

§ By this I mean that the farmers either did not respond or avoided the question—even after further explanation and questioning. Machiguenga are quite independent, and if they don't like a question or are confused, they often simply don't respond, or ignore the question. In this case, I inferred from facial expressions and ethology that some were confused by the question.
This "1" in A and B represents the same individual. He has spent a substantial amount of time in the mestizo towns doing wage labor. This acculturative experience may explain his divergent responses.

Data compiled by author.

directional force of cost-benefit decision, which can be quite helpful since our decisions are so wrought with mistakes.

Perhaps peasants acquire their behavioral strategies like MBA students (no offense to peasants). In a multiround investment experiment, MBA students had to divide their allotted money among three different investment options (A, B, and C). Each of these investment options had different mean returns and different amounts of variation on those returns. The returns between investments were sometimes correlated (e.g., a high yield in A probabilistically predicts a high yield in C), but these correlations changed as the game proceeded. Students were informed of all this and could also borrow money to invest (at interest). Students were highly motivated because their overall performance strongly affected their grade in the class. After each round, the experimenters posted a ranking of each student's performance (including both their allocations). As part of their analysis, these economists regressed the decisions made in each round by each individual against those of the top performer in the previous round and found strong evidence that students were "mimicking" the behavior of top performers (Kroll and Levy 1992).

Further, when Kroll and Levy compared the overall results of this experiment against a previous experiment in which results and rankings were not posted between rounds, they found that copying high performers allowed the whole group to move *much* closer to the optimal allocation behavior (as predicted by *Portfolio Theory*) compared to the no-copying control—which was very far from optimal, even after students had eighteen rounds of experience. Perhaps peasants, foragers, and horticulturalists possess well-adapted behavioral repertoires, not because they are each effective cost-benefit calculators, but because simple rules like "copy the most successful individual" generate well-adapted behavior in cultural evolutionary time.

People Rely on Biased Cultural Transmission

In an earlier version of this chapter I devoted considerable space to persuading readers that humans rely heavily on cultural transmission and imitation to acquire most of their behavior, beliefs, ideas, and values. After receiving feedback on this, I realized that what many anthropologists were missing was not that people rely heavily on cultural transmission, but that the nature of cultural learning processes can create behavioral and ideological change (cultural evolution), in the absence of cost-benefit decision making, by favoring the acquisition of ideas and behavior from certain people or by favoring particular kinds of ideas/behaviors. The next three sections address this as follows: (1) I briefly sketch the evidence for a substantial reliance on cultural transmission; (2) I show that this transmission is heavily biased in ways that can assemble and maintain adaptive behavioral repertoires—as well as create or maintain maladaptive practices under certain circumstances; and (3) I point out that when circumstances require flexible behavioral responses, biased cultural transmission can generate adaptive "rules of thumb" or context-specific heuristics over several generations.

Social Learning Theory

In his book *Social Learning Theory*, Bandura (1977) argues that psychologists must abandon approaches that emphasize reinforcement or internal drives and replace them with a cognitively detailed understanding of social learning—an understanding of how people acquire their behaviors, ideas, beliefs, and values from other people.[12] After more than two decades of research, Bandura concludes:

> The capacity to learn by observation [learn socially] enables people to acquire large, integrated patterns of behavior without having to acquire them gradually by tedious trial and error. . . . it is difficult to imagine a social transmission process in which the language, lifestyles, and institutional practices of a culture are taught to each new member by selective reinforcement of fortuitous behaviors, without the benefits of models who exemplify the cultural patterns. (1977: 12; brackets are mine)

Social learning research within psychology further shows that humans have the ability to infer abstract behavioral rules directly from observed behavior. Experiments demonstrated that:

> Modeling has been shown to be a highly effective means of establishing abstract or rule-governed behavior. On the basis of observationally derived rules, people learn, among other things, judgmental orientations, linguistic styles, conceptual schemes, information-processing strategies, cognitive operations, and standards of conduct. . . . Evidence that generalizable rules of thought and conduct can be induced through abstract modeling reveals the broad scope of observational learning. (1977: 42)

Bandura's work, and those of his fellow social learning theorists, shows that human cognition is strongly biased toward social learning. Humans will acquire behaviors and beliefs via social learning unconsciously, *without* positive reinforcement, and when they are unaware that a "correct" answer is sought or available. In experiments, individuals display the same propensity for social learning regardless of incentives or whether they are informed that correct imitation will be rewarded (Bandura and Walters

1963; Rosenthal and Zimmerman 1978). Bandura (1977: 38) writes, "one cannot keep people from learning what they have seen."

Anthropology and Child Development

In a recent paper that summarizes a great deal of research from cross-cultural studies of child development, Fiske (1998) argues that children learn most of what they need to know by observation and unconscious imitation, not from active instruction. Fiske finds the same patterns of imitation plus individual experimentation across time, space, and anthropological subfields. Children first imitate older siblings, peers, or adults, and then rehearse these imitations through play and practice. Children receive only the most general kind of negative feedback (in most places, adequate performances are expected). As with many things, Western society seems to be a strange aberration, where children may receive positive feedback and lots of active instruction (LeVine and LeVine 1977).

Children learn almost all of their adult behavior, including their economic practices and practical knowledge, by imitation and practice. In reference to rice agriculture in Okinawa, Maretzki and Maretzki (1966: 144) write, "Children learn by observing and experimenting. Whatever adults are doing, children are present to watch their activities and overhear their conversations" (see Titiev 1951: 91 for a similar observation among the Mapuche). Block (1994: 278, from Fiske 1998) gleans findings from a number of sources to make a similar point:

> In non-industrialized societies most of what takes people's time and energy—including such practices as how to wash both the body and clothes, how to cook, how to cultivate, etc.—are learned very gradually through imitation and tentative participation. . . . Knowledge transmission tends to occur in the context of everyday activities through observation and "hands-on" practices.

At first glance, "imitation plus experimentation" may sound like the standard model. But, as I show in the next section, there's good reason to believe the imitation process is biased. If children, for example, selectively copy *certain* peers, siblings, or adults, then the imitation process may generate cultural change prior to the experimentation component of the process—experimentation may then produce further change.

The Diffusion of Innovations

This interdisciplinary body of literature focuses on understanding why certain ideas, technologies, and practices spread, why some spread rapidly and others more slowly, and why some never spread. Rogers (1995, 18) summarizes some of the lessons from fifty years of research as follows:

> Diffusion investigations show that most individuals do not evaluate an innovation on the basis of scientific studies of its consequences, although such objective evaluations are not entirely irrelevant. . . . Instead, most people depend mainly upon a subjective evaluation of an innovation that is conveyed to them from other individuals like themselves who have previously adopted the innovation. This dependence on the experience of near peers suggests that the heart of the diffusion process consists of the modeling and imitation by potential adopters of their network partners.

According to Rogers, thousands of studies indicate that the costs and benefits of alternative practices, no matter how clearly observed, cannot explain the behavioral change process recorded in many places. In contrast, what does consistently emerge as essential to the diffusion process are the patterns of social interaction, modeling, and imitation.

Substantial Reliance on Social Learning Is Consistent with Evolutionary Models

Evolutionary anthropologists might wonder how imitative capacities could arise in a species if imitation sometimes causes individuals to do maladaptive things. In addressing this question, a number of theoretical evolutionary models have convincingly shown that natural selection favors the evolution of imitative capacities under a wide range of conditions (Boyd and Richerson 1985, 1988). Imitation acts like a shortcut to a good answer (but maybe not the best answer), and evolves because it saves the cost of individual experimentation and information gathering. Cultural transmission will evolve as long as the savings created by the shortcut exceeds the costs of occasionally acquiring maladaptive or less-adaptive traits. Henrich and Boyd (1998) constructed an evolutionary simulation model that allowed the degree of reliance on cultural transmission vs. individual learning (experimentation, etc.) to evolve in multiple subpopulations with migration and temporally changing environments. The model robustly shows that a strong reliance on cultural transmission will emerge from a population that begins with almost complete reliance on individual learning, under a wide range of conditions. Only when environments change very rapidly, or problems are very easy, does individual learning (cost-benefit analysis) predominate.

Parent-child Transmission Is Not the Dominant Mode of Cultural Learning

The standard model of cost-benefit decisions plus static transmission typically assumes (usually implicitly) that children acquire the cultural beliefs and practices of their parents. Although there are other transmission models that will produce static replication (e.g., if individuals copy people at random), most transmission processes generate cultural evolution. However, there are solid reasons to think that parent-child cultural transmission is relatively unimportant compared to other forms of transmission. In a recent book, Harris (1998) summarizes an enormous array of findings from across psychology, anthropology, and behavioral genetics to argue that children do not acquire their culture from their parents. Numerous behavioral-genetic studies comparing the behavior of parents and offspring show that parent-child transmission (or "common-family environment" more generally) accounts for little of the behavioral variation, once genetic similarities between parents and offspring are accounted for. Averaging over many behavioral/belief domains, common-family environment (which contains parent-child transmission) accounts for only 5 percent of the variation, the extra-family social world accounts for 45 percent (or 90 percent of the nongenetic influence), and genes account for 50 percent of the variation. Children do resemble their parents (behaviorally), but this similarity mostly arises from having the same genes. Anecdotal data focusing on the culture acquired by children raised by their immigrant families, but with a different cultural world outside the home, suggests that such children acquire their culture from their peers, not from their parents. A great deal of work in psychology is consistent with this finding. Anthropology's long-time assumption (Mead 1959: vii) that children acquire their culture from their parents is probably wrong.

Human Cognition Biases Cultural Transmission

There's an enormous number of ways that cultural transmission is, or could be, biased. Here, I focus on only two: *prestige-biased transmission* and *conformist transmission*. I selected these two transmission mechanisms for two reasons. First, both are content general—that is, as far as we know, they influence the transmission of ideas and behaviors across many domains. Domain-specific biases affect only beliefs about certain cultural domains, like "food," "animals," or "ghosts" (see Boyer 1994; Sperber 1996). And, second, both tend to favor adaptive behavior on average, but may favor maladaptive behavior under certain predictable conditions. Other examples of transmission biases that depend on the characteristics of the model (as opposed to the characteristics of the transmitted belief) cue off of such things as gender, age, and healthful appearance.

Prestige-biased transmission

Humans possess a strong propensity to preferentially copy the ideas, behaviors, values, and opinions of particularly prestigious or successful individuals in their social group—I term this cognitive mechanism *prestige-biased transmission*.[13] When sufficient information is available about who is the best hunter, forager, warrior, musician, or farmer (for example), people preferentially acquire his or her traits, beliefs, and practices. And, probably because the world is a noisy and uncertain place in which it's often difficult to tell why someone is so successful, people copy whole bundles of ideas, behaviors, linguistic patterns, and practices from successful individuals, even when the belief or practice's connection to the individual's success is unclear. In copying the best hunter, for example, it's difficult to tell whether his success results from his tracking techniques, his prayer rituals, his diet of carrots, or his habit of getting up early. Prestige-biased transmission, as a component of human cognition, biases cultural evolution in favor of those beliefs and practices possessed by successful individuals. On average, over many generations, it leads to the spread of those combinations of beliefs/practices that create successful individuals (i.e., good hunters, farmers, warriors, etc.). However, it can also drag along lots of maladaptive or neutral traits that happen to covary with those beliefs/practices that promote success (Boyd and Richerson 1985, chap. 8).

Prestige is important when individuals lack sufficient information about who are the most successful individuals in their group. Under these conditions, naïve individuals (children, young people, and immigrants) observe the deferential behavioral displays of others (noting to whom these displays are aimed) and use these as cues for whom to begin copying. These status-cues provide a shortcut means of exploiting the knowledge of others and figuring out whom to begin copying (see Henrich and Gil-White 2001 for details and an explanation of why).

A wide range of psychological, economic, and ethnographic literature confirms that people preferentially imitate prestigious individuals and overweigh their opinions in making judgments. In laboratory studies examining the social influence of prestigious individuals, Ryckman et al. (1972) and Ritchie and Phares (1969) found that individuals significantly shifted their opinion on "student activism" and "national budget priorities" (respectively) to match those of the prestigious individuals, even when the prestigious individuals would not know the subjects' opinion, and when the discussion topic was well outside of the prestigious individuals' domain of expertise. Similarly, in solving a maze game, Bauer et al. (1983) found that subjects copied the slow and "deliberate style" of a prestigious model, and thus performed worse than subjects exposed to no model or a low-prestige model.

Using real-world data from the vast literature on the diffusion of innovations, Rogers (1995) argues that the diffusion of new ideas, technologies, and practices is strongly influenced by "local opinion leaders." Compiling findings from many diffusion studies, Rogers describes these individuals as: (1) locally high in prestige (e.g., high prestige within the village); (2) well respected; (3) widely connected; and (4) effective social models for others (items 1, 2, and 4 are all parts of prestige-biased transmission). Consequently, the spread of novel technology depends on the prestige of whoever initially adopts it. Interestingly, Van den Ban (1963, from Rogers 1995) effectively demonstrates the pitfalls of prestige-biased transmission in his study of farmers in the Netherlands. He shows that small-scale farmers copied the mechanized farming practices of prestigious, large-scale farmers *even* when such practices were clearly inappropriate for their small-scale situations.

In the multiround investment game I mentioned earlier, Kroll and Levy (1992) found that MBA students tended to mimic the decisions of successful players even though rewards were distributed on a competitive basis. However, what I did not mention was that this imitation pattern caused several individuals to go "bust" as they repeatedly copied the margin-buying strategies of short-term winners. This experiment shows how prestige-biased imitation operates to adapt the overall behavior of the group, while simultaneously creating errors for those who too readily copy the short-run successes of lucky individuals. I explore this pattern further in my discussion of the Kantu of Borneo.

As I mentioned earlier, children acquire much of their culture via observation and imitation (Fiske 1998), probably by copying their peers (Harris 1998). However, psychological research on imitation (Brody and Stoneman 1981, 1985) indicates that children selectively copy their peers using both age and success (as demonstrated in "competence" for a specific task) as positive cues. Brody and Stoneman (1985) show that second-graders preferentially copy (in order of decreasing preference): same-age-high-competence, younger-high-competence, same-age-low-competence, younger-low-competence. This is true even when competence information comes from an *unrelated* task.

Conformist transmission

Under conformist transmission, individuals possess a propensity to preferentially adopt the cultural traits (ideas, beliefs, values, and behaviors) that are most frequent in the population. This psychological bias makes individuals more likely to adopt common traits than they would under static cultural transmission (the standard model). At the population level, conformist transmission causes more common traits to increase in frequency. If cultural transmission is static, then, barring the action of other forces, transmission will leave the frequency of the traits unchanged from one generation to the next. For example, if 60 percent of a population is performing a certain behavior, barring other forces, 60 percent of the population in the next generation will also perform that behavior. In contrast, conformist transmission increases the frequency of the trait from 60 percent in one generation to, say, 65 percent in the next generation. All other factors being equal, the frequency of the most prevalent trait will continually increase from one generation to the next. If it were the only transmission bias, conformist transmission would rapidly cause the most frequent cultural traits in the population to become the only cultural traits. Operating among other learning mechanisms (mechanisms that select, prioritize and evaluate different kinds of social and environmental information) and under constraining external conditions, conformist transmission creates a directional force that tends to establish and maintain cultural norms. When combined with prestige-biased transmission, conformist transmission provides a "brake" on an individual's tendency to copy "lucky" short-run successes.

There are both theoretical and empirical reasons for believing that conformist transmission exists. Theoretically, evolutionary models of social learning and conformist transmission demonstrate that natural selection favors the evolution of both a heavy reliance on social learning and a potent conformist effect, except when environments change very rapidly or the migration rate between groups is quite high (Henrich and Boyd 1998).

Empirically, numerous studies from psychology on social influence and conformity suggest that individuals rely on the judgments of others in making individual choices or decisions. Beginning with the famous Asch experiments in the 1950s, researchers from all over the world have demonstrated that people's perceptions and judgments are strongly influenced by others. Unfortunately, from my perspective, much of this work confounds by two different explanations. The more standard interpretation of these results, "normative conformity," proposes that people conform to the behavior of others because they want to appear similar to others, to be "a part of the group," and/or to curry favor with others or avoid punishment by agreeing. A less popular hypothesis consistent with conformist transmission suggests that people use the opinions, perceptions, and judgments of others as a source of information relevant to the issue at hand—as a means of improving one's chances of being correct.[14]

In a recent study sensitive to these two hypotheses, Baron et al. (1996) demonstrated two phenomena consistent with Henrich and Boyd's (1998) model of social learning and conformist transmission. In the experiment, subjects had to pick previously observed suspects out of a "criminal" line-up after hearing the selections of two others participants (confederates). Baron et al. varied both the problem difficulty and the compensation subjects received for correct answers. This study attempts to mitigate the influence of normative conformity by increasing compensation—presumably, the subjects' desire to appear like everyone else is balanced against their desire for cash. In the easy problem, which 97 percent of control subjects answered correctly without any social influence, conformity diminished when compensation increased—but some people still conformed to wrong answers. However, in a moderately difficult problem, which 76 percent of the control group got correct, subjects *increased* their conformity when compensation *increased*. This means that in problems with real monetary stakes, subjects rely *more* on social information as the problem difficulty *increases*. This finding concurs with our conformist model, which predicts that as a problem becomes more difficult, or environmental information becomes more ambiguous, subjects should shift their reliance from individual evaluations to biased transmission.

Insko et al. (1985) demonstrated that increasing the group size (the number of models) increases people's degree of conformity, *even* when responses are clearly private. Using a color perception task, these researchers varied the group size by using between one and four confederates, and varied the form of the response between public and private. Subjects either stated their responses aloud or wrote down their responses in secret. These results are consistent with conformist transmission in two respects: (1) they show an effect of group size (bigger groups should be a more salient cue); and (2) people remain conformists even when their responses are clearly secret—mitigating the effects of normative conformity.

In a study of the effect of social influence on common-pool resource games, Smith and Bell (1994) argue that players sometimes copy other players when they're uncertain of what to do. Two forms of a multiround common-goods game were used. In these games, one subject and two confederates make withdrawals of "points" from a common pool that initially contains fifteen points. The number of points in the pool doubles every other round, but cannot exceed fifteen. The game lasts until the common pool goes to zero, or for a maximum of fifteen rounds. In version one of the game, players receive "lottery tickets" (a chance of winning real money) according to their personal point totals at the end of the game; in version two, players receive "lottery tickets" according to their group's point total at the end of the game. In both versions, subjects show a significant reliance on mimicking the behavior of confederates. When confederates underutiltize the resources, subjects tend to underutiltize resources, and when confederates overutiltize resources, subjects tend to overutilitze resources. Because subjects behave similarly when their self-interest equates with the group-interest, and when it's opposed to the group, the authors argue that subjects mimic as a means of using social information under uncertainty, and not to compete with the other players (confederates). These results and conclusions are consistent with the predictions of conformist transmission and are important because they address economic decisions not related to perception. Wit (1999) produced similar findings using a voting game.

It's worth emphasizing that both conformist and prestige-biased transmission produce adaptive behavior under a wide range of conditions, and both are favored by natural selection over static transmission (Henrich and Gil-White 2001; Henrich and Boyd 1998; Boyd and Richerson 1985). Neither, however, involves the direct evaluation of information about the costs and benefits of alternative choices. Evolutionary models show that when environmental information is somewhat noisy or environments are variable, individuals who *selectively* acquire the behaviors, ideas, etc., from other members of their social group are better adapted than those who rely on experimentation and cost-benefit decision making.

Using formal cultural evolutionary models (Henrich forthcoming), I recently compared the dynamics generated by biased transmission (prestige-biased plus conformist transmission) with the "standard model" (experimentation plus static transmission). My analysis of the diffusion dynamics produced by these two approaches shows that the adoption of new ideas, practices, and techniques results primarily from biased cultural transmission, and not from the standard model. The diffusion of innovations literature robustly shows that adoption curves (frequency of adopters vs. time) form an "S-shape." These curves rise slowly, accelerate to a maximum adoption rate near the middle, and then taper offer toward the end of the adoption cycle (forming an S-like shape). Interestingly, formalizations of the standard model do not generally produce S-shaped adoption curves, while models of biased transmission always produce S-shapes. Combined models, which mix biased transmission with the standard model, do *not* produce the S-shapes, unless biased transmission is the dominant force. Consequently, this evidence (based on over 3,000 empirical studies) indicates that biased cultural transmission is likely to be important in any theory about the adoption of new techniques, technologies, and practices.[15]

Biased Cultural Transmission and Experimentation

Even when behavioral patterns are affected by experimental processes, biased transmission acts to reduce the range of possible experiments, thereby directing experimental efforts toward favorable possibilities, as well as to selectively spread the behavioral output of successful experiments (and lucky guesses). For example, Johnson (1971) describes how a Brazilian sharecropper, after observing a new method of planting bananas at a "technically advanced plantation," then performed a controlled experiment in which he planted alternating rows of bananas with the new and traditional methods—the traditionally planted rows acted as a control group for comparison with the new method. Here, the farmer first acquires an idea from a "prestigious cultural model," and then experiments with the idea, before incorporating it into his behavioral repertoire. He did not arrive at a new method *de novo*, through calculation. He copied a prestigious model, and then experimented.

In my work with Mapuche farmers I've found similar cases of prestige-biased transmission and experimentation. Although generally the Mapuche seem less inclined toward experimentation than Johnson's sharecroppers, the Mapuche sometimes acquire an idea from working at a local *fundo*, or from someone they trust, and then experiment with the idea. The readoption of barley that I described earlier fits this pattern, and I've seen similar examples with the sowing of spring wheat (vs. winter wheat) and the application of lime in soil management.

People Rely on Culturally Transmitted Scripts and Heuristics

Despite the continued emphasis on cost-benefit decision making in economic anthropology, ethnographic data soundly demonstrates that people rely heavily on tightly defined rules of thumb or context-specific heuristics when economic circumstances call for behavioral flexibility (e.g., Wilk 1996; Quinn 1978; Johnson 2000). Mapuche farmers, for example, decide when to sow winter wheat by watching for the initial emergence of weeds after the first rains of winter. This simple rule effectively accounts for both the variable timing of the winter rains and existing moisture in the soil. In sixty-three interviews, no farmer admits to having tried alternative rules—nobody, for example, has tried the rule "plant on June 3," or the rule "plant three days after the first winter rains." The theoretical question should be: Where do these rules and heuristics come from, or how did they evolve?

Do we think that the ancestors of each of these Mapuche farmers systematically experimented with a wide range of possible rules and all converged on this *one* rule, which was then passed down father to son? Or, if we think a few farmers occasionally experimented with modifications (which is currently what Mapuche do), then how do we account for the subsequent spread of this one rule through the population, especially since human cognition lacks both the data and the information-processing ability to accurately select among rules that are approximately equal in effectiveness? If rule selection was a product of cost-benefit decisions, then we should expect extreme heterogeneity in the rules used (which is sometimes the case). Biased cultural transmission, however, can spread and maintain such adaptive rules, even if people don't experiment but only occasionally misacquire the rule. Biased transmission takes advantage of the individual variation in a population, and allows for different rules to be recombined to form novel rules. If people sometimes vary in what they copy and from whom, then the transmission process can create novel combinations of cultural elements, which will probabilistically spread according to their influence on their possessor's success or prestige (Boyd and Richerson 2001).

Bird augury among the Kantu of Kalimantan

Dove's analysis (1993) of how the Kantu of Kalimantan use bird augury to select swidden garden locations provides an excellent example of both the systematic errors in human judgment and how cultural evolution can provide unconscious adaptation without individual cost-benefit decisions. Dove first points out how some Kantus reasoned that, because destructive floods had not occurred for several years, they should locate all their gardens on high ground (because a flood seemed "due"). In contrast to this classic exposition of the "gambler's fallacy," Dove writes:

> Cyclical resonance is a key heuristic device in many ecological models, in industrial societies as well as tribal societies. . . . But there is no evidence of cyclical patterns in rainfall or flooding in Kalimantan. Consequently, the nonoccurrence of a rice-destroying flood during a three-year period does not affect the statistical likelihood of such a flood during the following year: it is no more or less likely than in any other year. (1993: 147)

This means that interpreting floods as part of a cyclical process makes cultivators more likely to make mistakes. Cultural evolution, however, seems to have solved this problem: Kantu farmers rely on a system of cultural rules that effectively randomizes their interpretation of bird omens with respect to environmental and climatic factors, and thereby allows them to select garden sites without the negative influence of the gambler's fallacy (see Moore 1957 for a similar system). Decisions depend not only on seeing a particular species of bird in a particular location, but also on what type of call the bird makes.

Dove also notes how augury rules inhibit the operation of another important learning bias—prestige-biased transmission—which could cause cultivators to copy the short-term successes of lucky neighbors (which also occur in multiround investment games). He writes, "The Kantu are keen observers of one another's harvest successes and failures, and when one household enjoys conspicuous success, other households are tempted to copy its strategies" (1993: 147). Short-term strategies used by successful households in one particular year could be disastrous the following year. Cultural proscriptions, however, make the results of each household's bird augury a big secret, and the rules indicate that failure to heed one's own omens or the use of any others' omens will result in bad luck and a poor harvest. Copying short-term success would also tend to homogenize the group and deplete essential, risk-managing variation. So, these rules also promote interhousehold diversification, which acts as insurance against local failures of certain land types.

Interestingly, no rules prevent households from copying the bird augury *beliefs* themselves from successful neighbors. This system of bird augury seems to have evolved and spread throughout this region since the seventeenth century when rice cultivation was introduced—which makes good adaptive sense since it's rice cultivation that is most positively influenced by randomizing garden locations. It's possible that, with the introduction of rice cultivation, a few farmers began to use bird sightings as an indication of favorable garden sites. On average, over a lifetime, these farmers would do better (be more successful) than farmers who relied on the gambler's fallacy. Using prestige-biased imitation, individuals would copy whole sets of traits from successful individuals, including their rules and beliefs about garden selection. Consequently, within four hundred years, the bird augury system spread throughout the agricultural populations of the Borneo region, yet remains conspicuously missing or underdeveloped among local foraging groups and recent adopters of rice agriculture (illustrating a maladaptive temporal lag, as recent adopters of rice haven't yet acquired the bird augury beliefs), as well as among populations that rely on irrigation agriculture (e.g., the Rungus, who would experience no advantage from the omen beliefs). Here, cultural evolutionary processes seem to have retrofitted some rare beliefs about bird omens to deal with the problem of garden site selection (and avoid the gambler's fallacy), and adorned this belief system with prohibitions that prevent the short-term cascade effect sometimes generated by biased imitation.

Conclusion

In this chapter, I have argued that economic anthologists should incorporate an understanding of biased cultural transmission into their existing models of decision making. Laboratory evidence demonstrates that people (i.e., university students) lack the cognitive abilities to perform the kinds of analyses required by most cost-benefit models—without creating goal-averting mistakes. Similarly, field evidence shows that many behavioral patterns, despite being quite adaptive, cannot be products of cost-benefit decision making. Rather than relying on unrealistic cost-benefit models, we need to develop psychologically informed approaches that include both the relevant aspects of cultural transmission, as well as cost-benefit decision making. Most researchers would agree that people's behaviors, beliefs, values, and ideas result from a combination of cultural transmission, experimentation, and decision making. Individuals, standing on a body of culturally inherited rules, beliefs, and practices, use experimentation and their own decision-making abilities to adjust and adapt to their own circumstances. Most economic anthropologists, however, have focused on the "experimentation and decision making" part of the equation, which often accounts for much of the variation among individuals within social groups. I propose that we now consider how cultural learning processes have assembled the body of cultural stuff upon which individual decision makers stand. Such processes seem likely to illuminate much of the variation between social groups—i.e., variation among cultures instead of variation among individuals within cultures.

Notes

1. This model requires a source of variation—that is, some mechanism to create idiosyncratic differences among individuals. Such variation can be incorporated by imagining that creative individuals occasionally do experiments and/or cost-benefit analyses, or by simply assuming that people make errors through their cultural learning process.

2. Recent work in cognitive psychology shows that people may rely on domain-general heuristics that could help solve these kinds of information-poor dilemmas (Gigerenzer, Todd, and the ABC research group 1999).

3. The chances of another earthquake, given that one has recently occurred, are actually lower than the base rate of earthquakes because the stress has been temporally relieved.

4. For example, a general bias toward *availability* might even be adaptive if most events in the real world were autocorrelated. And, under specific circumstances, shorter memories that preferentially retain the most recent information actually outperform longer memories in accurately recognizing correlated patterns in the environment (Kareev 1995).

5. Positive autocorrelation means that the occurrence of an event increases the likelihood of that same event in the next trial or time period. For example, if coin flips were positively autocorrelated instead of independent, the appearance of "heads" on the first flip would increase the chance of heads on the next flip from 50 percent to, say, 60 percent.

6. Humans are also poor at searching for information. Economists have shown that people search too little, accept too soon, and respond too slowly to changes in the distribution of wage and price offers (Braunstein and Schotter 1982).

7. Nonhuman animals reason like humans. For example, while studying the economic decision making of bees, Real (1994) showed that, like humans, bees underweigh low probabilities and overweigh high probabilities in making risky decisions. Like humans, these animals also show an *availability bias*, in which they remember only the most recent or salient events (bees: Real 1994; starlings: Cuthill et al. 1990; Brunner et al. 1992, 1996). When researchers compare the human and nonhuman animal literatures they conclude that animals exhibit the same errors and biases that humans do (Camerer 1995; Davis and Holt 1993; Battalio et al. 1985).

8. Psychologists have shown that somewhat ambiguous data will actually drive people's opinions farther apart as individuals interpret new data in favor of their existing view (Lord et al. 1979).

9. More generally, the Mapuche are a growing indigenous group of approximately one million people. In the last fifty years, this population has been expanding out of the rural regions of central Chile (Bengoa 1997: 11).

10. This anecdotal finding is consistent with research from the "diffusion of innovations" literature (Rogers 1995).

11. If one wanted, one could use the machine to clear the garden (saving the cost of labor), and still leave some trees and branches behind to burn—thereby saving the labor and getting the nutrient fix. I suggested this during a few interviews, but the Machiguenga seemed to think it was a ridiculous suggestion. Why would one burn if one did not have to burn (i.e., it's both dangerous and extra work)? Of course we know that other groups use topical agricultural systems that do not involve burning (see Orejuela 1992).

12. Note, Bandura is arguing with psychologists, so he frames his argument for cultural transmission in opposition to the predominant approaches of the time in psychology—i.e., reinforcement learning and internal drives.

13. Many other researchers have noted this tendency, see Dove 1985; Hammel 1964; Rogers 1995; Moore 1957; Miller and Dollard 1941. This research is summarized in Henrich and Gil-White 2001.

14. These are not mutually exclusive hypotheses. I think both types of conformity are part of our cognition.

15. Admittedly, it's possible that my formalizations of the standard model missed some key element(s). Readers of Henrich (forthcoming) are encouraged to send me modifications. So far, however, no one has produced those "key elements."

References

Abelson, Robert P., and A. Levi
  1985 "Decision Making and Decision Theory." Pp. 231–309 in *Handbook of Social Psychology*, 3rd ed, G. Lindzey and E. Aronson, eds. New York: Random House.
Alcorn, Jan
  1989 "Process as Resource: The Traditional Agricultural Ideology of Bora Huastec Resource Managment and Its Implications for Research." Pp. 63–77 in *Resource Management in Amazonia: Indigenous and Folk Strategies*, Darrell A. Posey, and W. Balée, eds. Bronx, N.Y.: New York Botanical Garden.
Baksh, Michael George
  1984 "Cultural Ecology and Change of the Machiguenga Indians of the Peruvian Amazon." Dissertation, University of California at Los Angeles.
Bandura, Albert
  1977 *Social Learning Theory*. Englewood Cliffs, N.J.: Prentice-Hall.
Bandura, A., and R. H. Walters
  1963 *Social Learning and Personality Development*. New York: Holt, Reinhart and Winston.
Bar-Hillel, M., and W. Wagenaar
  1993 "The Perception of Randomness." Pp. 369–93 in *A Handbook for Data Analysis in the Behavioral Sciences: Methodological Issues*, G. Keren and C. Lewis, eds. Hillsdale, N.J.: L. Erlbaum Associates.
Baron, Robert, Joseph Vandello, and Bethany Brunsman
  1996 "The Forgotten Variable in Conformity Research: Impact of Task Importance on Social Influence." *Journal of Personality and Social Psychology* 71(5): 915–27.
Battalio, R. C., J. C. Kagel, and D. N. MacDonald
  1985 "Animals' Choices over Uncertain Outcomes: Some Initial Experimental Evidence." *American Economic Review* 75: 597–613.
Bauer, G.P., R. S. Schlottmann, J. V. Bates, and M. A. Masters
  1983 "Effects of State and Trait Anxiety and Prestige of Model on Imitation." *Psychology Reports* 52: 375–82.
Bengoa, Jose
  1997 *Los Mapuches: comunidades y localidades en Chile: Coleccion Estudios Sociales*. Chile: Instituto Nacional de Estadisticas.
Block, Marice
  1994 "Language, Anthropology, and Cognitive Science." Pp. 276–83 in *Assessing Cultural Anthropology*, Robert Borofsky, ed. New York: McGraw Hill.
Boyd, Robert, and Peter J. Richerson
  1985 *Culture and the Evolutionary Process*. Chicago: University of Chicago Press.
  1988 "An Evolutionary Model of Social Learning: the Effects of Spatial and Temporal Variation." Pp. 29–48 in *Social Learning: Psychological and Biological Perspectives*, Thomas R. Zentall and Bennett G. Galef, eds. Hillsdale, N.J.: Lawrence Erlbaum Associates.
  2001 "Norms and Bounded Rationality." Pp. 281–96 in *Bounded Rationality and the Adaptive Toolbox*, Gerd Gigerenzer and Reinhard Selten, eds. Cambridge, Mass.: MIT Press.

Boyer, P.
1994 *The Naturalness of Religious Ideas.* Berkeley: University of California Press.
Braunstein, Y. M., and A. Schotter
1982 "Labor Market Search: An Experimental Study." *Economic Inquiry* 20: 133–44.
Brehmer, B.
1980 "In One Word: Not from Experience." *Acta Psychologica* 45: 223–41.
Brody, G. H., and Z. Stoneman
1985 "Peer Imitation: An Examination of Status and Competence Hypotheses." *Journal of Genetic Psychology* 146(2): 161–70.
1981 "Selective Imitation of Same-Age, Older, and Younger Peer Models." *Child Development* 52(2): 717–20.
Brunner, Dani, Alex Kacelnik, and John Gibbon
1996 "Memory for Inter-Reinforcement Interval Variability and Patch Departure Decisions in the Starling, *Sturnus vulgaris.*" *Animal Behavior* 51: 1025–45.
Brunner, Dani, Alex Kacelnik, and John Gibbon
1992 "Optimal Foraging and Timing Processes in Starling, *Sturnus vulgaris*: Effect of Inter-capture Interval." *Animal Behaviour* 44: 597–613.
Camerer, Colin F.
1989 "Does the Basketball Market Believe in the 'Hot Hand'?" *American Economic Review* 79: 1257–61.
Camerer, Colin F.
1995 "Individual Decision Making." Pp. 587–703 in *The Handbook of Experimental Economics*, John H. Kagel and Alvin E. Roth, eds. Princeton, N.J.: Princeton University Press.
Castellan, N. J. Jr.
1977 "Decision Making with Multiple Probabilistic Cues." Pp. 143–59 in *Cognitive Theory*, vol. 2, N. J. Castellan Jr., D. Pisoni, and G. R. Potts, eds. Hillsdale, N.J.: Lawrence Erlbaum Associates.
Chapman, Loren J., and Jean Chapman
1982 "Test Results Are What You Think They Are." Pp. 239–48 in *Judgment under Uncertainty: Heustics and Biases.* Daniel Kahneman, Paul Slovic, and Amos Tversky, eds. Cambridge: Cambridge University Press.
Chibnik, Michael
1981 "The Evolution of Cultural Rules." *Journal of Anthropological Research* 37(3): 256–68.
Cuthill, Innes C., Alejandro Kacelnik, and John R. Kreb
1990 "Starling Exploiting Patches: The Effect of Recent Experience on Foraging Decisions." *Animal Behaviour* 40: 625–40.
Davis, Douglas D., and Charles A. Holt
1993 *Experimental Economics.* Princeton, N.J.: Princeton University Press.
Dawes, Robyn
1971 "A Case Study of Graduate Admissions: Application of Three Principles of Human Decision Making." *American Psychologist* 26: 180–88.
Dawes, Robyn M.
1982 "The Robust Beauty of Improper Linear Models in Decision Making." Pp. 391–407 in *Judgment under Uncertainty: Heuristics and Biases*, Daniel

Kahneman, Paul Slovic, and Amos Tversky, eds. Cambridge: Cambridge University Press.

Dawes, Robyn M., D. Faust, and P. E. Meehl
1989   "Clinical versus Actuarial Judgment." *Science* 243: 1668–74.

Dove, Michael
1993   "Uncertainty, Humility and Adaptation in the Tropical Forest: The Agricultural Augury of the Kantu." *Ethnology* 32(2): 145–67.

Environmental Resources Management
1996   "Camisea Appraisal Drilling Campaign: Environmental Impact Assessment." Lima, Peru: Royal Dutch Shell.

Fiske, Alan Page
1998   Learning a Culture the Way Informants Do: Observing, Imitating, and Participating. Unpublished manuscript, UCLA.

Freedman, R., and J. Papsdorf
1976   "Biofeedback and Progressive Relaxation Treatment of Insomnia: A Controlled All-night Investigation." *Biofeedback and Self-Regulation* 1: 253–71.

Garland, Eduardo Bedoya
1995   "The Social and Economic Causes of Deforestation in the Peruvian Amazon Basin: Native and Colonists." In *The Social Cause of Environmental Destruction in Latin America*, Michael Painter and William Durham, eds. Ann Arbor: University of Michigan.

Gigerenzer, Gerd, Peter M. Todd, and ABC Research Group
1999   *Simple Heuristics that Make Us Smart.* New York: Oxford University Press.

Gilovich, Thomas, Robert Vallone, and Amos Tversky
1985   "The Hot Hand in Basketball: on the Misperception of Random Sequences." *Cognitive Psychology* 17(3): 295–314.

Gladwin, Christina, and John Butler
1984   "Is Gardening an Adaptive Strategy for Florida Family Farmers?" *Human Organization* 43(3): 208–16.

Hammel, E.
1964   "Some Characteristics of Rural Village and Urban Slum Populations on the Coast of Peru." *Southwestern Journal of Anthropology* 20: 346–58.

Harris, Judith Rich
1998   *The Nurture Assumption: Why Children Turn Out the Way They Do.* New York: Touchstone.

Harris, Marvin
1979   *Cultural Materialism: The Struggle for a Science of Culture.* New York: Random House.

Henrich, Joseph
1997   "Market Incorporation, Agricultural Change and Sustainability Among the Machiguenga Indians of the Peruvian Amazon." *Human Ecology* 25(2): 319–51.

2000   "Does Culture Matter in Economic Behavior: Ultimatum Game Bargaining among the Machiguenga." *American Economic Review* 90(4).

forthcoming   "Cultural Transmission and the Diffusion of Innovations: Adoption Dynamics Indicate that Biased Cultural Transmission is the Predominant Force in Behavioral Change and Much of Sociocultural Evolution." *American Anthropologist.*

Henrich, Joe, and Robert Boyd
1998 "The Evolution of Conformist Transmission and the Emergence of Be-
tween-group Differences." *Evolution and Human Behavior* 19: 215–42.
Henrich, Joseph, and Richard McElreath
forthcoming "Peasant Are Not Risk Averse (In Fact, They Are Risk Prone)."
Current Anthropology.
Henrich, J., and F. Gil-White
2001 "The Evolution of Prestige: Freely Conferred Deference as a Mechanism
for Enhancing the Benefits of Cultural Transmission." *Evolution and Human
Behavior* 22(3): 165–96.
Insko, C. A., R. H. Smith, M. D. Alicke, J. Wade, and S. Taylor
1985 "Conformity and Group Size: The Concern with Being Right and the
Concern with Being Liked." *Personality & Social Psychology Bulletin* 11(1):
41–50.
Johnson, Allen
1971 *Sharecroppers of the Sertao: Economics and Dependence on a Brazilian Plantation.* Stanford, Calif.: Stanford University Press.
1983 "Machiguenga Gardens." Pp. 29–63 in *Adaptive Responses of Native
Amazonians,* Raymond Hames and William Vickers, eds. New York: Academic
Press.
2000 *The Matsigenka of the Peruvian Amazon: A Psychoecological Study.* Stanford:
Stanford University Press.
Kahneman, Daniel, Paul Slovic, and Amos Tversky, eds.
1982 *Judgment under Uncertainty: Heuristics and Biases.* Cambridge: Cambridge
University Press.
Kareev, Y.
1995 "Through a Narrow Window: Working Memory Capacity and the Detec-
tion of Covariation." *Cognition* 56: 263–69.
Kroll, Yoram, and Haim Levy
1992 "Further Tests of the Separation Theorem and the Capital Asset Pricing
Model." *American Economic Review* 82(3): 664–70.
Latcham, R. E.
1909 "Ethnology of the Araucanos." *Journal of the Royal Anthropological Institute* 39: 334–70.
LeVine, Robert A., and Barbara B. LeVine
1977 *Nyansongo: A Gussii Community in Kenya.* Six Culture Series. Huntington,
N.Y.: Robert E. Krieger.
Loomis, R. S., and D. J. Connor
1992 *Crop Ecology: Productivity and Management in Agricultural Systems.* Cambridge: Cambridge University Press.
Lord, Charles G., Lee Ross, and Mark R. Lepper
1979 "Biased Assimilation and Attitude Polarization: The Effects of Prior Theories on Subsequently Considered Evidence. *Journal of Personality and Social
Psychology* 37(1)1: 2098–109.
Maretzki, Thomas, and Hatsumi Maretzki
1966 *Taira: An Okinawan Village.* Six Cultures Series, v. 7. New York: Wiley.

Mead, Margaret
1959 *Preface to Ruth Benedict's Patterns of Culture*, 2nd ed. Boston: Houghton Mifflin.
Miller, N. E., and J. Dollard
1941 *Social Learning and Imitation*. New Haven, Conn.: Yale University Press.
Moore, O. K.
1957 "Divination: A New Perspective." *American Anthropologist* 59: 69–74.
Moran, Emilio F.
1993 *Through Amazonian Eyes: the Human Ecology of Amazonian Populations*. Iowa City: University of Iowa Press.
Nisbett, Richard E., and Lee Ross
1980 *Human Inference: Strategies and Shortcomings of Social Judgment*. Englewood Cliffs, N.J.: Prentice-Hall.
Orejuela, Jorge
1992 "Traditional Productive Systems of the Awa (Cuaiquer) Indians of Southwestern Columbia and Neighboring Ecuador." Pp. 58–82 in *Conservation of Neotropical Forest: Working from Traditional Resource Use*, Kent H. Redford and Christine Padoch, eds. New York: Columbia University Press.
Ortiz, Sutti
1980 "Forecasts, Decisions, and the Farmer's Response to Uncertain Environments." Pp. 313–34 in *Agricultural Decision Making: Anthropological Contributions to Rural Development*, Peggy F. Barlett, ed. New York: Academic Press.
Quinn, Naomi
1978 "Do Mfantse Fish Sellers Estimate Probabilities in Their Heads." *American Ethnologists* 5(2): 206–26.
Rabin, Matthew
1998 "Psychology and Economics." *Journal of Economic Literature* XXXVI: 11–46.
Real, Leslie A.
1994 "Information Processing and Evolutionary Ecology of Cognitive Architecture." Pp. 99–132 in *Behavioral Mechanisms in Evolutionary Ecology*, Leslie A. Real, ed. Chicago: University of Chicago Press.Rocha, Jorge M.
1996 "Rationality, Culture and Decision Making." Pp. 13–41 in *Research in Economic Anthropology*, vol. 17, Barry L. Isaac, ed. London: JAI Press.
Ritchie, E., and J. E. Phares
1969 "Attitude Change as a Function of Internal External Control and Communicator Status." *Journal of Personality* 37(3): 429–43.
Rogers, Everett M.
1995 *Diffusion of Innovations*. New York: Free Press.
Rosenthal, Ted L., and Barry J. Zimmerman
1978 *Social Learning and Cognition*. New York: Academic Press.
Ross, Michael, and Fiore Sicoly
1982 "Egocentric Biases in Availability and Attribution." Pp. 179–89 in *Judgement under Uncertainty: Heuristics and Biases*. Daniel Kahneman, Paul Slovic, and Amos Tversky, eds. Cambridge: Cambridge University Press.

Ryckman, R. M., W. C. Rodda, and M. F. Sherman
  1972 "Locus of Control and Expertise Relevance as Determinants of Changes in Opinions about Student Activism." *Journal of Social Psychology* 88: 107–14.
Sedlmeier, Peter, and Gerd Gigerenzer
  1997 "Intuitions about Sample Size: The Empirical Law of Large Numbers." *Journal of Behavioral Decision Making* 10(1): 33–51.
Smith, J. M., and P. A. Bell
  1994 "Conformity as a Determinant of Behavior in a Resource Dilemma." *Journal of Social Psychology* 134(2): 191–200.
Sperber, D.
  1996 *Explaining Culture: A Naturalistic Approach.* Cambridge, Mass.: Blackwell.
Stonich, Susan C.
  1993 *"I Am Destroying the Land!": The Political Ecology of Poverty and Environmental Destruction in Honduras.* Conflict and Social Change Series. Boulder, Colo.: Westview Press.
Stuchlik, Milan
  1976 *Life on a Half Share: Mechanisms of Social Recruitment among the Mapuche of Southern Chile.* London: C. Hurst.
Thaler, R. H.
  1987 "The Psychology of Choice and the Assumptions of Economics." In *Laboratory Experimentation in Economics: Six Points of View*, Alvin E. Roth, ed. Cambridge: Cambridge University Press.
Titiev, Mischa
  1951 *Araucanian Culture in Transition.* Ann Arbor: University of Michigan Press.
Tversky, Amos, and Daniel Kahneman
  1973 "Availability: A Heuristic for Judging Frequency and Probability." *Cognitive Psychology* 5(2): 207–32.
  1990 "Judgment under Uncertainty: Heuristics and Biases." Pp. 171–88 in P. K. Moser, *Rationality in Action: Contemporary Approaches.* New York: Cambridge University Press.
  1993 "Belief in the Law of Small Numbers." Pp. 341–49 in *A Handbook for Data Analysis in the Behavioral Sciences: Methodological Issues.*
Veblen, Thorstein
  1899 *The Theory of the Leisure Class: an Economic Study in the Evolution of Institutions.* New York: Macmillan.
Wilk, Richard R.
  1996 *Economies and Cultures: Foundations of Economic Anthropology.* Boulder, Colo: Westview Press.
Wilken, G. C.
  1987 *Good Farmers: Traditional Agricultural Resource Management in Mexico and Central America.* Berkeley: University of California Press.
Wit, J.
  1999 "Social Learning in a Common Interest Voting Game." *Games and Economic Behavior* 26: 131–56.

Author Index

Subject Index

About the Contributors

James M. Acheson is Professor of Anthropology and Marine Sciences at the University of Maine. He has done fieldwork in the Purepecha-speaking area of Mexico and in Maine fishing communities. He is author of a number of books including *The Lobster Gangs of Maine*; an edited volume *Anthropology and Institutional Economics*; and *The Question of the Commons* (with Bonnie McCay). In recent years he has focused on understanding the development of institutions to manage marine fisheries using concepts from institutional economics and rational choice theory.

Duran Bell developed his interest in Marx as an undergraduate at the University of California at Berkeley, having been introduced to theories of revolutionary change by a Trotskyist youth group. He received his Ph.D. in agricultural economics at Berkeley, and for a number of years pursued research in neoclassical economics. Since 1985, however, his work has been focused entirely on issues in economic anthropology, especially on the analysis of marriage and marriage payments, on the structure and functioning of corporate groups, and more recently on a cross-cultural examination of the nature and dynamics of wealth-assets.

Jeffrey H. Cohen is an assistant professor of cultural anthropology and demography at Pennsylvania State University. He is interested in patterns of migration and remittance outcomes as rural Mexicans migrate to the United States, as well as questions of economic development and ethnicity. He is the principal investigator for the NSF-CAREER project, "Transnational Migration and Remittances: A Longitudinal Study of Rural Oaxaca." He has published ethnography, *Cooperation and Community* (University of Texas Press 1999), and his articles have appeared in the journals *Human Organization*, *Economic Geography*, and the *American Anthropologist*.

E. Paul Durrenberger is Professor of Anthropology at Pennsylvania State University. He received a Ph.D. in anthropology from the University of Illinois at Urbana-Champaign in 1971. He was on the faculty of the University of Iowa for twenty-five years and was chair of the Anthropology Department when he left for Penn State in 1997. He has served on the executive board of the American Anthropological Association, and as president of Culture and Agriculture, the Society for Economic Anthropology, and the Council of Thai Studies. He has done ethnographic field-work in highland Southeast Asia, lowland Southeast Asia, Iceland, Mississippi, Alabama, Iowa, and Chicago. Recent books include *Gulf Coast Soundings* (University Press of Kansas 1996), *Dynamics of Medieval Iceland* (University of Iowa Press 1992), *It's All Politics* (University of Illinois Press 1992), *Icelandic Essays: Explorations in the Anthropology of Modern Life* (Rudi Publishing 1995) with Gísli Pálsson, *Images of Modern Iceland* (University of Iowa Press 1996) with Kendall Thu, *Pigs, Profits and Rural Communities* (State University of New York Press 1998), and *State and Community in Fisheries Management: Power, Policy, and Practice* (Bergin and Garvey 2000) with Tom King. With Suzan Erem he has recently published ethnographic work on union locals in Chicago in various anthropological journals. He has recently started working on sustainable agriculture in Pennsylvania.

Timothy Earle is Professor of Anthropology at Northwestern University, and received his Ph.D. from the University of Michigan in 1973. His research has focused on prehistoric economies and the evolution of complex societies. He has carried out fieldwork on the chiefdoms in Hawaii (1970, 1971–72, 1974), Peru (1968, 1977–79, 1982–83, 1986), Denmark (1990–97), and now Iceland (2000). The main goal of his research is to study cross-culturally the different routes to complexity as related to differences in regional political economies. In ongoing research in Iceland he investigates how Viking colonizers established a farming economy and competed with each other for regional control. Earle recently published *How Chiefs Come to Power* and *The Evolution of Human Societies* (2000, second edition). He is a member of the Executive Board of the American Anthropological Association.

Jean Ensminger received her Ph.D. in anthropology from Northwestern University in 1984. She is currently Professor of Anthropology at California Institute of Technology. She is a past president of the Society for Economic Anthropology and a current member of the MacArthur Foundation Preferences Network. Her current research focuses upon the use of experimental economics to help us understand economic decision making and the role of social norms in society. She has carried out extensive fieldwork with the pastoral-nomadic Orma of northeastern Kenya since 1978. She also works in the field of New Institutional Economics, which is applied to the Orma case study in her Cambridge University Press book *Making a Market: The Institutional Transformation of an African Society* (1992).

Jane I. Guyer is Professor of Anthropology at Northwestern University, having completed seven years as Director of its Program of African Studies. She has published in the economic anthropology and economic history of West and Equatorial Africa, based on field research carried out in Nigeria and Cameroon. One main theme of her work is the institutional and ecological dynamics of the food economies of urban hinterlands, with her latest book on this topic entitled *An African Niche Economy: Farming to Feed Ibada* (1997). The other theme concerns the history and anthropology of monetary valuation in the expanding commercial economies of the region, as in her edited book *Money Matters* (1995) and a set of essays in progress entitled "Marginal Gains: Analytical Essays on Transactions in Equatorial Africa."

Edwins Laban M. Gwako is Assistant Professor of Anthropology at Guilford College, with a Ph.D. from Washington University in Saint Louis. He is chair of the Department of Sociology and Anthropology at Guilford, and teaches courses in anthropological theory, ethnographic methods, economic anthropology, gender and development in Africa, and African cultures. His fieldwork has been in Kenya and his research centers on political economy and development, with a particular focus on property rights and gender in agricultural output. He has also conducted research on female circumcision, women's use of family planning methods, and reproductive behavior in western Kenya.

Karen Tranberg Hansen is Professor of Anthropology at Northwestern University. She has conducted most of her research in Zambia on the informal economy, wage labor, gender, and housing. Her most recent book focuses on consumption: *Salaula: The World of Secondhand Clothing and Zambia* (2000). She is also the author of *Distant Companions: Servants and Employers in Zambia 1900–1985* (1989) and *Keeping House in Lusaka* (1997), and she edited *African Encounters with Domesticity* (1992).

Joseph Henrich (Ph.D. UCLA, 1999) is currently a fellow at the Institute for Advanced Study (Wissenschaftskolleg) in Berlin and in the Society of Scholars at the University of Michigan. Beginning in the fall of 2002, he joins the faculty in the Department of Anthropology at Emory University. Henrich's research emphasizes a synthesis of evolutionary, cultural, economic, and psychological approaches to human behavior, and he has published in the *American Anthropologist*, the *American Economic Review*, and the *Journal of Theoretical Biology*, among others. He has also recently completed an edited volume, *The Foundations of Human Sociality: Experiments from 15 Small-Scale Societies*, which teams economists and anthropologists and pioneers an ethno-experimental approach to human social behavior.

Robert C. Hunt, Professor of Anthropology at Brandeis University, received his Ph.D. from Northwestern University in 1965 and is past president of the Society for Economic Anthropology. He has conducted field research in Mexico and the western states of the United States. His research interests have been focused on comparative issues, with a particular emphasis on the social organization and economics of irrigated agriculture.

Elena Obukhova is a Ph.D. student in the Department of Sociology at the University of Chicago. Her research interests include economic organization, transition economies, and social networks. She is currently working on a dissertation exploring the development of labor markets in the People's Republic of China.

Nicola Tannenbaum is Director of the Asian Studies Program and Professor of Anthropology at Lehigh University. She received her Ph.D. in anthropology from the University of Iowa in 1982. She is the former president of the Mid-Atlantic Region Association for Asian Studies. She has done fieldwork in Thailand on economic and cognitive anthropology and religion. She wrote *Who Can Compete Against the World? Power-Protection and Buddhism in Shan Worldview* (1995). She is one of the editors (with David B. Small) of a recent Society for Economic Anthropology (SEA) publication, *At the Interface: The Household and Beyond* (2000), and edited, with Cornelia Kammerer, *Founder's Cults in Southeast Asia: Ancestors, Agriculture, and Polity* (Yale University Southeast Asia Program Monograph Series). Her published articles can be found in various journals including *Ethnology*, *Ethnos*, the *American Ethnologist*, and the *Journal of Southeast Asian Studies*.

Richard Wilk is a cultural anthropologist with broad interests in both academic and applied areas of the discipline, particularly in areas of globalization, consumer culture, and the environment. He is presently chair of the anthropology department at Indiana University and president of the Society for Economic Anthropology. Most of his fieldwork has been conducted in Belize and the United States.

Deborah Winslow is Associate Professor of Anthropology at the University of New Hampshire. She writes primarily on economic and social change in Sri Lanka, where she has done research since 1973. Her most recent articles include "Potters' Progress: Hybridity and Accumulative Change" (forthcoming in *Human Organization*). She is co-editor (with Richard Blanton, Peter Peregrine, and Thomas Hall) of *Economic Analysis Beyond the Local System* (1995), volume 13 in the SEA Monographs in Economic Anthropology series.